Family Circle

Our Best RECIPES

Meredith® Books
Des Moines, Iowa

Family Circle® Our Best Recipes
Editor: Lois White
Contributing Editors: Jan Hazard, Carrie E. Holcomb, Annie Krumhardt,
    Spectrum Communications, Inc.
Contributing Writers: Nancy Byal, Wini Moranville
Associate Design Director: Todd Emerson Hanson
Photographers: Marty Baldwin, Jason Donnelly, Scott Little, Bryan McCay
Contributing Photographers: James Baigrie, Miki Duisterhof, Mark Ferri,
    Brian Hagiwara, Rita Maas, Susan Gentry McWhinney, Alison Miksch,
    Ellie Miller, Dean Powell, Alan Richardson, Charles Schiller,
    Ann Stratton, Mark Thomas, Dasha Wright
Copy Chief: Terri Fredrickson
Copy Editor: Kevin Cox
Publishing Operations Manager: Karen Schirm
Senior Editor, Asset and Information Management: Phillip Morgan
Edit and Design Production Coordinator: Mary Lee Gavin
Art and Editorial Sourcing Coordinator: Jackie Swartz
Editorial Assistant: Cheryl Eckert
Book Production Managers: Pam Kvitne, Marjorie J. Schenkelberg, Mark Weaver
Imaging Center Operator: Kristin E. Reese
Contributing Copy Editor: Carol DeMasters
Contributing Proofreaders: Sarah Enticknap, Elise Marton, Candy Meier
Contributing Indexer: Elizabeth T. Parsons
Food Stylist: Greg Luna
Contributing Food Stylists: Jill Lust, Janet Pittman, Charles Worthington
Contributing Prop Stylists: Lori Hellander, Sue Mitchell

Meredith® Books
Editor in Chief: Gregory H. Kayko
Executive Director, Design: Matt Strelecki
Managing Editor: Amy Tincher-Durik
Executive Editor: Jennifer Darling
Senior Editor/Group Manager: Jan Miller
Senior Associate Design Director: Ken Carlson

Executive Director, Marketing and New Business: Kevin Kacere
Director, Marketing and Publicity: Amy Nichols
Executive Director, Sales: Ken Zagor
Director, Operations: George A. Susral
Director, Production: Douglas M. Johnston
Business Director: Janice Croat

Senior Vice President: Karla Jeffries
Vice President and General Manager: Douglas J. Guendel

Family Circle® **Magazine**
Editor in Chief: Linda Fears
Editorial Director: Michael Lafavore
Creative Director: Karmen Lizzul
Food Director: Peggy Katalinich
Senior Food Editor: Julie Miltenberger
Associate Food Editor: Michael Tyrrell
Assistant Food Editor: Cindy Heller
Editorial Assistant: Katie Kemple
Test Kitchen Associate: Althea Needham

Meredith Publishing Group
President: Jack Griffin
Executive Vice President: Doug Olson
Vice President, Corporate Solutions: Michael Brownstein
Vice President, Manufacturing: Bruce Heston
Vice President, Consumer Marketing: David Ball
Consumer Product Marketing Director: Steve Swanson
Consumer Product Marketing Manager: Wendy Merical
Business Manager: Darren Tollefson

Meredith Corporation
Chairman of the Board: William T. Kerr
President and Chief Executive Officer: Stephen M. Lacy

In Memoriam: E.T. Meredith III (1933–2003)

Pictured on the front cover:
Caramel-Nut Brownie Delight (page 236).
Pictured on the back cover:
(clockwise from the top left):
Spicy Spaghetti and Meatballs (page 84),
Easy Microwave Nachos (page 147),
BBQ Bacon Cheeseburger (page 197),
Honey-Herbed Cornish Hens (page 290),
Chocolate Cheesecake (page 280) and
Jumbo Chocolate Chip Cookies (page 162).

Contents

A "healthy" icon next to the recipe nutrition facts means that the recipe meets certain calorie, fat, sodium and cholesterol guidelines. See page 336 for more information.

Our treasured heritage

For 75 years *Family Circle®* magazine has been helping families serve delicious, healthful meals for everyday and special occasions. This tradition continues from our kitchen to yours with *Our Best Recipes*. We reviewed nearly eight decades of food stories and chose 400 of our most requested recipes from the thousands we published. A few culinary milestones caught our eye and made us smile. We share them with you.

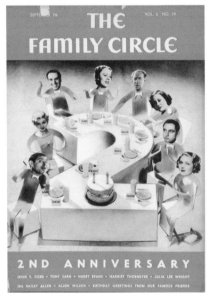

1934

1940

1930s—The first supermarket was launched in Long Island, New York, and grocery shoppers in mom-and-pop stores nationwide clamored for the first issues of *Family Circle* at the checkout counters. With family budgets tight because of the Great Depression, *Family Circle* editors offered tips for feeding a family of four on $13 to $15 a week. Hormel introduced SPAM®. Ruth Wakefield, owner of the Toll House Restaurant in Massachusetts, chopped a Nestlé® chocolate bar and stirred it into her cookie dough to create the Toll House cookie, the most popular version of the chocolate chip cookie in the United States today.

1940s—With American women working outside the home to help support the Allies in World War II, it was time to economize both money and time. Ingenuity was a cook's byword. *Family Circle* recipes that made the most of rationed foods (butter, sugar and eggs) gained in popularity. Thrifty meat and potato meals were dinnertime mainstays. When the war ended, America's culinary ingenuity turned to new products such as Tupperware® and new convenience foods, including cake mixes.

1956   1969   1977

1950s—Peacetime fueled prosperity that ushered in an era of new foods, new flavors and new kitchen appliances. U.S. servicemen returning from Italy brought back recipes for pizza. Nationwide, 15,000 pizzerias turned out the savory pies in 1953. Swanson dished up frozen TV dinners so families could enjoy a three-course turkey meal while watching Uncle Miltie (Milton Berle) on newly acquired television sets. *Family Circle* magazine turned the spotlight on family dining, featuring recipes ranging from Sunday roasts and fancy cheesecakes to weekday one-dish dinners and the magazine's first grilling recipes. The microwave oven debuted in 1955 when Tappan foresaw the need for speed in the kitchen.

1960s—Breakfast went a-go-go in the form of Kellogg's Pop-Tarts®. Teflon®-coated pans slipped onto stovetops. No-fuss casseroles appeared on party menus. Americans traveled worldwide and experienced international foods. *Family Circle* magazine began introducing home

cooks to exotic ingredients, such as curry powder (in modest amounts by today's standards), and showed how to prepare foreign foods like Senegalese chicken. Americans discovered their waistlines bulging too. Weight Watchers® diet program and Tab® low-calorie soft drink came to the rescue.

1970s—Women in droves opted for jobs away from home that resulted in the need for quick and easy cooking ideas. But with sky-high inflation, budgets were still tight. So *Family Circle* magazine showed how even a family of seven could eat deliciously for $50 a week and stir up 50-cent-per-serving main dishes. General Mills created a moneysaving meal with Hamburger Helper®. The simple, elegant style of cooking called *nouvelle cuisine* set restaurants on a new course with smaller portions, fresh ingredients, light seasonings and artful plate presentation.

1982   1991   2006

1980s—Men learned to love quiche at a time when *Family Circle* magazine provided recipes for more ethnic and regional food influences—Chinese and Pacific, Tex-Mex and Southern. Escalating time constraints brought microwave ovens center stage for all kinds of cooking. Tortilla sales soared (from 7.2 billion in 1980 to 36 billion in 1990) as Americans discovered these tasty flatbreads could wrap around all kinds of fillings—including PB&J.

1990s—Food label reading became a shopper's imperative thanks to the Nutrition Education and Labeling Act. Words such as "low fat" and "healthy" appeared everywhere because one-third of adults were overweight. *Family Circle* recipes kept up with the trend by offering nutrition analysis with every recipe to honor

readers' desire to feed their families nutritiously. Good-for-you became fun when families embraced the use of salsa and cooks expanded recipe ingredient lists to include other healthy foods.

2000s—Today *Family Circle* magazine editors think worldly, locally and healthfully by emphasizing nutritious, fresh ingredients and seasoning them with the flavors of the globe. Family meal preparation still eats up more time than most folks would like, so the magazine's food editors feature menu plans, shopping lists and prep/cook times with recipes. Even in an instant-message world, *Family Circle* continues to honor and celebrate great family cooking traditions like baking cookies for holiday events.

Express Lane **Meals**

Linguine with Zucchini Sauce p. 70

Taking about 30 minutes to prepare, each
one of these recipes is a winner every time.
Night after night, bite after bite, each proves
there's always time to share a nutritious,
satisfying meal with your family.

Philly Steak Pockets

1 **package (8 ounces) refrigerated crescent rolls**
4 **teaspoons yellow mustard**
4 **slices roast beef**
4 **slices American cheese**
1 **can (4 ounces) diced green chiles, drained**

1. Heat oven to 375°. Unroll dough into four rectangles. Spread each rectangle with 1 teaspoon mustard. Top each with 1 slice roast beef, 1 slice cheese and one quarter of the chiles.

2. Beginning at short ends, roll up. Pinch seams closed. Place, seam sides down, on baking sheet. Slash tops.

3. Bake at 375° for 15 to 20 minutes or until golden and crisp. Serve warm.

Crescent roll dough makes a fun way to wrap these luscious sandwiches. Green chiles add a little extra kick.

PREP: 10 minutes
BAKE: at 375° for 15 to 20 minutes
MAKES: 4 pockets

QUICK TIP

ALL DRESSED UP

One of the easiest go-withs for sandwiches is a crunchy tossed salad, and one of the easiest dressings is simply extra-virgin olive oil, vinegar, salt and black pepper. When dressing a salad, put the vinegar on first so the oil doesn't prevent the vinegar from reaching the greens.

Per pocket: 305 calories, 16 g total fat (6 g sat.), 30 mg cholesterol, 1,286 mg sodium, 23 g carbohydrate, 0 g fiber, 16 g protein.

Steak and Cheese Melt Pizza

1 tablespoon vegetable oil
2 large red onions (about 1 pound total), thinly sliced
1¼ teaspoons Montreal steak seasoning
2 boneless beef strip steaks (about 5 ounces each), ½ to ¾ inch thick
1 large (14 ounces) baked pizza crust (such as Boboli)
2 tablespoons deli-style mustard
1 cup shredded mild Cheddar cheese (4 ounces)
1 cup shredded provolone cheese (4 ounces)

1. Heat broiler. Coat broiler pan with nonstick cooking spray.

2. In nonstick skillet, heat oil over medium heat. Add onion and ½ teaspoon steak seasoning. Cook about 10 minutes or until translucent and lightly browned, stirring occasionally.

3. While onion is cooking, season steaks with remaining ¾ teaspoon steak seasoning. Broil for 4 minutes per side. Remove from broiler and slice thinly against the grain.

4. Place pizza crust on the broiler pan and spread with mustard. Sprinkle half of the Cheddar and provolone over the top; top with sliced steak and onion. Sprinkle remaining cheeses over steak. Broil about 1 minute or until cheese melts and steak is heated.

5. Remove to cutting board and cut into six slices.

Seasoned steak, two kinds of cheese and sautéed onions—if those sound like winning ingredients for a sandwich, wait until your family tries them on this hearty pizza!

PREP: 10 minutes
COOK: 10 minutes
BROIL: 9 minutes
MAKES: 6 servings

QUICK BITE

FLAVOR-PACKED BLENDS

Herb and spice blends, like the Montreal steak seasoning in this recipe, let you add a variety of flavors with just one measure. Keep a selection of blends on hand to transform simple broiled or grilled chicken, meat or fish into something irresistible.

Per serving: 490 calories, 23 g total fat (10 g sat.), 79 mg cholesterol, 849 mg sodium, 35 g carbohydrate, 3 g fiber, 34 g protein.

Curried Pepper Steak with Sweet Potatoes

3 tablespoons vegetable oil
1 pound beef top-round steak, cut across grain ¼ inch thick
1¼ teaspoons salt
2 sweet potatoes (1 pound), peeled, quartered lengthwise and sliced crosswise ½ inch thick
1 large onion, thinly sliced
2 green peppers, seeded and cut into thin strips
½ teaspoon curry powder
¼ teaspoon ground ginger
⅛ teaspoon cayenne pepper
½ cup water

1. In large skillet, heat 2 tablespoons oil over high heat. Season meat with ¼ teaspoon salt. Sauté for 2 minutes on each side. Transfer to plate; keep warm.

2. Add the remaining 1 tablespoon oil to skillet; sauté sweet potato and onion for 6 minutes. Add green peppers, curry powder, ginger, cayenne pepper and the remaining 1 teaspoon salt; sauté for 2 minutes. Add water; cover and cook about 6 minutes or until sweet potato is tender, stirring occasionally. Add meat; heat mixture through.

Give pepper steak a change of pace with a little extra seasoning and an unexpected vegetable.

PREP: 10 minutes
COOK: about 20 minutes
MAKES: 4 servings

QUICK TIP

PRODUCE POINTERS

The skin of a sweet potato can vary from brown to soft red to purple; white sweet potatoes have rough, mottled skin. Choose firm sweet potatoes without wrinkles, bruises, sprouts or decay. Handle sweet potatoes gently; they bruise easily. Buy only what you plan to eat within a few days or put sweet potatoes in a cool, well-ventilated place. Do not refrigerate sweet potatoes.

Per serving: 375 calories, 15 g total fat (2 g sat.), 71 mg cholesterol, 793 mg sodium, 31 g carbohydrate., 4 g fiber, 29 g protein.

Steak and Mushroom Burritos

- 2 **portabella mushroom caps, cleaned (about 8 ounces total)**
- 2 **teaspoons chili powder**
- ½ **teaspoon salt**
- ¼ **teaspoon black pepper**
- 1 **pound beef skirt steak or flank steak**
- 6 **fat-free burrito-size flour tortillas**
- 1 **can (16 ounces) fat-free refried beans**
- 3 **cups shredded iceberg lettuce**
- ¾ **cup bottled taco sauce**
- 2 **medium-size tomatoes, cored and diced**
  Salsa, warmed (optional)

1. Heat gas grill to medium-high or prepare charcoal grill with medium-hot coals.

2. Place mushroom caps on a sheet of waxed paper; coat tops with nonstick cooking spray.

3. In small bowl, mix together chili powder, salt and pepper. Liberally sprinkle chili powder mixture onto mushroom caps. Pat remaining chili powder mixture into skirt steak.

4. Place the mushroom caps on grill. Grill for 5 minutes (with grill closed). Uncover grill and flip over mushrooms. Add steak to grill. Grill, covered, for 3 minutes. Flip over meat and grill for 2 minutes longer.

5. Remove both meat and mushrooms from grill to a cutting board; let stand for 3 minutes. Slice steak and mushrooms into thin strips.

6. Place one tortilla on a plate. Spread about ¼ cup refried beans down center of tortilla. Microwave on HIGH for 30 to 40 seconds or until warm to the touch.

7. Top beans with ⅓ cup steak-mushroom mixture, ½ cup shredded lettuce, 2 tablespoons taco sauce and 3 tablespoons diced tomato. Fold up, envelope style, to enclose filling. Cover with foil to keep warm while preparing remaining burritos. If desired, serve with warm salsa.

One pound of beef serves six people when you tuck it into tortillas with plenty of other pleasing fillings.

PREP: 15 minutes
GRILL: 10 minutes
STAND: 3 minutes
MICROWAVE: 30 to 40 seconds per burrito
MAKES: 6 burritos

QUICK TIP

CLEANING MUSHROOMS

Did you know that you shouldn't soak fresh mushrooms? Because they are porous, washing with too much water makes them waterlogged and mushy. Instead, clean mushrooms with a quick wipe of a damp paper towel or use a mushroom brush to brush them off thoroughly.

Per burrito: 375 calories, 11 g total fat (4 g sat.), 51 mg cholesterol, 987 mg sodium, 40 g carbohydrate, 7 g fiber, 29 g protein.

Beef and Broccoli Stir-Fry

6 cups broccoli flowerets (from 1 bunch)
1 tablespoon ground ginger
1 teaspoon plus 1 tablespoon cornstarch
1 teaspoon garlic salt
½ teaspoon red pepper flakes
2 tablespoons vegetable oil
1 beef flank steak (about 2 pounds), thinly sliced
1 head bok choy (about 1½ pounds), chopped
½ cup orange juice
2 tablespoons teriyaki sauce
2 tablespoons water
6 medium-size scallions, trimmed and chopped (about ½ cup)
3 cups chow mein noodles
⅓ cup salted cashews, broken apart

1. Bring large pot of lightly salted water to a boil. Add broccoli flowerets; cook for 2 minutes. Remove with slotted spoon to a bowl.

2. In small bowl, mix together ginger, 1 teaspoon cornstarch, garlic salt and red pepper flakes.

3. In large skillet, heat oil over high heat. Place beef in medium-size bowl; sprinkle with ginger mixture and toss to coat. Add beef to hot oil; cook, stirring occasionally, about 3 minutes or until no longer pink. Add bok choy and blanched broccoli; cook for 3 minutes.

4. Meanwhile, in small bowl, whisk together orange juice, teriyaki sauce, water and remaining 1 tablespoon cornstarch. Add orange juice mixture to skillet. Cook about 2 minutes or until sauce in skillet is slightly thickened.

5. Remove skillet from heat. Add chopped scallion to skillet; carefully toss to combine. Serve over chow mein noodles. Top with the cashews. Serve immediately.

Broccoli, scallions and bok choy bring tempting colors and textures to this dish; orange juice adds a hint of citrus.

PREP: 20 minutes
COOK: 10 minutes
MAKES: 6 servings

QUICK TIP

BETTER BROWNING

When browning large amounts of meat, use a skillet or pot that looks too big. Forcing too much food into too small a pan results in rubbery texture and uneven browning.

Per serving: 446 calories, 24 g total fat (7 g sat.), 78 mg cholesterol, 821 mg sodium, 20 g carbohydrate, 4 g fiber, 38 g protein.

Sesame Beef and Asparagus Stir-Fry

¼ cup reduced-sodium soy sauce
3 tablespoons rice vinegar
2 tablespoons hoisin sauce
2 tablespoons brown sugar
1 tablespoon chopped fresh ginger
1 tablespoon dark Asian sesame oil
2 teaspoons cornstarch
¼ teaspoon red pepper flakes
2 cups water
2 packages (3 ounces each) beef-flavored ramen noodles
4 scallions, trimmed and sliced
2 tablespoons vegetable oil
1 pound boneless beef sirloin, thinly sliced across grain
3 cloves garlic, minced
1 pound fresh asparagus, diagonally cut into 1½-inch pieces
1 tablespoon sesame seeds, toasted

1. In cup, mix soy sauce, vinegar, hoisin sauce, brown sugar, ginger, 2 teaspoons sesame oil, the cornstarch and red pepper flakes. In medium-size saucepan, bring water to a boil. Add noodles with only one of the seasoning packets, the scallion and the remaining 1 teaspoon sesame oil. Remove from heat; let stand, covered.

2. In large skillet, heat 1 tablespoon vegetable oil over medium heat. Add beef and garlic. Stir-fry for 3 minutes. Remove beef. In same skillet, heat remaining 1 tablespoon vegetable oil. Add asparagus; stir-fry for 2 minutes. Stir soy sauce mixture. Add beef and soy sauce mixture to skillet. Stir-fry about 1 minute or until thickened. Sprinkle with sesame seeds. Serve with noodles.

A fascinating blend of flavorings lends intrigue to asparagus and beef, while ramen noodles bring speed.

PREP: 15 minutes
COOK: 6 minutes
MAKES: 4 servings

QUICK BITE

WHY NOT TRY ...

Hoisin sauce is a sweet, subtly tongue-tingling sauce made from fermented soybeans, molasses, vinegar, mustard, sesame seeds, garlic and chiles. It adds intrigue to Asian-style stir-fries. Another time, use it to fill in as a change-of-pace barbecue sauce. Find it alongside soy sauce at the supermarket.

Per serving: 503 calories., 24 g total fat (6 g sat.), 93 mg cholesterol, 1,338 mg sodium, 28 g carbohydrate, 2 g fiber, 38 g protein.

Thai Ground Beef Salad

⅓ cup vegetable oil
⅓ cup rice-wine vinegar
 1 tablespoon fish sauce
 1 teaspoon Asian chile paste (optional)
 1 tablespoon dark Asian sesame oil
 1 teaspoon sugar
 1 teaspoon ground ginger
¾ teaspoon garlic salt
 1 cup fresh cilantro leaves, chopped
 2 pounds ground beef chuck
 2 carrots, peeled and cut into
    1-inch-long pieces
 1 sweet red pepper, seeded and
    cut into 1-inch pieces
 3 scallions, trimmed and sliced
 2 bags (10 ounces each) European-blend
    salad greens

If you like taco salads, why not try a Thai twist? This is an equally enticing duo of hot meat served over cool greens.

PREP: 20 minutes
COOK: 7 minutes
MAKES: 6 servings

1. For dressing, in small bowl, whisk together vegetable oil, rice-wine vinegar, fish sauce, chile paste (if using), sesame oil, sugar, ginger and ¼ teaspoon garlic salt. Stir in cilantro.

2. Working in batches if necessary, in large skillet, cook meat over medium-high heat about 5 minutes or until browned. Drain off liquid. Season with remaining ½ teaspoon garlic salt.

3. Add carrot and sweet pepper to skillet; cook for 2 minutes.

4. Stir half of the dressing and the scallion into meat mixture. Remove from heat.

5. In serving bowl, toss salad greens with remaining half of the dressing. Spoon meat mixture over top.

QUICK BITE

WHY NOT TRY ...

Did you know that you can use rice vinegar, rice-wine vinegar and seasoned-rice vinegar interchangeably? Rice vinegar is made from fermented rice, while rice-wine vinegar is made from fermented rice wine. Seasoned rice-vinegar has added sugar and salt—if using this product, you may want to adjust the seasonings in the recipe.

Per serving: 515 calories, 39 g total fat (11 g sat.), 103 mg cholesterol, 551 mg sodium, 9 g carbohydrate, 3 g fiber, 31 g protein.

Tex-Mex Stew

1½ pounds lean ground beef
2¼ cups water
1 can (15½ ounces) black beans, drained and rinsed
1 can (11 ounces) corn niblets, drained
1 cup frozen chopped sweet red and green peppers
1 jar (4¼ ounces) diced green chiles
1 envelope (½ of a 2-ounce box) onion soup mix
1 tablespoon ground cumin
½ teaspoon salt
½ teaspoon dried oregano
¼ teaspoon cayenne pepper
2 tablespoons all-purpose flour
   Corn chips (optional)
   Fresh cilantro, for garnish (optional)

1. In 5- to 6-quart large, deep pot, cook beef over medium-high heat about 5 minutes or until browned, breaking up meat with wooden spoon but leaving some large pieces.

2. Add 2 cups water, beans, corn, sweet peppers, chiles, dry soup mix, cumin, salt, oregano and cayenne pepper. Simmer, covered, for 10 minutes. In small cup, stir remaining ¼ cup water into flour until smooth. Stir into stew; cook about 1 minute or until thickened. If desired, serve with corn chips and garnish with cilantro.

This recipe is as easy as a ground beef and bean chili but provides a nice change of pace. Onion soup mix is the secret ingredient.

PREP: 10 minutes
COOK: 16 minutes
MAKES: 6 servings

QUICK TIP

FREEZER FACTS

Soups and stews that make good candidates for freezing are those that do not include:
• Cheese, cream or other dairy products that may separate and curdle when thawed and reheated.
• Potatoes or pasta, which can become too soft when frozen and reheated.

Per serving: 260 calories, 9 g total fat (3 g sat.), 31 mg cholesterol, 1,155 mg sodium, 22 g carbohydrate, 5 g fiber, 23 g protein.

Beef Patties au Poivre

1 tablespoon green peppercorns in brine, drained
1 tablespoon butter
¼ cup chopped onion
2 tablespoons brandy
2 tablespoons all-purpose flour
1 cup beef broth
¼ cup heavy cream
1 pound lean ground beef, shaped into four ½-inch-thick patties
½ teaspoon salt
¼ teaspoon black pepper
4 hamburger buns

1. On clean work surface, crush half of the peppercorns with the back of a spoon.

2. For sauce, in small saucepan, melt butter over medium heat. Add onion and all of the peppercorns; sauté for 4 to 5 minutes or until browned. Carefully add brandy; scrape up any browned bits from bottom of pan with wooden spoon and cook for 30 seconds. Stir in flour; cook, stirring, for 2 minutes.

3. Add broth; bring to a boil, stirring. Reduce heat; simmer for 2 to 3 minutes. Add cream; cook, stirring, for 1 to 2 minutes. Remove from heat; cover sauce to keep warm.

4. Heat large nonstick skillet over medium heat. Season beef patties with salt and pepper. Add patties to skillet; cook for 9 to 12 minutes or until an instant-read meat thermometer inserted in centers registers 160°, turning once. Serve patties in buns with sauce.

A weeknight dinner takes on fine-dining flair when you dress up beef patties with green peppercorns, onion, brandy and cream.

PREP: 10 minutes
COOK: 18 to 24 minutes
MAKES: 4 servings

QUICK TIP

FREEZER FACTS

If you need to freeze leftover broth (or other liquid items), transfer it to plastic freezer bags and freeze flat. This strategy will revolutionize your freezer storage space!

Per serving: 390 calories, 16 g total fat (8 g sat.), 98 mg cholesterol, 980 mg sodium, 26 g carbohydrate, 2 g fiber, 30 g protein.

Individual Country Loaves

1 egg
½ pound ground beef
½ pound Italian sausage, casings removed
¾ cup packaged seasoned dry bread crumbs
2 tablespoons bottled barbecue sauce
2 tablespoons tomato paste
2 tablespoons Worcestershire sauce
1 tablespoon Dijon mustard
½ teaspoon garlic powder
½ teaspoon onion powder
¼ teaspoon salt
¼ teaspoon black pepper
1 box (10 ounces) frozen mixed vegetables, thawed and drained
1½ cups shredded mozzarella cheese
Accompaniment:
6 servings frozen mashed potatoes, cooked

1. Heat oven to 400°.

2. In large bowl, lightly beat egg. Add beef, sausage, bread crumbs, barbecue sauce, tomato paste, Worcestershire sauce, mustard, garlic powder, onion powder, salt and pepper.

3. In small bowl, mix together vegetables and mozzarella cheese.

4. Divide meat mixture into six equal portions. Pat one portion into 7-inch round on waxed paper. Spoon ½ cup of the vegetable mixture over center. Using waxed paper, lift sides of meat up over vegetable mixture; seal edges and ends and shape into oval. Place, seam side down, in 15½×10½×1-inch jelly-roll pan. Repeat with remaining meat and vegetables.

5. Bake at 400° about 20 minutes or until instant-read meat thermometer inserted in centers registers 160°. Serve with mashed potatoes.

If your kids love beef, sausage and cheese, they won't mind that you've tucked a few mixed vegetables into the loaves too!

PREP: 10 minutes
BAKE: at 400° for 20 minutes
MAKES: 6 loaves

QUICK TIP

STORE IT RIGHT

Refrigerate eggs (with the large ends up) in their carton so they don't absorb odors. Fresh eggs can be refrigerated for up to 5 weeks after the packaging date (this number is stamped on the carton from 1 to 365, with 1 representing January 1 and 365 representing December 31). Don't use dirty, cracked or leaking eggs—they may have become contaminated with harmful bacteria.

Per loaf: 494 calories, 24 g total fat (12 g sat.), 115 mg cholesterol, 1,201 mg sodium, 41 g carbohydrate, 4 g fiber, 27 g protein.

Stuffed Pork Chops

1 tablespoon plus 1 teaspoon extra-virgin olive oil
1 small red onion, chopped
1 Granny Smith apple, cored and chopped
2¼ cups water
4 cups herbed stuffing mix (from 16-ounce package)
½ teaspoon salt
4 thick-cut pork chops (2½ pounds total), each about 1½ inches thick
⅛ teaspoon black pepper
1 package (10 ounces) frozen honey-glazed carrots
Fresh herb sprigs, for garnish (optional)

Here stuffing mix doubles as a filling for the thick-cut chops and a comforting side dish.

PREP: 10 minutes
COOK: 25 minutes
MAKES: 4 servings

QUICK TIP

A PERFECT POCKET

To make a pocket in a chop, use a sharp knife to cut a 2-inch slit in its fatty side. Work the knife through the chop and almost to the other side, keeping the original slit as narrow as possible.

1. In large nonstick skillet, heat 1 tablespoon oil over medium-high heat. Add onion and apple; cook, stirring, about 5 minutes or until softened. Add 1¾ cups water and bring to a boil. Stir in stuffing mix and ¼ teaspoon salt. Place stuffing in microwave-safe bowl.

2. Cut slits in chops. Fill each with ¼ cup of the stuffing. Season chops with pepper and remaining ¼ teaspoon salt.

3. Wipe out skillet; heat 1 teaspoon olive oil over medium-high heat. Add chops; sauté for 5 minutes per side. Add remaining ½ cup water; cover and simmer on medium-low heat about 10 minutes or until instant-read meat thermometer inserted in thickest part of meat registers 160°.

4. Meanwhile, microwave carrots following package directions. Warm remaining stuffing in bowl in microwave. Stir in carrots and glaze. Serve chops with stuffing. Spoon cooking liquid on top. If desired, garnish with fresh herbs.

Per serving: 641 calories, 21 g total fat (5 g sat.), 125 mg cholesterol., 997 mg sodium, 59 g carbohydrate, 7 g fiber, 51 g protein.

Pork Saltimbocca

8 pork cutlets (1 pound total)
1 teaspoon salt
½ teaspoon dried sage
½ teaspoon black pepper
8 slices prosciutto (4 ounces total)
2 tablespoons butter
½ cup Marsala wine
½ cup beef broth
1 cup shredded fontina cheese (4 ounces)
Hot cooked pasta (optional)

1. Flatten pork cutlets; sprinkle each with some of the salt, sage and pepper.

2. Lay a slice of prosciutto on each cutlet. In large skillet, melt butter over medium-high heat. Working in batches if necessary, cook cutlets, starting with prosciutto sides down, in hot butter for 2 minutes per side. Remove.

3. Add wine and broth to skillet; cook for 2 minutes. Return cutlets to skillet, prosciutto sides up; top each with 2 tablespoons shredded fontina. Cover and cook about 2 minutes or until cheese melts. Transfer cutlets to platter.

4. Reduce sauce over medium-high heat about 4 minutes or until syrupy consistency. Spoon sauce over cutlets. If desired, serve over hot cooked pasta.

Traditionally, saltimbocca is a specialty made with veal; however, wine, prosciutto and sage work equally well with pork.

PREP: 10 minutes
COOK: 12 minutes
MAKES: 4 servings

QUICK BITE

ALLA ITALIA

Prosciutto is an Italian-style version of ham that has been seasoned, salt-cured and air-dried rather than smoked. Prosciutto di Parma (Parma ham from Italy) is considered to be the best. Sliced prosciutto dries out quickly and should be used within a day.

Per serving: 512 calories, 30 g total fat (14 g sat.), 167 mg cholesterol, 1,693 mg sodium, 4 g carbohydrate, 0 g fiber, 47 g protein.

Pork with Pear Salsa

Pear Salsa:
- 2 pears, cored and chopped
- ½ cup chopped toasted pecans
- ¼ cup crumbled blue cheese
- 2 tablespoons pear nectar
- 1 tablespoon brown sugar
- 1 teaspoon grated fresh ginger

Chops:
- 1 tablespoon vegetable oil
- 2 teaspoons sliced fresh ginger
- 4 rib pork chops, ½ inch thick
  (about 1½ pounds total)
- 1 teaspoon salt
- ¼ teaspoon black pepper
- ⅓ cup pear nectar
- Hot cooked egg noodles (optional)

Fry up some pork chops and top with a fresh and stylish pear, pecan and blue-cheese salsa.

PREP: 10 minutes
COOK: 10 minutes
MAKES: 4 servings

1. **Pear Salsa:** In medium-size bowl, combine pear, pecans, blue cheese, pear nectar, brown sugar and ginger. Set pear salsa aside.

2. **Chops:** In large skillet, heat oil over medium heat. Add ginger; cook about 1 minute or until crisp. Remove with slotted spoon and discard.

3. Sprinkle pork chops with salt and pepper. In same skillet, cook pork chops about 3 minutes or until browned; turn over and brown other side about 3 minutes or until instant-read meat thermometer inserted in centers registers 160°. Reduce heat to low; transfer chops to serving platter.

4. Add pear nectar to skillet, stirring to loosen browned bits. Simmer about 3 minutes or until thickened and syrupy. Pour over chops. Top with salsa. If desired, serve over egg noodles.

NICELY TOASTED NUTS

It's amazing how much flavor can be gained by giving nuts a stint in the oven. To toast nuts:
- Spread nuts in a single layer in a shallow baking pan.
- Bake in a 350° oven for 5 to 10 minutes or until the pieces are golden brown.
- Stir once or twice and check the nuts frequently because once they start to burn, they quickly become unsalvageable.

Per serving: 419 calories, 27 g total fat (7 g sat.), 64 mg cholesterol, 746 mg sodium, 23 g carbohydrate, 4 g fiber, 24 g protein.

Spicy BBQ Stew

1 container (18 ounces) prepared barbecue
    shredded pork
2 green peppers, seeded and coarsely
    chopped
1½ cups frozen corn, thawed
1 cup water
1 can (15 ounces) sweet potatoes in syrup
¼ cup shredded Cheddar cheese (1 ounce)

1. In large pot, combine shredded pork, pepper, corn and water. Heat, covered, over medium-high heat about 7 minutes or until pepper is crisp-tender, stirring occasionally.

2. Meanwhile, drain sweet potatoes and discard syrup. If whole, cut into bite-size pieces. Stir into stew and cook for 2 to 3 minutes longer or until heated through. Sprinkle with cheese.

Sweet potatoes balance the tang of prepared barbecue pork. Or try barbecue-flavored shredded chicken; it also tastes great in this recipe.

PREP: 5 minutes
COOK: 9 to 10 minutes
MAKES: 4 servings

QUICK TIP

GREEN PEPPER MATH

Green peppers come in a variety of sizes; two large peppers will give you roughly 2 cups of chopped peppers.

Per serving: 358 calories, 8 g total fat (3 g sat.), 42 mg cholesterol, 1,022 mg sodium, 53 g carbohydrate, 5 g fiber, 21 g protein.

Cassoulet in a Flash

1 pound kielbasa, cut into ½-inch-thick slices
1 medium-size red onion, sliced into
   thin wedges
1 clove garlic, finely chopped
1 can (19 ounces) white kidney beans,
   drained and rinsed
1 can (16 ounces) pork and beans in tomato
   sauce
1 teaspoon salt
1 teaspoon sugar
¾ teaspoon dried thyme
¼ teaspoon black pepper

1. In large skillet, cook kielbasa over medium heat for 3 to 4 minutes. Add red onion and garlic; cook, stirring occasionally, for 2 to 3 minutes.

2. Stir in kidney beans, pork and beans, salt, sugar, thyme and pepper. Bring to a boil. Reduce heat to low; simmer about 5 minutes or until heated through.

Cassoulet varies from region to region but most always combines white beans and meats for a hearty, warming stew.

PREP: 10 minutes
COOK: about 12 minutes
MAKES: 4 servings

QUICK BITE

WHAT'S IN A NAME?

White kidney beans are also known as cannellini beans. French and Italian cooks have traditionally used these nutty-flavored legumes to add texture and flavor to recipes. You'll find them sold under both names at the supermarket.

Per serving: 547 calories, 32 g total fat (12 g sat.), 84 mg cholesterol, 2,443 mg sodium, 40 g carbohydrate, 10 g fiber, 25 g protein.

Pasta Fagioli with Sausage

2 tablespoons extra-virgin olive oil
½ pound sweet Italian sausage, casings removed
3 cloves garlic, thinly sliced
3 large chicken bouillon cubes, dissolved in 6 cups hot water
1 can (28 ounces) crushed tomatoes
1 teaspoon dried Italian seasoning
¼ teaspoon onion salt
¼ teaspoon black pepper
1 pound ditalini pasta
2 cans (19 ounces each) cannellini beans, drained and rinsed
½ cup shredded Parmesan cheese

1. In large saucepan, heat oil over medium-high heat. Crumble sausage into saucepan; cook, stirring occasionally, about 5 minutes or until browned. Add garlic; cook for 1 minute.

2. Add dissolved bouillon cubes, tomatoes, Italian seasoning, onion salt and pepper. Bring to a boil over high heat. Stir in pasta. Reduce heat; simmer, stirring occasionally, for 10 to 11 minutes or until pasta is tender.

3. Stir in beans; cook about 1 minute or until beans are heated through. Serve immediately with cheese.

Fagioli refers to beans in general, which are a favorite ingredient in Tuscan cooking and a simple way to make a pasta dish more meaty—without adding more meat!

PREP: 10 minutes
COOK: about 18 minutes
MAKES: 8 servings

QUICK BITE

THE BIG CHEESE

One of the most famous cheeses in the world, Parmigiano-Reggiano is a rich, sharp cheese that can only come from specific areas within Italy. Products labeled "Parmesan" are the domestic versions of the cheese. While less expensive, domestic versions often lack the pronounced granular texture and complex flavors of the Italian version.

Per serving: 439 calories, 14 g total fat (4 g sat.), 22 mg cholesterol, 1,239 mg sodium, 60 g carbohydrate, 6 g fiber, 16 g protein.

Creamy Straw and Hay Fettuccine

12 ounces each regular and spinach fettuccine
 2 tablespoons extra-virgin olive oil
 1 package (8 ounces) sliced white mushrooms
1½ cups heavy cream
 1 box (10 ounces) frozen tiny peas, thawed
 ¼ cup sun-dried tomatoes in oil, drained and cut into thin strips
 ¼ pound prosciutto, cut into thin strips
 1 teaspoon salt
 ¼ teaspoon ground nutmeg
 ¼ teaspoon black pepper
 ¼ cup grated Parmesan cheese
   Shredded Parmesan cheese (optional)
   Fresh herbs, for garnish (optional)

1. Cook pasta following package directions. Drain well.

2. While pasta is cooking, in large skillet, heat oil over medium-high heat. Add mushrooms; sauté for 10 minutes.

3. Stir in cream, peas, sun-dried tomatoes, prosciutto, salt, nutmeg and pepper. Bring to a simmer. Stir in the ¼ cup Parmesan cheese.

4. Toss cooked pasta with sauce. If desired, sprinkle with additional Parmesan cheese and garnish with fresh herbs.

Peas, sun-dried tomatoes, prosciutto and mushrooms give color and personality to this easy pasta dish.

PREP: 10 minutes
COOK: about 15 minutes
MAKES: 10 servings

QUICK BITE
SPICE SAVVY

Nutmeg adds a slightly sweet and spicy note and aroma to dishes. While it's often used in cookies, cakes and custards, it has a role in savory foods too—chefs often put a pinch or two in a white sauce to add a nicely nutty flavor.

Per serving: 428 calories, 21 g total fat (10 g sat.), 59 mg cholesterol, 681 mg sodium, 49 g carbohydrate, 4 g fiber, 15 g protein.

Triple-Smoked Pasta

3 cups broccoli flowerets
1 pound penne pasta
1 tablespoon unsalted butter
1 tablespoon all-purpose flour
1 cup heavy cream
1 to 2 canned chipotle peppers in adobo
    sauce, chopped
½ teaspoon salt
¼ cup grated Parmesan cheese
½ pound smoked Gouda cheese (rind
    removed), shredded
½ pound smoked ham, cut into bite-size
    pieces

1. Bring a large pot of lightly salted water to a boil. Add broccoli and cook about 4 minutes or until crisp-tender. Remove with a slotted spoon and set aside.

2. Add penne to boiling water; cook following package directions. Drain, reserving 1 cup of the cooking water.

3. Meanwhile, in small saucepan, melt butter over medium-low heat. Add flour and cook for 1 minute. Whisk in cream and bring to a simmer. Add chipotle pepper and salt; cook for 1 minute. Remove saucepan from heat; stir in Parmesan cheese.

4. In large bowl, combine pasta, broccoli, Gouda, ham and cream sauce. Stir in ½ cup of the pasta cooking liquid. Cover and let stand for 5 minutes. Add more of the pasta cooking liquid if needed to attain creamy consistency.

Smoked Gouda, smoked ham and chipotle peppers—which are smoked jalapeños—add up to the trio of smoke-enhanced ingredients here.

PREP: 15 minutes
COOK: about 15 minutes
STAND: 5 minutes
MAKES: 8 servings

QUICK TIP

CHOPPING VERSUS DICING

Ever wonder about the difference between something that's chopped and something that's diced? To chop means to cut the food into fine, medium or coarse irregular pieces. To dice means to cut the food into uniform pieces, usually ¼ to ½ inch on all sides.

Per serving: 489 calories, 24 g total fat (14 g sat.), 95 mg cholesterol, 793 mg sodium, 47 g carbohydrate, 2 g fiber, 22 g protein.

Cobb Salad

1 large head romaine lettuce
1 large head chicory
1 small avocado, halved, pitted, peeled and cut lengthwise into thin wedges
2 ounces blue cheese, crumbled (about ½ cup)
1 cup cherry tomatoes, halved
6 strips turkey bacon (3 ounces total), cooked and coarsely crumbled
4 ounces cooked skinless, boneless turkey breast, cut into matchstick-size pieces
2 hard-cooked eggs, shelled and quartered
  Cranberry-Raspberry Vinaigrette (recipe follows)

The traditional presentation for Cobb salad is to arrange the ingredients in rows on top of the greens, but tossing them helps cut down on preparation time.

PREP: 20 minutes
MAKES: 8 servings

1. Tear romaine and chicory into bite-size pieces. Place in large shallow salad bowl.

2. Add the avocado, blue cheese, tomato, bacon and turkey to the lettuce mixture; toss gently. Top with egg. Serve with the vinaigrette.

Cranberry-Raspberry Vinaigrette: Place ¾ cup raspberries in sieve over bowl. Press to remove seeds; discard seeds. In food processor or blender, combine sieved raspberries, ½ cup cranberry juice, ½ cup wine vinegar, ¼ cup hot water, 1 tablespoon extra-virgin olive oil, ¾ teaspoon salt and ¼ teaspoon sugar. Whirl to blend. Makes 1½ cups.

QUICK TIP

PRODUCE POINTERS

The best place to store fresh tomatoes is in their original packaging in a cool, dry place, not on a sunny windowsill or in the refrigerator. Plan to use them within 1 to 2 days. Don't wash the tomatoes until just before using them because washing removes their sheen, causing them to ripen more quickly.

Per serving: 164 calories, 11 g total fat (3 g sat.), 82 mg cholesterol, 412 mg sodium, 7 g carbohydrate, 3 g fiber, 10 g protein.

Southwestern Burgers

2 pounds ground pork or meat loaf mix
1½ cups shredded pepper-Jack cheese
  (6 ounces)
¾ cup mayonnaise
1 can (4 ounces) diced pimientos, drained
6 onion buns, sliced and toasted
  Lettuce leaves (optional)
  Red onion, sliced (optional)

1. Heat broiler. Divide ground pork into 12 equal patties, each about 3½ inches in diameter. Place ¼ cup shredded pepper-Jack cheese in center of each of six of the patties. Top each with a patty; press the edges to seal.

2. Broil for 6 to 7 minutes per side or until instant-read meat thermometer inserted in centers registers 160°. In small bowl, combine mayonnaise and pimientos. If desired, line bun bottoms with lettuce and add onion slices. Add burgers. Top each burger with 1 tablespoon mayonnaise mixture; add bun tops. Pass remaining mayonnaise mixture.

Who can resist a little cheese tucked into a burger? A pimiento-spiked mayo makes this sandwich really take off.

PREP: 10 minutes
BROIL: 12 to 14 minutes
MAKES: 6 burgers

QUICK TIP

TOASTING SANDWICH BREADS

A toaster oven makes it easy to toast rolls and buns. But when you're broiling anyway, you might find it easier to toast with the broiler. Simply place the sliced rolls or buns, cut sides up, on a baking sheet. Broil 4 to 5 inches from heat for 1 to 2 minutes or until golden brown.

Per burger: 675 calories, 45 g total fat (17 g sat.), 136 mg cholesterol, 575 mg sodium, 26 g carbohydrate, 1 g fiber, 40 g protein.

Veracruz-Style Pork Chops

1 tablespoon vegetable oil
4 rib pork chops (about 8 ounces each)
½ teaspoon black pepper
⅛ teaspoon salt
1 medium-size red onion, halved and thinly sliced
3 large ribs celery, sliced
1 sweet yellow pepper, seeded and sliced
1 jar (14½ ounces) sliced tomatoes (such as Del Monte Garden Select Sliced Tomatoes)

1. In large nonstick skillet, heat oil over medium-high heat. Season pork chops with ¼ teaspoon black pepper and the salt. Sauté for 3 minutes per side. Transfer to a plate and set aside.

2. Add onion to the skillet and cook over medium-high heat for 3 minutes, stirring occasionally. Add the celery and sweet pepper; cook for 3 minutes longer.

3. Add tomatoes with their juice and the remaining ¼ teaspoon black pepper. Bring to a simmer. Tuck in the pork chops and pour any accumulated juices over. Cover and simmer on medium-low heat for 8 to 9 minutes or until instant-read meat thermometer inserted in centers of chops registers 160°.

"Veracruz" refers to a classic Mexican combo of onions, peppers and tomatoes. It often complements seafood but works beautifully with pork too.

PREP: 10 minutes
COOK: 20 to 21 minutes
MAKES: 4 servings

QUICK TIP

TOMATO POWER

The lycopene in tomatoes may help protect against cancer and may reduce the risk of cardiovascular disease. Scientists also believe the disease-fighting antioxidants in tomatoes can help bolster the immune system.

Per serving: 557 calories, 34 g total fat (11 g sat.), 136 mg cholesterol, 369 mg sodium, 11 g carbohydrate, 3 g fiber, 48 g protein.

Cherry Tomato Sauce

1 pound Italian sausage, casings removed
3 cloves garlic, thinly sliced
2 cans (8 ounces each) regular tomato sauce
    or basil, garlic and oregano tomato sauce
1 package (12 ounces) cherry tomatoes
    (about 2 cups), each tomato halved
½ teaspoon dried basil
½ teaspoon salt
¼ teaspoon black pepper
¾ pound spaghetti or capellini pasta
2 tablespoons shredded Parmesan
    or Romano cheese

1. Coat large nonstick skillet with nonstick cooking spray. Heat skillet over medium-high heat. Add sausage; cook, breaking up with wooden spoon, for 5 minutes. Add garlic; cook about 2 minutes or until sausage is browned. Stir in tomato sauce, cherry tomatoes, basil, salt and pepper; cook about 8 minutes or until slightly thickened and tomatoes are soft.

2. Meanwhile, cook spaghetti in large pot of lightly salted boiling water until al dente (firm yet tender). Drain.

3. Transfer spaghetti to large bowl or platter. Pour sauce over spaghetti. Sprinkle with cheese.

Liven up canned tomato sauce with fresh tomatoes and a couple of flavorful stir-ins.

PREP: 5 minutes
COOK: 15 minutes
MAKES: 6 servings

QUICK BITE
PRODUCE POINTERS

Small, round cherry tomatoes are available year-round, and their rich, sweet flavors make them a good find in winter, when fresh homegrown varieties aren't available. Thanks to their tender skins and tiny seeds, you generally don't have to peel or seed them before using.

Per serving: 533 calories, 26 g total fat (9 g sat.), 59 mg cholesterol, 1,442 mg sodium, 54 g carbohydrate, 5 g fiber, 21 g protein.

Mediterranean Pork Skewers

½ of 8-ounce package flavored feta cheese, crumbled
½ of 8-ounce container sour cream
1 small onion, diced
¼ teaspoon black pepper
1 seasoned pork tenderloin (about 1½ pounds), halved lengthwise and cut into 1-inch cubes
2 medium zucchini, halved lengthwise and cut into ½-inch-thick slices
12 cherry tomatoes
2 boxes (5.6 ounces each) flavored couscous
1 tablespoon chopped fresh flat-leaf parsley
Fresh flat-leaf parsley, for garnish (optional)

1. In food processor, process feta, sour cream, onion and pepper until smooth. Refrigerate until ready to serve.

2. Heat broiler. Coat broiler-pan rack with nonstick cooking spray.

3. On twelve 8-inch metal skewers, thread pork cubes with zucchini and tomatoes, leaving a ¼-inch space between pieces.

4. Place skewers on broiler pan; broil 5 inches from heat for 10 minutes, turning skewers over halfway through cooking.

5. While pork is broiling, cook couscous following package directions.

6. To serve, divide couscous among six dinner plates; top with skewers and sprinkle with chopped parsley. If desired, garnish with additional parsley. Serve sour cream mixture on the side.

Skewers give the quick-to-fix ingredients a festive look, and the flavored feta adds a windfall of great taste to the sauce.

PREP: 10 minutes
BROIL: 10 minutes
MAKES: 6 servings

QUICK BITE

BUILT-IN FLAVOR

Seasoned pork tenderloin is a cook's dream product. Options include lemon-pepper, Italian, chipotle and herb and garlic, to name a few. The tenderloins can be roasted whole or cut up or cubed for kabobs or stir-fries. Look for them in your grocer's meat section.

Per serving: 382 calories, 11 g total fat (6 g sat.), 59 mg cholesterol, 901 mg sodium, 47 g carbohydrate, 1 g fiber, 26 g protein.

Lemon Ginger Pork Stir-Fry

8 ounces angel hair pasta
1 pound pork tenderloin, cut into
   ¼-inch-thick slices
2 tablespoons vegetable oil
1 tablespoon cornstarch
¼ teaspoon salt
⅛ teaspoon black pepper
6 ounces fresh sugar-snap peas, trimmed
1 sweet red pepper, seeded and cut into
   ¼-inch-thick strips
½ cup sugar
½ cup lemon juice
2 tablespoons bottled chili sauce
1 teaspoon grated lemon zest
1 teaspoon grated fresh ginger
¼ cup coarsely chopped scallions

1. Cook pasta following package directions. Drain; rinse with cold water and set aside. In large bowl, combine pork, 1 tablespoon oil, cornstarch, salt and black pepper.

2. In large skillet, heat the remaining 1 tablespoon oil over high heat. Add pork; stir-fry about 3 minutes or until browned. Add peas and pepper strips; stir-fry for 3 minutes longer. Transfer to large bowl.

3. In same skillet, boil sugar and ¼ cup lemon juice about 3 minutes or until caramel colored. Add remaining ¼ cup lemon juice, chili sauce, lemon zest and ginger. Add pork-vegetable mixture, scallions and pasta; heat through.

Zippy lemon juice, chili sauce and fresh ginger perk up lean pork tenderloin.

PREP: 15 minutes
COOK: about 10 minutes
MAKES: 4 servings

QUICK TIP

FREEZER FACTS

The next time a recipe calls for citrus juice, if you have any left over, freeze it in ice cube trays. Then transfer the cubes to a freezer container or bag. Seal, label and store in the freezer for future use.

Per serving: 575 calories, 12 g total fat (2 g sat.), 67 mg cholesterol, 442 mg sodium, 83 g carbohydrate, 5 g fiber, 33 g protein.

Spaetzle has a delightfully chewy texture and makes an easy alternative to egg noodles.

PREP: 15 minutes
MICROWAVE: 5 minutes
COOK: about 12 minutes
MAKES: 6 servings

QUICK TIP

MAKING DRY BREAD CRUMBS

Packaged dry bread crumbs are handier to use in recipes; however, if you've run out, make dry bread crumbs from scratch. Simply arrange ½-inch bread cubes in a single layer on a baking pan. Bake in a 300° oven for 10 to 15 minutes or until dry, stirring twice. Let cool. Place in a food processor or blender; process into fine crumbs. One slice yields ¼ cup fine dry crumbs.

Per serving: 540 calories, 20 g total fat (10 g sat.), 234 mg cholesterol, 967 mg sodium, 49 g carbohydrate, 4 g fiber, 36 g protein.

Veal Meatballs Stroganoff

1 box (10½ ounces) spaetzle
1½ pounds ground veal
½ cup packaged plain dry bread crumbs
2 eggs, lightly beaten
2 tablespoons dried onion flakes
1 teaspoon dried thyme
¾ teaspoon salt
¼ teaspoon black pepper
2 tablespoons unsalted butter
3 tablespoons all-purpose flour
2 cups beef broth
1 can (4 ounces) sliced mushrooms, drained
⅔ cup sour cream
1 tablespoon Dijon mustard
¼ cup chopped fresh parsley leaves

1. Prepare the spaetzle following package directions. Drain.

2. Meanwhile, in large bowl, mix together veal, bread crumbs, eggs, onion flakes, thyme, salt and pepper. Form into 24 meatballs, about 2 tablespoons each. Coat a 13×9×2-inch microwave-safe baking dish with nonstick cooking spray. Add meatballs to dish and cover with plastic wrap. Microwave, covered, on HIGH for 5 minutes.

3. In large nonstick skillet, melt butter. Add flour and cook for 1 minute. Whisk in broth; simmer for 1 minute. Add meatballs and mushrooms. Cover and simmer about 8 minutes or until instant-read meat thermometer inserted in centers of meatballs registers 160°, stirring once halfway through cooking time.

4. Over low heat, stir in sour cream, mustard and parsley. Heat through. Serve meatballs over cooked spaetzle.

Greek-Style Lamb Chops

8 rib lamb chops
½ teaspoon salt
¼ teaspoon black pepper
1 tablespoon extra-virgin olive oil
½ pound orzo pasta
1 cup chicken broth
2 cloves garlic, peeled and sliced
1 cup grape tomatoes, halved
½ cup kalamata olives, pitted and chopped
¼ cup chopped fresh mint leaves
1 tablespoon chopped fresh oregano leaves
1 teaspoon grated lemon zest
1 tablespoon lemon juice
Fresh oregano, for garnish (optional)

1. Bring a large pot of salted water to a boil (to cook the orzo).

2. Season lamb chops with ¼ teaspoon salt and ⅛ teaspoon pepper.

3. Heat 12-inch nonstick sauté pan or skillet briefly over medium-high heat; add oil. When oil sizzles, add lamb chops and sauté for 3 minutes per side. Remove from pan; keep warm.

4. Meanwhile, add the orzo to the boiling water and cook following package directions.

5. Add ½ cup broth to the sauté pan or skillet. Cook over medium-high heat, scraping up any browned bits from the bottom. Add garlic and cook for 1 minute. Add tomato, olives, remaining ½ cup broth, ¼ teaspoon salt and ⅛ teaspoon pepper. Cook for 2 minutes. Add mint, the chopped oregano, lemon zest and lemon juice. Cook for 1 minute longer.

6. Drain orzo and spoon onto four dinner plates. Spoon tomato and olive mixture over orzo. Arrange the lamb chops on top. If desired, garnish with additional oregano.

Olives, oregano, lemon juice, tomatoes—many of the ingredients that make a Greek salad so irresistible make lamb chops equally enticing.

PREP: 15 minutes
COOK: 10 minutes
MAKES: 4 servings

QUICK BITE

WHY NOT TRY ...

Orzo pasta, sometimes called rosamarina, is a must-have staple for busy families. This almond-shape pasta satisfies just like rice but cooks up more quickly.

Per serving: 500 calories, 15 g total fat (5 g sat.), 66 mg cholesterol, 1,153 mg sodium, 52 g carbohydrate, 3 g fiber, 34 g protein.

Ground Lamb Gyros

Yogurt Sauce:
- 1 cup plain yogurt
- ½ large cucumber, thinly sliced
- 2 teaspoons lemon juice
- ⅛ teaspoon salt

Filling:
- 1½ pounds ground lamb or beef
- ¼ cup chopped fresh mint leaves
- 1 teaspoon dried oregano
- ½ teaspoon salt
- ¼ teaspoon black pepper
- Zest from 1 lemon

Gyros:
- 6 large pitas, warmed slightly
- 1 container (10½ ounces) herb-flavored feta cheese
- 3 cups shredded iceberg lettuce

1. **Yogurt Sauce:** In small bowl, mix together yogurt, cucumber, lemon juice and salt. Cover and refrigerate until ready to use.

2. **Filling:** Heat broiler. In large bowl, mix together lamb, mint, oregano, salt, pepper and lemon zest. Form into six patties, each 1 inch thick. Broil 5 inches from heat for 7 minutes per side or until an instant-read meat thermometer inserted in centers registers 160°. Remove from broiler.

3. **Gyros:** Slice patties. Evenly divide cooked lamb, feta and lettuce among the pitas.

4. Fold sides of pitas over the filling in the centers. Secure with parchment paper or with toothpicks. Serve with yogurt sauce.

If you're a fan of the ever-popular Greek sandwich, you can make this tasty version at home, no problem.

PREP: 15 minutes
BROIL: 14 minutes
MAKES: 6 servings

QUICK BITE

HERB KNOW-HOW

Sweet, refreshing mint adds a cool aftertaste to recipes. Peppermint is more intense than spearmint, which is delicate. Snip leftover leaves into salads (they go especially well with salads that include orange slices) or use them as a garnish for desserts.

Per serving: 554 calories, 28 g total fat (15 g sat.), 126 mg cholesterol, 1,236 mg sodium, 40 g carbohydrate, 2 g fiber, 34 g protein.

Teriyaki Chicken and Noodles

1 package (8 ounces) thin rice noodles
1 can (14 ounces) reduced-fat coconut milk
1 bag (12 ounces) broccoli slaw
1 sweet red pepper, seeded and cut into thin strips
7 tablespoons teriyaki sauce
¼ teaspoon salt
1½ pounds thin-sliced boneless, skinless chicken breasts
3 egg whites, lightly beaten
1¼ cups panko crumbs or packaged plain dry bread crumbs
¼ cup vegetable oil

1. Soak noodles in enough warm water to cover for 15 minutes. Meanwhile, in large saucepan, heat coconut milk, broccoli slaw, sweet pepper, 4 tablespoons teriyaki sauce and the salt over medium heat until broccoli and pepper are heated through. Set aside.

2. Brush chicken with the remaining 3 tablespoons teriyaki sauce. Dip each slice in egg white, then coat completely with panko crumbs.

3. In large nonstick skillet, heat oil over high heat. Sauté chicken for 2 to 3 minutes, then turn and cook for 2 minutes longer or until an instant-read meat thermometer inserted in centers registers 160° and crumbs are crisp.

4. Meanwhile, drain noodles and add to coconut milk-teriyaki sauce in saucepan; reheat as needed. Serve noodles with chicken.

When a taste of Asia would hit the spot, remember these crunchy chicken breasts served with teriyaki-seasoned veggies and rice noodles.

PREP: 15 minutes
COOK: 4 to 5 minutes
MAKES: 6 servings

QUICK BITE

MORE CRUMB CRUNCH

Panko crumbs are Japanese-style bread crumbs that are coarser than traditional American bread crumbs. They give breaded dishes a surprising crunchiness. Find panko crumbs in the Asian food aisle of the supermarket or at Asian food stores.

Per serving: 500 calories, 15 g total fat (5 g sat.), 66 mg cholesterol, 1,153 mg sodium, 52 g carbohydrate, 3 g fiber, 34 g protein.

Lemon Chicken

¼ cup slivered almonds
6 small boneless, skinless chicken breast halves (1 pound total)
½ teaspoon lemon pepper
2 tablespoons vegetable oil
1 package (20 ounces) refrigerated diced potatoes and onions
1 cup water
1 package (24 ounces) frozen green beans in garlic-butter sauce
3 tablespoons lemon juice

1. In large dry skillet, toast almonds for 4 minutes; transfer to small dish. Sprinkle chicken with lemon-pepper seasoning. In large skillet, heat oil over medium heat. Add chicken; cook about 4 minutes or until lightly browned.

2. Flip chicken; cook for 4 minutes longer. Transfer to plate. Add potatoes and onions and water to skillet; cook, covered, for 5 minutes.

3. Add green beans and lemon juice; cover and cook for 10 to 12 minutes or until potatoes are tender. Place chicken on top; cover and cook until heated through, about 3 minutes. Sprinkle individual servings with almonds.

Green beans with toasted almonds and lemon are a winning combination. Now team the trio with chicken and potatoes for a speedy main dish.

PREP: 5 minutes
COOK: about 30 minutes
MAKES: 6 servings

QUICK TIP

LOTS OF LEMON JUICE

To get more juice from lemons or limes, heat them in the microwave for 10 seconds before squeezing them.

Per serving: 291 calories, 11 g total fat (2 g sat.), 47 mg cholesterol, 728 mg sodium, 8 g carbohydrate, 5 g fiber, 21 g protein.

Chicken-Pineapple Kabobs

1½ pounds boneless, skinless chicken thighs, fat removed and chicken cut into 1-inch pieces
12 strips turkey bacon
3 cups fresh pineapple chunks (1-inch cubes)
⅓ cup hickory-smoked barbecue sauce
⅓ cup pineapple preserves
2 pouches (8.8 ounces each) fully cooked white rice (such as Zatarain's)

1. Soak eight short bamboo skewers in water for 30 minutes (or use four long metal skewers). Place chicken on microwave-safe plate and microwave on HIGH for 5 minutes, stirring once halfway through cooking time. Cut bacon crosswise into 2-inch-long pieces. Thread skewers with chicken, folded bacon and pineapple chunks, leaving a ¼-inch space between pieces.

2. Heat gas grill to medium-high or prepare charcoal grill with medium-hot coals. Place skewers on grill and cook for 6 minutes; turn and grill for 6 minutes longer.

3. Meanwhile, in small microwave-safe bowl, stir together barbecue sauce and pineapple preserves; microwave on HIGH for 1 to 2 minutes or until warm. Microwave cooked rice following package directions.

4. Remove skewers from grill. Brush with warm barbecue sauce mixture. Serve with hot rice and remaining barbecue sauce mixture on the side.

Kids love fruity kabobs slathered with tangy barbecue sauce.

PREP: 10 minutes
MICROWAVE: 7 minutes
GRILL: 12 minutes
MAKES: 4 servings

QUICK TIP

KEEP IT CLEAN

To prevent the spread of bacteria when cooking chicken or turkey:
• Immediately after handling raw poultry, wash work surfaces and utensils in hot, soapy water.
• Use separate cutting boards for raw poultry and other food.
• Never use the same plate for uncooked and cooked poultry.

Per serving: 659 calories, 18 g total fat (4 g sat.), 179 mg cholesterol, 989 mg sodium, 79 g carbohydrate, 2 g fiber, 44 g protein.

Thanks to convenience products, paprika chicken—one of Hungary's most famous dishes—gets transformed into an any-night soup.

PREP: 10 minutes
COOK: 15 minutes
MAKES: 6 servings

Chicken Paprikash Soup

¼ cup all-purpose flour
2 tablespoons paprika
½ teaspoon salt
¼ teaspoon black pepper
1½ pounds chicken tenders, cut in half
2 cans (14 ounces each) chicken broth
1 tablespoon peanut oil
1 cup chopped onion
2 teaspoons bottled chopped garlic
½ of a 1½-pound package refrigerated partially cooked potato slices (see note)
6 tablespoons sour cream
Paprika, for garnish (optional)

1. In plastic food-storage bag, combine flour, the 2 tablespoons paprika, the salt and pepper. Add half of the chicken; shake to coat. Place flour-coated chicken on plate. Repeat the coating process with remaining chicken.

2. In small bowl, stir together remaining flour from plastic bag and 3 tablespoons chicken broth. Set aside.

3. In large nonstick saucepan, heat oil over medium heat. Add chicken; brown for 4 minutes. Add onion and garlic; cook for 1 minute. Add remaining broth; simmer for 2 minutes.

4. Add potatoes; cook for 5 minutes.

5. Stir in flour mixture; bring to a boil. Cook, stirring, about 2 minutes longer or until slightly thickened.

6. Serve each portion with dollop of sour cream. If desired, sprinkle with additional paprika.

Note: One can (15 ounces) sliced white potatoes, drained, can be substituted for the packaged refrigerated potatoes.

Per serving: 262 calories, 11 g total fat (4 g sat.), 72 mg cholesterol, 821 mg sodium, 16 g carbohydrate, 2 g fiber, 26 g protein.

Country Captain Soup

2 teaspoons extra-virgin olive oil
1 onion, chopped
1 green pepper, seeded and chopped
1 Granny Smith apple, peeled, cored and
   chopped
1 teaspoon bottled minced garlic
1 tablespoon curry powder
1 teaspoon grated fresh ginger
1¼ pounds boneless, skinless chicken
   thighs, fat removed and chicken cut
   into 1-inch pieces
2 cans (14 ounces each) chicken broth
1 can (14½ ounces) chopped tomatoes
   with jalapeños

1. In large saucepan, heat oil over medium heat. Add onion, green pepper, apple and garlic; sauté about 4 minutes or until softened. Add curry powder and ginger; sauté for 1 minute.

2. Add chicken, broth and tomatoes. Simmer, covered, for 15 minutes.

This dish was named for a British army officer who discovered the recipe while stationed in India— that explains the use of the curry.

PREP: 10 minutes
COOK: 20 minutes
MAKES: 6 servings

QUICK BITE
SPICE SAVVY

Consider curry a pantry staple. This fragrant ingredient blends up to 20 spices, letting you add a windfall of exotic flavor with just one measure. It's often used in Indian and Asian cooking.

Per serving: 225 calories, 11 g total fat (3 g sat.), 67 mg cholesterol, 909 mg sodium, 11 g carbohydrate, 2 g fiber, 20 g protein.

Orange-Chicken Salad

With canned mandarin oranges on the shelf, you can serve a fruit-studded chicken salad any time of year.

PREP: 10 minutes
COOK: 10 minutes
MAKES: 4 servings

4 boneless, skinless chicken breast halves (1¼ pounds total)
1 clove garlic, smashed
2 cups chicken broth
1 pound whole fresh green beans, trimmed
1 head red-leaf lettuce, washed and dried
1 can (15 ounces) mandarin oranges, drained, 2 tablespoons juice reserved for dressing
½ cup red grapes, halved
½ cup coarsely chopped candied walnuts (such as Emerald brand)
Dressing:
  ⅓ cup reduced-fat sour cream
  2 tablespoons reserved mandarin orange juice
  2 teaspoons maple syrup
  1 teaspoon lemon juice
  ¼ teaspoon salt
  ⅛ teaspoon black pepper
  ⅛ teaspoon hot-pepper sauce

1. In large saucepan, combine chicken and garlic. Lightly brown chicken; add broth. Bring to a boil over medium-high heat; reduce to simmer. Cook about 10 minutes or until chicken is done, adding beans during last 5 minutes of cooking.

2. **Dressing:** Stir together sour cream, mandarin orange juice, maple syrup, lemon juice, salt, black pepper and hot-pepper sauce.

3. Line a platter with lettuce. Arrange chicken, beans, oranges and grapes on top of lettuce; top with chopped walnuts and serve with dressing.

Per serving: 427 calories, 12 g total fat (2 g sat.), 91 mg cholesterol, 856 mg sodium, 41 g carbohydrate, 3 g fiber, 38 g protein.

Springtime Pasta

- 1 **pound cavatappi or other corkscrew-shape pasta**
- 1 **tablespoon extra-virgin olive oil**
- 1½ **pounds boneless, skinless chicken breast halves, cut into 1-inch pieces**
- 1 **sweet yellow pepper, seeded and cut into thin strips**
- 1 **bunch (1 pound) fresh asparagus, trimmed and cut into 2-inch pieces**
- 1 **pint cherry tomatoes, halved**
- 1 **package (5.2 ounces) spreadable herb cheese (such as Boursin brand)**
- ¼ **teaspoon salt**
- ¼ **teaspoon black pepper**

1. Bring a large pot of lightly salted water to a boil. Add pasta and return to a boil. Cook for 6 minutes.

2. Meanwhile, heat large nonstick skillet over medium-high heat. Add oil and tilt skillet to coat. Add chicken. Cook for 6 minutes, stirring occasionally. During last minute of cooking, add yellow pepper to skillet. Remove from heat.

3. Once pasta has cooked for 6 minutes, add asparagus and cook 2 minutes longer. Scoop out ¼ cup pasta water, then drain pasta.

4. In large bowl, toss together hot pasta and asparagus, chicken and yellow pepper, tomatoes, herbed cheese, reserved ¼ cup pasta water, salt and black pepper until well blended and cheese is melted.

Herbed cheese and a little cooking water combine to make a creamy pasta sauce that's a bit lighter than usual.

PREP: 15 minutes
COOK: about 10 minutes
MAKES: 8 servings

QUICK TIP

PASTA MAKEOVERS

Your favorite pasta dishes can tip the scale at over 600 calories apiece. Here are a few ways to reshape recipes:
- When using tomato-based sauces from a jar, check ingredient labels to find brands with 50 to 80 calories per ½-cup serving—just the right amount for 1½ cups cooked pasta.
- Bulk up your bowl with high-fiber vegetables such as cauliflower and broccoli. It will help you stay full longer and also cut calories per serving.
- If you normally start with oil in the pan, switch to a nonstick skillet and use half the original amount of oil.

Per serving: 395 calories, 10 g total fat (5 g sat.), 74 mg cholesterol, 248 mg sodium, 47 g carbohydrate, 3 g fiber, 30 g protein.

Speedy Chicken Scarpariello

1 tablespoon extra-virgin olive oil
2 pounds boneless, skinless chicken thighs, fat removed and chicken cut into 1-inch pieces
¾ teaspoon salt
¾ teaspoon dried Italian seasoning
½ teaspoon black pepper
1 package (12 ounces) fully cooked Italian-flavored chicken sausage
1 pound refrigerated packaged precooked potato wedges
2 sweet peppers (any color), seeded and cut up
2 cloves garlic, chopped
¼ cup bottled Italian salad dressing

1. In large nonstick skillet, heat the oil over medium-high heat. Season the chicken with ¼ teaspoon each of the salt, Italian seasoning and black pepper. Sauté chicken for 5 minutes, stirring occasionally.

2. Cut sausage into ½-inch pieces. Add to skillet along with potatoes, sweet pepper and garlic. Stir in remaining ½ teaspoon salt, ½ teaspoon Italian seasoning and ¼ teaspoon black pepper. Add Italian dressing; stir to combine.

3. Cover skillet and cook over medium-high heat for 15 minutes, stirring occasionally.

4. Remove skillet from heat and let stand for 5 minutes before serving.

There are many versions of Chicken Scarpariello; some, like this one, call for sausage, making the dish a hearty mainstay.

PREP: 10 minutes
COOK: 20 minutes
STAND: 5 minutes
MAKES: 6 servings

QUICK BITE

PRODUCE POINTERS

Choose firm, smooth, glossy peppers without dings or cracks; stems should be green and not too dried out. Sweet peppers can be stored, unwrapped, in the refrigerator for up to 5 days.

Per serving: 363 calories, 11 g total fat (2 g sat.), 148 mg cholesterol, 866 mg sodium, 19 g carbohydrate, 2 g fiber, 46 g protein.

Chicken and Sun-Dried Tomato Cream

1½ pounds thin-sliced boneless, skinless
  chicken breasts
¼ teaspoon salt
⅛ teaspoon black pepper
2 tablespoons extra-virgin olive oil
¼ teaspoon red pepper flakes
1 small onion, diced
¼ cup dry white wine
1 cup chicken broth
½ cup heavy cream
½ cup purchased sun-dried tomato pesto
¼ cup kalamata or niçoise olives, pitted
  and halved
  Fresh rosemary sprigs, for garnish
  (optional)

1. Season both sides of each chicken piece
with salt and pepper. In large skillet, heat
1 tablespoon oil over medium-high heat. Add
half of the chicken; cook for 3 minutes per side
or until an instant-read meat thermometer
inserted in centers registers 160°. Transfer to
platter; keep warm. Repeat with remaining oil
and chicken.

2. Add red pepper flakes and onion to skillet;
cook for 3 minutes. Add wine; cook for
1 minute, stirring to dissolve browned bits. Add
broth, cream and pesto. Bring to a boil; cook,
uncovered, about 4 minutes or until slightly
thickened. Pour sauce over chicken. Sprinkle
with olives. Serve immediately. If desired,
garnish with fresh rosemary.

With a wine-based cream sauce flecked with sun-dried tomato pesto, this is a handy pick if you want to enjoy something weekend-worthy on a weeknight.

PREP: 10 minutes
COOK: 20 minutes
MAKES: 6 servings

QUICK TIP

STORE IT RIGHT

Keep olive oil in a cool, dark place for up to 6 months or refrigerate it for up to 1 year. Chilled olive oil becomes thick and cloudy; before using, let it stand at room temperature until it becomes liquid and clear.

Per serving: 304 calories, 19 g total fat (7 g sat.), 91 mg cholesterol, 746 mg sodium, 7 g carbohydrate, 1 g fiber, 25 g protein.

Pepper- and Cheese-Stuffed Chicken

4 boneless, skinless chicken breast halves
   (1½ pounds total)
1 jar (7 ounces) roasted red peppers,
   drained and chopped
4 tablespoons herb-flavored cheese spread
¼ cup all-purpose flour
1 teaspoon salt
¼ teaspoon black pepper
2 eggs
⅔ cup packaged seasoned dry bread crumbs
   Hot cooked noodles tossed with butter
    and chopped fresh flat-leaf parsley
    leaves (optional)
   Fresh flat-leaf parsley, for garnish
   (optional)

Chicken again? Here's another delicious approach to one of our favorite go-to ingredients.

PREP: 10 minutes
BAKE: at 375° for 20 minutes
MAKES: 4 servings

1. Heat oven to 375°. Line a 13×9×2-inch baking dish with aluminum foil; coat with nonstick cooking spray.

2. Insert sharp paring knife into thicker side of each chicken breast and cut a pocket lengthwise, carefully making it as wide as possible without puncturing sides.

3. Divide roasted red peppers into four equal portions; spoon one portion into each pocket. Spread 1 tablespoon herb cheese on top of roasted red pepper in each pocket. Secure sides with wooden toothpicks.

4. On waxed paper, combine flour, salt and black pepper. Beat eggs lightly in a pie plate. Dip chicken into flour mixture; shake off excess. Dip in egg; coat with bread crumbs. Place in prepared baking pan; coat chicken breast tops with nonstick cooking spray.

5. Bake at 375° about 20 minutes or until golden and instant-read meat thermometer inserted in centers registers 160°. Remove toothpicks. If desired, serve with noodles and garnish with additional parsley.

QUICK TIP

EXTRA ROASTED RED PEPPERS?

Jars of roasted red peppers shave prep time (no more roasting and peeling your own!) while adding color and spark to meals. If you purchase a larger jar than the 7-ounce jar called for in this recipe, refrigerate the extras to use as a garnish for dips, to stir into scrambled eggs or to tuck into sandwiches.

Per serving: 371 calories, 11 g total fat (4 g sat.), 215 mg cholesterol, 1,373 mg sodium, 25 g carbohydrate, 1 g fiber, 42 g protein.

Chicken Soft Tacos

1 tablespoon extra-virgin olive oil
2 chorizo sausages, cut into ½-inch pieces
1 pound ground chicken
2 small zucchini, chopped
1 small yellow squash, chopped
1 tablespoon hot chili powder
½ teaspoon salt
⅛ teaspoon cayenne pepper
½ cup sour cream
1 ripe avocado
3 tablespoons bottled salsa
1 tablespoon lime juice
1 package (9 ounces) white corn tortillas (12 tortillas total)
Lime wedges, for garnish (optional)

1. In large nonstick skillet, heat oil over medium-high heat. Add chorizo and chicken; cook for 3 minutes. Add zucchini, squash, chili powder, salt and cayenne pepper; stir to combine. Add sour cream and reduce heat to medium; cook for 5 to 8 minutes longer or until zucchini is tender and sauce has reduced.

2. Peel and remove pit from avocado. In a bowl, mash avocado with fork. Stir in salsa and lime juice. Heat tortillas according to package directions. Serve chicken wrapped in tortillas with avocado salsa on the side. If desired, garnish with lime wedges.

Craving a little spice? Chorizo is a highly seasoned pork sausage that's favored in Mexican and Spanish cuisines. The avocado salsa comes together with just three ingredients.

PREP: 10 minutes
COOK: about 11 minutes
MAKES: 12 tacos

QUICK BITE
PRODUCE POINTERS

Choose young, small, fresh and firm zucchini with no blemishes or soft spots. Store in a plastic storage bag in the refrigerator for up to 4 days.

Per taco: 227 calories, 14 g total fat (5 g sat.), 63 mg cholesterol, 300 mg sodium, 14 g carbohydrate, 2 g fiber, 11 g protein.

White and Wild Rice Chicken Salad

1 box (6 ounces) white-and-wild-rice mix
3 tablespoons tarragon-flavored vinegar
1 tablespoon honey-Dijon mustard
¼ teaspoon salt
¼ teaspoon black pepper
¼ cup plus 1 tablespoon vegetable oil
1 pound boneless, skinless chicken breast, cut into ¼-inch-wide strips
1 Gala apple, cored and chopped
6 scallions, trimmed and chopped
2 large ribs celery, sliced
½ cup toasted pecan pieces
½ cup dried cranberries
  Lettuce leaves, for garnish (optional)

1. Prepare rice mix following package directions, using very hot water.

2. Meanwhile, in small bowl, mix vinegar, mustard, salt and pepper. Whisk in ¼ cup oil. Set aside.

3. In large skillet, heat 1 tablespoon oil over high heat. Add chicken strips; sauté for 4 to 6 minutes or until cooked through and lightly browned. Remove chicken to bowl; cover.

4. In large bowl, combine apple, scallion, celery, pecans and cranberries. Add hot rice, chicken and vinegar mixture.

5. If desired, line a serving bowl with lettuce leaves; spoon salad into bowl. Serve immediately or refrigerate and serve cold.

The white-and-wild-rice mix lets you get a jump-start on this satisfying fruit-and-nut salad.

PREP: 15 minutes
COOK: 4 to 6 minutes
MAKES: 6 servings

QUICK TIP

NUT SUBSTITUTIONS

In recipes, specific nuts are often selected for their particular flavor and appearance. However, in general, walnuts may be substituted for pecans and vice versa.

Per serving: 406 calories, 20 g total fat (2 g sat.), 44 mg cholesterol, 560 mg sodium, 36 g carbohydrate, 3 g fiber, 21 g protein.

Turkey Bolognese and Polenta

2 tablespoons extra-virgin olive oil
1 package (4 ounces) sliced mixed mushrooms
1¼ pounds ground turkey
1 teaspoon dried basil
¼ teaspoon salt
¼ teaspoon black pepper
1 jar (24 ounces) marinara sauce
⅓ cup heavy cream
1 package (24 ounces) heat-and-serve polenta (such as San Gennaro brand), cut into ½-inch-thick slices
6 tablespoons shredded Parmesan cheese
Fresh basil sprigs, for garnish (optional)

1. In large nonstick skillet, heat oil over medium-high heat. Add mushrooms and cook for 3 minutes. Crumble in ground turkey and add dried basil, salt and pepper. Cook for 5 minutes longer, stirring occasionally.

2. Stir in marinara sauce and cook over medium heat, stirring occasionally, for 5 minutes longer. Stir in cream.

3. While sauce is cooking, heat a grill pan and grill the polenta slices until heated through. Serve sauce with polenta slices. Sprinkle each serving with shredded cheese. If desired, garnish with fresh basil.

Sliced mixed mushrooms and prepared polenta are two shortcuts that allow you to serve this hearty dish in less than 30 minutes.

PREP: 10 minutes
COOK: 13 minutes
MAKES: 6 servings

JAZZ UP MARINARA

Marinara sauce is a great staple to keep on hand for quick meals anytime. To perk up this everyday sauce, call on any of the following: smashed capers, chopped black olives, flaked tuna, chopped fresh mozzarella, sautéed zucchini coins, crisp bacon bits or slivers of prosciutto.

Per serving: 388 calories, 23 g total fat (7 g sat.), 98 mg cholesterol, 960 mg sodium, 22 g carbohydrate, 3 g fiber, 26 g protein.

White Pizza with Smoked Turkey

2 large (10 ounces each) baked thin pizza
   crusts (such as Boboli brand)
2 cups shredded Italian-blend cheese
   (8 ounces)
4 ounces thinly sliced smoked turkey,
   cut into ½-inch-wide strips
1 container (15 ounces) ricotta cheese
1 container (4 ounces) garlic-and-herb
   cheese spread
¼ cup fresh basil leaves

1. Heat oven to 450°. Place each pizza shell on a baking sheet. Sprinkle 1 cup shredded cheese over each pizza shell. Evenly distribute turkey over pizza shells.

2. In small bowl, mix ricotta and cheese spread. Dollop evenly over pizzas.

3. Bake at 450° about 10 minutes or until heated through and cheese is melted. Sprinkle basil over pizzas. To serve the pizzas, cut each into six wedges.

Smoked sausage doesn't need precooking, and the ready-to-use crusts and cheeses need no prep either. Dinner doesn't get much faster than this!

PREP: 5 minutes
BAKE: at 450° for 10 minutes
MAKES: 12 wedges

QUICK BITE

HERB KNOW-HOW

Fresh basil adds an irresistibly minty and clovelike aroma to foods. In a pinch, substitute oregano or thyme. Look for the smallest basil leaves or stack several large ones, roll them, then slice into thin strips for garnish.

Per wedge: 302 calories, 15 g total fat (8 g sat.), 48 mg cholesterol, 583 mg sodium, 25 g carbohydrate, 1 g fiber, 15 g protein.

Couscous Paella

2 tablespoons extra-virgin olive oil
1 pound turkey cutlets, cut into
  ½-inch pieces
½ pound medium-size shrimp, shelled
  and deveined
¾ teaspoon salt
2 cups chicken broth
1 cup frozen peas
½ cup chopped roasted red pepper
1 tablespoon dried onion flakes
1 box (10 ounces) couscous
1 jar (6½ ounces) marinated artichokes
½ cup sliced pepperoni
½ cup stuffed olives
2 tablespoons lemon juice
⅛ teaspoon cayenne pepper

1. In a large nonstick skillet, heat oil over medium heat. Add turkey to skillet. Sauté for 2 minutes. Add shrimp and cook about 3 minutes or until turkey is no longer pink and shrimp turns pink. Season with ¼ teaspoon salt. With a slotted spoon, transfer to a large bowl.

2. In same skillet, mix broth, peas, red pepper and onion flakes. Cover and bring to a boil. Remove from heat and stir in couscous. Cover and let stand for 5 minutes.

3. Drain marinated artichokes, reserving liquid. Add artichokes, pepperoni and olives to bowl with turkey and shrimp. Fluff couscous mixture and add to bowl.

4. In small bowl, whisk together reserved artichoke marinade, the lemon juice, cayenne pepper and the remaining ½ teaspoon salt. Toss with couscous mixture. Serve warm or at room temperature.

A traditional party dish becomes weeknight easy when you call on nearly instant couscous instead of rice.

PREP: 15 minutes
COOK: about 7 minutes
STAND: 5 minutes
MAKES: 6 servings

QUICK TIP

GETTING THE KIDS TO HELP

To transform kitchen time into together time, get the kids involved. Depending on their ages, here are ways they can help you with meals:

- Measuring ingredients.
- Whisking and stirring dry ingredients and batters.
- Flattening dough into pastry crusts.
- Tearing herbs; grating cheese.
- Spreading breads with toppings.
- Dredging ingredients.

Per serving: 494 calories, 19 g total fat (4 g sat.), 107 mg cholesterol, 1,354 mg sodium, 46 g carbohydrate, 5 g fiber, 35 g protein.

Peanut Noodles and Turkey Skewers

Peanut Sauce:
- ½ cup creamy peanut butter
- ½ cup warm water
- 2 tablespoons lemon juice
- 2 tablespoons reduced-sodium soy sauce
- 2 teaspoons chopped fresh ginger
- 2 cloves garlic, chopped
- 1 teaspoon sesame oil
- ½ teaspoon sugar
- ¼ teaspoon red pepper flakes

Noodles and Turkey:
- 8 ounces wide lo mein noodles
- 2 carrots, coarsely shredded
- 3 scallions, trimmed and sliced
- 1 pound turkey or chicken cutlets

1. Heat broiler. Coat broiler pan with nonstick cooking spray. Bring large pot of water to a boil.

2. **Peanut Sauce:** In small bowl, whisk together peanut butter, water, lemon juice, soy sauce, ginger, garlic, sesame oil, sugar and red pepper flakes. Set aside.

3. **Noodles and Turkey:** Cook noodles following package directions. Rinse under cold water. Toss with 1 cup of the peanut sauce, the carrot and scallion.

4. Cut each turkey cutlet crosswise into six pieces. Thread onto 8 metal skewers. Brush liberally with remaining peanut sauce. Broil for 2 minutes. Turn and broil for 2 minutes longer.

5. Serve immediately with noodle mixture.

A lush peanut sauce coats wide noodles and also gets brushed onto the turkey skewers.

PREP: 20 minutes
COOK: 5 minutes
BROIL: 4 minutes
MAKES: 4 servings

QUICK BITE
WHY NOT TRY ...

Flat and wide, lo mein noodles are a popular shape of Chinese wheat noodles that are often cooked, then stir-fried with other ingredients. Dried lo mein noodles will keep indefinitely in the pantry. If you find fresh lo mein noodles in an Asian market, use within 3 days.

Per serving: 583 calories, 21 g total fat (4 g sat.), 136 mg cholesterol, 531 mg sodium, 54 g carbohydrate, 4 g fiber, 47 g protein.

Turkey Lo Mein

2 tablespoons vegetable oil

2 pounds turkey cutlets, cut into thin strips

1 package (8 ounces) sliced mixed mushrooms

2 cups frozen mixed-pepper strips (from a 1-pound package)

⅔ cup bottled stir-fry sauce (see Note)

1 pound linguine, cooked following package directions

1. Heat a large nonstick wok or large skillet over high heat. Add 1 tablespoon oil. In two batches, stir-fry turkey strips about 3 minutes or until lightly browned. Transfer to a plate; set aside.

2. Wipe out wok or skillet and heat remaining 1 tablespoon oil; add mushrooms and stir-fry for 4 minutes. Add pepper strips and stir-fry for 2 minutes longer. Add turkey and stir-fry sauce and heat through.

3. Place cooked pasta on large platter; spoon turkey mixture on top.

Note: We suggest one of the following sauces: House of Tsang Imperial Citrus Sauce or Sweet and Sour Stir-Fry Sauce or San-J Polynesian Sweet and Tangy Stir-Fry Sauce.

Colorful, fresh, family friendly— and fast! Yes, it can be done, thanks to the combined convenience of frozen mixed-pepper strips, presliced mushrooms and stir-fry sauce.

PREP: 10 minutes
COOK: 12 minutes
MAKES: 6 servings

QUICK BITE
TEMPTING TURKEY CUTLETS

Why wait for Thanksgiving to enjoy turkey? Turkey cutlets are a lean and luscious option for any-night meals. Also turn to this cut when you are looking for a substitute for thin-sliced chicken cutlets or veal cutlets.

Per serving: 467 calories, 7 g total fat (1 g sat.), 109 mg cholesterol, 1,149 mg sodium, 51 g carbohydrate, 3 g fiber, 50 g protein.

Sweet-and-Sour Turkey Meatballs

1 can (20 ounces) pineapple chunks with juice
1 can (14 ounces) chicken broth
1 green pepper, seeded and cut into strips
1 sweet red pepper, seeded and cut into small squares
1 cup ketchup
¼ cup packed light-brown sugar
¼ cup cider vinegar
1 package (24 ounces) refrigerated turkey meatballs
6 scallions, trimmed and cut into 1-inch pieces
2½ cups instant rice, cooked following package directions

1. In large skillet, combine pineapple and juice, broth, green pepper strips, red pepper squares, ketchup, brown sugar and vinegar. Bring to a simmer over medium-high heat, stirring to dissolve sugar.

2. Add the meatballs; simmer, covered, for 10 minutes. Stir in scallion. Serve over rice.

There's no need to turn to takeout when you can have this homemade sweet-and-sour dish on the table in minutes.

PREP: 10 minutes
COOK: about 15 minutes
MAKES: 8 servings

QUICK TIP

MORE WAYS WITH MEATBALLS

Here are more ideas for transforming meatballs into quick weeknight meals:
• Add meatballs to a can of minestrone soup; sprinkle with Parmesan cheese.
• Sliced prepared meatballs make for a kid-pleasing pizza topper; simply keep prepared crusts, pizza sauce and cheese on hand for an anytime dinner.
• Pasta and meatballs with red sauce is a classic, but for a change, try purchased Alfredo sauce instead.
• Heat with barbecue sauce and tuck into toasted hoagie buns.

Per serving: 358 calories, 8 g total fat (3 g sat.), 46 mg cholesterol, 602 mg sodium, 57 g carbohydrate, 3 g fiber, 16 g protein.

Piquant Turkey Cutlets

⅓ cup all-purpose flour
½ teaspoon salt
⅛ teaspoon black pepper
4 turkey cutlets (1 to 1¼ pounds total)
2 tablespoons extra-virgin olive oil
¾ cup dry white wine
1¼ cups chicken broth
1 jar (7½ ounces) sun-dried tomatoes in oil, drained and thinly sliced
1½ tablespoons drained capers
1½ teaspoons dried marjoram
1½ tablespoons butter
Hot cooked pasta (optional)

1. In plastic food-storage bag, combine flour, salt and pepper. Cut each turkey cutlet into 3 or 4 pieces. Add half of the turkey pieces to bag; seal and shake to coat. Remove turkey pieces from bag; set aside. Repeat with remaining turkey pieces.

2. In large skillet, heat oil over medium-high heat. Add half of the turkey pieces; sauté for 2 to 3 minutes per side or until browned. Transfer to plate. Repeat with remaining turkey pieces. Drain fat from skillet.

3. Add wine to skillet; cook over high heat for 2 minutes. Add broth, sun-dried tomatoes, capers and marjoram. Gently boil about 4 minutes or until slightly reduced. Return turkey pieces to skillet; cook over medium heat for 2 minutes. Add butter, swirling just until melted. If desired, serve with pasta.

Sun-dried tomatoes and capers add spark and color to done-in-a flash turkey cutlets.

PREP: 10 minutes
COOK: about 16 minutes
MAKES: 4 servings

QUICK BITE
WHY NOT TRY ...

Capers have a taste that can be best described as a cross between citrus fruit and olives, with a bonus of tangy flavor from the salt and vinegar of their packaging brine. Look for them next to the olives in the supermarket. You might spot jars of smaller buds alongside jars of larger buds; while they can be used interchangeably in recipes, smaller buds have more flavor.

Per serving: 382 calories, 23 g total fat (6 g sat.), 87 mg cholesterol, 822 mg sodium, 13 g carbohydrate, 2 g fiber, 27 g protein.

Nutty Turkey Cutlets

¾ cup honey- or spice-flavored almonds
½ cup honey
¼ cup light soy sauce
4 turkey or chicken cutlets (about
    1 pound total)
1 box (5.8 ounces) garlic-flavored couscous
    Scallions, trimmed and chopped,
    for garnish (optional)

1. Set aside a few nuts for garnish. Place remaining nuts in food processor and pulse once or twice or just until nuts are chopped. Do not overprocess. Place chopped nuts on waxed paper.

2. In shallow bowl, stir together honey and soy sauce. Dip cutlets in honey-soy sauce mixture, allowing excess to drip back into bowl. Dip cutlets into chopped nuts, patting nuts firmly onto both sides. Transfer to a plate and refrigerate for 10 minutes.

3. Meanwhile, prepare the couscous following package directions. Cover and keep warm.

4. Place remaining honey-soy sauce mixture in small saucepan and bring to a boil; cook for 3 minutes, then remove from heat; set aside.

5. Heat broiler. Coat broiler pan with nonstick cooking spray. Place cutlets on broiler pan; broil 6 inches from heat for 2 to 3 minutes; turn and cook 2 to 3 minutes longer. Serve with couscous; drizzle honey-soy sauce mixture on top. Garnish with reserved nuts and, if desired, chopped scallions.

A brief stint in the refrigerator will ensure that the nutty coating stays in place. Use that time to stir up the couscous and a salad.

PREP: 10 minutes
CHILL: 10 minutes
BROIL: 4 to 6 minutes
MAKES: 4 servings

QUICK BITE
HONEY VARIETIES

Bees often make honey from clover, but other sources include lavender, thyme, orange blossom, apple, cherry, buckwheat and tupelo. Generally, the lighter the color, the milder the flavor. Store honey at room temperature in a dark place.

Per serving: 470 calories, 10 g total fat (2 g sat.), 74 mg cholesterol, 1,032 mg sodium, 67 g carbohydrate, 2 g fiber, 32 g protein.

Zesty Fish Soup

2 cans (14 ounces each) chicken broth
⅔ cup instant rice
1 package (10 ounces) frozen corn
1½ cups bottled chunky salsa
1 pound mild-flavored fish fillets (haddock, cod or halibut), cut into 2-inch pieces
 Fresh lime pieces, for garnish (optional)

1. In deep pot, combine broth with enough water to make 6 cups; bring to a boil. Add rice; simmer, covered, for 5 minutes.

2. Add corn and salsa. Bring to a boil. Add fish pieces. Cook, covered, about 5 minutes or until fish flakes easily when tested with a fork. If desired, garnish with lime.

Keep chicken broth, rice and salsa in the cupboard and frozen corn in the freezer. Then, with just one stop at a fish market, you can make this satisfying soup supper.

PREP: 5 minutes
COOK: 15 minutes
MAKES: 4 servings

QUICK TIP

STORE IT RIGHT

It's best if you cook fish the same day you buy it. Otherwise, wrap it loosely in plastic wrap and store it in the coldest part of the refrigerator. Use it within 2 days. Cover and chill leftover cooked fish and use it within 2 days.

Per serving: 292 calories, 5 g total fat (1 g sat.), 76 mg cholesterol, 1,346 mg sodium, 34 g carbohydrate, 4 g fiber, 29 g protein.

Spicy Tuna and Linguine

3 tablespoons extra-virgin olive oil
4 cloves garlic, chopped
1 can (28 ounces) recipe-ready crushed
   tomatoes with Italian herbs
½ teaspoon salt
½ teaspoon red pepper flakes
4 tuna steaks, ¾ inch thick (6 ounces each)
3 tablespoons drained capers
1 bunch Broccolini, cut into 1-inch pieces
12 ounces fresh spinach linguine
2 tablespoons shredded Parmesan cheese
   (optional)

1. Bring large pot of salted water to a boil.

2. In large skillet, heat oil over medium heat. Add garlic; sauté for 1 minute. Add tomatoes, salt and red pepper flakes. Bring to simmer. Add tuna steaks; cover and simmer for 5 minutes. Turn tuna over; add capers. Simmer, covered, for 3 minutes longer.

3. Meanwhile, add Broccolini to the pot of boiling water; cook for 8 minutes. Add linguine; cook for 2 to 3 minutes longer or just until pasta is tender. Drain. Serve tuna and sauce over linguine and Broccolini. If desired, sprinkle with Parmesan cheese.

When you're in the mood for a full-flavored pasta dish but are pressed for time, tuna steaks and refrigerated fresh pasta are the way to go!

PREP: 10 minutes
COOK: about 20 minutes
MAKES: 4 servings

QUICK BITE
PRODUCE POINTERS

With its thin stems and small, tender buds, Broccolini looks like a slender cousin to broccoli. Because of its slim figure, some cooks think the veggie is a cross between asparagus and broccoli; however, it's actually a hybrid of broccoli and a Chinese vegetable called gai lan. Broccolini has a sweet taste with a touch of mustard and becomes less peppery and more sweet as it's cooked. It's terrific blanched, steamed, sautéed, stir-fried or served raw with dip.

Per serving: 666 calories, 14 g total fat (3 g sat.), 164 mg cholesterol, 1,225 mg sodium, 68 g carbohydrate, 6 g fiber, 64 g protein.

Lemon Flounder with Garlicky Shrimp

- 1 package (8.8 ounces) cooked long-grain rice
- 4 flounder fillets (about 4 ounces each)
- ½ teaspoon salt
- ¼ teaspoon black pepper
- ¼ cup Wondra flour (see Note)
- 4 tablespoons extra-virgin olive oil
- 4 tablespoons (½ stick) unsalted butter
- ½ pound small shrimp, shelled and deveined (if desired, leave tails intact)
- 3 cloves garlic, chopped
- ¼ cup lemon juice
- ¼ cup chopped fresh parsley leaves
- 2 tablespoons drained capers
- Fresh parsley and lemon slices, for garnish

1. Prepare long-grain rice following package directions. Keep warm.

2. Season the fish with ¼ teaspoon salt and ⅛ teaspoon black pepper. Coat both sides of fish with the flour, shaking off excess.

3. Heat a 12-inch nonstick sauté pan or skillet briefly over medium-high heat; add 1 tablespoon oil and 1 tablespoon butter. When oil-butter mixture sizzles, add two of the flounder fillets; sauté for 2 minutes per side. Remove to a plate and keep warm. Add an additional tablespoon each of oil and butter. Add the remaining flounder fillets and sauté. Remove to the plate.

4. Add shrimp and garlic and sauté for 2 minutes. Stir after 1 minute so garlic does not burn and shrimp are evenly cooked. Add lemon juice, chopped parsley, capers and the remaining 2 tablespoons each of oil and butter. Heat for 1 minute. Stir in the remaining ¼ teaspoon salt and ⅛ teaspoon pepper.

5. To serve, divide rice among plates. Top with flounder. Spoon shrimp and caper mixture, including all accumulated liquid, over flounder. Garnish with additional parsley and lemon.

Note: Wondra flour is a granulated variety that tends to form a good coating; however, regular white unbleached flour can be substituted.

If you can't find flounder, try mild tilapia in this elegant presentation instead. A good side dish would be buttered green beans with toasted almonds.

PREP: 10 minutes
COOK: about 12 minutes
MAKES: 4 servings

QUICK TIP

HANDLING SHRIMP

To shell and devein a fresh shrimp, start at the head end and use your fingers to peel off the shell. If desired, gently pull on the tail portion of the shell to remove it. Then use a sharp knife to make a shallow slit from head to tail along the back of the shrimp. Rinse under cold running water to remove the vein, using the tip of the knife to dislodge the vein, if necessary.

Per serving: 510 calories, 28 g total fat (10 g sat.), 172 mg cholesterol, 630 mg sodium, 27 g carbohydrate, 1 g fiber, 36 g protein.

Lime Snapper

4 red snapper fillets (6 ounces each)
½ teaspoon salt
¼ teaspoon black pepper
3 tablespoons all-purpose flour
½ cup water
1 tablespoon Asian fish sauce
1 tablespoon sugar
   Juice of 1 lime
1 teaspoon Asian chili paste
3 tablespoons vegetable oil
3 cloves garlic, minced
3 scallions, trimmed and sliced
2 cups frozen Asian vegetables, cooked
   and drained

1. Season red snapper fillets with salt and pepper. Coat with flour.

2. In small bowl, combine water, fish sauce, sugar, lime juice and Asian chili paste.

3. In large nonstick skillet, heat oil over medium heat. Add fish; sauté for 5 minutes per side. Transfer to serving platter; keep warm. Add garlic, scallion and fish sauce mixture to skillet. Boil for 1 minute; pour over fish. Serve with Asian vegetables.

In the time it takes to make the usual sautéed fish, you can have an intriguing Asian-inspired dish instead.

PREP: 10 minutes
COOK: about 11 minutes
MAKES: 4 servings

QUICK TIP

RED SNAPPER SUBSTITUTIONS

Red snapper is a firm, mild to moderately flavored fish that works well for sautéing. If red snapper fillets aren't available, use grouper, lake trout, ocean perch or whitefish fillets.

Per serving: 359 calories, 13 g total fat (1 g sat.), 63 mg cholesterol, 813 mg sodium, 22 g carbohydrate, 5 g fiber, 39 g protein.

Chipotle Salmon Tacos

1¼ pounds salmon fillet (with skin)
¼ teaspoon salt
1 canned chipotle pepper in adobo sauce, seeded, chopped and mixed with 1 tablespoon adobo sauce
8 hard taco shells
1 can (11 ounces) Mexicali corn
1 cup bottled medium-hot salsa

1. Heat oven to 450°.

2. Place salmon, skin side down, in 11×7×2-inch baking dish. Season with salt and chipotle pepper mixture.

3. Bake at 450° about 18 minutes or until salmon is cooked through and flakes easily when tested with fork. Heat the taco shells in oven for the last 3 minutes of baking time.

4. Heat corn in microwave oven or small saucepan; drain. Flake salmon.

5. To serve, divide corn and salmon among taco shells; serve with salsa.

If your kids haven't graduated to fish yet, try tucking some into taco shells—that might get them started!

PREP: 10 minutes
BAKE: at 450° for 18 minutes
MAKES: 4 servings (8 tacos)

QUICK TIP

PICKING THE BEST

Fresh fish from the sea should smell pleasantly briny, not fishy. When buying fillets, choose those that are springy to the touch and have firm, translucent flesh without tears or blemishes. Avoid raggedly cut fillets.

Per serving: 349 calories, 10 g total fat (2 g sat.), 66 mg cholesterol, 1,079 mg sodium, 31 g carbohydrate, 5 g fiber, 32 g protein.

Baked Fish in White Wine

When you don't want to fuss with flipping delicate fish fillets in a frying pan, baking them is a super way to go!

PREP: 10 minutes
BAKE: at 450° for 17 to 18 minutes
MAKES: 4 servings

Fish:
- 2 large ripe tomatoes, seeded and chopped
- ⅓ cup dry white wine
- 3 tablespoons drained capers, chopped
- 3 tablespoons chopped fresh mint leaves
- 4 tilapia fillets (1 to 1¼ pounds total) or flounder or sole fillets
- ¼ teaspoon salt
- ⅛ teaspoon black pepper
- 4 thin slices lemon
- 2 tablespoons unsalted butter

Couscous:
- 1½ cups plain couscous
- 1½ cups water
- 2 tablespoons unsalted butter
- ¼ teaspoon salt
- ⅛ teaspoon black pepper
- Fresh herb sprigs, for garnish (optional)

1. Heat oven to 450°. Coat baking pan just large enough to hold the fish in single layer with nonstick cooking spray.

2. **Fish:** In medium-size bowl, gently stir together tomatoes, wine, capers and mint.

3. Season fish with salt and pepper. Place in prepared baking dish. Pour tomato mixture over fish. Place a lemon slice on each fillet.

4. Bake at 450° for 17 to 18 minutes or until fish is cooked through and flakes easily when tested with fork. Remove fish to warm serving dish. Whisk butter into pan juices.

5. **Couscous:** While fish is cooking, prepare couscous following package directions, using the water, butter, salt and pepper.

6. To serve, divide couscous among four plates; top with fish. Spoon sauce from baking pan over couscous and fish. If desired, garnish with fresh herb sprigs.

QUICK BITE

WHY WINE?

Ever wonder how wine works to add so much richness and body to recipes? Part of its effect comes from the flavor of the wine, but the rest is due to wine's ability to pull flavor from other ingredients. Wine's alcohol is a hardworking flavor extractor that grabs great tastes that other liquids, such as oil and water, cannot. This marvelous molecular activity imbues foods with mouthwatering complexity.

Per serving: 492 calories, 14 g total fat (8 g sat.), 98 mg cholesterol, 599 mg sodium, 55 g carbohydrate, 4 g fiber, 33 g protein.

Salmon with Peach Chutney

2 pounds salmon fillet (about 1¼ inches thick), cut into 6 equal pieces
¼ teaspoon salt

Chutney:
1 medium-size red onion, diced
4 scallions, trimmed and sliced
1 jalapeño chile, seeded and diced
2 tablespoons vegetable oil
1 teaspoon curry powder
¼ teaspoon cayenne pepper
1 jar (12 ounces) peach preserves
1 mango, peeled, pitted and diced
1 teaspoon salt

Rice:
3 cups quick-cooking rice
1 box (10 ounces) frozen peas, thawed

1. Heat oven to 450°. Coat 13×9×2-inch baking dish with nonstick cooking spray. Place salmon in dish. Season with salt.

2. Roast at 450° about 13 minutes or until fish is cooked through and flakes easily when tested with fork.

3. Chutney: Meanwhile, in small saucepan, sauté onion, half of the scallion and the jalapeño chile in oil for 3 minutes. Add curry powder and cayenne pepper; cook for 1 minute. Add preserves, mango and salt; cook for 5 minutes. Remove chutney from heat.

4. Rice: Cook rice following package directions. Stir peas into rice.

5. Serve salmon with rice. Spoon a little chutney over salmon. Top with remaining scallion. Serve chutney on side.

Fresh homemade chutney can be ready in minutes; check out how great it tastes on salmon!

PREP: 15 minutes
BAKE: at 450° for 13 minutes
MAKES: 6 servings

QUICK TIP

CUTTING UP A MANGO

Because of the fruit's pithy seed, cutting up a mango requires a little know-how. First start by looking at its shape. You'll see a broad, flat side. That shows you the shape of the seed inside. Using a sharp knife, slice all the way through the mango next to the seed. Repeat on the other side of the seed, resulting in two large pieces of fruit. Cut away all the fruit that remains around the seed. Slice or score the flesh and cut off cubes.

Per serving: 596 calories, 10 g total fat (1 g sat.), 74 mg cholesterol, 644 mg sodium, 90 g carbohydrate, 5 g fiber, 35 g protein.

Curried Swordfish Kabobs

2 teaspoons curry powder
½ cup pineapple preserves
¼ cup (½ stick) unsalted butter
1 tablespoon grated lime zest
1 tablespoon lime juice
½ teaspoon salt
¼ teaspoon cayenne pepper
¼ pound fresh snow peas or sugar-snap peas
1½ pounds swordfish steaks (1 inch thick)
1 large sweet red pepper, seeded and cut into 1-inch pieces
½ fresh pineapple, peeled, cored and cut into 1-inch pieces

1. Soak six 15-inch bamboo skewers in water for 30 minutes.

2. In small saucepan, heat curry powder over medium-high heat about 1 minute or until fragrant. Add pineapple preserves and butter; melt, stirring. Remove from heat; stir in lime zest, lime juice, salt and cayenne pepper.

3. In saucepan of boiling water, cook snow peas for 1 minute. Drain; rinse with cold water. Remove skin from swordfish; cut steaks into 1-inch pieces.

4. Heat gas grill to medium-low to medium or prepare charcoal grill with medium-low to medium coals. On skewers, alternately thread snow peas, swordfish pieces, sweet pepper pieces and pineapple pieces, leaving a ¼-inch space between pieces.

5. Grill skewers about 10 minutes or until fish is cooked through and flakes easily when tested with fork, turning every 2 minutes and brushing with curry mixture during the last 2 minutes of grilling. Serve with remaining curry mixture.

Charged with appealing curry and fruit flavors but blessedly uncomplicated—how's that for tonight's catch?

PREP: 15 minutes
GRILL: 10 minutes
MAKES: 6 servings

QUICK BITE

EITHER OPTION WORKS

Unsalted and salted butter can be used interchangeably in recipes; however, if you use salted butter in place of unsalted butter, you may want to decrease any salt called for in a recipe. Because the unsalted version is more perishable, you might want to freeze it for long-term storage.

Per serving: 264 calories, 11 g total fat (6 g sat.), 51 mg cholesterol, 277 mg sodium, 26 g carbohydrate, 2 g fiber, 17 g protein.

Farfalle Niçoise

1 pound farfalle (bow tie) pasta
2 tablespoons extra-virgin olive oil
¾ pound fresh green beans, trimmed
  and cut up
1 medium-size red onion, sliced
2 cans (6 ounces each) solid white albacore
  tuna in water, undrained
¾ cup bottled red-wine vinaigrette dressing
½ cup pitted kalamata olives, halved
½ cup diced roasted red peppers
2 tablespoons lemon juice
¼ teaspoon black pepper

1. Bring a large pot of lightly salted water to a boil. Cook pasta following package directions. Drain; keep warm.

2. Meanwhile, in a large skillet, heat olive oil over medium-high heat. Add green beans and sauté 3 minutes. Stir in red onion and cook 5 minutes longer.

3. Stir in tuna with its liquid, vinaigrette, olives, red peppers and lemon juice. Cook to heat through. Toss with warm pasta and black pepper.

Green beans, tuna and kalamata olives give farfalle a Mediterranean accent.

PREP: 10 minutes
COOK: about 15 minutes
MAKES: 6 servings

QUICK TIP

PASTA PAIRINGS

Enhance the flavor and appearance of sauces by teaming them with the right pasta. Here's a simple rule of thumb: Match a delicate sauce with a delicate pasta and a chunky veggie or meat sauce with a sturdy pasta. For example, pair a light cream sauce with angel hair pasta and a rich meat sauce with mostaccioli, rigatoni or penne pasta.

Per serving: 521 calories, 19 g total fat (3 g sat.), 35 mg cholesterol, 901 mg sodium, 59 g carbohydrate, 4 g fiber, 25 g protein.

Basque-Style Scallops

3 tablespoons extra-virgin olive oil
3 sweet peppers (assorted colors), seeded and cut into strips
2 large onions, cut into strips
1 can (28 ounces) whole peeled tomatoes with juice, broken up
3 cloves garlic, crushed
1 teaspoon salt
½ teaspoon black pepper
1½ pounds sea scallops
½ cup fresh flat-leaf parsley leaves
1 pound pappardelle pasta

1. In large skillet, heat oil over medium-high heat. Add sweet pepper strips and onion strips; sauté about 10 minutes or until softened. Add tomatoes, garlic, salt and black pepper; simmer for 10 minutes over medium-high heat, stirring occasionally.

2. Tuck sea scallops into pepper mixture; cook, turning scallops over once, about 6 minutes or just until scallops are cooked through. Stir in parsley leaves.

3. Meanwhile, cook pasta following package directions; drain well. Serve scallop mixture with cooked pasta.

The traditional Basque trio of sweet peppers, tomatoes and olive oil makes a lively sauce for scallops.

PREP: 10 minutes
COOK: 26 minutes
MAKES: 6 servings

QUICK BITE

HERB KNOW-HOW

Though it was once considered a garnish, cooks are discovering that parsley makes a terrific seasoning. It brings a fresh, mild taste to almost any dish. Flat-leaf parsley, also called Italian parsley, has a milder flavor than the curly-leaf variety. However, in a pinch, you can substitute one for the other in recipes.

Per serving: 476 calories, 9 g total fat (1 g sat.), 37 mg cholesterol, 786 mg sodium, 66 g carbohydrate, 6 g fiber, 30 g protein.

Soba and Shrimp Salad

Dressing:
- ¼ cup extra-virgin olive oil
- 3 tablespoons reduced-sodium soy sauce
- 3 tablespoons mirin
- 2 teaspoons grated fresh ginger
- 1 teaspoon sugar
- ½ teaspoon hot-pepper sauce

Shrimp and Noodles:
- 2 teaspoons vegetable oil
- 1½ pounds medium-size shrimp, shelled and deveined (if desired, leave tails intact)
- 4 cloves garlic, chopped
- 2 tablespoons lemon juice
- ⅛ teaspoon salt
- 1 package (12 ounces) soba noodles
- 1 seedless cucumber, sliced
- 1 sweet red pepper, seeded and thinly sliced
- ⅓ cup fresh cilantro leaves, for garnish

1. **Dressing:** In large bowl, whisk together olive oil, soy sauce, mirin, ginger, sugar and hot-pepper sauce. Set aside.

2. **Shrimp and Noodles:** In large nonstick skillet, heat oil over medium-high heat. Add shrimp and garlic; sauté for 3 to 4 minutes or until shrimp turns pink, turning shrimp occasionally. Add lemon juice and salt. Remove from heat.

3. Cook noodles following package directions. Drain; rinse under cool water. Toss noodles, cucumber and sweet pepper with dressing. Add shrimp and any liquid. Toss gently. Serve warm or at room temperature. Garnish with cilantro.

Stir-fried shrimp with soba noodles in a sweet ginger dressing—it's a great way to introduce your family to a whole new noodle.

PREP: 15 minutes
COOK: about 10 minutes
MAKES: 6 servings

QUICK BITE

WHY NOT TRY ...

Rich in protein and fiber, soba noodles get a nutty taste from buckwheat flour. These Japanese noodles are often served cold. Substitute whole wheat spaghetti, if necessary.

Per serving: 444 calories, 13 g total fat (2 g sat.), 172 mg cholesterol, 971 mg sodium, 51 g carbohydrate, 1 g fiber, 32 g protein.

Shrimp and Spinach Casseroles

¾ pound shelled and deveined medium-size shrimp, cut into thirds
1 package (10 ounces) frozen chopped spinach, thawed and squeezed dry
¾ cup mayonnaise
½ cup chopped onion
¼ cup grated Parmesan cheese
1 tablespoon lemon juice
⅛ teaspoon black pepper
3 egg whites
½ teaspoon salt
   Lemon wedges (optional)

1. Heat oven to 375°. Coat four 12-ounce shallow gratin dishes with nonstick cooking spray. In large bowl, combine shrimp, spinach, mayonnaise, onion, Parmesan cheese, lemon juice and pepper.

2. In medium-size bowl, with electric mixer on medium to high speed, beat egg whites and salt until stiff peaks form. Fold into shrimp mixture. Spoon into prepared dishes. Bake at 375° about 15 minutes or until browned and puffed. If desired, serve with lemon wedges.

Glam up your weeknight—there's something special about serving main dishes in individual casseroles!

PREP: 10 minutes
BAKE: at 375° for 15 minutes
MAKES: 4 servings

QUICK TIP

STORE IT RIGHT

• You can refrigerate unbroken raw egg yolks covered with water in a tightly covered container for up to 2 days; however, you should not freeze them.
• Raw egg whites can be stored in a tightly covered container for up to 4 days. Or place them in a freezer container and store for up to 1 year—be sure to specify on the label how many egg whites are in the container.

Per serving: 419 calories, 36 g total fat (6 g sat.), 150 mg cholesterol, 864 mg sodium, 6 g carbohydrate, 2 g fiber, 20 g protein.

Seafood Skillet

3 strips bacon, chopped
1 pound small bay scallops
¼ pound medium-size shrimp, shelled
    and deveined (if desired, leave tails intact)
2 cloves garlic, finely chopped
1 can (11.8 ounces) coconut water
¼ cup water
2 teaspoons chicken bouillon granules
½ teaspoon salt
¼ teaspoon red pepper flakes
1 bag (1 pound) frozen mixed peppers,
    thawed and coarsely chopped
2 cups instant rice

1. In large nonstick skillet, cook bacon over medium heat for 4 minutes. Add bay scallops, shrimp and garlic; cook over medium-high heat for 4 minutes. Add coconut water, the water, bouillon granules, salt and red pepper flakes. Bring to a boil.

2. Add mixed peppers; simmer for 3 minutes. Stir in instant rice; cover and remove from heat. Let stand, stirring occasionally, about 5 minutes or until liquid is absorbed.

Bacon, scallops and shrimp are a fabulous combination— the meat's smokiness and the seafood's sweetness meld deliciously.

PREP: 10 minutes
COOK: about 15 minutes
STAND: 5 minutes
MAKES: 6 servings

QUICK TIP

PICKING THE BEST

Scallops should be firm and moist, retaining their shape when touched. Their meat should be plump and free of shell particles or grit. The liquor should not exceed 10% of the total volume. The scallops should have a fresh, oceanlike scent, not a sour or sulfurlike odor. Refrigerate scallops, covered with their liquor, for up to 2 days or store them in the freezer for up to 3 months.

Per serving: 267 calories, 7 g total fat (2 g sat.), 43 mg cholesterol, 843 mg sodium, 34 g carbohydrate, 4 g fiber, 15 g protein.

Silky onions in a rich broth topped with melty Swiss cheese—it's a classic!

PREP: 15 minutes
COOK: 20 minutes
BROIL: 3 minutes
MAKES: 4 servings

QUICK TIP

HOW SWEET IT IS

For a change, try sweet onions in recipes. These varieties generally have at least 6% sugar—and can go as high as 15%—compared with the normal 3% to 5%. Use them when you want a milder flavor. Look for Oso, Vidalia, Maui or Walla Walla.

Quick Onion Soup

¼ cup (½ stick) unsalted butter
4 large white onions (2 pounds total), halved and thinly sliced (4 cups)
1 teaspoon sugar
1 tablespoon all-purpose flour
3 cans (10½ ounces each) condensed beef broth
¼ cup dry red wine
1⅓ cups garlic-flavored croutons
4 slices Swiss cheese (about 3 ounces total)

1. Heat broiler. In 5-quart saucepan, melt butter over medium-high heat. Add onion; stir to coat with butter. Cover; cook for 8 minutes, stirring occasionally. Add sugar; cook, uncovered, stirring, about 6 minutes or until slightly golden. Add flour; cook for 1 minute longer. Stir in broth, 1 broth can of water and the red wine. Simmer, covered, for 5 minutes.

2. Place four 2-cup broilerproof bowls on a baking sheet. Put ⅓ cup croutons in each bowl. Evenly divide soup over croutons in each bowl (about 1¾ cups each). Top each with slice of cheese. Broil about 3 minutes or until cheese is melted.

Per serving: 443 calories, 27 g total fat (12 g sat.), 54 mg cholesterol, 744 mg sodium, 34 g carbohydrate, 2 g fiber, 14 g protein.

Penne à la Siciliana

3 tablespoons extra-virgin olive oil
1 eggplant (1¼ pounds), cut into ½-inch dice
1 large onion, sliced
2 cloves garlic, chopped
1 can (28 ounces) crushed tomatoes
¼ cup dry red wine
1 teaspoon chopped fresh rosemary
    or ½ teaspoon dried rosemary
1 teaspoon dried oregano
1½ teaspoons salt
¼ teaspoon red pepper flakes
1 pound penne pasta
¾ cup shredded smoked mozzarella cheese
    (3 ounces)

1. In large skillet, heat oil over medium-high heat. Add eggplant, onion and garlic. Sauté about 5 minutes or until softened, stirring frequently.

2. Add tomatoes, dry red wine, rosemary, oregano, salt and red pepper flakes. Bring mixture to a simmer. Simmer, uncovered, for 15 minutes, stirring occasionally.

3. While sauce is simmering, cook pasta following package directions. Drain.

4. Spoon eggplant mixture over pasta. Top with smoked mozzarella and let melt slightly.

This recipe may be meatless, but it offers all the bold, robust flavors you'd expect from anything inspired by Sicily!

PREP: 10 minutes
COOK: 20 minutes
MAKES: 6 servings

QUICK TIP

WINE ON RESERVE

When calling on a wine for recipes, you needn't pull out your very best bottle, but don't use an inferior wine either. The general rule is that any wine you use in cooking should be good enough to drink. Consider using the same wine you plan to drink with dinner in your recipe. Or next time you enjoy a wine—but don't quite finish the bottle—pour the remaining wine into a smaller container (air is the culprit that makes good wine go stale). Store it in the refrigerator to help keep it fresh.

Per serving: 427 calories, 12 g total fat (3 g sat.), 10 mg cholesterol, 866 mg sodium, 67 g carbohydrate, 8 g fiber, 15 g protein.

Linguine with Zucchini Sauce

- 1 pound linguine
- 2 tablespoons extra-virgin olive oil
- 3 cloves garlic, thinly sliced
- 2 pounds zucchini, coarsely shredded
- ½ teaspoon salt
- ⅛ teaspoon black pepper
- 1 cup shredded sharp Cheddar cheese (4 ounces)
- ½ cup purchased Alfredo sauce
  Fresh basil, for garnish (optional)

1. Cook pasta following package directions. Drain; keep warm. In large skillet, heat oil over medium-high heat. Add garlic; cook, stirring, about 30 seconds or until lightly browned.

2. Increase heat to high. Stir in zucchini, salt and pepper. Cook, stirring often, about 3 minutes or until tender. Add cheese and Alfredo sauce; heat through. Transfer to large bowl; toss with pasta. If desired, garnish with basil.

Just a handful of ingredients goes into this quick pasta toss— it's a great way to take advantage of a bumper crop of zucchini.

PREP: 15 minutes
COOK: about 5 minutes
MAKES: 6 servings

Per serving: 378 calories, 15 g total fat (6 g sat.), 28 mg cholesterol, 593 mg sodium, 48 g carbohydrate, 4 g fiber, 16 g protein.

Falafel

1 can (19 ounces) chickpeas, rinsed
   and drained
½ onion, coarsely chopped
⅓ cup packaged plain dry bread crumbs
2 tablespoons chopped fresh flat-leaf
   parsley leaves
1 teaspoon ground cumin
2 cloves garlic, smashed
¼ teaspoon salt
⅛ teaspoon black pepper
1 cup fat-free plain yogurt
¼ cup tahini
2½ tablespoons lemon juice
1 clove garlic, chopped
¼ teaspoon salt
⅛ teaspoon black pepper
½ cucumber, diced
4 small pitas
2 cups shredded iceberg lettuce

1. In food processor, combine chickpeas, onion, bread crumbs, parsley, cumin, the smashed garlic, ¼ teaspoon salt and ⅛ teaspoon pepper. Whirl until well blended. Divide into 12 equal portions. Roll each into a ball; flatten slightly.

2. Coat nonstick skillet with nonstick cooking spray. Heat over medium heat. Add chickpea balls; cook for 2 to 3 minutes per side or until lightly browned. Set aside.

3. In food processor, combine yogurt, tahini, lemon juice, the chopped garlic, ¼ teaspoon salt and ⅛ teaspoon pepper. Whirl until smooth. Stir in diced cucumber.

4. Split each pita halfway down side. Put ½ cup lettuce inside each pita; add 3 chickpea balls and top with some of the cucumber mixture.

Sautéing this Middle-Eastern treat in a nonstick skillet means less cleanup and fewer fat calories too.

PREP: 15 minutes
COOK: 4 to 6 minutes
MAKES: 4 servings

QUICK TIP

THE CUTTING EDGE

A good set of sharp knives makes cooking faster, easier and more enjoyable. To keep your knives in their best shape:
• Always cut on a cutting board.
• Wash knives in hot, soapy water immediately after using them. Do not let them soak and do not put them in the dishwasher.
• Store knives in a block or protective case rather than in a drawer mixed with other utensils.

Per serving: 672 calories, 14 g total fat (2 g sat.), 1 mg cholesterol, 765 mg sodium, 107 g carbohydrate, 16 g fiber, 33 g protein.

Classic Ham and Cheese Omelet

  1 tablespoon unsalted butter
  4 eggs
  2 egg whites
1½ teaspoons Dijon mustard
  ½ teaspoon dried tarragon
  ⅛ teaspoon salt
     Pinch of black pepper
     Pinch of ground nutmeg
  3 thin slices Black Forest ham
  ⅔ cup grated Gruyère cheese
     Fresh chives, chopped, for garnish
     (optional)

No matter how busy your day has been, you usually have enough energy to make an omelet. Serve with crusty bread and you're set.

PREP: 5 minutes
COOK: about 6 minutes
MAKES: 2 servings

1. Heat 10-inch nonstick skillet over medium heat. Add butter; heat until melted. Swirl pan to coat.

2. In medium-size bowl, whisk together eggs, egg whites, mustard, tarragon, salt, pepper and nutmeg. When butter is melted, add eggs to skillet. Cook, pushing cooked edges into center of skillet and tilting skillet to coat with uncooked mixture. Continue cooking for 5 minutes.

3. Layer ham and cheese onto half of the omelet. Tent skillet with aluminum foil; cook about 1 minute longer or until eggs are cooked and cheese is melted. Fold untopped half over filling; slide omelet onto a plate. Cut in half and move one portion to second plate. If desired, sprinkle with chives.

QUICK TIP

SEPARATING EGGS SAFELY

It's no longer considered safe to separate egg yolks from whites by passing the yolk between the two halves of the shell. Instead use an egg separator so that any bacteria present on the shell won't contaminate the yolk or the white. When cracking eggs, avoid getting eggshell into the raw eggs.

Per serving: 392 calories, 28 g total fat (14 g sat.), 489 mg cholesterol, 778 mg sodium, 3 g carbohydrate, 0 g fiber, 30 g protein.

Broccoli and Cheese Campanelle

1 pound campanelle or rotini pasta
2 tablespoons onion flakes
1 bag (12 ounces) fresh broccoli flowerets
1 jar (1 pound) double Cheddar sauce
   (such as Ragú brand)
1 package (8 ounces) diced ham
1 cup grated pepper-Jack cheese

1. Bring large pot of lightly salted water to a boil. Add pasta and onion flakes; cook for 4 minutes. Add broccoli; cook for 5 minutes longer.

2. Meanwhile, in medium-size saucepan, heat Cheddar sauce, ham and pepper-Jack cheese, stirring occasionally. Drain pasta and broccoli and return to pot. Stir in cheese sauce mixture until combined. Serve warm.

Here's a way to get kids to eat their broccoli—pour on a sauce full of one of their favorite ingredients: cheese!

PREP: 5 minutes
COOK: about 10 minutes
MAKES: 6 servings

QUICK TIP

YOU'RE THE CHEF

Most quick-cooking pasta dishes leave plenty of room for innovation, so go ahead and experiment with your favorite ingredients (or whatever you have on hand). For example, in this recipe, you could substitute Alfredo sauce for the Cheddar. Not a fan of pepper-Jack cheese? Use Monterey Jack or provolone. And if red meat isn't your thing, go for diced cooked chicken instead of ham.

Per serving: 379 calories, 14 g total fat (7 g sat.), 32 mg cholesterol, 999 mg sodium, 44 g carbohydrate, 3 g fiber, 20 g protein.

Bow Ties and Veggies with Pesto

12 ounces farfalle (bow tie) pasta
1 tablespoon extra-virgin olive oil
½ pound fresh green beans or asparagus, trimmed and cut into 2-inch pieces
1 yellow pepper, seeded and diced
1 small zucchini, trimmed, halved lengthwise and cut into ¼-inch-thick half moons
2 cloves garlic, sliced
½ cup purchased basil pesto
¼ cup heavy cream
1 cup cherry or grape tomatoes, halved or quartered
½ teaspoon salt

1. Bring large pot of salted water to a boil. Add pasta and cook following package directions for 8 minutes. Drain.

2. Meanwhile, in large nonstick skillet, heat oil over medium to medium-high heat. Add green beans and pepper; cook for 5 minutes. Add zucchini and garlic. Cook for 2 minutes. Stir in pesto and cream; cook for 1 minute. Stir in tomatoes and salt. Remove from heat.

3. Add cooked bow ties to sauce; toss well to combine. Divide among bowls; serve.

Beans and yellow peppers add crunch to a basil-based sauce. A quarter cup of heavy cream gives just a touch of richness.

PREP: 15 minutes
COOK: 8 minutes
MAKES: 6 servings

QUICK TIP

PREPPING BEANS

Getting beans ready for cooking is a snap! After thoroughly washing, remove ends and strings. You can leave them whole or cut into pieces. For French-cut beans, slice lengthwise.

Per serving: 397 calories, 18 g total fat (5 g sat.), 19 mg cholesterol, 372 mg sodium, 50 g carbohydrate, 4 g fiber, 12 g protein.

Black Bean and Corn Soup

1 medium-size red onion, chopped
2 tablespoons vegetable oil
2 cans (15 ounces each) black beans, drained
1 can (14 ounces) chicken broth
1 can (11 ounces) corn niblets, drained
1 cup bottled chunky salsa
1 tablespoon lime juice
½ teaspoon salt
⅛ teaspoon black pepper
  Sour cream, for garnish (optional)
  Lime wedges, for garnish (optional)

1. In large saucepan, sauté onion in oil over low heat about 5 minutes or until tender. In small bowl, mash 1 cup of the beans.

2. Stir mashed beans, whole beans, broth, corn, salsa, lime juice, salt and pepper into saucepan; simmer, uncovered, about 10 minutes or until heated through. If desired, serve with sour cream and lime wedges.

Use your favorite brand of chunky salsa as well as canned beans, corn and broth to keep the prep to a mere 5 minutes. Corn bread muffins provide a winning side.

PREP: 5 minutes
COOK: 15 minutes
MAKES: 6 servings

QUICK BITE
THE BENEFITS OF BEANS

If you'd like to go meatless more often, stock up on beans. They're hearty, filling, almost fat-free and a terrific source of fiber, protein and iron. Conveniently, they're also an inexpensive and satisfying substitute for meat.

Per serving: 191 calories, 7 g total fat (1 g sat.), 2 mg cholesterol, 1,171 mg sodium, 25 g carbohydrate, 7 g fiber, 8 g protein.

Bean Burgers

2 cans (15½ ounces each) pinto beans, drained and rinsed
½ cup packaged plain dry bread crumbs
½ cup bottled salsa
1 egg
1 teaspoon chili powder
½ teaspoon ground cumin
½ cup coarsely crushed baked tortilla chips
3 (4-inch) pitas (2 ounces each), halved
12 lettuce leaves
12 slices tomato
   Bottled salsa (optional)

1. Heat broiler. Lightly coat broiler-pan rack with nonstick cooking spray. Set aside.

2. Reserve 1 cup of the pinto beans. Whirl remaining beans in a food processor or mash with fork in large bowl until smooth.

3. In large bowl, combine the reserved 1 cup beans, the pureed beans, bread crumbs, the ½ cup salsa, egg, chili powder and cumin. Stir in crushed chips. Shape bean mixture into six patties. Coat both sides of each patty with nonstick cooking spray.

4. Broil about 4 inches from heat, turning once, about 10 minutes or until instant-read thermometer inserted in centers registers 160°. Serve in pita pocket halves with lettuce and tomato. If desired, serve with additional salsa.

When one of your children suddenly announces that he or she is a vegetarian, serve these wholesome, healthy burgers.

PREP: 10 minutes
BROIL: 10 minutes
MAKES: 6 burgers

QUICK TIP

SODIUM CONTROL

Ready to use in recipes, canned beans save you time. However, with their added salt, they can tip the scale on sodium in recipes. Rinsing and draining beans in a colander under cold running water helps eliminate the salty packing liquid. Be sure to drain the beans well.

Per burger: 282 calories, 3 g total fat (0 g sat.), 35 mg cholesterol, 738 mg sodium, 54 g carbohydrate, 8 g fiber, 11 g protein.

Slow & Simple Meals

Spicy Spaghetti and Meatballs p. 84

Here's the best in "hands off" cooking.
Spend just a little time prepping these soups,
stews, casseroles and other hearty, full-flavored
foods, then take it easy while your oven,
stove or slow cooker does the work.

Spicy Beef Short Ribs

6   beef chuck short ribs (4 to 5 pounds total)
2   cans (12 ounces each) beer
1   cup ketchup
⅓   cup lemon juice
¼   cup packed light-brown sugar
¼   cup vinegar
3   tablespoons unsalted butter
1   tablespoon Worcestershire sauce
1   tablespoon yellow mustard
1   teaspoon onion powder
½   teaspoon celery seeds
½   teaspoon hot-pepper sauce

1. Trim any excess fat from ribs. Place ribs in flameproof casserole. Add beer to cover. Cover with lid.

2. Bring to a boil over high heat. Reduce heat to low; simmer, covered, about 1½ hours or until fork tender.

3. Meanwhile, in medium-size saucepan, stir together ketchup, lemon juice, brown sugar, vinegar, butter, Worcestershire sauce, mustard, onion powder, celery seeds and hot-pepper sauce. Simmer over medium heat for 15 minutes. Set aside until cool, then divide, using half for basting and half for dipping.

4. Heat broiler. Brush ribs with sauce. Place on greased broiler-pan rack. Broil for 8 minutes. Turn ribs over; brush with more sauce. Broil about 7 minutes longer or until crisped.

5. Heat reserved half of the ketchup mixture for dipping. Serve with ribs.

Simmering short ribs in beer makes them tender. Then broiling them with a homemade sauce makes them even better.

PREP: 10 minutes
COOK: 1½ hours
BROIL: 15 minutes
MAKES: 6 servings

Per serving: 295 calories, 16 g total fat (6 g sat.), 73 mg cholesterol, 725 mg sodium, 11 g carbohydrate, 1 g fiber, 26 g protein.

Classic Pot Roast

- 1 **large onion, diced**
- 1 **cup peeled baby carrots, sliced ¼ inch thick**
- 1 **rib celery, sliced ¼ inch thick**
- 2 **cloves garlic, chopped**
- 1 **boneless beef chuck roast (about 3 pounds), tied**
- 1 **teaspoon extra-virgin olive oil**
- 1 **teaspoon salt**
- ¼ **teaspoon black pepper**
- 2 **cups sliced white button mushrooms**
- 4 **sprigs fresh thyme**
- 1 **bay leaf**
- 1 **cup beef broth**
- ½ **cup dry red wine**
- 2 **tablespoons tomato paste**
- 2 **tablespoons extra-virgin olive oil**
- 3 **tablespoons all-purpose flour**
- 1 **pound egg noodles**

1. In 5- to 5½-quart slow cooker, layer onion, carrot, celery and garlic. Rub roast all over with 1 teaspoon olive oil; season roast with the salt and pepper. Scatter mushrooms over vegetables in slow cooker; place roast on top. Tuck thyme sprigs and bay leaf into mixture.

2. In medium-size bowl, whisk together broth, wine and tomato paste; pour over meat.

3. Cover slow cooker; cook on high-heat setting for 6 hours.

4. Remove roast from slow cooker; keep warm.

5. Pour liquid with vegetable mixture from slow cooker into medium-size saucepan; remove and discard thyme sprigs and bay leaf. Bring to a boil.

6. In small cup, stir together the 2 tablespoons oil and the flour until well blended and smooth. Stir flour mixture into liquid in saucepan. Boil, stirring, about 1 minute or until liquid is slightly thickened.

7. Meanwhile, cook noodles in large pot of lightly salted boiling water following package directions. Drain noodles well.

8. Slice roast. Serve with gravy and cooked noodles.

If you've forgotten how good a succulent, long-cooking pot roast can be, remind yourself with this traditional version.

PREP: 10 minutes
SLOW COOK: 6 hours on high-heat setting
MAKES: 10 servings

CONVENTIONAL METHOD

Heat oven to 300°. Heat 2 tablespoons oil in large heavy pot over medium-high heat. Brown meat on all sides; remove from pot. Reduce heat to medium; add onion, carrots, celery and garlic; cook 5 minutes. Add mushrooms; cook 5 minutes more. Stir in salt, pepper, thyme, bay leaf, broth, wine and tomato paste. Bring to boil; reduce heat and simmer 5 minutes. Add beef; cover. Bake 3 to 4 hours, turning meat every hour. Remove roast; keep warm. Reduce flour to 2 tablespoons and blend with 3 tablespoons water; add to liquid. Cook and stir over medium heat until thickened. Serve as directed.

Per serving: 545 calories, 30 g total fat (10 g sat.), 130 mg cholesterol., 433 mg sodium, 34 g carbohydrate, 2 g fiber, 33 g protein.

Asian Beef Stew

2 large onions, sliced
2 pounds beef round steak, sliced for stir-fry
2 ribs celery, sliced ¼ inch thick
1 cup peeled baby carrots
1 cup plus 2 tablespoons beef broth
1 cup orange juice
3 tablespoons soy sauce
2 tablespoons hoisin sauce
1½ teaspoons Chinese five-spice powder
1 teaspoon Asian chili paste
3 tablespoons cornstarch
1 package (10 ounces) frozen peas, thawed
6 cups cooked white rice

1. In 5- or 5½-quart slow cooker, layer onions, beef, celery and carrots.

2. In medium-size bowl, whisk together 1 cup broth, the orange juice, soy sauce, hoisin sauce, five-spice powder and Asian chili paste. Pour into slow cooker.

3. Cover slow cooker; cook on high-heat setting for 5 hours.

4. In cup, mix the remaining 2 tablespoons broth and the cornstarch. Stir into slow cooker; cover and cook for 30 minutes longer.

5. Stir in peas; cook about 5 minutes longer or until heated through. Serve with rice.

Conventional Method: In large skillet, heat 1 tablespoon vegetable oil over medium-high heat. Add steak; cook about 3 minutes or until steak is still slightly pink. Remove from skillet and set aside. In bowl, whisk together 1 cup beef broth, the orange juice, soy sauce, hoisin sauce, five-spice powder and Asian chili paste. Place onions, celery and carrots in skillet and pour in broth mixture. Bring to a boil; reduce heat to medium-low and simmer about 15 minutes or until carrots are tender. In cup, stir together 2 tablespoons beef broth and the cornstarch. Return steak to skillet. Add cornstarch mixture and stir until combined. Boil over high heat for 2 to 3 minutes or until sauce has thickened and steak is fully cooked. Stir in peas and heat through. Serve with rice.

When you're craving both the slow-cooked convenience of stew and the appeal of Asian food, this recipe offers the best of both worlds.

PREP: 10 minutes
SLOW COOK: 5 hours 35 minutes on high-heat setting
MAKES: 8 servings

QUICK TIP

DON'T LIFT THAT LID!

When preparing foods in a slow cooker, remember not to peek (lift the lid) during the recommended cooking time. Even if the lid is off for only a few seconds, the cooker will lose heat quickly, and that could affect the time needed to cook the dish.

Per serving: 365 calories, 5 g total fat (2 g sat.), 65 mg cholesterol, 728 mg sodium, 45 g carbohydrate, 4 g fiber, 32 g protein.

Barbecue Chili

1 tablespoon vegetable oil
1 pound ground beef
1 cup chopped onion
2 cloves garlic, finely chopped
¼ cup chili powder
1 tablespoon ground cumin
1 can (16 ounces) stewed tomatoes
1 cup ketchup
⅓ cup packed brown sugar
¼ cup molasses
¼ cup Worcestershire sauce
1 tablespoon dry mustard
2 cans (15¼ ounces each) dark-red kidney
 beans, drained
2 cans (15 ounces each) pinto beans, drained
1 can (15 ounces) cannellini beans, drained
12 cooked bacon strips, for garnish (optional)
 Jalapeño pepper slices, for garnish
 (optional)

1. In large Dutch oven, heat oil over medium-high heat. Add meat, onion, garlic, chili powder and cumin; cook, stirring to break up meat, about 10 minutes or until meat is no longer pink and onion is tender.

2. Stir in tomatoes, ketchup, brown sugar, molasses, Worcestershire sauce and mustard; cover and simmer, stirring occasionally, for 20 minutes. Stir in kidney, pinto and cannellini beans; cover and simmer, stirring occasionally, for 30 minutes to blend flavors.

3. To serve, ladle chili into bowls. If desired, garnish each serving with a strip of bacon and jalapeño slices.

If you love barbecue and you love chili, you'll love how great they taste together in one bowl!

PREP: 15 minutes
COOK: 1 hour
MAKES: 12 servings

QUICK BITE

BROWN SUGAR SUBSTITUTION

If you're out of brown sugar and need a quick substitution, use 1 cup granulated sugar plus 2 tablespoons molasses for every cup of packed brown sugar called for in the recipe. (For this recipe, you'd use ⅓ cup granulated sugar plus 2 teaspoons molasses.)

Per serving: 343 calories, 6 g total fat (2 g sat.), 14 mg cholesterol, 675 mg sodium, 53 g carbohydrate, 14 g fiber, 20 g protein.

Best-Ever Roast Beef

2 large onions, cut in ¼-inch-thick rings
1 cup dry red wine
1 beef eye of round roast (3 pounds)
¼ cup ketchup
2 tablespoons bottled teriyaki sauce
2 tablespoons Dijon mustard
1 tablespoon balsamic vinegar
½ cup cold water
3 tablespoons all-purpose flour
2 cups beef broth

1. Heat oven to 400°. Coat small, flameproof roasting pan with nonstick cooking spray. Scatter onion rings over bottom of pan. Pour red wine into the pan. Place roast in center of pan on top of onion.

2. In small bowl, stir together ketchup, teriyaki sauce, mustard and balsamic vinegar until well blended. Remove 2 tablespoons of the ketchup mixture to another small bowl; reserve for making the gravy. Brush some of the remaining ketchup mixture over top and sides of roast.

3. Roast at 400°, basting occasionally with rest of ketchup mixture, about 1¼ hours or until instant-read meat thermometer inserted in thickest part of roast registers 140° for medium-rare (internal temperature will continue to rise another 5° to 10° during standing).

4. Remove roast to cutting board; cover loosely with aluminum foil. Remove onions from roasting pan to small bowl; cover with aluminum foil.

5. Add water to reserved 2 tablespoons ketchup mixture; whisk in flour until well blended and smooth. Place roasting pan over medium-high heat on the stovetop. Add broth; cook for 2 minutes, stirring and scraping up any browned bits from bottom of pan. Slowly whisk in flour mixture; cook, stirring, about 3 minutes or until thickened. Pour into small serving bowl. Thinly slice roast. Serve with onions and gravy.

Teriyaki sauce, mustard and balsamic vinegar do double duty as a coating on the roast and a key element in the gravy.

PREP: 15 minutes
ROAST: at 400° for 1¼ hours
COOK: about 5 minutes
MAKES: 12 servings

QUICK BITE

BALSAMIC PINCH HITTER

While there's no true substitute for the rich, complex flavor of balsamic vinegar, in a pinch, you can use 1 tablespoon cider vinegar or red-wine vinegar plus ½ teaspoon of sugar for each tablespoon of balsamic vinegar called for in a recipe.

Per serving: 251 calories, 12 g total fat (5 g sat.), 60 mg cholesterol, 457 mg sodium, 7 g carbohydrate, 1 g fiber, 24 g protein.

Cheese-Stuffed Flank Steak

2 tablespoons grated Parmesan cheese
1 tablespoon chopped fresh parsley leaves
1 tablespoon extra-virgin olive oil
2 cloves garlic, chopped
½ teaspoon salt
½ teaspoon dried Italian seasoning
¼ teaspoon black pepper
¼ teaspoon red pepper flakes
1 beef flank steak (1½ pounds)
½ pound sliced provolone cheese
   (10 to 12 slices)
1 jar (7 ounces) roasted red peppers, drained
6 red onions, quartered

1. In small bowl, mix Parmesan cheese, parsley, oil, garlic, salt, Italian seasoning, black pepper and red pepper flakes to form paste.

2. Lay steak on work surface. Holding sharp knife parallel to work surface and starting at long side, slice flank steak in half to opposite long side, without cutting all the way through; open up steak like a book.

3. Rub steak on both sides with seasoning paste. Arrange slices of provolone over surface of steak, leaving 1-inch border around edges. Top with roasted peppers. Starting at short end, roll up steak to enclose filling. Tie steak roll at 1-inch intervals with kitchen twine. Wrap in plastic wrap. Refrigerate for 2 hours or overnight.

4. Heat oven to 425°. Remove plastic wrap from steak. Let meat stand at room temperature while oven is heating, but no more than 30 minutes. Place steak on broiler-pan rack in broiler pan. Arrange onion quarters around steak on rack.

5. Roast steak and onions at 425° for 25 minutes. Turn on oven broiler. Broil steak and onions 4 inches from heat about 15 minutes or until instant-read meat thermometer inserted in center of steak registers 150°. Let stand for 15 minutes. Remove twine. Slice crosswise.

A relatively inexpensive beef cut becomes company-special thanks to this impressive presentation.

PREP: 20 minutes
CHILL: 2 hours or overnight
ROAST: at 425° for 25 minutes
BROIL: 15 minutes
STAND: up to 45 minutes
MAKES: 6 servings

QUICK BITE

QUICK FIXES WITH ROASTED PEPPERS

Keep roasted red peppers on hand to add zip and color to meals: Stir ½ cup chopped peppers with ¾ cup corn into cooked rice pilaf mix; whirl ½ cup with 1 tablespoon lemon juice in a blender, then brush on broiled shrimp.

Per serving: 402 calories, 23 g total fat (11 g sat.), 93 mg cholesterol, 522 mg sodium, 12 g carbohydrate, 2 g fiber, 35 g protein.

Spicy Spaghetti and Meatballs

Spicy Meatballs (recipe, left)
Sauce and Spaghetti:
 2 tablespoons extra-virgin olive oil
 1 cup chopped onion
 ½ cup chopped fennel (about half of a
   medium-size bulb)
 2 cans (28 ounces each) plum tomatoes in
   thick puree
 1 can (14½ ounces) diced tomatoes
 ½ cup dry red wine
 4 cloves garlic, lightly crushed
 2 teaspoons sugar
 ½ teaspoon salt
 ½ teaspoon dried oregano
 ½ teaspoon dried sage
 ¼ teaspoon black pepper
 1 box (1 pound) spaghetti
   Fresh parsley sprigs, for garnish (optional)

1. Prepare Spicy Meatballs.

2. **Sauce and Spaghetti:** In large, deep, heavy pot, heat oil over medium heat. Add onion and fennel; sauté about 7 minutes or until softened. Add plum tomatoes, diced tomatoes, red wine, garlic, sugar, salt, oregano, sage and pepper, breaking up tomatoes with wooden spoon. Simmer, uncovered, over medium-high heat for 10 minutes (you should have about 9 cups sauce).

3. Carefully add cooked meatballs to sauce, submerging them, if possible. Cover and simmer about 15 minutes or until instant-read meat thermometer inserted into centers of meatballs registers 160°.

4. Meanwhile, cook spaghetti following package directions. Drain pasta; transfer to large serving dish. Top with meatballs and sauce. If desired, garnish with parsley.

This boldly seasoned version of the classic Italian-American dish rivals anything you can get at a restaurant!

PREP: 30 minutes
COOK: about 1 hour
MAKES: 8 servings

SPICY MEATBALLS

Preheat oven to 325°. In medium-size nonstick skillet, heat 1 tablespoon olive oil over medium heat. Add 1 small onion, chopped, and ½ cup chopped fennel; cook about 10 minutes or until soft. In bowl, combine 2½ pounds lean ground beef, 1 cup packaged seasoned dry bread crumbs, 2 eggs, ½ cup milk, 2 teaspoons Italian seasoning, 1¼ teaspoons hot-pepper sauce, 1 teaspoon garlic salt, ½ teaspoon black pepper and onion mixture. Shape mixture into thirty-six 2-inch meatballs. Arrange meatballs in a single layer in two 15×10×2-inch baking pans. Bake at 325° for 20 minutes.

Per serving spaghetti and meatballs: 619 calories, 15 g total fat (5 g sat.), 141 mg cholesterol, 1,638 mg sodium, 71 g carbohydrate, 7 g fiber, 46 g protein.

Pork with Lemon-Rosemary Rub

Pork Roast:
- 1 center-cut pork loin roast with 6 ribs (4 to 4½ pounds)
- ½ teaspoon salt
- ⅛ teaspoon black pepper
- 1 tablespoon lemon juice
- 1 tablespoon extra-virgin olive oil
- 1 tablespoon Dijon mustard
- 1 tablespoon chopped fresh rosemary leaves
- 1 teaspoon grated lemon zest
- 4 cloves garlic, chopped

Gravy:
- ⅓ cup dry white wine
- 3 tablespoons all-purpose flour
- 3 cups chicken broth
- 2 tablespoons apricot preserves

1. Heat oven to 450°.

2. **Pork Roast:** Season roast with salt and pepper. In small bowl, mix lemon juice, oil, mustard, rosemary, lemon zest and garlic.

3. Rub pork roast with lemon-rosemary mixture. Place on a rack in a large roasting pan. Roast at 450° for 20 minutes. Reduce oven temperature to 325° and roast about 65 minutes longer or until instant-read meat thermometer inserted in center of roast registers 150°. Let stand in warm place for 10 minutes before slicing (internal temperature should reach 160°).

4. **Gravy:** Pour off all but 1 tablespoon of the fat in roasting pan. Place pan over medium heat and add wine. Cook for 1 minute, scraping up any browned bits from bottom of pan. Sprinkle flour into pan and cook for 1 minute. Gradually whisk in chicken broth and bring to a boil. Cook for 2 minutes, whisking constantly. Whisk in apricot preserves. Strain into a small saucepan; keep warm.

5. Slice meat and serve with the warm gravy on the side.

Rosemary, garlic, lemon and mustard make pork a truly memorable meal.

PREP: 15 minutes
ROAST: at 450° for 20 minutes; at 325° for 65 minutes
STAND: 10 minutes
MAKES: 8 servings

QUICK BITE

BROTH IN A PINCH

Instant bouillon takes up very little space and comes in handy when you run out of broth. To substitute bouillon for broth, simply use 1 teaspoon or 1 cube of beef or chicken bouillon plus 1 cup hot water for each cup of beef or chicken broth called for in a recipe.

Per serving: 343 calories, 20 g total fat (7 g sat.), 81 mg cholesterol, 621 mg sodium, 7 g carbohydrate, 0 g fiber, 31 g protein.

Double-Cut Pork Chops

3 strips bacon, chopped
1 small onion, diced
1 small zucchini, shredded
1 teaspoon chopped fresh rosemary
2 cloves garlic, sliced
¼ teaspoon black pepper, plus extra for seasoning chops
⅛ teaspoon salt, plus extra for seasoning chops
2 slices white bread, crumbled to make fresh bread crumbs (about 1¼ cups)
¼ cup grated Parmesan cheese
6 double-cut pork chops about 1¼ inches thick (about 5 pounds total) (consult your butcher for these)
1 tablespoon vegetable oil
¾ cup dry white wine

1. Heat oven to 350°. For stuffing, in nonstick large skillet, cook bacon over medium-high heat until it begins to sizzle. Reduce heat to medium. Add onion; cook about 6 minutes or until softened. Add zucchini, rosemary, garlic, ¼ teaspoon pepper and ⅛ teaspoon salt; cook about 5 minutes or until most of the liquid evaporates.

2. Remove skillet from heat. Add bread crumbs and Parmesan cheese to skillet; stir to mix. Transfer to small bowl. Wipe out skillet with paper towels.

3. Season chops on both sides with salt and pepper. Using tip of a sharp knife, cut pocket in each chop, cutting all the way through to bone. Place packed ⅓ cup stuffing into each pocket, pressing gently to flatten.

4. In the large nonstick skillet, heat oil over medium-high heat. Add 3 chops and brown about 2 minutes per side. Transfer browned chops to large shallow roasting pan or 15×10×1-inch jelly-roll pan. Repeat with remaining chops, adding more oil if needed. Pour wine into roasting pan.

5. Bake chops at 350° about 45 minutes or until instant-read meat thermometer inserted in thickest part of meat registers 150° to 155°. Remove from oven (internal temperature will increase to 160°). Serve warm.

The stuffing brims with vegetables and smoky bacon. Steamed green beans are a winning accompaniment.

PREP: 15 minutes
COOK: 20 minutes
BAKE: at 350° for 45 minutes
MAKES: 6 servings

QUICK BITE

GOOD WHITES FOR COOKING

When a recipe calls for dry white wine, good options include Chardonnay, Sauvignon Blanc and Pinot Grigio. If you'd rather not cook with wine, substitute chicken broth in savory cooking, or apple or white grape juice in dessert recipes.

Per serving: 519 calories, 26 g total fat (9 g sat.), 149 mg cholesterol, 504 mg sodium, 9 g carbohydrate, 1 g fiber, 56 g protein.

Jerk-Seasoned Pork Roast and Polenta

¼ cup extra-virgin olive oil
   Grated zest from 1 lime (about 1 teaspoon)
   Juice from 1 lime (about 2 tablespoons)
4 cloves garlic, chopped
2 tablespoons plus 1 teaspoon jerk
   seasoning
1 boneless pork loin roast (3 to 3½ pounds)
5 tablespoons butter
1 cup diced sweet peppers (assorted colors)
1 quart (4 cups) milk
1½ teaspoons garlic salt
1⅓ cups instant polenta
¼ teaspoon black pepper
   Lime wedges (optional)

1. In large plastic food-storage bag, combine oil, lime zest, lime juice, garlic and 2 tablespoons jerk seasoning. Add pork roast; turn to coat completely. Refrigerate overnight.

2. Heat oven to 425°. Place pork roast on rack in large roasting pan. Rub remaining 1 teaspoon jerk seasoning over pork.

3. Roast at 425° for 15 minutes. Reduce oven temperature to 350°. Roast for 55 to 60 minutes or until instant-read meat thermometer inserted in center of roast registers 150°. Let roast stand in warm place for 10 minutes before slicing (internal temperature should reach 160°).

4. While meat is standing, in large pot, melt 1 tablespoon butter over medium heat. Add sweet peppers; sauté about 3 minutes or until peppers are softened. Add milk and garlic salt. Bring to a boil.

5. Slowly pour in polenta, stirring constantly. Cook, over medium heat, stirring constantly, about 3 minutes or until polenta pulls away from sides of pot, taking care not to let the polenta stick. Stir in the remaining 4 tablespoons butter and the black pepper; cook until butter is completely melted.

6. Serve polenta immediately with sliced pork roast. If desired, serve with lime wedges.

Olive oil sparked with lime juice, garlic and jerk seasoning makes a lively marinade for pork roast.

PREP: 15 minutes
CHILL: overnight
ROAST: at 425° for 15 minutes;
at 350° for 55 to 60 minutes
STAND: 10 minutes
COOK: 6 minutes
MAKES: 8 servings

QUICK BITE

GARLIC SUBSTITUTE

Fresh garlic is best, but if you find yourself without any garlic cloves, substitute ½ teaspoon bottled minced garlic or ⅛ teaspoon garlic powder for each clove called for in a recipe.

Per serving: 663 calories, 38 g total fat (15 g sat.), 149 mg cholesterol, 608 mg sodium, 33 g carbohydrate, 2 g fiber, 44 g protein.

Kielbasa and Apple Pasta Bake

1 pound rigatoni pasta
2 tablespoons extra-virgin olive oil
1 large onion, sliced
¼ cup all-purpose flour
1 quart (4 cups) milk
1 block (10 ounces) extra-sharp Cheddar cheese, shredded (3 cups)
1 teaspoon hot-pepper sauce
1 teaspoon salt
1 package fully cooked kielbasa (14 ounces), sliced into ¼-inch-thick coins
3 Fuji apples, cored and cut into ½-inch cubes
2 scallions, trimmed and thinly sliced

1. Heat oven to 350°. Coat 10-cup baking dish with nonstick cooking spray.

2. In large deep pot of lightly salted boiling water, cook pasta until al dente, firm but tender, following package directions. Drain.

3. Meanwhile, in large heavy-bottomed saucepan, heat oil over medium-high heat. Add onion; cook for 5 to 7 minutes or until softened. Stir in flour; cook for 1 minute. Gradually whisk in milk. Bring to a boil, stirring continuously; boil about 1 minute or until thickened. Remove from heat.

4. Set aside 1 cup cheese for topping the casserole. Stir remaining 2 cups cheese, the hot-pepper sauce and salt into milk mixture until smooth.

5. In pasta cooking pot, toss together pasta, cheese sauce, kielbasa and apples. Spoon into prepared baking dish, mounding mixture slightly. Cover.

6. Bake, covered, at 350° for 30 minutes. Uncover. Stir pasta mixture. Sprinkle top with the reserved 1 cup cheese. Bake about 10 minutes longer or until cheese is melted. Let stand for 10 minutes. Sprinkle with scallions.

Apples and Cheddar cheese are a natural together, so it's no surprise they taste terrific baked into a casserole.

PREP: 25 minutes
COOK: 8 minutes
BAKE: at 350° for 40 minutes
STAND: 10 minutes
MAKES: 8 servings

QUICK BITE

KIELBASA FOR SWIFT SUPPERS

Because kielbasa usually has a long shelf life when stored in the fridge, it's easy to keep on hand for a quick supper anytime. Serve with interesting mustards such as grainy, hot, sweet and flavored for an exceptional meal.

Per serving: 485 calories, 20 g total fat (11 g sat.), 54 mg cholesterol, 577 mg sodium, 56 g carbohydrate, 4 g fiber, 20 g protein.

Chipotle Mac and Cheese

- 1 **pound medium-size pasta shells**
- 2 **tablespoons butter**
- 2 **tablespoons all-purpose flour**
- 2 **cups half-and-half**
- 1 **package (8 ounces) shredded Monterey Jack cheese**
- 1 **package (8 ounces) shredded sharp Cheddar cheese**
- ¾ **teaspoon chipotle seasoning or salt-free seasoning blend (such as Mrs. Dash or McCormick)**
- ½ **teaspoon salt**
- 1 **ham steak (about 1 pound), trimmed of excess fat and meat cut into ¼-inch dice**

1. Heat oven to 350°. Coat 13×9×2-inch baking dish with nonstick cooking spray.

2. Cook shells in lightly salted boiling water following package directions. Drain. Return pasta to hot pan.

3. In large heavy-bottomed saucepan (not nonstick), melt butter over medium heat. Stir in flour until well blended; cook for 1 minute. Whisk in 1 cup half-and-half; cook, whisking continuously, until very smooth. Whisk in remaining 1 cup half-and-half; continue to cook, whisking about 6 minutes or until thickened and smooth. Remove from heat. Stir in 1 cup Jack cheese, 1 cup Cheddar cheese, chipotle seasoning and salt until smooth.

4. Stir ham and cheese sauce into pasta. Spoon into prepared dish. Top with remaining cheeses.

5. Bake at 350° about 30 minutes or until bubbly and lightly golden brown on top. Remove from oven to wire rack; let stand for 10 minutes before serving.

Here's an all-new take on a comfort-food classic, with ham for heartiness and two kinds of cheese for richness.

PREP: 15 minutes
COOK: about 20 minutes
BAKE: at 350° for 30 minutes
STAND: 10 minutes
MAKES: 12 servings

QUICK BITE

CHEESE PLEASE: MONTEREY JACK

Monterey Jack is named after David Jacks, a cheesemaker who lived near Monterey, California, and invented the cheese in the 19th century. The mild-flavor, semisoft cheese works well for snacking and melting; in a pinch, substitute an American Muenster. Do not confuse it with Dry Jack, a renowned aged California cheese with a deep, sharp, nutty flavor.

Per serving: 348 calories, 19 g total fat (11 g sat.), 64 mg cholesterol, 401 mg sodium, 28 g carbohydrate, 1 g fiber, 16 g protein.

Ham-and-Pineapple Bread Pudding

- ¼ cup (½ stick) unsalted butter
- 1 medium-size carrot, peeled and shredded
- 1 rib celery, chopped
- 1 small green pepper, seeded and chopped
- 1 small onion, chopped
- 6 eggs
- 1 can (20 ounces) crushed pineapple in syrup
- ½ cup milk
- 1 tablespoon Dijon mustard
- 1 loaf Italian bread (about 6 ounces), cut into ½-inch cubes (6 cups)
- 1 pound piece boiled ham, cut into ½-inch cubes (2¾ cups)
- 1 cup shredded Swiss cheese (4 ounces)

1. Heat oven to 375°. In large nonstick skillet, melt butter over medium heat. Add carrot, celery, green pepper and onion; sauté about 3 minutes or until slightly softened. Remove from heat.

2. In large bowl, stir together eggs, pineapple with its syrup, milk and mustard until blended. Stir in bread, ham, cheese and cooked vegetables. Pour into 3-quart casserole; use spatula to level off top.

3. Bake at 375° about 40 minutes or until set and golden brown.

Swiss cheese, Dijon mustard and pineapple are favorite accompaniments for ham, and this casserole combines them all.

PREP: 15 minutes
COOK: 3 minutes
BAKE: at 375° for 40 minutes
MAKES: 8 servings

Per serving: 412 calories, 22 g total fat (10 g sat.), 220 mg cholesterol, 1,059 mg sodium, 30 g carbohydrate, 2 g fiber, 23 g protein.

Mexican Pulled-Pork Tacos

- 1 medium-size onion, coarsely chopped
- 1 boneless pork shoulder roast or picnic roast (about 3½ pounds)
- 1 medium-size sweet red pepper, seeded and cut into ¼-inch squares
- 1 medium-size green pepper, seeded and cut into ¼-inch squares
- 1 can (14½ ounces) jalapeño-flavored diced tomatoes
- 2 teaspoons ground cumin
- 1½ teaspoons garlic salt
- 1½ teaspoons dried oregano
- ½ teaspoon cayenne pepper
- 1 can (11 ounces) corn kernels, drained
- 1 jar (4 ounces) diced green chiles, drained
- 3 tablespoons tomato paste
- 16 corn tortillas (about 6 inches each), warmed following package directions
  Sour cream, for garnish (optional)

1. In 5- or 5½-quart slow cooker, layer onion, pork roast, red pepper and green pepper. In medium-size bowl, stir together tomatoes, cumin, garlic salt, oregano and cayenne pepper. Pour evenly over the mixture in the slow cooker. Add corn and chiles.

2. Cover slow cooker; cook on high-heat setting for 5 hours. Remove pork roast to cutting board; keep warm.

3. Remove 1½ cups of the liquid from slow cooker and discard. Stir tomato paste into vegetable mixture in the slow cooker. Cover and cook for 30 minutes longer.

4. Meanwhile, cut pork roast into slices. Shred slices using two forks to pull the meat apart. Add shredded pork to mixture in slow cooker; heat through.

5. To serve, wrap pork mixture in warmed corn tortillas, dividing the mixture equally among the tortillas. If desired, garnish each serving with sour cream.

Pork shoulder is an inexpensive cut of meat that cooks up into a moist, tender filling.

PREP: 10 minutes
SLOW COOK: 5½ hours on high-heat setting
MAKES: 8 servings

CONVENTIONAL METHOD

Heat oven to 350°. Heat 2 tablespoons oil in large heavy pot over medium heat; add onion and peppers. Cook for 5 minutes or until softened. Add diced tomatoes, cumin, salt, oregano, cayenne, corn, green chiles and tomato paste. Bring to boil; reduce heat to medium and simmer for 5 minutes. Heat oven to 350°. Coat large deep pot with nonstick cooking spray; add pork. Bake for 30 minutes. Add sauce; cover and reduce heat to 300°. Bake about 3 hours or until instant-read meat thermometer registers 170°, basting meat occasionally. Remove pork to cutting board and shred. Return to sauce in pan. Continue with step 5.

Per serving: 590 calories, 32 g total fat (11 g sat.), 138 mg cholesterol, 836 mg sodium, 35 g carbohydrate, 5 g fiber, 40 g protein.

Spiced Country Ribs

Pork ribs marry beautifully with stewed fruits and spices.

PREP: 20 minutes
SLOW COOK: 5 to 6 hours on high-heat or 10 to 11 hours on low-heat setting, plus 5 to 10 minutes on high-heat setting
MAKES: 4 servings

1¼ cups chopped carrot
1 cup chopped parsnip
1 large onion, coarsely chopped
1 cup (6-ounce package) dried apricots, each apricot halved
½ cup pitted prunes (3½ ounces), each prune halved
2 cloves garlic, minced
1 cinnamon stick (3 inches)
4 whole cloves
4 whole allspice berries
1 square (6-inch) cheesecloth
3 pounds country-style pork ribs
1½ cups chicken broth
½ cup orange juice
2 tablespoons balsamic vinegar
1 teaspoon salt
⅛ teaspoon black pepper
¼ cup all-purpose flour
Hot cooked rice or couscous (optional)

1. In 5- or 5½-quart slow cooker, layer carrot, parsnip, onion, apricots, prunes and garlic. Place cinnamon, cloves and allspice on clean cheesecloth square. Tie the ends together with kitchen twine to form a bundle. Place the ribs and spice packet on top of the vegetables.

2. In 2-cup measure, stir together 1 cup broth, the orange juice, vinegar, salt and pepper until well blended; pour evenly over ribs.

3. Cover slow cooker; cook on high-heat setting for 5 to 6 hours or on low-heat setting for 10 to 11 hours or until the vegetables and ribs are tender.

4. Remove ribs to a large platter; cover with aluminum foil to keep warm. Discard spice packet. If necessary, raise temperature to high-heat setting.

5. In 1-cup measure, stir together remaining ½ cup broth and the flour until well blended and smooth. Stir into the liquid in the slow cooker. Cover slow cooker; cook on high-heat setting for 5 to 10 minutes or until liquid is thickened. Serve vegetable mixture from slow cooker with ribs. If desired, serve with rice or couscous on the side for soaking up the juices.

CONVENTIONAL METHOD

Cook ribs in 1 tablespoon oil in large heavy pot about 10 minutes or until browned all over. Remove to a plate. Add carrot, parsnip, onion, garlic and 2 tablespoons water to pot. Cook 3 to 4 minutes. Place ribs on top of vegetables. Stir in apricots and prunes. Add 1 cup chicken broth, the orange juice, vinegar, spice packet, salt and pepper. Cover; simmer over medium-low heat about 1½ hours or until ribs are tender. Remove ribs to large platter; keep warm. Follow step 5, cooking about 1 to 2 minutes or until thick. Spoon mixture over ribs.

Per serving: 622 calories, 23 g total fat (8 g sat.), 133 mg cholesterol, 1,094 mg sodium, 61 g carbohydrate, 9 g fiber, 45 g protein.

Pork Chop 'n' Rice Casserole

- 4 bone-in loin pork chops (about 1½ pounds total)
- ½ teaspoon salt
- ¼ teaspoon black pepper
- 2 tablespoons vegetable oil
- ⅔ cup long-grain white rice
- 1 can (14½ ounces) jalapeño-flavored diced tomatoes
- 1 cup water
- 2 medium-size green peppers, seeded and sliced into thin strips
- 1 cup shredded taco-blend cheese (4 ounces)

1. Heat oven to 350°.

2. Season pork chops with ¼ teaspoon salt and ⅛ teaspoon black pepper. In large skillet, heat oil over medium-high heat. Add chops; cook about 2 minutes per side or until lightly browned. Remove skillet from heat.

3. Coat 2½-quart oval baking dish with nonstick cooking spray. Add rice, tomatoes, water and remaining ¼ teaspoon salt and ⅛ teaspoon black pepper; stir to combine. Place pork chops on rice mixture; scatter green pepper over top. Cover dish with aluminum foil.

4. Bake at 350° about 50 minutes or until rice is tender and most of the liquid has been absorbed. Remove foil from dish; sprinkle cheese over top. Bake about 5 minutes longer or until cheese melts. Let stand for 10 minutes before serving.

Graduate your kids from tacos to this more adult pork chop dish—it has plenty of taco-like seasonings to make the transition smooth.

PREP: 10 minutes
COOK: 4 minutes
BAKE: at 350° for 55 minutes
STAND: 10 minutes
MAKES: 4 servings

QUICK TIP

FREEZER FACTS

If you have a green pepper in the fridge that you're not going to use before it's past its prime, consider freezing it. To do this, chop the green pepper, seal in a freezer bag, then label and freeze for up to 2 months. The tidbits will thaw quickly, so when you're ready to use them they can be stirred directly into the recipe.

Per serving: 508 calories, 23 g total fat (8 g sat.), 87 mg cholesterol, 1,034 mg sodium, 39 g carbohydrate, 3 g fiber, 35 g protein.

Zesty Minestrone Soup

3 cups packaged coleslaw mix
  (from 1-pound bag)
1 large onion, chopped
3 medium-size carrots, peeled and chopped
1 medium-size yellow squash, halved
  lengthwise and sliced crosswise
  ¼ inch thick
1 medium-size zucchini, halved lengthwise
  and sliced crosswise ¼ inch thick
1 can (28 ounces) diced tomatoes
2 cans (14 ounces each) chicken broth
1 can (15 ounces) red kidney beans, drained
  and rinsed
2 cups water
¼ pound thinly sliced prosciutto, chopped
2 cloves garlic, chopped
1½ teaspoons dried Italian seasoning
1 teaspoon salt
½ teaspoon black pepper
¼ teaspoon red pepper flakes
1 cup ditalini pasta
  Shaved Parmesan cheese (optional)

1. In 5- or 5½-quart slow cooker, stir together coleslaw mix, onion, carrot, squash, zucchini, tomatoes, broth, beans, water, prosciutto, garlic, Italian seasoning, salt, black pepper and red pepper flakes.

2. Cover slow cooker; cook on high-heat setting for 4½ hours.

3. Stir uncooked ditalini into mixture in slow cooker. Cover; cook for 30 minutes longer.

4. To serve, spoon into bowls. If desired, top with Parmesan cheese.

Conventional Method: In large pot or Dutch oven, stir together coleslaw mix, onion, carrot, squash, zucchini, tomatoes, broth, beans, water, prosciutto, garlic, Italian seasoning, salt, black pepper and red pepper flakes. Cover and bring to a boil over high heat. Reduce heat to medium. Simmer, covered, for 10 minutes, stirring occasionally. Add uncooked ditalini; cook for 10 minutes longer, stirring occasionally. To serve, spoon into bowls. If desired, sprinkle with Parmesan cheese.

A little prosciutto adds a lot of pizzazz to this veggie-packed soup. Serve with cheesy garlic toast for a satisfying one-dish meal.

PREP: 15 minutes
SLOW COOK: 5 hours on high-heat setting
MAKES: 8 servings

Per serving: 222 calories, 4 g total fat (1 g sat.), 12 mg cholesterol, 1,367 mg sodium, 34 g carbohydrate, 9 g fiber, 13 g protein.

Bacon 'n' Cheese Strata

8 slices firm white bread

2 scallions, trimmed and chopped (including some of the green)

8 strips precooked bacon, chopped

1 cup shredded sharp Cheddar cheese (4 ounces)

1 can (14½ ounces) diced tomatoes, drained and patted dry

3 eggs

1½ cups milk

⅛ teaspoon black pepper

⅛ teaspoon hot-pepper sauce

1. Coat shallow 2-quart baking dish with nonstick cooking spray. Arrange half of the bread in single layer in dish, cutting to fit. Cover with half of the scallion, bacon, cheese and tomatoes. Repeat for a second layer.

2. Heat oven to 375°. In small bowl, combine eggs, milk, black pepper and hot-pepper sauce. Pour over casserole.

3. Bake, uncovered, at 375° about 45 minutes or until lightly browned. If browning too quickly, cover loosely with aluminum foil.

Make Ahead: Prepare as directed, except do not bake. Cover and refrigerate for up to 2 hours. Bake as directed.

On weekend mornings, instead of making eggs every which way for everyone, make one egg dish everyone will like.

PREP: 10 minutes
BAKE: at 375° for 45 minutes
MAKES: 6 servings

QUICK TIP

THE PROPER PAN

For recipes with eggs or acidic ingredients such as tomatoes and lemon, use glass or ceramic baking dishes. Pans made of aluminum, iron and tin can react with these foods, causing them to discolor.

Per serving: 313 calories, 13 g total fat (6 g sat.), 134 mg cholesterol, 778 mg sodium, 34 g carbohydrate, 3 g fiber, 17 g protein.

Pork Chops with Apple Cream Sauce

4 medium-size sweet potatoes, scrubbed
4 thick bone-in center-cut loin pork chops (about 2 pounds total)
½ teaspoon salt
½ teaspoon dried thyme
¼ teaspoon black pepper
1 tablespoon extra-virgin olive oil
2 large Vidalia onions, cut in half, then sliced about ¼ inch thick
1½ cups apple juice or cider
1½ cups chicken broth
½ cup heavy cream
4 teaspoons Dijon mustard

1. Heat oven to 375°. Place sweet potatoes on baking sheet and bake at 375° about 45 minutes or until tender.

2. While sweet potatoes bake, season both sides of chops with salt, thyme and pepper. Heat nonstick skillet large enough to hold the chops in a single layer over medium-high heat. Add oil, then chops; cook about 4 minutes per side or until lightly browned. Remove to a plate.

3. Reduce heat to medium-low; add onion and cook, stirring, about 3 minutes or until onion softens. Stir in ⅔ cup apple juice. Place chops on top of onion; cover and cook over medium heat about 15 minutes or until instant-read meat thermometer inserted in centers of chops registers 155°.

4. Place chops on serving plate; remove onion with a slotted spoon and place alongside chops or in separate bowl. Cover loosely with aluminum foil. Increase heat to high; add remaining apple juice and the broth to skillet. Cook over high heat, stirring, for 5 to 8 minutes or until slightly reduced. Add cream and cook for 5 minutes longer. Remove from heat; stir in mustard. Serve sauce with chops, onion and sweet potatoes.

The pork chop bake— old-fashioned comfort food— gets a bistro-style update.

PREP: 10 minutes
BAKE: at 375° for 45 minutes
COOK: about 36 minutes
MAKES: 4 servings

QUICK BITE
HERB KNOW-HOW

An old cook's adage exclaims, "When in doubt, use thyme!" Indeed, this herb's slightly minty, slightly lemony flavor nicely seasons chicken, meats, vegetables and a variety of sauces. If you like, you may substitute basil, marjoram, oregano or savory for thyme.

Per serving: 624 calories, 28 g total fat (12 g sat.), 153 mg cholesterol, 913 mg sodium, 50 g carbohydrate, 3 g fiber, 43 g protein.

Chicken Stew with Potato Dumplings

- 3 pounds bone-in chicken thighs, skin removed
- 2 large carrots, peeled and cut into ½-inch coins
- 2 ribs celery, cut into ½-inch pieces
- 3 medium-size parsnips, peeled and cut into ½-inch coins
- 1 large sweet potato (about 1 pound), peeled and cut into 1-inch cubes
- 4 scallions, trimmed and chopped
- 1 quart (4 cups) chicken broth
- 1 cup water
- ½ teaspoon dried sage leaves
- ¼ teaspoon salt
- ¼ teaspoon black pepper
- 1 package (1.1 pounds) shelf-stable fully cooked gnocchi (dumplings)
- 2 tablespoons cornstarch mixed with ¼ cup cold water
- Hot-pepper sauce, to taste

1. Place chicken in a 6-quart slow cooker. Top with carrot, celery, parsnip, sweet potato and scallion. Pour chicken broth and 1 cup water over; season with sage, salt and pepper.

2. Cover slow cooker. Cook on high-heat setting for 4 hours or on low-heat setting for 6 hours.

3. Uncover slow cooker and remove chicken to a cutting board. If necessary, raise temperature to high-heat setting. Add gnocchi to slow cooker; cover and cook for 10 minutes. Meanwhile, let chicken cool slightly, then shred meat from bones, discarding bones.

4. When gnocchi are cooked, return chicken to slow cooker. Stir cornstarch-water mixture; stir into slow cooker. Cover and cook for 10 to 20 minutes or until thickened slightly. Add hot-pepper sauce to taste before serving.

Conventional Method: In large deep pot, combine chicken, carrot, celery, parsnip, sweet potato and scallion. Pour chicken broth and water over; season with sage, salt and pepper. Bring to boil; reduce heat to medium-low. Simmer, covered, 25 minutes or until vegetables are tender. Remove chicken to a cutting board. Add gnocchi to pot; cover and cook 10 minutes. Meanwhile, let chicken cool slightly, then shred meat from bones; discard bones. When gnocchi are cooked, return chicken to pot. Stir cornstarch-water mixture; stir into pot. Cover and cook for 10 to 20 minutes or until thickened. Add hot sauce to taste.

Shelf-stable cooked gnocchi are your ticket to no-prep dumplings in this stick-to-your-ribs stew.

PREP: 10 minutes
SLOW COOK: 4 hours on high-heat or 6 hours on low-heat setting, plus 20 to 30 minutes on high-heat setting
MAKES: 8 servings

QUICK TIP

HOW TO SKIN CHICKEN

Don't be daunted by the idea of skinning chicken. It's easy. Using a paper towel, grip the chicken piece with one hand. Grasp the skin end of the chicken with your other hand and simply pull the skin toward the bone end, twisting as necessary to fully loosen it.

Per serving: 362 calories, 10 g total fat (3 g sat.), 72 mg cholesterol, 881 mg sodium, 45 g carbohydrate, 4 g fiber, 23 g protein.

Four-Cheese Baked Macaroni

1 pound rotelle pasta
2 cups shredded sharp Cheddar cheese (8 ounces)
1 cup shredded mozzarella cheese (4 ounces)
½ cup shredded Jarlsberg cheese (2 ounces)
½ cup grated Parmesan cheese
¼ cup (½ stick) unsalted butter
¼ cup all-purpose flour
4 cups milk
1 teaspoon salt
¼ teaspoon ground nutmeg
⅛ teaspoon cayenne pepper
2 large ripe tomatoes, thinly sliced

Macaroni and cheese can only get better when you use four ever-popular cheeses in the mix.

PREP: 20 minutes
COOK: about 8 minutes
BAKE: at 350° for 45 minutes
STAND: 10 minutes
MAKES: 12 servings

1. Heat oven to 350°. Coat bottom and sides of 13×9×2-inch glass baking dish with nonstick cooking spray.

2. In large pot of lightly salted boiling water, cook pasta following the package directions. Drain pasta well.

3. Meanwhile, in large bowl, mix together Cheddar, mozzarella, Jarlsberg and Parmesan cheeses.

4. Over medium heat, melt butter in the pot in which pasta was cooked. Whisk flour into melted butter until well blended; continue to cook, whisking constantly, for 2 minutes to eliminate flour taste. Whisk in 1 cup milk until well blended. Gradually whisk in the remaining 3 cups milk, 1 cup at a time, whisking after each addition until well blended. Stir in salt, nutmeg and cayenne pepper. Bring mixture to simmering; cook, whisking constantly, about 2 minutes or until thickened and smooth. Remove saucepan from heat. Stir in 2 cups of the cheese mixture, whisking until the sauce is very smooth.

5. Add cooked pasta to cheese sauce in the pot; toss together until well blended.

6. Sprinkle ½ cup of the remaining cheese mixture evenly over the bottom of the prepared baking dish. Spoon half of the pasta mixture into baking dish, spreading evenly. Sprinkle 1 cup of the remaining cheese mixture over the pasta. Spoon the remaining pasta mixture over cheese mixture. Sprinkle remaining cheese mixture on top of pasta. Arrange sliced tomato on top.

7. Bake at 350° about 45 minutes or until the top of the macaroni is lightly golden. Let dish stand for at least 10 minutes before serving.

QUICK TIP

WHITE SAUCE SECRETS

Making a lump-free white sauce is easy when you follow these tips: When adding the flour to the melted butter, avoid high heat so the butter-flour mixture doesn't cook too fast and form clumps or burn. Add the milk or cream gradually, whisking after each addition until well blended.

Per serving: 361 calories, 18 g total fat (11 g sat.), 56 mg cholesterol, 463 mg sodium, 33 g carbohydrate, 2 g fiber, 17 g protein.

Orange-Flavored Roast Chicken

1 cup hot water
½ cup kosher or coarse salt
½ cup packed dark-brown sugar
3 cups orange juice
1 large onion, halved and thinly sliced
3 cloves garlic, crushed
1 tablespoon ground cumin
¼ teaspoon black pepper
1 whole roasting chicken (about 4 pounds)
   Orange wedges, for garnish (optional)
   Fresh parsley sprigs, for garnish (optional)

1. In 3-quart glass bowl, combine hot water, salt and brown sugar; stir to dissolve salt and brown sugar. Add orange juice, onion, garlic, cumin and pepper; stir to combine. Place chicken, breast side down, in the bowl. Cover; refrigerate overnight.

2. Heat oven to 400°. With slotted spoon or hands, remove half of the sliced onion from liquid; place in bottom of a roasting pan. Remove chicken, letting excess liquid drain into bowl. Discard liquid and remaining onion. Place chicken, breast side up, on top of onion in pan. Roast, uncovered, at 400° about 1 hour or until instant-read meat thermometer inserted into the thigh registers 165°. After 30 minutes, use aluminum foil to cover wing tips and any other areas of the chicken that may be browning too quickly.

3. Remove chicken from oven; let stand, tented with aluminum foil, for 10 minutes before carving. If desired, garnish serving platter with orange wedges and parsley.

Brining the chicken in the orange juice mixture ensures that even the breast meat will remain extra moist.

PREP: 10 minutes
CHILL: overnight
BAKE: at 400° for 1 hour
STAND: 10 minutes
MAKES: 6 servings

QUICK TIP

TAKING THE TEMP

When using a digital instant-read thermometer, keep in mind that its sensor is in the tip. You can use this type of thermometer to verify internal temperatures of thin or thick foods. On the other hand, the sensor of a dial instant-read thermometer is in the stem, not the tip, so you must insert the stem at least 2 inches into the food you are testing for an accurate reading. For thinner cuts, you may need to insert the thermometer sideways into the food.

Per serving: 372 calories, 19 g total fat (5 g sat.), 149 mg cholesterol, 1,054 mg sodium, 11 g carbohydrate, 1 g fiber, 38 g protein.

Roast Chicken with Vegetables

Roast chicken has made a comeback in recent years as cooks have discovered how easy it is to make and how good it can be with just the right seasonings.

PREP: 15 minutes
ROAST: at 450° for 30 minutes; at 350° for 60 minutes
STAND: 5 to 7 minutes
MAKES: 6 servings

HERB KNOW-HOW

Often used in French cooking, tarragon brings an aromatic, licoricelike appeal to dishes. It shines best with poultry, fish and in vinaigrette dressings. If necessary, substitute chervil or a dash of crushed fennel seeds or crushed anise seeds.

Per serving: 456 calories, 19 g total fat (5 g sat.), 105 mg cholesterol, 412 mg sodium, 33 g carbohydrate, 4 g fiber, 37 g protein.

---

1 roasting chicken (3 to 4 pounds)
½ teaspoon salt
¼ teaspoon black pepper
2 sprigs each fresh tarragon and thyme or ½ teaspoon dried of each
1 pound red-skin potatoes, scrubbed and cut into quarters or halves if large
1 basket (10 ounces) small white onions, peeled
2 large carrots, peeled and cut into thick slices
12 ounces fresh mushrooms, quartered
½ cup chicken broth or water

1. Heat oven to 450°. Dry chicken with paper towels. Remove excess fat. Sprinkle chicken with salt and pepper inside and out. Place tarragon and thyme in cavity of chicken. Slip tips of chicken wings under bird. Tie legs closely together. Place chicken, breast side down, in roasting pan large enough to hold vegetables heaped around it. Place potato, onions and carrot around chicken.

2. Roast at 450° for 30 minutes. Reduce oven temperature to 350°. Turn chicken breast side up. Add mushrooms around chicken in pan; add broth. Roast for 45 minutes longer or until an instant-read meat thermometer registers 165°. Remove chicken to platter; let stand for 5 to 7 minutes before cutting into portions. Meanwhile, return roasting pan with vegetables to oven about 15 minutes longer or until tender.

Variations:

• With or without herbs, place halves of lemon or orange in cavity of chicken before roasting.
• Vary vegetables by using parsnips, winter squash and turnips.
• Add fresh tomatoes when they are in season locally, as well as sweet red and green peppers.
• Roast 2 or 3 chickens without vegetables and chill for summertime dinners, picnics and easy-to-eat leftovers.

Rice-Noodle Chicken Soup

Broth:

- 3 quarts (12 cups) chicken broth
- 1 whole chicken (about 3½ pounds), rinsed, skin removed
- 1 large carrot, peeled and cut into chunks
- 1 large onion, cut into chunks
- 2 ribs celery, cut into chunks
- 1 piece (1 inch) fresh ginger, peeled and coarsely chopped

Soup:

- ½ head Napa cabbage, rinsed, hard core removed and cabbage cut into 1-inch-wide strips (about 8 cups)
- 2 large carrots, peeled and thinly sliced
- 2 large ribs celery, thinly sliced
- ¼ pound pad thai or broad rice noodles
- 1 can (8 ounces) sliced water chestnuts, drained
- ¼ cup reduced-sodium soy sauce
- ¼ cup fresh cilantro leaves
- 2 tablespoons hoisin sauce
  Fresh parsley sprigs, for garnish (optional)

1. **Broth:** In large pot, combine broth, chicken, carrot, onion, celery and ginger. Bring to a boil. Partially cover; reduce heat to medium and simmer for 1 hour.

2. Strain liquid through sieve into large pot; reserve. Set chicken aside; discard other solids. When chicken is cool enough to handle, remove meat, discarding bones. Shred meat.

3. **Soup:** Bring broth to a simmer. Add cabbage, carrot and celery; simmer for 4 minutes.

4. Add the noodles; simmer for 3 to 4 minutes or until noodles are cooked, stirring occasionally.

5. Add shredded chicken, the water chestnuts, soy sauce, cilantro and hoisin sauce; simmer about 2 minutes or until heated through. If desired, garnish each serving with parsley.

If your chicken and noodle soup needs perking up, try this colorful Asian-spiced version.

PREP: 30 minutes
COOK: 1 hour 10 minutes
MAKES: 9 servings

QUICK BITE

PRODUCE POINTERS

With its thin, crisp, crinkly white and pale green leaves, Napa cabbage adds crunch to stir-fries and also tastes great baked, braised or added to soups. To prepare this large, cylindrical Chinese cabbage, cut off bottom core; rinse leaves in cold water and pat dry. Refrigerate in a plastic storage bag for up to 3 days.

Per serving: 319 calories, 11 g total fat (3 g sat.), 85 mg cholesterol, 1,761 mg sodium, 22 g carbohydrate, 4 g fiber, 32 g protein.

Smoky Baked Ziti and Sausage

1 pound ziti or penne pasta
1½ cups shredded mozzarella cheese (6 ounces)
5 ounces Parmesan cheese, shredded (about 1¼ cups)
¾ teaspoon garlic salt
½ teaspoon dried basil
¼ teaspoon black pepper
1 can (28 ounces) fire-roasted diced tomatoes (such as Muir Glen), drained
1 jar (25½ ounces) basil and tomato pasta sauce
1 package (12 ounces) fully cooked fire-roasted chicken-and-turkey sausage (such as Applegate Farms), cut into coins
1 sweet red pepper, seeded and chopped

1. Heat oven to 375°. Grease a 13×9×2-inch baking dish. Set aside.

2. In large pot of lightly salted boiling water, cook pasta for 9 minutes. Drain.

3. In medium-size bowl, stir together the cheeses, garlic salt, basil and black pepper.

4. In large bowl, stir together cooked pasta, half of the cheese mixture, half of the drained tomatoes, half of the pasta sauce, the sausage and sweet pepper.

5. Spoon pasta mixture into prepared baking dish. Top with remaining drained tomatoes, pasta sauce and cheese mixture.

6. Cover; bake at 375° for 30 minutes. Uncover; bake about 15 minutes longer or until bubbly. Let stand for 10 minutes before serving.

You can always count on a baked sausage, pasta and cheese casserole to satisfy. Now add some smoky fire-roasted tomatoes to jazz things up.

PREP: 15 minutes
BAKE: at 375° for 45 minutes
STAND: 10 minutes
MAKES: 8 servings

QUICK TIP

PERFECT PASTA

Did you know it's best not to rinse pasta after cooking? If you do, the sauce won't cling to it very well. The exception is when preparing pasta for a salad.

Per serving: 448 calories, 14 g total fat (7 g sat.), 71 mg cholesterol, 804 mg sodium, 56 g carbohydrate, 3 g fiber, 27 g protein.

Jambalaya

1 large onion, chopped
2 ribs celery, sliced
1 green pepper, seeded and chopped
1 sweet red pepper, seeded and chopped
3 cloves garlic, chopped
1 package (10 ounces) frozen corn kernels, thawed
½ pound chorizo, cut into ½-inch pieces
1 can (6½ ounces) chopped clams, drained
1 can (15½ ounces) red kidney beans, drained
1 can (14½ ounces) stewed tomatoes
1 cup vegetable broth
1 can (8 ounces) tomato sauce
1½ teaspoons Cajun seasoning
½ teaspoon salt
½ pound cooked, shelled and deveined small shrimp with tails
1½ cups instant brown rice
3 scallions, trimmed and sliced

1. In 5- or 5½-quart slow cooker, layer onion, celery, peppers, garlic, corn, chorizo, clams and kidney beans.

2. In large bowl, mix tomatoes, broth, tomato sauce, Cajun seasoning and salt. Pour into slow cooker.

3. Cover slow cooker; cook on high-heat setting for 5 hours.

4. For last 10 minutes of cooking, stir in shrimp and instant brown rice.

5. To serve, sprinkle with scallion.

Conventional Method: In large nonstick skillet, heat 1 tablespoon vegetable oil over medium-high heat. Add onion, celery, peppers, garlic and chorizo. Sauté for 10 minutes, stirring occasionally. Add corn, clams, kidney beans, tomatoes, broth, tomato sauce, Cajun seasoning and salt. Bring to a boil. Lower heat and simmer, covered, for 10 minutes, stirring occasionally. Turn off heat and stir in shrimp. Let stand about 5 minutes or until heated through. Serve with cooked brown rice and sprinkle with scallion.

When you're looking to liven up a weeknight meal, you can't go wrong with this Cajun-seasoned stew!

PREP: 15 minutes
SLOW COOK: 5 hours on high-heat setting
MAKES: 8 servings

QUICK TIP

A SLICK WAY TO CHOP SWEET PEPPER

Here's a nifty way to seed and chop a sweet pepper. Hold the pepper upright on a cutting surface. With a sharp knife, slice each of the sides from the pepper. You should have 4 large, flat pieces. The stems, seeds and ribs will all be in one unit that can be easily discarded. Then simply chop the flat pieces of pepper.

Per serving: 360 calories, 13 g total fat (4 g sat.), 70 mg cholesterol, 980 mg sodium, 43 g carbohydrate, 8 g fiber, 21 g protein.

Greek Meatballs and Orzo

Meatballs:
- 1 pound ground turkey
- ½ pound fresh white button mushrooms, cleaned and finely chopped
- ½ cup fat-free plain yogurt
- 3 tablespoons chopped fresh mint leaves
- 1½ teaspoons dried oregano
- ¾ teaspoon lemon pepper
- ¾ teaspoon salt

Orzo:
- 1 tablespoon extra-virgin olive oil
- ½ small onion, chopped
- ¾ cup orzo pasta
- 2 large cloves garlic, chopped
- 1 can (14 ounces) chicken broth
- ¼ teaspoon salt
- ⅛ teaspoon black pepper
- 1 bag (6 ounces) baby spinach leaves
- ½ cup cherry tomatoes (about 8), cut into halves
- 2 tablespoons chopped fresh mint (optional)

1. Heat oven to 350°. Line 15×11×1-inch jelly-roll pan with aluminum foil.

2. Meatballs: In large bowl, mix together turkey, mushrooms, yogurt, mint, oregano, lemon pepper and salt. Shape into 28 meatballs, using 1 slightly rounded tablespoon for each. Place meatballs on prepared pan.

3. Bake at 350° about 40 minutes or until browned and an instant-read meat thermometer inserted in center of meatball registers 165°.

4. Orzo: While meatballs are baking, in medium-size saucepan, heat oil over medium heat. Add onion; cook, stirring, about 3 minutes or until slightly softened. Add uncooked orzo and garlic; cook, stirring, about 3 minutes longer or until orzo is coated and onion is softened. Add broth, salt and pepper. Simmer, covered, about 15 minutes or until orzo is tender. Stir in spinach, tomato and, if desired, mint; cook about 1 minute or until spinach is wilted and tomato is heated through. Serve meatballs with orzo mixture.

Meatball lovers, take note. Here's another way to enjoy those always-satisfying, always-kid-pleasing gems.

PREP: 20 minutes
BAKE: at 350° for 40 minutes
COOK: 22 minutes
MAKES: 4 servings (7 meatballs each)

QUICK BITE

SPICE SAVVY

Bringing a delicate lemon flavor to dishes, lemon-pepper consists mostly of salt, with black pepper and dried grated lemon peel (although some brands are salt free). In a pinch, use a mixture of salt, pepper and lemon zest in place of the purchased seasoning.

Per serving: 342 calories, 13 g total fat (3 g sat.), 90 mg cholesterol, 999 mg sodium, 28 g carbohydrate, 3 g fiber, 27 g protein.

Spicy Turkey Lasagna

- 1 pound ground turkey
- 1 teaspoon dried oregano
- ½ teaspoon salt
- ¼ teaspoon red pepper flakes
- 1 container (15 ounces) ricotta cheese
- 2 cups shredded Italian-blend cheese (8-ounce package)
- 1 package (10 ounces) frozen chopped spinach, thawed and squeezed dry
- 12 lasagna noodles, uncooked and broken in half
- 1 jar (26 ounces) chunky pasta sauce with mushrooms and green pepper
- ½ cup water
  Grated Parmesan cheese (optional)

1. In nonstick skillet, brown turkey over medium-high heat, breaking up clumps, for 5 to 7 minutes or until no longer pink. Season with oregano, salt and red pepper flakes. Remove from heat.

2. In medium-size bowl, mix ricotta cheese, cheese blend and spinach.

3. In oval 5½-quart slow cooker, layer half of the noodles, overlapping as necessary. Spoon on half of the turkey mixture. Pour on half of the pasta sauce and half of the water. Spread half of the cheese mixture on top. Repeat layering.

4. Cover slow cooker; cook on low-heat setting for 4½ hours. To serve, cut into 8 equal pieces. If desired, sprinkle with Parmesan cheese.

Conventional Method: Heat oven to 375°. Coat 13×9×2-inch baking dish with nonstick cooking spray. In nonstick skillet, brown turkey over medium-high heat, breaking up clumps, for 5 to 7 minutes or until no longer pink. Season with oregano, salt and red pepper flakes. Remove from heat. In bowl, combine ricotta cheese, cheese blend and spinach. Substitute 12 no-cook lasagna noodles for the regular lasagna noodles. Place 3 noodles in bottom of the prepared baking dish. Spoon one-third of the meat mixture, ¾ cup of pasta sauce and one-third of the cheese mixture over noodles in baking dish; sprinkle with 3 tablespoons water. Repeat layers twice more. Top with remaining 3 noodles and remaining sauce. If desired, sprinkle with 2 tablespoons Parmesan cheese. Cover with aluminum foil; bake at 375° for 30 minutes. Remove foil; bake for 15 minutes longer.

Preshredded cheese and ready-made pasta sauce help shave the prep time to just 15 minutes.

PREP: 15 minutes
SLOW COOK: 4½ hours on low-heat setting
MAKES: 8 servings

QUICK BITE

CHEESE, PLEASE: RICOTTA

This white, slightly grainy, moist cheese with a slightly sweet taste is used in many savory dishes such as lasagna or manicotti. Ricottas are made from the whey drained from other cheeses such as provolone or mozzarella. In the United States, ricotta is typically made with a combination of whey and whole, low-fat or fat-free milk.

Per serving: 452 calories, 20 g total fat (10 g sat.), 92 mg cholesterol, 781 mg sodium, 39 g carbohydrate, 4 g fiber, 29 g protein.

Turkey-Black Bean Chili Pie

Chili:
- 6 strips bacon, chopped
- 1 large onion, chopped
- 6 cloves garlic, minced
- 1½ pounds turkey breast cutlets, cut into ½-inch pieces
- ¼ cup chili powder
- 1½ teaspoons ground cumin
- 3 cans (15 ounces each) black beans, drained and rinsed
- 1 can (12 ounces) beer
- ½ cup ketchup
- 1½ teaspoons dried oregano
- ¾ teaspoon salt
- ¼ teaspoon black pepper

Topping:
- 1½ cups yellow cornmeal
- 1 tablespoon baking powder
- ¾ teaspoon salt
- 1 cup milk
- 1 egg
- 1½ teaspoons light-brown sugar
- 6 ounces shredded Cheddar cheese (1½ cups)

Cheesy biscuits top a bacon-infused black-bean chili for a hearty and robust winter warmer if ever there was one!

PREP: 20 minutes
COOK: 50 minutes
BAKE: at 425° for 25 minutes
STAND: 10 minutes
MAKES: 12 servings

QUICK TIP

MAKE AHEAD

The chili may be prepared through step 1 and refrigerated, covered, for up to 3 days. Reheat; continue with step 2.

1. **Chili:** In non-aluminum large pot, sauté bacon for 5 to 6 minutes or until crispy. Add onion and garlic; cook about 10 minutes or until softened. Add turkey; cook about 5 minutes or until almost cooked through. Add chili powder and cumin; cook for 1 minute. Add beans, beer, ketchup, oregano, salt and pepper. Cover and bring to a boil. Reduce heat to low; simmer for 30 minutes.

2. Pour chili into shallow 3-quart casserole or 13×9×2-inch glass baking dish.

3. Heat oven to 425°. **Topping:** Sift cornmeal, baking powder and salt into medium-size bowl. In small bowl, whisk milk, egg and brown sugar. Stir milk mixture into cornmeal mixture. Stir in cheese. Spoon dollops of mixture over warm chili.

4. Bake at 425° about 25 minutes or until the topping is golden brown. Let stand for 10 minutes before serving.

Per serving: 315 calories, 9 g total fat (4 g sat.), 79 mg cholesterol, 897 mg sodium, 30 g carbohydrate, 6 g fiber, 26 g protein.

Turkey and Curried Vegetables

1 tablespoon curry powder
2 teaspoons ground ginger
½ teaspoon salt
¼ teaspoon black pepper
1 cup chicken broth
1 tablespoon sugar
8 large cauliflower pieces (from a 2-pound head), cut up
1 can (15 ounces) chickpeas, drained and rinsed
½ cup dried apricots, coarsely chopped
½ cup golden raisins
1 cinnamon stick
1 bone-in turkey breast half (2½ to 3 pounds), skin removed
1 box (10 ounces) frozen green beans, thawed
2 tablespoons cornstarch mixed with 2 tablespoons cold water
1 jar (12 ounces) mango chutney (optional)

1. In small bowl, stir together curry powder, ginger, salt and pepper. Stir 2 teaspoons of the spice mixture into broth along with the sugar.

2. In 6-quart slow cooker, combine cauliflower, chickpeas, apricot and golden raisins. Tuck in cinnamon stick. Rub remaining spice mixture onto turkey breast. Place turkey on top of vegetables. Pour broth mixture around turkey. Cover; cook on high-heat setting for 4½ hours or on low-heat setting for 8 hours.

3. Remove turkey to a cutting board; cover loosely with aluminum foil and let stand for 10 minutes. If necessary, raise temperature to high-heat setting. Stir green beans and cornstarch-water mixture into slow cooker; cover and cook about 10 minutes or until beans are tender.

4. Cut turkey into ¼-inch-thick slices. Pour a little of the cooking juices on top; serve with vegetables and, if desired, chutney.

A hint of curry adds spice to winter vegetables and tender turkey breast for a wholesome meal with attitude!

PREP: 15 minutes
COOK: 4½ hours on high-heat or 8 hours on low-heat setting, plus 10 minutes on high-heat setting
STAND: 10 minutes
MAKES: 6 servings

QUICK BITE

A GOOD GLASS OF WINE

It can be a bit tricky to pair wines with spicy foods, especially curry. However, a good bet is Riesling because of its pleasant fruitiness and refreshing acidity. You also can't go wrong with a sparkling wine, which will prove refreshing alongside warm spices. Pairing reds with spicy foods is also tricky. Try a lighter-bodied Syrah if you do prefer a red. Cabernet Sauvignon can make the spices play even warmer on the palate.

Per serving: 423 calories, 4 g total fat (1 g sat.), 130 mg cholesterol, 621 mg sodium, 44 g carbohydrate, 7 g fiber, 54 g protein.

Cajun Meat Loaf with Roasted Sweet Potatoes

- **2** tablespoons vegetable oil
- **2** pounds ground turkey
- **1** large green pepper, seeded and finely chopped
- **2** ribs celery, finely chopped
- **⅓** cup ketchup
- **1** tablespoon Cajun seasoning
- **½** teaspoon onion salt
- **½** teaspoon hot-pepper sauce
- **2** pounds sweet potatoes, peeled and cut into 1-inch-thick half-moons
- **½** teaspoon salt
- **¼** teaspoon black pepper
- **¼** cup prepared salsa

1. Heat oven to 350°. Coat large roasting pan with 1 tablespoon oil.

2. In large bowl, combine turkey, green pepper, celery, ketchup, Cajun seasoning, onion salt and hot-pepper sauce. Shape into 9×4-inch oval loaf. Place meat loaf in roasting pan.

3. In another large bowl, combine sweet potato, remaining 1 tablespoon oil, the salt and black pepper. Spoon sweet potato mixture around the meat loaf in the pan.

4. Bake at 350° for 65 to 70 minutes or until instant-read meat thermometer inserted in center of meat loaf registers 160° and potatoes are tender. For last 10 minutes of baking, spoon salsa evenly over top of the meat loaf.

Sweet potatoes roast alongside the meat loaf for a one-pan meal. Serve with your favorite green vegetable and you're set.

PREP: 25 minutes
BAKE: at 350° for 65 to 70 minutes
MAKES: 6 servings

CAJUN SEASONING SUBSTITUTE

If you find yourself out of Cajun seasoning, combine the following for each tablespoon needed: ½ teaspoon white pepper, ½ teaspoon garlic powder, ½ teaspoon onion powder, ½ teaspoon cayenne pepper, ½ teaspoon paprika and ½ teaspoon black pepper.

Per serving: 437 calories, 18 g total fat (4 g sat.), 119 mg cholesterol, 981 mg sodium, 40 g carbohydrate, 3 g fiber, 30 g protein.

Basque-Style Fish Bake

- 2 onions, halved and sliced ½ inch thick
- 2 sweet red peppers, seeded and sliced ½ inch thick
- 2 green peppers, seeded and sliced ½ inch thick
- 1 pound red potatoes, sliced ⅛ inch thick
- 3 tablespoons extra-virgin olive oil
- 1 teaspoon salt
- ½ teaspoon black pepper
- 2 cans (14½ ounces each) diced tomatoes
- 4 cloves garlic, smashed
- 2 tablespoons lemon juice
- ½ teaspoon hot-pepper sauce
- 1½ pounds cod fillets

1. Heat oven to 375°. In large bowl, toss onion slices, red and green pepper slices and potato slices with oil and half of the salt and black pepper. Spread the mixture in a 13×9×2-inch baking dish.

2. Bake, uncovered, at 375° for 40 minutes, stirring halfway through cooking.

3. After 40 minutes, add 1 can tomatoes, the garlic, lemon juice and hot-pepper sauce to baking dish; stir to combine.

4. Season fish with remaining salt and pepper. Cut fish into six servings. Arrange over top of potato mixture. Spoon remaining can of tomatoes over fish and vegetables.

5. Cover; bake for 30 minutes longer. Let covered baking dish stand for 10 minutes before serving.

What's so Basque about this dish? It's the tasty use of tomatoes, sweet peppers and olive oil—hallmarks of the classic Basque dish pipérade.

PREP: 15 minutes
BAKE: at 375° for 1 hour 10 minutes
STAND: 10 minutes
MAKES: 6 servings

QUICK TIP

TESTING FISH FOR DONENESS

To check if fish fillets or steaks are done, peek between the flakes with the tip of a thin-bladed knife; the fish should not look raw or translucent. For a whole fish, check that the meat near the bone is opaque.

Per serving: 240 calories, 8 g total fat (1 g sat.), 30 mg cholesterol, 612 mg sodium, 27 g carbohydrate, 6 g fiber, 17 g protein.

Lobster Corn Pudding

4 frozen lobster tails in shells, thawed (about 7 ounces each, 4 cups meat total) or
    4 cups surimi (imitation seafood blend)
4 medium-size ears corn, husked and silked
2 cups half-and-half
2 tablespoons unsalted butter
½ sweet red pepper, seeded and finely chopped
4 scallions, trimmed and chopped
6 eggs
¼ cup all-purpose flour
1 tablespoon chopped fresh cilantro leaves
1½ teaspoons salt
1 teaspoon sugar
1 cup shredded pepper-Jack cheese

1. Heat oven to 350°. Coat eight 8-ounce individual casseroles or one shallow 2-quart casserole with nonstick cooking spray.

2. In large pot of boiling water, boil lobster tails for 8 to 10 minutes or until heated through. Drain; rinse in cold water. Remove meat; discard shells. Chop meat (should have 4 cups).

3. Holding corn on end, with knife, cut down each ear to remove kernels. In food processor, puree half of the corn with ½ cup half-and-half.

4. In large skillet, melt butter over medium-high heat. Add remaining corn kernels, sweet pepper and scallion; sauté for 5 minutes.

5. In bowl, whisk remaining 1½ cups half-and-half, the eggs, flour, cilantro, salt and sugar. Stir in lobster, pureed corn, sautéed vegetables and ½ cup cheese. Divide among individual casseroles or pour into large casserole. Top with remaining ½ cup cheese.

6. Set individual casseroles or large casserole in baking pan. Place in oven; pour hot water into baking pan to 1-inch depth.

7. Bake at 350° about 35 minutes for individual casseroles (or about 45 minutes for large casserole) or until knife inserted in center comes out clean. Let stand for 10 minutes before serving.

Sweet corn and sweet lobster pair nicely for a scrumptious brunch or luncheon entrée.

PREP: 20 minutes
COOK: 10 minutes
BAKE: at 350° for 35 minutes for small puddings, or 45 minutes for large casserole
STAND: 10 minutes
MAKES: 8 servings

QUICK TIP

MAKE AHEAD

Step 2 can be completed a day ahead; refrigerate the lobster. The pudding can be prepared through step 5 earlier in the day that you plan to serve them; cover and refrigerate. To serve, bake as directed in steps 6 and 7, allowing extra time since pudding is cold from the refrigerator.

Per serving: 351 calories, 18 g total fat (10 g sat.), 267 mg cholesterol, 898 mg sodium, 18 g carbohydrate, 2 g fiber, 28 g protein.

On the Side

Corn Bread-Stuffed Peppers p. 128

Whether you want to show off a bundle
of spring-fresh asparagus or a basket of home-grown
tomatoes—or you simply want to jazz up dinner
with a sensational side—you'll find plenty
of inspiration here.

Broccoli and Carrot Sauté

½ cup pine nuts
¼ cup extra-virgin olive oil
4 cloves garlic, sliced
1 head broccoli (about 1½ pounds), trimmed into flowerets
1 bag (10 ounces) matchstick carrots
½ teaspoon salt
½ teaspoon dried Italian seasoning
2 tablespoons lemon juice
¼ teaspoon black pepper

1. In large skillet, toast pine nuts over medium heat, stirring frequently, about 4 minutes or until golden brown. Remove pine nuts to small bowl. Set aside.

2. In same skillet, heat oil over medium heat. Add garlic; sauté about 1 minute or just until garlic starts to color. Add broccoli, carrots, salt and Italian seasoning. Increase heat to medium-high; sauté for 12 to 15 minutes or until vegetables are cooked but still slightly crisp. (If vegetables start to stick, add a few tablespoons water.)

3. To serve, place vegetables in serving bowl; toss with lemon juice, pepper and pine nuts.

Broccoli and carrots always make a vibrant duo—now amp up the veggies with a garlicky, lemony dressing and a few pine nuts.

PREP: 10 minutes
COOK: about 20 minutes
MAKES: 8 servings

QUICK TIP

SAUTÉ SUGGESTIONS

Sauté comes from the French word, *sauter,* which means "to jump." Sautéed food is cooked and stirred in a small amount of fat over fairly high heat in a shallow pan. For best results and even cooking, cut food in uniform-size pieces when you sauté.

Per serving: 151 calories, 11 g total fat (2 g sat.), 0 mg cholesterol, 181 mg sodium, 10 g carbohydrate, 4 g fiber, 5 g protein.

Corn and Lima Beans with Potatoes

1 tablespoon butter
2 scallions, trimmed and chopped
2 tomatoes (about ¾ pound), seeded and chopped
1 cup water
1 cup mashed potatoes (about 2 potatoes)
1 cup fresh lima beans or fresh butter beans or half of a 10-ounce box frozen lima beans, thawed
7 ears corn, husked, silked, and kernels cut from cob
1 teaspoon salt
¼ teaspoon black pepper

1. In large skillet, heat butter over medium heat. Add scallion; sauté for 1 minute. Add tomato, water, potatoes and beans. Cover and simmer gently about 30 minutes or until beans are tender. (If using frozen beans, reduce cooking time to about 20 minutes.)

2. During the last 5 to 10 minutes of cooking time, add the corn. Season with salt and pepper. If mixture becomes too dry, add a little water and correct the seasonings to taste, adding more salt and pepper as needed. The mixture should be thick but not dry. Serve warm.

Corn and lima beans are a classic combo (known as succotash in the South). Mashed potatoes add heartiness.

PREP: 30 minutes
COOK: about 30 minutes
MAKES: 6 servings

QUICK TIP

PRODUCE POINTERS

Unless corn is labeled "supersweet," the sugar in it will start to turn to starch the minute it is picked. Your best bet? Head to a farmer's market, buy early in the morning and use it quickly. Choose ears with fresh, firm, green husks. Do not strip ears; rather look for pale and silky tassels with only a little brown at the top. Corn can be refrigerated, with the husks on, for one day.

Per serving: 260 calories, 3 g total fat (1 g sat.), 5 mg cholesterol, 414 mg sodium, 53 g carbohydrate, 10 g fiber, 11 g protein.

Sesame Broccoli

1 bunch fresh broccoli (about 1 pound), cut into flowerets (about 4 cups)
1 medium-size sweet red pepper, seeded and cut into ¼-inch-wide strips
2 teaspoons vegetable oil
1 teaspoon dark Asian sesame oil
1 clove garlic, minced
1 piece (1 inch) fresh ginger, peeled and cut into very thin slivers
3 tablespoons reduced-sodium teriyaki sauce
1 teaspoon lemon juice
1 tablespoon sesame seeds, toasted

1. Steam broccoli and sweet pepper for 5 to 7 minutes or until vegetables are crisp-tender.

2. Meanwhile, in nonstick skillet, heat vegetable oil and sesame oil. Add garlic and ginger; stir-fry about 30 seconds or until fragrant. Stir in teriyaki sauce and lemon juice; heat through. Toss vegetables in sauce to coat. Sprinkle with sesame seeds.

Sesame oil and seeds, along with garlic and ginger, make this an utterly fascinating take on broccoli.

PREP: 10 minutes
COOK: 5 to 7 minutes
MAKES: 4 servings

QUICK TIP

KIDS AND VEGGIES

Kids love choices. To help get them to eat their vegetables, take them grocery shopping and instead of asking, "Do you want any fruits and vegetables?" ask, "Which fruits and vegetables would you like this week?" They may not pick broccoli, but at least they might grab an orange!

Per serving: 83 calories, 5 g total fat (1 g sat.), 0 mg cholesterol, 261 mg sodium, 9 g carbohydrate, 3 g fiber, 4 g protein.

New-Wave Green Beans

2 tablespoons butter

1½ pounds fresh green beans, trimmed

1 package (10 ounces) cremini mushrooms, cleaned and sliced

⅓ cup heavy cream

½ teaspoon salt

¼ teaspoon black pepper

1 package (8 ounces) Brie, rind removed and cheese cut into pieces

3 tablespoons walnuts, toasted and chopped (see Note)

1. In large skillet, melt butter over medium-high heat. Add green beans; cook, stirring occasionally, about 7 minutes or until beans are crisp-tender.

2. Add mushrooms to skillet; cook about 5 minutes or just until beans are tender. Add cream, salt and pepper. Remove skillet from heat. Stir in Brie pieces until melted. Top with toasted walnuts. Serve immediately.

Note: To toast walnuts, heat oven to 350°. Spread walnuts on baking sheet and toast at 350° for 7 to 10 minutes or until light golden brown. Let cool slightly; chop.

Heavy cream and Brie cheese combine to make a melty, rich sauce for beans and mushrooms.

PREP: 15 minutes
COOK: about 15 minutes
MAKES: 8 servings

QUICK BITE

BEYOND THE BASIC

Tan to brown in color, cremini mushrooms are similar in shape but richer and earthier in flavor than white button mushrooms. Use them the same way you would white mushrooms.

Per serving: 183 calories, 15 g total fat (8 g sat.), 43 mg cholesterol, 288 mg sodium, 8 g carbohydrate, 3 g fiber, 7 g protein.

Casablanca Couscous

1 red onion, halved and thinly sliced
1½ teaspoons ground cumin
½ teaspoon ground ginger
⅛ teaspoon ground cloves
⅛ teaspoon cayenne pepper
2 tablespoons extra-virgin olive oil
1 sweet red pepper, seeded and
  cut into 1-inch pieces
1 medium-size zucchini, halved lengthwise
  and cut into chunks
1 can (19 ounces) chickpeas, drained
  and rinsed
½ cup chopped dates
1 teaspoon salt
1 teaspoon grated orange zest
2 cups water
⅓ cup orange juice
1 box (10 ounces) plain couscous
2 tablespoons chopped fresh mint leaves

1. In large pot, cook onion, cumin, ginger, cloves and cayenne pepper in hot oil over medium-low heat about 5 minutes or until onion is softened, stirring often.

2. Add sweet pepper, zucchini, chickpeas, dates, salt and orange zest, stirring to combine. Add water and orange juice. Increase heat to high. Bring to a boil. Stir in couscous. Remove from heat; cover and let stand for 5 minutes. Fluff with fork; stir in mint. Serve warm.

Cumin, ginger, cloves and cayenne pepper combine with orange zest and fresh mint to make this couscous really stand out.

PREP: 20 minutes
COOK: about 7 minutes
STAND: 5 minutes
MAKES: 6 servings

QUICK TIP

ALL ABOUT GINGER

Here are different types of ginger that you'll find in the marketplace.
• **Powdered:** ground from dried fresh ginger. Its flavor fades, so discard after 6 months.
• **Fresh:** firm and plump. To store, wrap in a paper towel, place in loosely closed plastic bag and refrigerate up to 1 month.
• **Candied:** fresh ginger that has been boiled in a sugar solution; has a sweet-tart flavor. Keeps indefinitely at room temperature if tightly sealed.

Per serving: 368 calories, 7 g total fat (1 g sat.), 0 mg cholesterol, 590 mg sodium, 67 g carbohydrate, 8 g fiber, 11 g protein.

Garlic-Roasted Potatoes

2½ pounds small new potatoes, scrubbed
 2 packages (9 ounces each) frozen artichoke hearts, thawed
 8 cloves garlic, halved
 ¼ cup extra-virgin olive oil
 ¾ teaspoon salt
 ¼ teaspoon black pepper
 1 tablespoon grated lemon zest
 ¼ cup lemon juice
 2 tablespoons chopped fresh parsley leaves

1. Heat oven to 425°. Cut potatoes into quarters (larger ones into eighths).

2. In large roasting pan, toss potatoes, artichoke hearts, garlic, oil, salt and pepper.

3. Roast at 425° for 30 to 40 minutes or until potatoes are tender and browned, tossing once. Remove to large bowl; toss with lemon zest, lemon juice and chopped parsley. Serve warm or at room temperature.

Artichoke hearts and fresh, aromatic seasonings elevate oven-roasted potatoes to company-worthy status.

PREP: 15 minutes
BAKE: at 425° for 30 to 40 minutes
MAKES: 10 servings

QUICK TIP

CITRUS MATH

Pick up two medium-size lemons for the lemon juice and zest in this recipe. One medium lemon will yield about 3 tablespoons of juice and 2 teaspoons grated zest. One medium-size orange will yield about 1 tablespoon of grated orange zest and about ⅓ cup juice.

Per serving: 141 calories, 6 g total fat (1 g sat.), 0 mg cholesterol, 202 mg sodium, 19 g carbohydrate, 4 g fiber, 4 g protein.

Tomato-Cheese Gratin

2½ pounds tomatoes, cored and cut
    into ⅜-inch-thick slices
1 teaspoon coarse salt
1 cup part-skim ricotta cheese
½ cup packed fresh basil leaves, chopped
2 egg yolks
1 tablespoon all-purpose flour
½ teaspoon onion salt
4 ounces Gruyère cheese, grated
    (about 1 cup)
2 English muffins, well toasted
1 tablespoon extra-virgin olive oil

1. Spread tomato slices on paper towel-lined baking sheet. Sprinkle both sides with coarse salt. Let drain slightly (about 15 minutes).

2. Heat oven to 375°. Coat 2-quart casserole with nonstick cooking spray. In medium-size bowl, stir together ricotta cheese, basil, egg yolks, flour and onion salt. Stir in ½ cup grated cheese.

3. In food processor, process English muffins until coarse crumbs are formed (about 1¼ cups). Sprinkle ½ cup crumbs over bottom of prepared casserole.

4. Place single layer of tomato slices, including the ends, on top of crumbs. Carefully spread half of the ricotta cheese mixture over tomatoes. Add another layer of tomatoes and the remaining ricotta cheese mixture. Sprinkle with 2 tablespoons English muffin crumbs. Top with remaining tomato slices, slightly overlapping. Brush with oil.

5. Bake at 375° for 30 minutes. Sprinkle with remaining English muffin crumbs and remaining ½ cup grated cheese. Bake about 15 minutes longer or until cheese is melted and topping is lightly browned. Let stand for 5 minutes before serving.

When summer brings you a bumper crop of tomatoes, here's how to star them front and center in a savory bake.

PREP: 20 minutes
BAKE: at 375° for 45 minutes
STAND: 5 minutes
MAKES: 6 servings

QUICK TIP

HEIRLOOM TOMATOES

In the summer months check out farmer's markets for old-time heirloom tomato varieties, prized for their intense flavors. Scout out unblemished globes and buy a few days before you plan to use. Ripen on the counter—though not by a sunny window; to speed the process, place in a paper bag. Only cut tomatoes should be refrigerated. Use those within a few days.

Per serving: 265 calories, 14 g total fat (7 g sat.), 104 mg cholesterol, 687 mg sodium, 21 g carbohydrate, 3 g fiber, 15 g protein.

Chipotle-Cheddar Mashed Potatoes

2½ pounds Yukon gold potatoes, with skins, scrubbed and cut into 1-inch cubes

2½ teaspoons salt

1 cup milk

2 tablespoons butter

⅛ teaspoon ground cinnamon

1 cup shredded sharp white Cheddar cheese (4 ounces)

2 canned chipotle chiles in adobo sauce, chopped (1 tablespoon)

1 teaspoon adobo sauce from canned chipotles

Fresh cilantro sprigs, for garnish (optional)

1. In large saucepan, combine potatoes, 2 teaspoons salt and enough cold water to cover potatoes. Bring to a boil over high heat. Reduce heat to medium; gently boil about 30 minutes or until fork-tender.

2. In small saucepan, combine milk, butter, cinnamon and remaining ½ teaspoon salt. Bring to a boil. Set aside.

3. Drain potatoes. Return potatoes to saucepan. Place over medium heat; toss about 1 minute to dry out. Remove from heat. Add cheese; stir to combine. Add milk mixture, chipotles and adobo sauce. Mash. If desired, garnish each serving with cilantro.

Chefs often come up with creative add-ins for mashed potatoes. This recipe follows their lead!

PREP: 10 minutes
COOK: about 30 minutes
MAKES: 8 servings

QUICK TIP

STORE IT RIGHT

Did you know that you shouldn't refrigerate potatoes? Doing so causes them to become overly sweet and to darken when cooked. Instead, store potatoes up to several weeks in a dark, well-ventilated, cool place that is slightly humid but not wet. Store away from bright light, which can cause the potatoes to develop green patches that have a bitter flavor.

Per serving: 216 calories, 9 g total fat (6 g sat.), 27 mg cholesterol, 878 mg sodium, 28 g carbohydrate, 3 g fiber, 8 g protein.

Brown-Sugar Sweet Potato Wedges

6 small sweet potatoes (about 6 ounces each), scrubbed
1 tablespoon butter
¼ cup walnuts, chopped
¼ cup plus 2 tablespoons packed light-brown sugar
2 tablespoons cider vinegar
½ teaspoon salt
¼ teaspoon black pepper
¼ teaspoon ground allspice

1. Heat gas grill to medium-high or prepare charcoal grill with medium-hot coals or use Stovetop Method (below).

2. Pierce sweet potatoes with fork. Place potatoes on paper towels in microwave oven. Microwave on HIGH about 10 minutes or until partially cooked but still very firm, turning over halfway through cooking.

3. When sweet potatoes are cool enough to handle, cut each lengthwise into quarters.

4. Meanwhile, in small skillet, melt butter over medium heat. Add walnuts, brown sugar, vinegar, salt, pepper and allspice; cook, stirring, about 2 minutes or until brown sugar is melted. Remove the skillet from heat. Brush cut sides of sweet potatoes with brown sugar mixture, leaving nuts in skillet.

5. Grill potatoes, cut sides down, uncovered, for 5 minutes. Turn the wedges so second cut sides are facing down; grill for 5 minutes. Turn the wedges, skin sides down. Brush the cut sides with brown sugar mixture. Grill about 5 minutes or until sweet potatoes are tender. Transfer sweet potatoes to a serving platter. Spoon remaining brown sugar mixture with nuts over sweet potato wedges.

Stovetop Method: Heat a stovetop grill pan over medium-high heat. Cook sweet potato wedges as directed in step 5 on the grill pan instead of on the grill.

Next time you fire up the coals, save a little room on the rack for this clever sweet potato recipe!

PREP: 10 minutes
MICROWAVE: 10 minutes
GRILL: 15 minutes
MAKES: 8 servings

QUICK TIP

SWEET POTATO VERSUS YAM

A nutrition powerhouse, the sweet potato is a great source of vitamins A and C. Sweet potatoes are frequently mislabeled "yams," a different species not often sold in U.S. markets. When selecting sweet potatoes, choose those that are firm, smooth and without wrinkles or bruises. Handle sweet potatoes gently as they tend to bruise easily. Store in a cool, dark, well-ventilated place; do not refrigerate.

Per serving: 173 calories, 4 g total fat (1 g sat.), 4 mg cholesterol, 159 mg sodium, 33 g carbohydrate, 4 g fiber, 2 g protein.

Eggplant Rollatini

2 medium-size eggplants (about 2¼ pounds total)

½ teaspoon salt

1½ cups shredded part-skim mozzarella cheese (6 ounces)

1 cup part-skim ricotta cheese

1 egg yolk

⅛ teaspoon dried Italian seasoning

⅛ teaspoon black pepper

1 jar (12 ounces) roasted red peppers, drained

1½ cups prepared low-fat marinara sauce

2 tablespoons grated Parmesan cheese

1. Trim tops and bottoms from eggplants. Cut each eggplant into six lengthwise slices, about ½ inch thick. Arrange slices on two large baking sheets lined with paper towels. Sprinkle slices with ¼ teaspoon salt, then turn slices over and sprinkle with remaining ¼ teaspoon salt. Let stand for 15 minutes, flipping slices halfway through standing time.

2. Heat gas grill or stovetop grill pan to medium-high or prepare charcoal grill with medium-hot coals. Quickly rinse eggplant slices under running water; pat dry. Spray both sides of each eggplant slice with nonstick cooking spray. Grill slices about 4 minutes per side or until softened and nicely marked. Return slices (do not overlap) to large baking sheets (without paper towels).

3. Heat oven to 350° and coat a 13×9×2-inch baking dish with nonstick cooking spray. In small bowl, stir together ¾ cup mozzarella, the ricotta, egg yolk, Italian seasoning and black pepper. Stir until well mixed.

4. Divide roasted pepper pieces evenly among eggplant slices, placing them on the wider end of each slice. Top each pepper piece with a heaping tablespoon of the cheese mixture. Spread ½ cup marinara sauce on the bottom of the prepared baking dish. Roll up eggplant slices, starting at the wide ends and enclosing filling. Place in baking dish. Top with remaining 1 cup marinara sauce, remaining ¾ cup mozzarella and the grated Parmesan cheese.

5. Bake at 350° for 25 minutes. Remove baking dish to wire rack; let stand for 10 minutes before serving. Add salt to taste.

A quick stint on the grill gives eggplant slices a pleasing hint of smoke. Serve with a tartly dressed green salad.

PREP: 20 minutes
STAND: 25 minutes
GRILL: eggplant slices for 8 minutes
BAKE: at 350° for 25 minutes
MAKES: 12 rollatini

QUICK TIP

PRODUCE POINTERS

Eggplants are available year-round, though the peak time to buy them is July through September. Look for plump, glossy eggplants with fresh, mold-free caps. Avoid those that are scarred or bruised. Refrigerate whole eggplants up to 2 days; slice just before using in a recipe (they discolor easily). Eggplant can have a bitter taste; salting it and letting it rest can help round out the flavor.

Per rollatine: 114 calories, 5 g total fat (3 g sat.), 33 mg cholesterol, 347 mg sodium, 10 g carbohydrate, 3 g fiber, 8 g protein.

Zucchini Parmesan

½ cup all-purpose flour
¾ teaspoon garlic powder
½ teaspoon salt
½ teaspoon black pepper
4 large zucchini (about 2 pounds total), trimmed and cut lengthwise into ¼-inch-thick slices
¼ cup vegetable oil
2 cans (14½ ounces each) Italian-seasoned recipe-ready diced tomatoes
¼ teaspoon red pepper flakes
1¼ cups shredded mozzarella cheese (5 ounces)
½ cup shredded Asiago cheese (2 ounces)
¼ cup grated Parmesan cheese
Fresh basil, cut in strips, for garnish (optional)

Though this makes a terrific accompaniment to grilled meats or chicken, you could also serve it as a main dish for a light summer supper.

PREP: 30 minutes
COOK: 18 minutes
BAKE: at 375° for 15 to 20 minutes for au gratin dishes, or about 30 minutes for baking dish
STAND: 10 minutes
MAKES: 8 servings

1. Heat oven to 375°. Coat eight au gratin dishes or a 13×9×2-inch glass baking dish with nonstick cooking spray.

2. In shallow plate, mix together flour, ¼ teaspoon garlic powder, the salt and ¼ teaspoon black pepper. Dredge zucchini slices in flour mixture to coat, tapping off excess.

3. In large nonstick skillet, heat 2 tablespoons oil over medium-high heat. Working in three batches, add zucchini and sauté about 3 minutes on each side or until lightly browned, adding more oil as needed to prevent sticking. Transfer zucchini to work surface or baking sheet lined with paper towels.

4. In medium-size bowl, combine tomatoes, red pepper flakes, the remaining ½ teaspoon garlic powder and ¼ teaspoon black pepper.

5. In second bowl, combine mozzarella, Asiago and Parmesan cheeses.

6. Spread small amount of tomato mixture over bottom of prepared au gratin dishes or baking dish. Arrange half of the zucchini in a single layer in the au gratin dishes or baking dish. Spoon half of the remaining tomato mixture over zucchini; sprinkle with half of the cheese mixture. Repeat the layering with zucchini, tomato mixture and cheese mixture.

7. Bake, uncovered, at 375° for 15 to 20 minutes for au gratin dishes (about 30 minutes for baking dish) or until heated through and cheese is melted. Let stand for 10 minutes before serving. If desired, garnish with fresh basil.

Per serving: 240 calories, 14 g total fat (5 g sat.), 24 mg cholesterol, 694 mg sodium, 19 g carbohydrate, 1 g fiber, 10 g protein.

Asparagus Gratin

**1 pound fresh asparagus, tough ends
    trimmed and stems peeled 1 inch
    from bottom**
6 slices prosciutto or thin-sliced deli ham
3 tablespoons butter
½ cup fresh bread crumbs
½ cup shredded Gruyère cheese (2 ounces)

1. In large pot, cook asparagus in simmering water for 7 to 9 minutes or until tender. Drain.

2. Divide asparagus into six equal bundles. Wrap each bundle with a slice of the prosciutto; place in shallow flameproof dish.

3. In small saucepan, melt butter over medium-low heat. Add bread crumbs; cook, stirring, for 1 minute. Spoon bread crumb mixture over bundles. Top with Gruyère cheese.

4. Heat broiler. Broil about 1 minute or until cheese lightly browns.

When you serve these elegant spears, you can keep the entrée simple. Try them with roast chicken or pork.

PREP: 15 minutes
COOK: 9 minutes
BROIL: 1 minute
MAKES: 6 servings

QUICK BITE
CHEESE, PLEASE: GRUYÈRE

Gruyère cheese brings sharp, complex flavors to recipes. Known for its rich, nutty flavor and fruity aroma, Gruyère is a great melting cheese (try it in sandwiches or anytime you'd use Swiss). Gruyère hails from Switzerland or France (those from France are often labeled French Gruyère or Comté). Gruyère may cost a bit more than domestic Swiss, but a little goes a long way in recipes.

Per serving: 179 calories, 11 g total fat (6 g sat.), 35 mg cholesterol, 474 mg sodium, 10 g carbohydrate, 2 g fiber, 9 g protein.

Butternut Squash and Tomato Soup

Here's your chance to make the sort of bright, colorful soup you might find at a fresh-focused neighborhood corner bistro.

PREP: 20 minutes
BAKE: at 350° for 30 minutes
COOK: about 45 minutes
MAKES: 8 servings

Per serving: 187 calories, 11 g total fat (6 g sat.), 27 mg cholesterol, 1,120 mg sodium, 21 g carbohydrate, 4 g fiber, 4 g protein.

1 small butternut, acorn or other winter squash (1½ to 2 pounds)
2 tablespoons unsalted butter
1 large onion, chopped
2 tomatoes (about 1 pound total), skinned, seeded and chopped
2 ribs celery, chopped
2 carrots, peeled and chopped
4 cups chicken broth
1 cup apple cider
  Bouquet garni (6 sprigs fresh parsley and 1 teaspoon dried thyme, tied in cheesecloth bag)
1 bay leaf
½ teaspoon ground ginger
½ teaspoon ground cumin
1½ cups half-and-half or milk
1½ teaspoons salt
¼ teaspoon black pepper
  Fresh sage leaves, for garnish
  Diced tomato, for garnish

1. Heat oven to 350°. Place whole squash in roasting pan with 1 inch of water.

2. Bake squash at 350° for 30 minutes. Cool in cold water. Quarter squash and remove seeds; peel. Cut squash into chunks.

3. In 4-quart pot, heat butter over medium heat. Add onion; cook about 3 minutes or until glazed. Add squash, tomato, celery and carrot; cook for 5 minutes. Add broth, cider, bouquet garni, bay leaf, ginger and cumin. Cover; simmer about 35 minutes or until vegetables are tender. Discard bouquet garni and bay leaf.

4. Working in batches, puree soup in blender or food processor. Pour back into pot. Stir in half-and-half, salt and pepper. Serve hot. Garnish with fresh sage and diced tomato.

Spinach Soufflés

2 packages (10 ounces each) fresh whole-leaf
   spinach, trimmed and washed
1 bunch scallions (about 6) or other small
   spring onions, trimmed and
   halved crosswise
3 tablespoons butter
6 tablespoons all-purpose flour
1¼ cups milk
1¼ teaspoons salt
⅛ teaspoon ground nutmeg
   Pinch of cayenne pepper
4 ounces Havarti cheese with dill, shredded
¼ cup packaged plain dry bread crumbs
6 eggs, separated into yolks and whites
2 teaspoons lemon juice

1. Bring large pot of water to a boil. Add spinach and scallion, stirring and submerging; cook 2 minutes or until wilted; drain. When cool, squeeze out excess water. Finely chop.

2. In medium-size saucepan, melt butter over medium heat. Sprinkle with 3 tablespoons flour; whisk 1 minute or until blended and cooked slightly. Add milk, whisking to prevent lumps. Cook over medium heat 3 minutes or until mixture reaches a low boil; whisk in 1 teaspoon salt, the nutmeg and cayenne pepper. Remove saucepan from heat. Whisk in cheese; let cool slightly.

3. Heat oven to 375°. Lightly coat eight (about 6-ounce) individual soufflé dishes or one 10-cup soufflé dish with nonstick cooking spray. Sprinkle with bread crumbs, tilting to coat.

4. In large bowl, whisk half of the cheese mixture into egg yolks. With wooden spoon, vigorously stir in remaining cheese mixture and the spinach mixture.

5. In large clean bowl, beat together egg whites, lemon juice and remaining ¼ teaspoon salt until stiff peaks form. Sift remaining 3 tablespoons flour over egg whites and gently fold in. Stir one-quarter of beaten egg white mixture into spinach mixture. Gently fold in remaining egg white mixture. Spoon about 1 cup into each individual dish or scrape whole amount into large soufflé dish. Place individual dishes on baking sheet.

6. Bake individual soufflés at 375° about 25 minutes or until golden brown and puffed (or bake for 35 to 40 minutes for large soufflé dish). Serve immediately.

Here's a terrific choice when you want to pull out all the stops with an elegant entrée, such as beef tenderloin.

PREP: 35 minutes
BAKE: at 375° for 25 minutes for individual soufflés or 35 to 40 minutes for large soufflé
MAKES: 8 individual soufflés or 1 large soufflé

QUICK BITE

CHEESE, PLEASE: HAVARTI

Originally from Denmark, Havarti is a semisoft cheese with a buttery yet tangy flavor. A terrific melting cheese, it works well in sauces and grilled sandwiches. When serving as part of an hors d'oeuvres spread, a full-bodied Chardonnay makes a good wine pairing.

Per individual soufflé: 414 calories, 15 g total fat (8 g sat.), 241 mg cholesterol, 560 mg sodium, 50 g carbohydrate, 3 g fiber, 19 g protein.

Scalloped Potatoes

Everyone needs a top-notch recipe for creamy scalloped potatoes. Here's yours. Serve with anything from broiled steaks to pan-fried chicken breasts.

PREP: 20 minutes
BAKE: at 450° for 40 minutes
STAND: 10 minutes
MAKES: 6 servings

QUICK TIP

A GOOD SPUD

Medium-starch potatoes—such as Yukon gold, long white or yellow—work well for scalloped potato dishes. They contain more moisture than high-starch potatoes, so they won't fall apart as easily.

2 pounds all-purpose potatoes, peeled and thinly sliced
1 tablespoon vegetable oil
½ teaspoon salt
⅛ teaspoon black pepper
1 cup low-fat (1%) milk
1 jar (7 ounces) roasted red peppers, drained and chopped
1 cup shredded reduced-fat Jarlsberg cheese (4 ounces)
¼ cup grated Parmesan cheese
¼ cup chopped fresh parsley leaves

1. Heat oven to 450°. Coat 8×8×2-inch or 11×7×2-inch baking dish with nonstick cooking spray.

2. Arrange potato slices in overlapping rows in prepared baking dish. Drizzle with oil; sprinkle with salt and pepper.

3. Bake at 450° for 15 minutes. Remove from oven.

4. Meanwhile, in small saucepan, heat milk to a slow boil; pour over potatoes. Sprinkle with red peppers; top with cheeses. Return to oven.

5. Bake at 450° about 25 minutes longer or until potatoes are tender and cheese is golden brown. Sprinkle with parsley. Let stand for 10 minutes before cutting and serving.

Per serving: 253 calories, 9 g total fat (4 g sat.), 21 mg cholesterol, 433 mg sodium, 32 g carbohydrate, 3 g fiber, 13 g protein.

Roasted Cauliflower with Cheese Sauce

Cauliflower:
- 2 small heads cauliflower (4½ pounds total), trimmed and cut into flowerets
- ¼ cup extra-virgin olive oil
- ¾ teaspoon salt
- ½ teaspoon black pepper

Sauce:
- 3 tablespoons butter
- 3 tablespoons all-purpose flour
- 1½ cups milk
- 1 teaspoon salt
- ¼ teaspoon white pepper
- Pinch of ground nutmeg
- 6 ounces Gruyère cheese, shredded (about 1½ cups)
- Pinch of cayenne pepper

1. **Cauliflower:** Heat oven to 400°. In large bowl, toss together cauliflower, oil, salt and black pepper until cauliflower is well coated.

2. Transfer to large rimmed baking sheet, at least 15×10×1 inches. Roast the cauliflower at 400°, stirring occasionally, about 30 minutes or until tender and evenly browned.

3. **Sauce:** Near end of the roasting time, in medium-size saucepan, melt butter over medium heat. Sprinkle the flour over the butter; whisk about 3 minutes or until the flour and butter are blended and the mixture is slightly brown. Gradually whisk in the milk until smooth. Add salt, white pepper and nutmeg; simmer, whisking occasionally, for 3 minutes. Remove the saucepan from the heat. Whisk in cheese and cayenne pepper until the cheese is melted and well blended.

4. Transfer cauliflower to a large serving platter. Spoon sauce over the cauliflower.

Make Ahead: Prepare the cauliflower and cheese sauce as directed; refrigerate separately for up to 2 days. Gently reheat sauce in a microwave oven or in a saucepan on the stovetop over low heat until smooth. Reheat cauliflower in microwave oven until warm to touch. Serve as directed above.

Your kids may say they don't like cauliflower, but they may become converts when it's topped with a cheese sauce.

PREP: 10 minutes
ROAST: at 400° for 30 minutes
COOK: about 10 minutes
MAKES: 8 servings

QUICK TIP

MASTERING A MORNAY

Congratulations! If you've made the sauce in this recipe, you've mastered a Mornay, one of the most classic French sauces. At its most basic, a Mornay sauce is a white sauce to which cheese has been added. To allow the cheese to melt evenly into the sauce, be sure the cheese is shredded and stir it in a little bit at a time with the pan off the heat.

Per serving: 250 calories, 20 g total fat (9 g sat.), 41 mg cholesterol, 633 mg sodium, 10 g carbohydrate, 3 g fiber, 10 g protein.

Corn Bread-Stuffed Peppers

3 **large sweet red peppers**
1½ **cups warm water**
2 **tablespoons unsalted butter**
1 **ear corn, husked, silked and kernels
   cut from cob**
1 **small onion, chopped**
4 **links hot Italian turkey sausage
   (¾ pound total), casings removed**
1 **box (6 ounces) corn bread stuffing mix**
2 **tablespoons chopped fresh parsley leaves**
¾ **cup shredded pepper-Jack cheese
   (3 ounces)**

1. Heat oven to 350°. Slice sweet peppers in half from stems to bottoms. Remove seeds and membranes. Place pepper halves, cut sides down, in microwave-safe 13×9×2-inch baking dish and add ½ cup water to the dish. Cover dish with plastic wrap; microwave on HIGH for 4 minutes. Remove dish from microwave; carefully remove plastic wrap; drain off water.

2. In medium-size pot, melt butter over medium to medium-high heat. Add corn and onion and cook for 4 minutes. Add sausage, breaking apart with a wooden spoon. Cook about 5 minutes or until meat is browned. Add remaining 1 cup water and bring to a simmer. Add stuffing mix and stir to combine. Remove from heat and cover. Let stand for 5 minutes. Uncover; gently stir in parsley.

3. Flip pepper halves over. Divide filling among pepper halves, mounding mixture slightly (about 1 cup for each pepper half). Top with shredded cheese (about 1½ tablespoons for each stuffed pepper half).

4. Bake peppers at 350° for 18 to 20 minutes or until cheese is melted and peppers are tender. Serve warm.

A spicy filling of sausage and corn is topped with pepper-Jack cheese for even more zip.

PREP: 15 minutes
MICROWAVE: 4 minutes
BAKE: at 350° for 18 to 20 minutes
MAKES: 6 servings

QUICK TIP

RED PEPPERS FOR HEALTH

Next time you have an extra sweet red pepper in your veggie drawer, add it to pasta sauce for extra vitamins A and C. Simply sauté 1 cup chopped sweet red pepper, then stir it into prepared marinara sauce as you're heating it.

Per serving: 318 calories, 13 g total fat (5 g sat.), 63 mg cholesterol, 980 mg sodium, 37 g carbohydrate, 4 g fiber, 19 g protein.

Winter Squash with Apple Stuffing

3 acorn squash (about 3½ pounds total), cut lengthwise and seeded
2 tablespoons maple syrup
½ cup walnuts, chopped
2 teaspoons corn oil
1 large onion, finely chopped
1 large rib celery, thinly sliced
1 Granny Smith apple (peeled if desired), cut into ¼-inch cubes
¾ cup fat-free, reduced-sodium chicken broth
⅓ cup golden raisins, chopped
¼ cup bulgur wheat
¼ teaspoon salt
¼ teaspoon ground cinnamon

1. Heat oven to 400°. Grease 15½×10½×1-inch jelly-roll pan. Brush cut surfaces and inside of squash with 1 tablespoon syrup. Arrange squash, cut sides down, on pan.

2. Bake squash at 400° for 30 to 40 minutes or until tender.

3. Meanwhile, in nonstick skillet, toast walnuts over medium heat, stirring, about 5 minutes or until golden brown and fragrant. Transfer to paper towel.

4. In same skillet, heat oil over medium-high heat. Add onion and celery; sauté about 3 minutes or just until tender. Add apple, broth, raisins, uncooked bulgur wheat, salt and cinnamon. Cover and simmer about 15 minutes or until bulgur wheat is tender and liquid is absorbed. Stir in toasted walnuts.

5. Reduce oven temperature to 375°. Turn squash cut sides up. Fill with apple mixture. Drizzle with remaining 1 tablespoon syrup. Bake at 375° for 15 minutes.

Maple syrup, nuts, apples, raisins and cinnamon are unbelievably good complements to sweet winter squash.

PREP: 15 minutes
BAKE: at 400° for 30 to 40 minutes; at 375° for 15 minutes
COOK: about 25 minutes
MAKES: 6 servings

QUICK TIP

GOING FOR THE GRAIN

Whole grains are a category of nutrient-dense foods that contain all of the nutrient-rich parts of a grain kernel. Consisting of wheat kernels that have been boiled, dried and cracked, bulgur is a delicious way to add whole grain to your diet. It has an earthy flavor and tender, chewy texture.

Per serving: 238 calories, 7 g total fat (1 g sat.), 0 mg cholesterol, 169 mg sodium, 44 g carbohydrate, 6 g fiber, 5 g protein.

Layered Eggplant

1 large eggplant (about 2 pounds), trimmed
½ cup all-purpose flour
½ teaspoon salt
½ teaspoon black pepper
¾ cup vegetable oil
1 pound cottage cheese or ricotta cheese
4 ounces sharp Cheddar cheese, shredded (1 cup)
1 tablespoon finely chopped fresh parsley leaves
1 teaspoon finely chopped fresh marjoram leaves
2 tablespoons fresh bread crumbs
Fresh Tomato Sauce (recipe follows)
Fresh basil leaves, for garnish (optional)

Here's a dish that's a little like Eggplant Parmesan but with two kid-friendly cheeses for broad appeal.

PREP: 20 minutes
COOK: about 15 minutes
BAKE: at 400° for 10 minutes
MAKES: 6 servings

1. Heat oven to 400°. Cut eggplant crosswise into 18 slices. Pat dry with paper towels. Spread out more paper towels for blotting. In shallow dish or on waxed paper, mix together flour, salt and ¼ teaspoon pepper.

2. In each of two large skillets, heat ¼ cup oil over medium-high heat. Dredge each eggplant slice in flour mixture to coat both sides.

3. Fry 2 or 3 slices of eggplant per skillet about 4 minutes total or until browned on both sides. Transfer to paper towels to drain. Repeat until all slices are fried, adding more oil as needed.

4. In large bowl, mix cottage cheese, Cheddar cheese, parsley, marjoram and remaining ¼ teaspoon pepper.

5. To assemble stacks: In large baking dish, place 1 slice eggplant. Spread on 3 tablespoons of the cottage cheese mixture; top with a second eggplant slice, 3 more tablespoons of the cottage cheese mixture and a third slice of eggplant. Repeat with remaining eggplant slices and cottage cheese mixture to make six stacks. Sprinkle with bread crumbs.

6. Bake, uncovered, at 400° for 10 minutes. Serve immediately with Fresh Tomato Sauce. If desired, garnish with basil leaves.

Fresh Tomato Sauce: In small bowl, mix together 1 large tomato, seeded and diced; 3 tablespoons sliced fresh basil leaves; 3 tablespoons balsamic vinegar; 3 tablespoons extra-virgin olive oil; ¼ teaspoon salt; and ⅛ teaspoon freshly ground black pepper. Makes about 1½ cups sauce.

QUICK BITE

HERB KNOW-HOW

Marjoram is similar to oregano but with a sweeter, milder flavor. Use any extra chopped and served over tomatoes with salt, black pepper and olive oil. If you can't find marjoram, substitute oregano (but use a little less because oregano is more pungent).

Per serving: 456 calories, 35 g total fat (8 g sat.), 31 mg cholesterol, 706 mg sodium, 21 g carbohydrate, 4 g fiber, 17 g protein.

Polenta and Roasted Vegetable Casserole

Roasted Vegetables:
- 2 parsnips (about ½ pound total), peeled and cut into 1-inch pieces
- 5 carrots (about ½ pound total), peeled and cut into 1-inch pieces
- 3 large sweet red and/or yellow peppers, cored, seeded and cut into 1-inch-wide strips
- 1 bulb fennel (about ½ pound), rinsed, trimmed and sliced in 1-inch-wide strips
- 1 red onion, cut into ½-inch wedges
- 2 tablespoons extra-virgin olive oil
- ½ teaspoon salt
- ¼ teaspoon black pepper

Polenta:
- 4 cups milk
- 1 cup hot water
- 1 teaspoon garlic powder
- 1 teaspoon salt
- ¼ teaspoon black pepper
- 1½ cups cornmeal
- ½ cup grated Parmesan cheese
- ⅓ cup fresh basil leaves, shredded

Topping:
- ¼ cup heavy cream
- ½ cup shredded fontina cheese (2 ounces)
- 1 teaspoon chopped fresh thyme leaves

1. Roasted Vegetables: Heat oven to 375°. In large bowl, mix parsnip, carrot, sweet pepper, fennel, onion, oil, salt and black pepper. Spread in single layer in large roasting pan.

2. Roast at 375° for 45 minutes, stirring halfway through cooking.

3. Polenta: In large saucepan, combine milk, water, garlic powder, salt and black pepper. Bring to a simmer over medium-high heat. Whisk in cornmeal; cook, whisking, about 3 minutes or until thick and smooth. If too thick, add a little more hot water. Stir in Parmesan cheese and basil.

4. Coat a 2-quart baking dish with nonstick cooking spray. Spread polenta in baking dish. Arrange vegetables over polenta.

5. Topping: Drizzle cream on top. Sprinkle with fontina cheese and thyme. Bake at 375° for 25 minutes. Let cool slightly before cutting.

Serve this great dish to vegetarians—or anyone who loves sweet, mellow roasted vegetables.

PREP: 30 minutes
BAKE: vegetables at 375° for 45 minutes; casserole at 375° for 25 minutes
MAKES: 8 servings

QUICK TIP

PRODUCE POINTERS

Look for dry bulb onions that are firm, spot-free and not sprouting. Store them in a cool, dry, well-ventilated place for several weeks.

Per serving: 386 calories, 15 g total fat (7 g sat.), 40 mg cholesterol, 706 mg sodium, 52 g carbohydrate, 7 g fiber, 13 g protein.

New Potato Salad

3 cups plain low-fat yogurt
3 pounds small new potatoes, scrubbed and cut into quarters
3 teaspoons salt
⅓ cup sour cream
3 scallions, trimmed and finely chopped
¼ cup chopped fresh chives
3 tablespoons lemon juice
1 tablespoon sugar
1 tablespoon bottled horseradish
¼ teaspoon black pepper

1. Line medium-size colander with 100%-cotton cheesecloth or two layers of paper towels; place colander over a bowl. Add yogurt to colander; drain for 2 hours or refrigerate overnight. You should have about 2 cups solid yogurt and ⅔ cup liquid; discard liquid.

2. Place potatoes in large pot. Add enough cold water to cover. Add 2 teaspoons salt. Boil about 12 minutes or until knife-tender. Drain; cool.

3. In large bowl, whisk together drained yogurt, sour cream, scallion, 3 tablespoons of the chives, the lemon juice, sugar, horseradish, pepper and remaining 1 teaspoon salt. Add potatoes to dressing. Stir gently until all pieces are coated. Refrigerate until ready to serve. Garnish with remaining 1 tablespoon chives.

A little sour cream and horseradish are the secrets to the rich, zesty yogurt dressing.

PREP: 15 minutes
STAND: 2 hours or refrigerate overnight
COOK: about 12 minutes
MAKES: 12 servings

QUICK BITE

REACH FOR THE NEW

New potatoes are young potatoes of any variety, whether white, red, yellow or purple, that haven't matured long enough to fully convert their sugars into starch. Prized for their thinner skins and tender, sweet flesh, new potatoes also hold their shape better than other potatoes, making them an ideal choice for salads and roasting.

Per serving: 101 calories, 3 g total fat (2 g sat.), 7 mg cholesterol, 521 mg sodium, 15 g carbohydrate, 2 g fiber, 4 g protein.

Spinach and Arugula Salad

Dressing:
- 2 tablespoons red-wine vinegar
- 1 tablespoon grainy Dijon mustard
- 1 tablespoon lemon juice
- 2 teaspoons dried oregano
- 1 teaspoon garlic powder
- ¾ teaspoon salt
- ¼ teaspoon black pepper
- ½ cup extra-virgin olive oil

Salad:
- ½ of 12-ounce package turkey bacon
- 1 package (10 ounces) white button mushrooms, cleaned and sliced
- 6 ounces fresh baby spinach leaves, washed and dried
- 6 ounces arugula, trimmed, rinsed and dried
- 1 medium-size red onion, cut into thin rings
- 3 hard-cooked eggs, cut into quarters

1. **Dressing:** In small bowl, whisk together vinegar, mustard, lemon juice, oregano, garlic powder, salt and pepper until salt is dissolved and mixture is smooth. Gradually whisk in oil in a thin, steady stream. Continue to whisk the mixture until the oil is thoroughly incorporated and the dressing is thickened. Cover bowl with plastic wrap until ready to use.

2. **Salad:** Heat large skillet over medium-high heat. Add bacon; cook about 3 minutes per side or until crispy. Remove bacon from skillet to plate; reserve.

3. To the same skillet, add mushrooms; sauté about 5 minutes or until softened. Remove mushrooms from skillet to plate; let cool.

4. In large serving bowl, toss together spinach, arugula, onion and cooled mushrooms. Crumble cooked bacon and sprinkle over top of salad. Toss with about ⅓ cup of the dressing. Arrange hard-cooked egg pieces alongside each serving. Serve with remaining dressing on the side. (Extra dressing can be refrigerated, covered, for up to 5 days. Let come to room temperature before using and whisk thoroughly.)

Arugula joins all the other ingredients so loved in a classic spinach salad—bacon, mushrooms and hard-cooked eggs.

PREP: 20 minutes
COOK: about 10 minutes
MAKES: 6 servings or 12 appetizer/first-course servings

QUICK TIP

PREPARING GREENS

To get greens ready for the table, remove and discard roots and any brown-edged, bruised or wilted leaves. Swirl the leaves around in a bowl or clean sink filled with cold water for about 30 seconds. Remove the leaves and shake them gently to let any remaining dirt, sand or other debris fall back into the water. Repeat until the water remains clear. Use a salad spinner to dry the greens or pat each leaf dry with a clean paper towel.

Per serving: 305 calories, 26 g total fat (5 g sat.), 131 mg cholesterol, 789 mg sodium, 7 g carbohydrate, 2 g fiber, 11 g protein.

Green Salad with Walnut Vinaigrette

Dressing:
- 2 tablespoons balsamic vinegar
- 2 tablespoons fresh raspberries
- 1 tablespoon walnut pieces
- 1 teaspoon chopped fresh parsley leaves
- ½ teaspoon sugar
- ¼ teaspoon salt
- ¼ teaspoon black pepper
- ¼ cup canola oil
- ¼ cup walnut oil

Salad:
- 8 cups assorted greens, washed, dried and torn into bite-size pieces
- ½ cup cherry tomatoes, halved
- ½ cup fresh raspberries
- ½ cup walnuts, toasted

1. **Dressing:** In food processor, puree vinegar, berries, walnuts, parsley, sugar, salt and pepper. With machine running, slowly add oils until combined.

2. **Salad:** Place greens on four plates; top with tomatoes and berries. Drizzle each with 2 tablespoons dressing. Sprinkle with nuts.

Walnuts and walnut oil offer a double dose of nutty richness.

PREP: 15 minutes
MAKES: 6 servings

QUICK BITE

LETTUCE VARIETIES

The best salads include a variety of greens—mix up crunchy and tender and toss in a bit of bite. Crunchy varieties include iceberg and romaine. For a tender touch, use green leaf, Boston, Bibb or mâche. Arugula will add a peppery bite to a salad and green chicory will add a sharp note. For color, toss in some radicchio or red leaf lettuce.

Per serving: 250 calories, 24 g total fat (2 g sat.), 0 mg cholesterol, 109 mg sodium, 8 g carbohydrate, 3 g fiber, 3 g protein.

Potato Salad with Honey-Dill Dressing

1½ pounds small red-skin new potatoes
4 strips bacon
1 medium-size red onion, chopped
6 tablespoons honey
6 tablespoons cider vinegar
½ teaspoon cornstarch mixed with ½ teaspoon cold water
2 tablespoons chopped fresh dill or 1 tablespoon dried dill
1 bunch watercress, trimmed, rinsed and dried

1. In large saucepan, cook potatoes in 1 quart lightly salted boiling water for 15 to 20 minutes or until tender but still firm. Drain. When the potatoes are cool enough to handle, cut potatoes in half or quarters, depending on size. Place potatoes in large bowl.

2. Meanwhile, for dressing, in medium-size skillet, sauté bacon until slightly crisp. With slotted spoon, transfer bacon to paper towels to drain. Sauté onion in bacon drippings about 3 minutes or until softened. Add honey and cider vinegar; cook over medium heat for 2 minutes. Stir in cornstarch mixture. Bring to boiling; cook, stirring, about 2 minutes or until thickened. Remove from heat. Crumble bacon; stir into dressing along with dill.

3. Tear watercress into bite-size pieces; add to potatoes in bowl. Pour warm dressing over; gently toss. Serve immediately.

Peppery watercress provides a wonderful contrast to the earthy potatoes in this exquisite salad.

PREP: 10 minutes
COOK: 15 to 20 minutes
MAKES: 6 servings

QUICK BITE
BIG AND BOLD

No wonder watercress has a bold, peppery bite—it's a member of the mustard family of greens. Similar to arugula, watercress is used to flavor soups, sandwiches and salads; if you have any left over, tuck it into a sandwich instead of lettuce for extra flavor. Or sprinkle it on a fresh-baked pizza for a little extra texture and taste.

Per serving: 242 calories, 9 g total fat (3 g sat.), 10 mg cholesterol, 130 mg sodium, 38 g carbohydrate, 3 g fiber, 4 g protein.

Grilled Corn Salsa

4 ears corn, husked and silked
½ medium-size sweet red pepper, seeded and chopped
1 small red onion, chopped
1 jalapeño chile, seeded and chopped
¼ cup chopped fresh cilantro leaves
2 tablespoons lime juice
2 tablespoons extra-virgin olive oil
½ teaspoon salt
¼ teaspoon black pepper
    Corn tortillas, for garnish (optional)
    Lime or lemon wedges, for garnish (optional)

1. Heat gas grill to high or prepare charcoal grill with hot coals. Coat ears of corn with nonstick cooking spray.

2. Grill corn over direct heat, covered, for 3 to 4 minutes on each side or use Broiler Method (below). Remove from heat. When cool enough to handle, cut kernels from cobs. (You should have about 2 cups kernels.)

3. In large bowl, combine corn, sweet pepper, onion, jalapeño, cilantro, lime juice, oil, salt and black pepper. Cover and refrigerate. If desired, serve in a corn tortilla-lined serving dish with lime or lemon wedges.

Broiler Method: Heat broiler. Place corn on rack of broiler pan. Broil 4 to 6 inches from heat for 3 to 4 minutes on each side. Proceed as above.

A jalapeño chile adds heat to a colorful salsa.

PREP: 10 minutes
GRILL: 12 to 16 minutes
MAKES: 2 cups salsa

HANDLE WITH CARE

Jalapeños and other hot chiles contain volatile oils that can burn your skin and eyes. Avoid direct contact with them as much as possible. When working with hot chiles, wear plastic or rubber gloves. If your bare hands do touch the chiles, wash your hands well with soap and warm water.

Per ¼ cup: 99 calories, 4 g total fat (1 g sat.), 0 mg cholesterol, 157 mg sodium, 15 g carbohydrate, 2 g fiber, 3 g protein.

Summer Bean Sauté

1 pound each **fresh yellow wax beans
    and green beans, trimmed**
⅓ **cup fresh basil leaves**
3 **tablespoons butter**
1 **pint grape tomatoes, halved**
¾ **teaspoon salt**
½ **teaspoon black pepper**
3 **tablespoons balsamic vinegar**

1. Bring a large pot of water to a boil. Add beans; boil about 8 minutes or until crisp-tender. Drain well in a colander.

2. Meanwhile, cut basil leaves into thin strips (chiffonade). In very large skillet, melt butter over medium-high heat. Add beans; cook for 8 to 10 minutes or until they begin to brown. Add tomato, salt and pepper; cook about 3 minutes or until tomato begins to soften. Stir in balsamic vinegar. Remove skillet from heat. Stir in basil. Serve immediately or cool to room temperature.

The secret to cooking the best green beans ever is right here—first you boil, then you sauté.

PREP: 15 minutes
COOK: about 20 minutes
MAKES: 8 servings

QUICK TIP

WHY VEGGIES COUNT

The health benefits of eating a wide variety of vegetables—fruits too—are profound, lowering the risk of many chronic diseases including type 2 diabetes. Recent studies show that dishes rich in veggies help dieters succeed by creating a sense of fullness and could help keep brain function sharp.

Per serving: 87 calories, 5 g total fat (3 g sat.), 12 mg cholesterol, 227 mg sodium, 11 g carbohydrate, 4 g fiber, 2 g protein.

Bean and Mozzarella Salad

¼ cup sherry-wine vinegar
2 teaspoons Dijon mustard
2 teaspoons honey
¾ teaspoon salt
¼ teaspoon black pepper
⅔ cup extra-virgin olive oil
8 ounces fresh mozzarella cheese
1 pound mixed fresh green and yellow beans
1 cup grape tomatoes, halved
8 cups torn Boston lettuce

1. For dressing, in medium-size bowl, whisk together vinegar, mustard, honey, salt and pepper until smooth. Gradually whisk in the oil and continue whisking until thickened. Set aside. Cut mozzarella cheese into ½-inch pieces. Set aside.

2. Bring medium-size pot of salted water to a boil. Add beans and cook for 5 minutes. Drain beans and place in a glass bowl. Toss with ¼ cup of the dressing. Allow to cool about 30 minutes or until room temperature.

3. In large bowl, toss together tomato, lettuce, mozzarella cheese, beans and another ¼ cup of the dressing.

4. Serve salad immediately with the remaining dressing on the side.

This salad is as satisfying as it is colorful. Try it with fresh-off-the-grill chicken breasts.

PREP: 10 minutes
COOK: 5 minutes
COOL: 30 minutes
MAKES: 6 servings

QUICK TIP

PRODUCE POINTERS

Intensely sweet, both red and yellow grape tomatoes add a burst of juice to salads. They also make a pretty garnish. Another time, sauté them in extra-virgin olive oil with fresh herbs.

Per serving: 367 calories, 33 g total fat (9 g sat.), 30 mg cholesterol, 401 mg sodium, 11 g carbohydrate, 4 g fiber, 9 g protein.

Chopped Salad

2 ribs celery, chopped (about 1 cup)
8 radishes, chopped (about 1 cup)
1 large (about 1 pound) seedless cucumber, peeled and chopped (about 2 cups)
2 hard-cooked eggs
3 tablespoons extra-virgin olive oil
2 tablespoons jarred mayonnaise-style salad dressing
½ teaspoon sugar
½ teaspoon salt
¼ teaspoon black pepper
3 tablespoons lemon juice
1 tablespoon white-wine vinegar

1. In large bowl, combine celery, radishes and cucumber. Peel hard-cooked eggs. Separate egg whites from yolks; chop whites. Stir whites into vegetable mixture in bowl.

2. In small bowl, mash hard-cooked yolks until smooth. Whisk in oil, salad dressing, sugar, salt and pepper until smooth. Continue to whisk, adding lemon juice and vinegar until well blended. Toss with vegetable mixture.

Here's a bright and crunchy salad that will add a fresh contrast to meaty, long-simmered dishes.

PREP: 20 minutes
MAKES: 4 servings

QUICK TIP

HARD-COOKED EGGS

To hard-cook eggs, place the eggs in a single layer in a large saucepan. Add enough cold water to cover by 1 inch. Bring to a rapid boil over high heat. Remove from the heat; cover and let stand for 15 minutes. Drain. Immediately run cold water over the eggs or place in ice water until cool enough to handle.

Per serving: 198 calories, 17 g total fat (3 g sat.), 109 mg cholesterol, 412 mg sodium, 9 g carbohydrate, 2 g fiber, 4 g protein.

Herbed Vinaigrette

⅔ cup extra-virgin olive oil
2 tablespoons balsamic vinegar
2 tablespoons chopped onion
½ cup loosely packed fresh parsley leaves
1 tablespoon Dijon mustard
1 small clove garlic
7 cornichons (tiny French pickles)
1 teaspoon Worcestershire sauce
⅛ teaspoon black pepper

1. Place oil, vinegar, onion, parsley, mustard, garlic, cornichons, Worcestershire sauce and pepper in food processor or blender. Puree until well blended. Refrigerate for up to 1 week.

Everyone needs a reliable, versatile "house vinaigrette" to call on again and again. Consider this one yours!

PREP: 5 minutes
MAKES: 1¼ cups

Per 2-tablespoon serving: 75 calories, 7 g total fat (1 g sat.), 0 mg cholesterol, 47 mg sodium, 2 g carbohydrate, 0 g fiber, 0 g protein.

Broiled Tomato and Blue Cheese Salad

Extra-virgin olive oil
6 plum tomatoes (1¼ pounds total), cored and cut in half from top to bottom
⅛ teaspoon salt
Large pinch of black pepper
6 ounces blue cheese (Roquefort, Maytag blue, Gorgonzola or Stilton)
1 large head Bibb or Boston lettuce, leaves pulled from the core intact
¼ cup bottled vinaigrette dressing
3 tablespoons chopped fresh chives or parsley leaves, for garnish (optional)

1. Heat broiler and adjust the oven rack so it's about 4 inches from heat source. Brush a baking sheet with olive oil. Put tomatoes, cut sides up, on baking sheet. If the tomatoes won't lie flat, use a spatula or your hand to gently press them until they are stable. Sprinkle with salt and pepper.

2. Crumble blue cheese into large pieces, flatten with your fingers, if necessary, and put the pieces on top of tomatoes. Broil for 3 to 4 minutes or until cheese is golden brown and bubbly. Remove from oven and let tomatoes cool down in the pan for a bit to set.

3. Divide lettuce leaves among four serving plates. Top each with three tomato halves and drizzle with vinaigrette. If desired, garnish with chives. (Or arrange everything on one platter and serve family-style.)

Top plum tomatoes with tangy blue cheese and broil until bubbly for an irresistible salad. Try it with grilled or broiled steak.

PREP: 10 minutes
BROIL: 3 to 4 minutes
MAKES: 4 servings

QUICK TIP

PRODUCE POINTERS

When choosing tomatoes, look for those that are unblemished with no cracks or bruises. Hold them in your hands—they should feel firm but not hard. For best results, select tomatoes that are bright-colored for the variety.

Per serving: 260 calories, 20 g total fat (9 g sat.), 32 mg cholesterol, 799 mg sodium, 11 g carbohydrate, 2 g fiber, 12 g protein.

Wild Rice Pilaf

- 2 cans (14 ounces each) chicken broth
- 1 package (8 ounces) wild rice
- ⅓ cup converted long-grain white rice
- 3 tablespoons butter
- ½ pound fresh green beans, trimmed and halved
- 1 small onion, chopped
- ¾ pound assorted mushrooms (such as shiitake, portabella and white button), cleaned and sliced into bite-size pieces
- ½ teaspoon salt
- ¼ teaspoon black pepper
- 3 tablespoons dry sherry

1. In 5-quart saucepan, bring broth to a boil. Add wild rice. Cover; reduce heat to medium-low. Simmer for 40 minutes. Add white rice; cover and cook about 20 minutes longer or until wild rice grains have popped and are tender. Let stand, covered, for 5 minutes.

2. In large skillet, heat 2 tablespoons butter over medium heat. Add beans and onion; cook, stirring, for 5 minutes. Add mushrooms; cook about 5 minutes or until mushrooms release their liquid. Season with salt and pepper. Add sherry; cook for 4 minutes. Stir in rice (or combine mushroom mixture with rice in large bowl). Stir in remaining 1 tablespoon butter.

Roast pork or turkey, as well as a creamy chicken or seafood dish—all would go well with this hearty combo.

PREP: 20 minutes
COOK: about 1¼ hours
STAND: 5 minutes
MAKES: 6 servings

Per serving: 293 calories, 9 g total fat (4 g sat.), 18 mg cholesterol, 783 mg sodium, 46 g carbohydrate, 5 g fiber, 9 g protein.

Minted Pea and Orzo Pilaf

1¼ cups orzo pasta (half of a 1-pound box)
2 tablespoons butter
1 tablespoon extra-virgin olive oil
1 small onion, chopped
2 cloves garlic, finely chopped
2 teaspoons finely chopped fresh ginger
1 box (10 ounces) frozen peas, thawed
½ cup chicken broth
1 teaspoon salt
¼ teaspoon black pepper
½ cup packed fresh mint leaves, chopped
2 tablespoons lemon juice
Lemon wedges, for garnish (optional)

1. Cook orzo following package directions. Drain.

2. In large skillet, heat 1 tablespoon butter and the oil over medium heat. Add onion, garlic and ginger; sauté about 10 minutes or until onion is softened. Stir in peas, broth, salt and pepper. Bring to a boil over high heat. Stir in cooked orzo. Reduce heat to medium-low; cook about 3 minutes or until heated through.

3. Stir in mint, lemon juice and the remaining 1 tablespoon butter. If desired, garnish with lemon wedges.

Lemon juice and mint leaves add extra freshness, while peas add sweetness to this satisfying side.

PREP: 10 minutes
COOK: about 20 minutes
MAKES: 4 servings

QUICK TIP

STORE IT RIGHT

Keep garlic in a cool, dry, dark place rather than in the refrigerator, which can diminish the bulb's flavor. Because individual cloves dry out quickly, store garlic bulbs whole.

Per serving: 394 calories, 14 g total fat (6 g sat.), 24 mg cholesterol, 796 mg sodium, 56 g carbohydrate, 6 g fiber, 12 g protein.

Cold Asparagus Salad

2 bunches fresh asparagus (about
   2 pounds total), tough ends
   trimmed and stems peeled
   1½ inches from bottom
   Grated zest of 1 lemon
   Juice of 1 lemon (about 2¼ tablespoons)
1 small shallot, trimmed and finely chopped
1½ teaspoons sugar (superfine, if available)
¼ teaspoon salt
⅛ teaspoon black pepper
¼ cup extra-virgin olive oil
1 small romaine heart, leaves separated,
   rinsed and patted dry
   Sliced lemon, for garnish (optional)

1. Steam asparagus about 4 minutes or until stem ends can be pierced with tip of knife and still offer some resistance. Using tongs, transfer asparagus to shallow dish with ice and small amount of water. Place in refrigerator to chill.

2. Meanwhile, for dressing, in small bowl, whisk together lemon zest, lemon juice, shallot, sugar, salt and pepper. While whisking, add oil in a thin stream and continue to whisk until dressing is thick and smooth.

3. To serve, spread romaine leaves on large platter. Pat chilled asparagus dry with paper towels; arrange on romaine. Drizzle with dressing. If desired, garnish with lemon slices. Serve immediately.

Asparagus dressed in a sprightly lemon and olive oil dressing is a classic—and classy—side dish.

PREP: 20 minutes
COOK: 4 minutes
MAKES: 6 servings

QUICK BITE

SEA SALT SAVVY

You've likely spotted sea salt beside the table salt at the supermarket. What's the difference? Some people feel they can detect the additives present in table salt and the hints of minerals present in sea salt (depending on its origin). The best way to tell which you prefer is to taste it for yourself by sprinkling the same amount of sea salt and table salt on a tomato wedge.

Per serving: 110 calories, 9 g total fat (1 g sat.), 0 mg cholesterol, 108 mg sodium, 6 g carbohydrate, 2 g fiber, 2 g protein.

Kid-Pleasing Foods

Easy Microwave Nachos p. 147

From granola bars and guacamole to nachos and pizza, we have recipes to feed everyone from finicky preschoolers to always-hungry teens whether you're on the go or around the table.

Guacamole

2 scallions, trimmed and cut into 1-inch lengths
1 tablespoon chopped fresh cilantro or parsley leaves
2 ripe avocados
2 tablespoons lime juice (2 limes)
1 tablespoon medium or medium-hot picante sauce or salsa
½ teaspoon salt
⅛ teaspoon hot-pepper sauce
Scallions, sliced, for garnish (optional)

1. In food processor, combine the 2 scallions and the cilantro; whirl until evenly chopped.

2. Halve avocados. Peel and pit. Cut avocados into 2-inch pieces. Add about half of the avocado to scallion mixture in food processor. Add lime juice, picante sauce, salt and hot-pepper sauce. Whirl, using on-and-off pulses, until mixture is finely chopped.

3. Add remaining avocado to mixture in food processor. Whirl, using on-and-off pulses, until desired consistency.

4. Scrape guacamole into a serving dish. If desired, sprinkle with additional scallions. Serve with tortilla chips.

Make Ahead: The guacamole can be prepared up to 4 hours ahead and refrigerated, tightly covered, with plastic wrap.

Kids seem to really take to guacamole. Maybe this will help them muster up the courage to try other green foods!

PREP: 20 minutes
MAKES: 1⅔ cups

QUICK TIP

OUTSMARTING PICKY EATERS

When you're trying to introduce a food new to your child, use these strategies:
• Place a new food in front of your child at mealtime without making a big deal about it. Chances are, he or she will go for at least one bite.
• Introduce new foods one at a time in small amounts. At mealtime, offer one or two favorite foods along with something new.
• Wait until your child is hungry to introduce something new, such as pineapple or mango chunks.

Per 1 tablespoon guacamole: 31 calories, 3 g total fat (0 g sat.), 0 mg cholesterol, 63 mg sodium, 2 g carbohydrate, 1 g fiber, 1 g protein.

Easy Microwave Nachos

1 bag (8½ ounces) baked tortilla chips
1 jar (15½ ounces) medium-hot salsa con queso (such as Tostitos restaurant-style)
1 package (3½ ounces) sliced pepperoni
1 can (4¼ ounces) diced green chiles, drained
1 can (2¼ ounces) sliced black olives, drained
4 scallions

1. Spread half of the tortilla chips over the bottom of a large microwave-safe serving platter. Spoon half of the salsa over chips. Evenly distribute half of the pepperoni, half of the green chiles and half of the black olives on top.

2. Using scissors, snip two of the scallions over the nachos. Microwave on HIGH for 2 to 3 minutes.

3. Repeat with remaining ingredients on a second platter. Serve warm.

Show older kids how to prepare these quick nachos and they can make them for after-school or sleepover snacks themselves.

PREP: 10 minutes
MICROWAVE: 2 to 3 minutes per batch
MAKES: 8 servings

QUICK TIP

NACHO CITY

Vary the nacho ingredients to include some bites your family enjoys best. Use the recipe above as a guideline for ingredient measures. Good combos include:
- Mozzarella cheese with prosciutto, tomatoes and green or sweet red peppers.
- Monterey Jack cheese with salsa, cooked chorizo sausage and canned mild green chiles (drained).
- Cheddar cheese with crumbled cooked bacon, tomatoes and scallions.

Per serving: 381 calories, 23 g total fat (13 g sat.), 96 mg cholesterol, 139 mg sodium, 38 g carbohydrate, 2 g fiber, 5 g protein.

Strawberry Lemonade

¾ to 1 cup sugar
1 package (3 ounces) strawberry-flavored gelatin
1 cup boiling water
6 cups cold water
1 cup lemon juice
  Lemon slices, for garnish (optional)
  Whole fresh strawberries, for garnish (optional)

1. In 3-quart heatproof pitcher, stir together sugar and gelatin. Stir in boiling water, stirring until sugar and gelatin dissolve. Stir in cold water and lemon juice. Chill at least 2 hours. If desired, garnish each serving with a lemon slice and a fresh strawberry.

Treat kids to this pretty-as-can-be sipper at parties or simply as a summertime thirst quencher.

PREP: 10 minutes
CHILL: 2 hours
MAKES: 10 servings

QUICK TIP

A NO-MESS PARTY

Here's an easy way to protect your house from spills when hosting kids at a party: Spread a plastic liner on the floor and let the kids sit and eat on the floor, picnic-style. Roll up the plastic liner and throw away the mess when they're finished.

Per serving: 95 calories, 0 g total fat (0 g sat.), 0 mg cholesterol, 20 mg sodium, 24 g carbohydrate, 0 g fiber, 1 g protein.

Caramel Popcorn Mix

10 cups popped popcorn
2 cups wheat cereal squares
1 cup roasted peanuts
1 cup salted wheat crackers, broken into bite-size pieces
½ cup (1 stick) unsalted butter
1 cup packed dark-brown sugar
½ cup light corn syrup
¼ teaspoon baking soda
½ teaspoon vanilla extract

1. Heat oven to 250°. In large roasting pan, mix popcorn, cereal, peanuts and crackers.

2. In medium-size saucepan, melt butter over low heat. Add brown sugar and corn syrup. Bring mixture to boiling, stirring constantly. Gently boil, without stirring, for 5 minutes. Remove from heat. Stir in baking soda and vanilla.

3. Pour corn syrup mixture over popcorn mixture in roasting pan; toss to coat evenly.

4. Bake at 250° for 1 hour, stirring every 15 minutes. Remove from oven and transfer to aluminum foil. Break popcorn mix into small clusters; cool. Store in airtight container for up to 1 week.

What's good gets even better! Wheat cereal squares and crackers lend a little wholesomeness to popcorn mix.

PREP: 10 minutes
BAKE: at 250° for 1 hour
MAKES: 14 cups

QUICK TIP

WHAT MAKES POPCORN POP?

Kids are bound to ask. The short answer: Water is encircled in hard starch by a popcorn kernel. When the kernel is heated, the water turns to steam and builds up pressure. When the starch gives way, the kernel explodes. The starch pops out, the kernel turns inside out and steam is released.

Per cup: 251 calories, 12 g total fat (5 g sat.), 18 mg cholesterol, 160 mg sodium, 35 g carbohydrate, 2 g fiber, 3 g protein.

Taco Dip and Chips

1 container (8 ounces) whipped cream cheese
1 package (1.25 ounces) taco seasoning
1 cup bottled medium-hot salsa
¼ head lettuce, shredded
1 large tomato, seeded, chopped and drained on paper towels
1 medium-size onion, chopped
1 cup shredded Cheddar cheese

1. In medium-size bowl, mix cream cheese, taco seasoning and 2 tablespoons salsa. Spread over bottom of a large serving platter. Top with remaining salsa. Layer lettuce, tomato, onion and Cheddar cheese over salsa. Serve with tortilla chips.

Make Ahead: Prepare cream cheese mixture a day ahead and refrigerate, covered.

Taco seasonings have such a warm personality—kids usually buddy up to them just fine!

PREP: 10 minutes
MAKES: 8 servings

QUICK TIP

INTRODUCING ... NEW CHEESES!

To get the kids hip to new kinds of cheese, use a few different varieties on this dip. Sprinkle thick, separate strips of Cheddar, Monterey Jack, brick and/or colby and talk about which cheeses everyone likes best.

Per serving of dip: 193 calories, 13 g total fat (9 g sat.), 41 mg cholesterol, 826 mg sodium, 10 g carbohydrate, 1 g fiber, 8 g protein.

Take-Your-Choice Dips

Cheese Dip

PREP: 10 minutes

1. In medium-size bowl, stir together half of an 8-ounce package cream cheese (4 ounces), at room temperature; 6 ounces Brie cheese, trimmed, at room temperature; 2 scallions, trimmed, both green and white parts chopped; 1 teaspoon Dijon mustard; 2 drops hot-pepper sauce; pinch of salt; and pinch of black pepper. Serve with assorted fruit or vegetable dippers. Makes 1 cup.

Per 1 tablespoon dip: 61 calories, 5 g total fat (3 g sat.), 18 mg cholesterol, 105 mg sodium, 0 g carbohydrate, 0 g fiber, 3 g protein.

Peanut Butter Dip

PREP: 10 minutes

1. In medium-size bowl, combine ½ cup creamy or chunky peanut butter, ¼ cup chopped honey-roasted peanuts, ¼ cup raisins, 2 tablespoons honey, 1 tablespoon water and ½ teaspoon ground cinnamon. Serve with apple wedges. Makes 1 cup.

Per 1 tablespoon dip: 75 calories, 5 g total fat (1 g sat.), 0 mg cholesterol, 46 mg sodium, 6 g carbohydrate, 1 g fiber, 3 g protein.

Spiced Chocolate Dip

PREP: 20 minutes

1. Prepare 1 package (3⅛ ounces) cook-and-serve chocolate pudding and pie filling following package directions. To pudding, add ½ cup bottled hot fudge sauce, 1 teaspoon ground cinnamon and ⅛ teaspoon ground cloves, stirring until well blended. Serve warm or chill until mixture is of puddinglike consistency. Serve with apple wedges. Makes 2 cups.

Per 1 tablespoon dip: 38 calories, 1 g total fat (1 g sat.), 2 mg cholesterol, 42 mg sodium, 7 g carbohydrate, 0 g fiber, 1 g protein.

It's no big deal to get the kids to eat fruits and vegetables after school when you serve this trio of dips.

QUICK TIP

DIFFERENT DIPPERS

If you're looking to move beyond carrot and celery sticks, try these ideas for dippers:
- Chicken drummies: These are the part of a chicken wing that looks like a mini drumstick. Roast some up—they work beautifully as dippers on a hearty appetizer spread.
- Chicken breast strips: Marinate and grill or broil chicken breasts and cut them into strips. Serve warm or chill and serve cold.
- Belgian endive: The sturdy, curved leaves of this pleasantly bitter veggie are made for scooping!

Nutritional information provided with each recipe.

South-of-the-Border Snack Mix

4 cups bite-size baked tortilla chips
3 cups multibran cereal squares
2 cups fish-shape crackers
2 cups fat-free mini pretzel twists
1½ cups dry-roasted unsalted peanuts
¼ cup (½ stick) butter or margarine, melted
2 tablespoons Worcestershire sauce
1 tablespoon chili powder
2 teaspoons ground cumin
1 teaspoon garlic powder
1 teaspoon seasoned salt
1 teaspoon cayenne pepper, or to taste

1. Position oven racks in second and third levels in oven. Heat oven to 250°.

2. In large bowl, toss together tortilla chips, cereal, fish-shape crackers, pretzels and unsalted peanuts until well mixed.

3. In small bowl, stir together melted butter, Worcestershire sauce, chili powder, cumin, garlic powder, seasoned salt and cayenne pepper until well mixed. Pour butter mixture over tortilla chip mixture, tossing until the mix is evenly and lightly moistened with the butter mixture. Turn the snack mix into two ungreased 15×10×1-inch jelly-roll pans.

4. Bake at 250° about 30 minutes or until the coating on the snack mix begins to darken slightly; stir the snack mix every 10 minutes and turn and reverse the jelly-roll pans halfway through the baking time. Let the snack mix cool completely in the pans on wire racks.

Consider putting this in little take-home bags as a party favor for your next celebration.

PREP: 15 minutes
BAKE: at 250° for 30 minutes
MAKES: about 12½ cups

QUICK TIP

PARTY BAGS

Kids love to receive take-home bags at parties, but you don't need to fill them with elaborate or costly contents. Rather than focusing on numerous tiny trinkets, give each child one fancifully wrapped nice item that ties in with the party theme. Ideas include a set of sidewalk chalk tied in a bundle from an artsy party, bubble solution or a book of fairy tales from a fairy-tale party, an inflatable beach ball from a swimming party or perhaps a take-away bag with some of the most-fun food served at the party.

Per ¼ cup: 74 calories, 4 g total fat (1 g sat.), 3 mg cholesterol, 126 mg sodium, 9 g carbohydrate, 1 g fiber, 2 g protein.

Caramel Candy Apples

12 small McIntosh apples (about
    3 pounds total)
12 wooden ice cream sticks
 2 packages (14 ounces each) soft caramels
    (such as Kraft brand)
 3 tablespoons water
¼ cup shelled pistachios, coarsely chopped
¼ cup peanuts, coarsely chopped
 3 tablespoons chocolate sprinkles
 3 tablespoons vanilla sprinkles
 1 ounce semisweet chocolate, broken up
½ teaspoon solid vegetable shortening

1. Line a large baking sheet with nonstick aluminum foil. Coat the foil with nonstick cooking spray.

2. Remove stems from apples; wash and dry apples. Insert wooden stick into stem end of each apple.

3. Place unwrapped caramels in medium-size saucepan. Add water; heat over medium-low heat, stirring occasionally, until caramels are melted and smooth.

4. Working quickly with one apple at a time, and keeping caramel over low heat, dip the apple into the caramel, turning to coat apple completely (tilt saucepan slightly for easier dipping). Remove apple from caramel, letting excess caramel drip back into saucepan. Scrape bottom of apple on edge of saucepan and transfer to prepared baking sheet. Repeat with all apples.

5. Press pistachios, peanuts or sprinkles onto bottoms of apples and 1 inch up the sides; place in cupcake liners on another baking sheet. Refrigerate about 10 minutes or until caramel is cool.

6. Meanwhile, in small microwave-safe bowl, microwave chocolate with shortening on HIGH about 1 minute or until melted. Stir until smooth. Transfer to a small plastic bag; snip off corner. Drizzle over apples. Refrigerate about 20 minutes or until hardened. Store in the refrigerator.

When it's time to treat your family to something really special, dress caramel apples up in all kinds of nut-and-candy finery!

PREP: 15 minutes
COOK: about 15 minutes
CHILL: 30 minutes
MAKES: 12 caramel apples

QUICK TIP

APPLE ADVANTAGE

Can an apple a day really keep the doctor away? It sure can help! Apples are packed with antioxidants and fiber, which may help prevent everything from cancer to memory loss, asthma, heart disease and obesity. So keep plenty on hand for cooking and snacking too.

Per apple: 378 calories, 9 g total fat (5 g sat.), 5 mg cholesterol, 182 mg sodium, 74 g carbohydrate, 4 g fiber, 5 g protein.

Strawberry Smoothie Pops

4 containers (8 ounces each) vanilla yogurt
1 bag (12 ounces) frozen strawberries
3 tablespoons honey

1. In blender, combine yogurt, strawberries and honey; puree until smooth.

2. Pour into ice pop molds and freeze overnight.

Talk about convenient—smoothies ready to go in a fun-to-lick frozen form.

PREP: 10 minutes
FREEZE: overnight
MAKES: 20 small ice pops

QUICK TIP

FREEZER FACTS

For a safe and effective freezer, make sure it's set at 0° or below. To check the temperature, put a thermometer between frozen food packages. Wait 8 hours. If the temperature is above 0°, adjust the control and check again after 5 to 8 hours. And don't overstuff the freezer. Air should circulate around the packages.

Per ice pop: 61 calories, 1 g total fat (1 g sat.), 4 mg cholesterol, 30 mg sodium, 10 g carbohydrate, 0 g fiber, 2 g protein.

Cheese-Filled Empanadas

1 cup part-skim ricotta cheese
1 cup shredded mozzarella cheese (4 ounces)
¼ cup chopped turkey pepperoni
½ teaspoon dried Italian seasoning
1 package (14 ounces) frozen empanada
    wrappers (such as Goya brand), thawed
1 egg, lightly beaten
    Warmed spaghetti sauce (optional)

1. Heat oven to 375°. Coat two large baking sheets with nonstick cooking spray.

2. In small bowl, stir together ricotta, mozzarella, pepperoni and Italian seasoning.

3. Spread one empanada wrapper on a work surface. Brush the rim with egg. Dollop 2 tablespoons of the ricotta mixture into center; fold dough over to form half-moon shape. Press edge together firmly and seal with the tines of a fork. Repeat, using remaining ingredients.

4. Transfer empanadas to prepared baking sheets. Brush tops with egg.

5. Bake at 375° about 20 minutes or until lightly browned. Remove to rack to cool. If desired, serve with warmed spaghetti sauce.

No time to stop to eat before the big game? These totally totable packets are mini pizzas to go.

PREP: 10 minutes
BAKE: at 375° for 20 minutes
MAKES: 10 empanadas

QUICK BITE
SOUTH OF THE BORDER

If your kids enjoy Italian-style empanadas, introduce them to more authentic ones: In a large nonstick skillet, heat 1 tablespoon vegetable oil over medium-high heat. Add 1 small onion, chopped, and 2 poblano chiles, seeded and chopped. Cook and stir 5 minutes. Add 1¼ pounds ground turkey, breaking apart with a wooden spoon. Cook for 5 minutes. Stir in ½ cup dark seedless raisins; ¼ cup small pimiento-stuffed olives, chopped; 2 tablespoons tomato paste; 2 teaspoons ground cinnamon; 1 teaspoon sugar; ½ teaspoon salt; and ¼ teaspoon black pepper. Cook 1 minute. Fill as directed, using 2 tablespoons per empanada.

Per empanada: 195 calories, 9 g total fat (5 g sat.), 46 mg cholesterol, 376 mg sodium, 21 g carbohydrate, 1 g fiber, 9 g protein.

Mexican Pizzas

12 (6-inch) corn tortillas
1 pound ground beef sirloin
1 green pepper, seeded and sliced into thin strips
1 sweet red pepper, seeded and sliced into thin strips
1 packet (1.25 ounces) taco seasoning
1½ cups canned refried beans or bean dip
1½ cups shredded taco cheese blend (6 ounces)
 Lime wedges
 Sour cream

This easy-on-you, yummy-for-the-kids recipe is a winner.

PREP: 10 minutes
BAKE: at 425° for 16 minutes
COOK: 8 minutes
MAKES: 12 pizzas

1. Heat oven to 425°. Place tortillas, overlapping slightly, on two baking sheets. Coat with nonstick cooking spray; flip over and coat bottoms. Bake at 425° for 7 minutes. Flip tortillas over; rotate sheets. Bake about 7 minutes longer or until crisp and lightly browned.

2. In large nonstick skillet, brown ground sirloin for 4 minutes, breaking up clumps. Stir in green and red pepper strips and taco seasoning; cook for 4 minutes.

3. Spread each tortilla with 2 tablespoons of the refried beans or bean dip. Top each with heaping ¼ cup of the meat mixture and 2 tablespoons of the cheese. Bake for 2 minutes to melt cheese. Serve with lime wedges and sour cream on the side.

QUICK TIP

READY-TO-EAT SNACKS

Help stave off hunger pangs while dinner is being warmed up. Take a few minutes in the morning to do a little prep, then place the goods up front in the fridge:
• Slice carrots, celery or peppers into strips and load a plastic container with ranch dressing for easy dipping.
• Wash red and green grapes, pull off stems, then stash in groups of a dozen or so in containers or plastic bags.
• Stock up on string or presliced cheese to pair with whole grain crackers.

Per pizza: 260 calories, 13 g total fat (6 g sat.), 53 mg cholesterol, 584 mg sodium, 18 g carbohydrate, 3 g fiber, 17 g protein.

Wraps to Pack

4 (10-inch) flour tortillas
1/3 cup fat-free ranch, bacon-ranch or
   Thousand Island dressing
8 slices honey-baked ham (4 ounces total)
8 slices American cheese (4 ounces total)
2 cups shredded iceberg lettuce

1. Lay out tortillas on clean surface. Spread evenly with dressing. Top with ham, cheese and lettuce, dividing evenly. Fold in two sides of each tortilla; roll up tightly like a burrito. If desired, slice in half; wrap in plastic wrap. Keep refrigerated or chilled until serving.

What did we ever do without wraps? They're among the neatest ways to take sandwiches with you just about anywhere.

PREP: 5 minutes
MAKES: 4 wraps

QUICK TIP

PINT-SIZE PORTIONS

When it comes to serving portions, one size doesn't fit all. Here are a few examples of what constitutes one serving for children 6 to 12 years old:
• Cereal: An amount of cold cereal the size of a tennis ball.
• Fruit: Any fresh fruit that is about the size of a baseball.

Per wrap: 394 calories, 13 g total fat (6 g sat.), 33 mg cholesterol, 1,215 mg sodium, 51 g carbohydrate, 3 g fiber, 17 g protein.

Sloppy Joes

1 tablespoon vegetable oil
1 medium-size onion, diced
1½ pounds lean ground beef
½ teaspoon chili powder
1 can (8 ounces) tomato sauce
1 can (4 ounces) chopped green
   chiles, drained
⅓ cup ketchup
1 tablespoon sugar
¼ teaspoon salt
⅛ teaspoon black pepper
   Hamburger buns
   Sweet pickles

1. In large skillet, heat oil over medium heat. Add onion; cook for 5 minutes.

2. Increase heat to medium-high. Add beef and chili powder; cook about 5 minutes or until meat is browned.

3. Stir in tomato sauce, green chiles, ketchup, sugar, salt and black pepper. Increase heat to high; simmer about 5 minutes or until thickened. Serve on hamburger buns with sweet pickles.

Why not designate one night a week as sloppy joe night at your house—they're so simple and well-liked, it's almost like a "cook's night off."

PREP: 15 minutes
COOK: 15 minutes
MAKES: 8 servings

QUICK TIP

SAFE LEFTOVERS

When a recipe makes more servings than you need, stash the extras in the freezer so you can pull a meal together fast. Here's how to thaw and reheat leftovers:

• Thaw all foods other than baked goods in the refrigerator. Baked goods can thaw at room temperature.
• Heat foods to a safe serving temperature before serving. Bring soups, sauces and gravies to a full boil and heat all other leftovers to 165°.

Per serving: 346 calories, 12 g total fat (4 g sat.), 31 mg cholesterol, 808 mg sodium, 37 g carbohydrate, 2 g fiber, 21 g protein.

Pepperoni Pizza Pockets

- **2** tomatoes (6 ounces each), seeded and chopped
- **8** ounces fresh mozzarella cheese, cut into ½-inch cubes
- **2** ounces pepperoni slices, cut into strips
- **1** tablespoon packaged seasoned dry bread crumbs
- **6** teaspoons prepared basil pesto
- **6** precut pita bread pockets
  Fresh basil, for garnish

1. Pat chopped tomato dry with paper towels. In medium-size bowl, combine tomato, mozzarella, pepperoni and bread crumbs. Stir to combine.

2. Spread 1 teaspoon pesto on inside of each pita pocket. Divide tomato and mozzarella cheese mixture among pita pockets.

3. Place upright in a small microwave-safe baking dish; microwave on HIGH about 1 minute or until warm.

4. Garnish with basil and serve immediately.

Cheese and pepperoni—two ingredients most kids love—get wrapped up into one fun pocket!

PREP: 10 minutes
MICROWAVE: 1 minute
MAKES: 6 servings

QUICK TIP

TWO KINDS OF EATERS?

Many families gather both picky and non-picky eaters around their tables. How do you cook a meal that isn't too scary for a timid palate but not too boring for the rest of the family? Consider having the kids participate in mealtime prep, letting them choose which ingredients will go into their serving. For example, in the above recipe, the picky eater might want fewer (or no) pepperoni strips, while the adventuresome might add some olives or use a fancier kind of cheese. Keep a lot of options on hand, and you may be pleasantly surprised at what ends up on the plate.

Per serving: 299 calories, 16 g total fat (8 g sat.), 43 mg cholesterol, 500 mg sodium, 25 g carbohydrate, 1 g fiber, 13 g protein.

Oatmeal-Raisin Muffins

- 2 cups all-purpose flour
- ½ cup packed light-brown sugar
- ½ cup granulated sugar
- 1 tablespoon baking powder
- ¾ teaspoon salt
- ¼ teaspoon ground allspice
- 1 cup quick-cooking oatmeal
- ½ cup raisins
- ½ cup chopped walnuts
- 1 egg
- 1¼ cups milk
- ⅓ cup vegetable oil
- 1 teaspoon vanilla extract
- Quick-cooking oatmeal (optional)

1. Heat oven to 375°. Coat the cups of standard-size 12-cup muffin pan with nonstick cooking spray.

2. In large bowl, whisk together flour, brown sugar, granulated sugar, baking powder, salt and allspice. Stir in the 1 cup oatmeal, the raisins and nuts. In medium-size bowl, lightly beat egg. Stir in milk, oil and vanilla to combine. Stir gently into flour mixture; do not overmix.

3. Fill muffin cups two-thirds full. If desired, sprinkle with additional oatmeal. Bake at 375° about 25 minutes or until golden brown on top. Remove to wire rack and let cool.

These muffins will come in handy when everyone needs a boost of energy.

PREP: 10 minutes
BAKE: at 375° for 25 minutes
MAKES: 12 muffins

QUICK TIP

GOOD-FOR-YOU OATMEAL

Don't tell the kids, but as a whole grain food, oatmeal is good for you. Among its advantages (according to research):
• As a source of fiber, oatmeal may also help slow the rate of digestion, which may help maintain healthy blood sugar levels, curb appetite and sustain your energy level through the morning.
• When included as part of a diet low in saturated fat and cholesterol, the soluble fiber from oatmeal may reduce the risk of heart disease.

Per muffin: 297 calories, 11 g total fat (2 g sat.), 21 mg cholesterol, 317 mg sodium, 45 g carbohydrate, 2 g fiber, 5 g protein.

Hot Chocolate

⅓ cup sugar
3 tablespoons unsweetened cocoa powder
Pinch of salt
¼ cup water
1¾ cups half-and-half
1 cup milk
2 ounces semisweet or bittersweet chocolate, chopped
⅛ teaspoon ground cinnamon
½ teaspoon vanilla extract
Marshmallows (optional)

1. In medium-size saucepan, combine sugar, cocoa powder and salt. Whisk in water until well blended.

2. Stir over medium-high heat until boiling; boil for 2 minutes. Add half-and-half, milk, chopped chocolate and cinnamon, stirring just until chocolate is melted and liquid is heated through; do not boil. Remove from heat; stir in vanilla. If desired, top individual servings with marshmallows.

A chill in the air? Seize the moment and treat your family to a creamy cup of real homemade hot chocolate.

PREP: 5 minutes
COOK: 5 minutes
MAKES: 4 servings

QUICK TIP

FROZEN HOT CHOCOLATE

When the weather's nice, offer kids of all ages this variation. Prepare Hot Chocolate as directed and let cool completely. Pour mixture into ice cube trays and cover well. Freeze for at least 6 hours or overnight (up to 1 week). To serve, place the cubes in a food processor fitted with a steel blade. Process with a few tablespoons of milk until no lumps remain. Serve with spoons. Or refreeze until solid; scoop and serve frozen.

Per serving: 321 calories, 19 g total fat (12 g sat.), 47 mg cholesterol, 147 mg sodium, 35 g carbohydrate, 3 g fiber, 7 g protein.

Jumbo Chocolate Chip Cookies

2¼ cups all-purpose flour
1 teaspoon baking soda
1 teaspoon salt
1 cup (2 sticks) unsalted butter or margarine, at room temperature
⅔ cup creamy peanut butter
1 cup granulated sugar
1 cup packed light-brown sugar
2 eggs
2 teaspoons vanilla extract
1 bag (12 ounces) semisweet chocolate chunks or 1 bag (10 ounces) oversize semisweet chocolate chips
1¼ cups coarsely chopped pecans

1. Heat oven to 325°. In medium-size bowl, combine flour, baking soda and salt.

2. In large bowl, with electric mixer on medium speed, beat together butter, peanut butter, granulated sugar and brown sugar about 3 minutes or until light and fluffy. Beat in eggs and vanilla until blended. Stir in flour mixture until blended and dough forms. Stir in chocolate chunks and pecans.

3. Using a ¼-cup measure, drop dough by slightly rounded mounds onto large ungreased cookie sheets, spacing cookies about 2 inches apart.

4. Bake at 325° for 15 to 17 minutes or until golden brown around edges and lightly colored on top.

5. Remove the cookie sheets to a wire rack to cool about 3 minutes. Transfer the cookies with a metal spatula from the cookie sheets to a wire rack and cool completely.

These extra-big cookies are just the thing when someone you know has been extra good.

PREP: 20 minutes
BAKE: at 325° for 15 to 17 minutes per batch
COOL: 3 minutes
MAKES: 24 cookies

QUICK TIP

THE SCOOP ON COOKIES

If you make drop cookies often, it may be worth your while to invest in a small ice cream scoop. It will make slick work of getting the dough from the bowl to the cookie sheet; it will also ensure that every mound of dough will be the same size for even baking and the cookies will have the same round shape. Purchase ice cream scoops in the appropriate sizes for the cookies you bake most often.

Per cookie: 323 calories, 20 g total fat (8 g sat.), 39 mg cholesterol, 186 mg sodium, 35 g carbohydrate, 2 g fiber, 5 g protein.

Peanut Butter Popcorn Balls

⅔ cup reduced-fat or regular peanut butter
½ cup caramel syrup
½ cup semisweet chocolate chips
½ cup chopped peanuts
4 cups popped popcorn

1. In small bowl, combine peanut butter and caramel syrup. Fold in chocolate chips and chopped peanuts.

2. Place popcorn in large bowl. Pour caramel mixture over top; mix with hands (mixture will be sticky).

3. Using plastic wrap to prevent sticking, compress about 2 tablespoons of the popcorn mixture into a 2-inch ball. Transfer to waxed paper. Continue with the remaining mixture. Refrigerate if desired.

Making popcorn balls is a rite of childhood! Here's a recipe to share the experience with the next generation of cooks.

PREP: 15 minutes
MAKES: 24 popcorn balls

QUICK TIP

HEALTHY POPPIN'

Studded with candy, nuts and/or chocolate, popcorn balls are a special-occasion treat. However, popcorn without the trimmings is a good-for-you snack if it's not loaded up with sodium and fat; choose wisely and you get healthy whole grains with lots of fiber. For example, when purchasing microwave popcorn, look for labels that boast "94% fat-free." Pay attention to the "percent of daily value" for total fat, saturated fat, trans fat, cholesterol and sodium. Anything above 20% is high.

Per popcorn ball: 92 calories, 5 g total fat (1 g sat.), 0 mg cholesterol, 64 mg sodium, 11 g carbohydrate, 1 g fiber, 3 g protein.

Chocolate-Chip Cookie Pizza

1 tube (18 ounces) refrigerated
   chocolate-chip cookie dough
½ cup raspberry preserves
¼ cup multicolored candy-coated
   chocolate pieces
2 tablespoons peanuts, chopped
2 tablespoons shredded flake coconut

1. Heat oven to 350°. Coat nonstick 12-inch pizza pan with nonstick cooking spray. Spread cookie dough out evenly on prepared pan, pressing with fingers to flatten.

2. Bake at 350° about 17 minutes or until the cookie dough is lightly browned. Let cool completely in pizza pan on a wire rack.

3. To decorate: Spread raspberry preserves evenly over cookie pizza to within 1 inch of edge of pizza. Sprinkle chocolate pieces, peanuts and flake coconut evenly over the preserves. Cut cookie pizza into 12 wedges.

On "planet kid," when it comes to dessert the sweeter the better, and few desserts are sweeter than a cookie pizza.

PREP: 10 minutes
BAKE: at 350° for 17 minutes
MAKES: 12 slices

QUICK TIP

FRUIT PIZZA PIZZAZZ

This same cookie base can be topped with assorted fruit. Bake the cookie dough as directed. Let cool in pan on wire rack. In a small bowl, combine ½ cup lemon yogurt and ½ cup thawed frozen whipped topping. Spread onto cookie crust. Slice 12 strawberries. Peel and slice 2 bananas and 1 kiwifruit. Arrange fruit on top of crust in a decorative pattern. Chill for at least 10 minutes or up to 2 hours.

Per slice: 248 calories, 10 g total fat (4 g sat.), 10 mg cholesterol, 98 mg sodium, 38 g carbohydrate, 2 g fiber, 3 g protein.

Triple-Chocolate Chewy Brownies

Brownies:
- 6 tablespoons (¾ stick) unsalted butter
- 3 squares (1 ounce each) unsweetened chocolate, chopped (½ cup)
- 1 cup granulated sugar
- 2 eggs
- 1½ teaspoons vanilla extract
- ⅛ teaspoon salt
- 1 cup all-purpose flour
- 1 cup white-chocolate chips

Frosting:
- ½ cup chopped milk-chocolate bar (3 ounces), melted
- 2 tablespoons unsalted butter, at room temperature
- 2 tablespoons milk
- ½ teaspoon vanilla extract
- ¼ teaspoon salt
- 2 cups confectioners' sugar

1. **Brownies:** Heat oven to 325°. Line 8×8×2-inch baking pan with nonstick aluminum foil, leaving an overhang.

2. In small saucepan, melt butter and unsweetened chocolate over low heat, stirring. Remove from heat. Stir in granulated sugar, eggs, vanilla and salt until smooth. Stir in flour and white-chocolate chips. Spread into prepared pan.

3. Bake at 325° about 30 minutes or until set in center. Let cool in pan on wire rack. Cut into shapes or squares.

4. **Frosting:** In medium-size bowl, cool melted chocolate bar slightly. With electric mixer on low to medium speed, beat in butter, milk, vanilla and salt; beat in ½ cup confectioners' sugar until creamy. Beat in the remaining 1½ cups confectioners' sugar until a drizzling consistency. Drizzle over brownies.

With sophisticated white chocolate for the adults and plenty of sweet, creamy frosting for the kids, this is a best-of-both-worlds brownie!

PREP: 15 minutes
BAKE: at 325° for 30 minutes
MAKES: 16 brownies

QUICK TIP

PACING A PARTY

When you're hosting kids for a party, bring out one or two snacks and treats between games instead of setting out all the food at once. This eliminates interruptions, keeps the kids focused on the game at hand and gives them something to anticipate.

Per brownie: 310 calories, 15 g total fat (9 g sat.), 6 mg cholesterol, 79 mg sodium, 44 g carbohydrate, 1 g fiber, 3 g protein.

Surprise Cupcakes

The surprise is a rich orange-cream cheese filling that tastes heavenly with the chocolate in the cake and frosting.

PREP: 15 minutes
BAKE: at 350° for 24 minutes
MAKES: 24 cupcakes

QUICK TIP

FREEZER FACTS

Like many cakes, cupcakes freeze well. Freeze them unfrosted. Place the cooled cupcakes on baking sheets and freeze until firm. Transfer to freezer bags or wrap and seal in freezer wrap. Freeze for up to 4 months.

Per cupcake: 243 calories, 14 g total fat (6 g sat.), 49 mg cholesterol, 201 mg sodium, 27 g carbohydrate, 1 g fiber, 4 g protein.

Cupcakes:
- 1 large orange
- 6 ounces cream cheese, at room temperature
- ¼ cup sugar
- 4 eggs
- 1 box (17.59 ounces) dark-chocolate cake mix
- ⅓ cup vegetable oil
- 1 teaspoon ground cinnamon

Frosting:
- 1 package (11.5 ounces) milk-chocolate chips
- ¾ cup sour cream

1. **Cupcakes:** Heat oven to 350°. Line the cups of two standard-size 12-cup muffin pans with paper liners.

2. Grate the zest from the orange (about 2 teaspoons). Squeeze juice from orange into a 1-cup measuring cup. Add water to measuring cup to equal 1 cup liquid; set aside.

3. In medium-size bowl, with electric mixer on medium speed, beat cream cheese, sugar, 1 egg and 1 teaspoon orange zest about 1 minute or until smooth; set aside.

4. In large bowl, combine cake mix, remaining 3 eggs, orange juice-water mixture, oil, remaining orange zest, cinnamon and chocolate syrup packet if included in cake mix box. With same beaters, beat on low speed for 30 seconds to moisten. Beat on medium speed for 2 minutes.

5. Fill each prepared muffin cup with scant ¼ cup of the chocolate cake batter. Spoon cream cheese mixture into large pastry bag fitted with ¼-inch plain round tip. Insert tip into batter of each cupcake. Squeeze some filling into center of each (top will bulge slightly).

6. Bake at 350° about 24 minutes or until wooden toothpick inserted in centers comes out clean. Remove cupcakes from muffin cups to wire racks; let cool.

7. While cupcakes are baking, make **Frosting:** In large microwave-safe glass bowl, microwave chocolate chips on HIGH for 1 to 2 minutes, stirring to melt. With electric mixer on medium speed, beat in sour cream until fluffy and good spreading consistency. Let frosting sit at room temperature until cupcakes are cooled. Frost each cupcake with 1 tablespoon of the frosting. Store cupcakes, covered, in refrigerator for up to 3 days.

Honeyed Peach à la Mode

1 freestone peach, halved and pitted,
    or 2 canned peach halves, in juice
    or light syrup, drained
1 tablespoon honey
½ cup low-fat frozen vanilla yogurt
    or light ice cream
1 tablespoon chopped toasted almonds
    or walnuts (see Note)

1. Heat toaster oven to broil. Place peach halves, cut sides up, on broiler tray; drizzle with half of the honey.

2. Broil for 8 to 10 minutes or until lightly browned. Cut into slices. Place in two small dessert bowls.

3. Top each peach half with ¼ cup frozen yogurt. Sprinkle with toasted nuts. Drizzle with the remaining honey and serve.

Note: To toast almonds or walnuts, place nuts in small, heavy skillet over medium-low heat. Cook, stirring, about 3 minutes or until aromatic and just lightly colored. Transfer the nuts to paper towels to cool before chopping.

Dessert on a weeknight? You'll always have time when you keep the ingredients for this recipe on hand.

PREP: 5 minutes
BROIL: 8 to 10 minutes
MAKES: 2 servings

QUICK TIP

PEACH PANACHE

Having a can of peaches on hand means you're only a few minutes away from dessert. Kids will enjoy this dreamy treat: In a small bowl, mix together 10 crushed vanilla wafers, 1 teaspoon butter at room temperature, 1 tablespoon packed dark-brown sugar and ¼ teaspoon ground cinnamon. Drain one 15-ounce can peach halves in juice. Place the peaches, hollow sides up, in a broilerproof pie plate. Sprinkle with the vanilla wafer mixture. Broil about 1 minute or until sugar is melted and bubbly.

Per serving: 135 calories, 3 g total fat (1 g sat.), 3 mg cholesterol, 23 mg sodium, 25 g carbohydrate, 2 g fiber, 3 g protein.

Toasted Pound Cake S'mores

1 package (12 ounces) pound cake, cut into 12 equal slices, each about ½ inch thick
¾ cup marshmallow cream (from 7½-ounce jar)
3 milk chocolate bars (1.55 ounces each), cut in half crosswise

1. Heat gas grill to medium-high or prepare charcoal grill with medium-hot coals or use Stovetop Method (below).

2. Toast pound cake on grill about 2 minutes per side. Remove from grill.

3. Spread each of six slices with 2 tablespoons marshmallow cream. Place one of the chocolate squares on top of marshmallow cream on each pound cake slice; top with a slice of the remaining pound cake.

4. Place each s'more over indirect heat just until chocolate starts to melt (1 minute or less). Serve immediately.

Stovetop Method: Heat stovetop grill pan over medium-high heat. Place pound cake slices on pan; toast about 2 minutes per side. Continue with step 3 above. Heat over low heat just until chocolate starts to melt. Serve immediately.

Buttery pound cake, sweet and oozy marshmallow cream and melty milk chocolate—it's almost too good to be true!

PREP: 5 minutes
GRILL: about 5 minutes
MAKES: 6 servings

QUICK TIP

POUND CAKE PLUS

Pick your child's favorite jelly to use for this quick-fix snack: Trim the rounded top and brown sides from 1 prepared pound cake. Slice cake lengthwise into 4 equal slices. Broil cake slices for 2 to 3 minutes, turning over once. Spread each slice with 2 tablespoons of jelly. Drizzle slices with 2 ounces white or milk chocolate, melted. Cut each slice into thirds, then cut each third in half diagonally.

Per serving: 449 calories, 16 g total fat (9 g sat.), 86 mg cholesterol, 243 mg sodium, 72 g carbohydrate, 2 g fiber, 6 g protein.

After-School Dip

1 package (8 ounces) fat-free cream cheese
1 tablespoon fat-free milk
3 tablespoons dark-brown sugar
¼ teaspoon pumpkin pie spice
⅓ cup raisins
  Apple wedges, pear wedges, carrot sticks
  and ginger cookies, for dipping

1. In food processor or blender, combine cream cheese and milk. Pulse until creamy; do not overbeat. Add brown sugar and pumpkin pie spice. Whirl until blended.

2. Remove mixture to small bowl; stir in raisins. Serve with dippers. Refrigerate unused portion of dip.

Brown sugar and pumpkin pie spice make this dip irresistible.

PREP: 5 minutes
MAKES: 1⅓ cups dip

QUICK TIP

NO-FUSS SNACKS

Kids ages 3 and older need to refuel their bodies several times a day, especially when they're active, and because they have smaller stomachs than adults, they may need to refuel more often. Here are some healthful, interesting foods to keep on hand to satisfy their needs:

- Fruit (banana or chopped apple)
- Nuts (almonds)
- Yogurt
- Cut-up veggies
- Peanut butter crackers
- Cheese sticks or slices
- Whole grain crackers
- Applesauce

Per 1 tablespoon dip: 23 calories, 0 g total fat (0 g sat.), 2 mg cholesterol, 66 mg sodium, 4 g carbohydrate, 0 g fiber, 2 g protein.

Thick Chocolate Banana Shakes

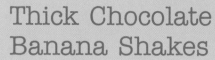

4 ice cubes, crushed
2 cups chocolate sorbet
2 cups fat-free milk
2 large ripe bananas, cut into chunks
1 teaspoon vanilla extract

1. In blender, pulse crushed ice, sorbet, milk, banana and vanilla until thick and smooth (if necessary, prepare mixture half at a time). Pour into four tall glasses.

One of the best ways to get children to eat their fruit may be to have them drink it!

PREP: 5 minutes
MAKES: 4 servings

SHAKE 'EM UP

Once the blender's going, you can turn out shakes in a jiffy. Here are two more options: Whirl 2 cups hulled strawberries, 1½ cups cubed honeydew melon and 2 tablespoons honey in blender. Add 1 cup ice, one cube at a time; whirl until smooth. Add 6 ounces vanilla yogurt; whirl just to blend. Or in a blender, combine 4 ice cubes, crushed; 1¼ cups fat-free milk; 3 tablespoons creamy peanut butter; and 1 ripe banana, peeled and cut into chunks. Pulse until mixture is smooth. Add 1½ cups fat-free vanilla ice cream, softened. Whirl until shake is thick and creamy.

Per serving: 168 calories, 1 g total fat (0 g sat.), 2 mg cholesterol, 110 mg sodium, 36 g carbohydrate, 1 g fiber, 6 g protein.

Classics **101**

Eggs Benedict p. 174

Now you're the expert! Thanks to foolproof step-by-step instructions and helpful how-to photos, it's a cinch to make some of the world's best recipes—from a rich crème brûlée to an airy soufflé.

Beef Tenderloin with Roasted Wild Mushroom Sauce

1 whole beef tenderloin (about 4½ pounds), trimmed and tied for roasting
3 tablespoons extra-virgin olive oil
1 teaspoon salt
½ teaspoon black pepper
2 cloves garlic, finely chopped
½ pound assorted fresh mushrooms (such as cremini, shiitake, oyster and portabella)
2 tablespoons all-purpose flour
1 can (14¾ ounces) beef broth
¼ cup heavy cream
½ teaspoon chopped fresh tarragon leaves or ¼ teaspoon dried tarragon

Few foods impress as much as beef tenderloin. Follow these steps and it will really wow your guests!

PREP: 15 minutes
ROAST: at 425° for 45 minutes
STAND: 10 minutes
MAKES: 8 servings

1. Heat oven to 425°.

2. Rub tenderloin with 1 tablespoon oil. Season all sides with salt and pepper. Press chopped garlic onto all sides of tenderloin. Place tenderloin on rack in large flameproof roasting pan.

3. In medium-size bowl, toss together mushrooms and the remaining 2 tablespoons oil. Arrange mushrooms around tenderloin in roasting pan.

4. Roast at 425° about 45 minutes or until an instant-read meat thermometer inserted in thickest part of tenderloin registers 135° for medium rare.

5. Remove tenderloin from pan; tent with aluminum foil and let stand for 10 minutes in warm place.

6. Meanwhile, prepare mushroom sauce: Place roasting pan on top of stove over two burners. Remove rack from pan. Scrape any mushrooms remaining on rack into the roasting pan. Using a sieve, sprinkle flour over mushrooms in pan. Cook for 1 minute over medium-high heat, scraping up any browned bits from bottom of pan with metal spatula.

7. Gradually stir broth into mushroom mixture in roasting pan, continuously stirring and scraping bottom of pan with spatula. Bring to a boil; cook about 1 minute or until sauce is thickened. Stir in cream and tarragon. Return to a boil. Remove from heat.

8. Remove string from tenderloin. Slice tenderloin. Pour mushroom sauce into gravy boat and serve with the sliced tenderloin.

Per serving: 487 calories, 28 g total fat (10 g sat.), 170 mg cholesterol, 610 mg sodium, 2 g carbohydrate, 0 g fiber, 54 g protein.

How to
Prep meat

Tie one end of a 4-foot length of kitchen string around thicker part of tenderloin. Continue until meat is neatly tied.

Chicken Caprese

3 large plum tomatoes (3 to 4 pounds total),
   cored, seeds squeezed out and diced

6 ounces fresh mozzarella cheese, cut into
   small cubes

5 tablespoons extra-virgin olive oil

3 tablespoons chopped fresh basil

1 tablespoon balsamic vinegar

½ teaspoon salt

¼ teaspoon black pepper

½ cup all-purpose flour

2 eggs

½ cup packaged plain dry bread crumbs

4 boneless, skinless chicken breasts (about
   1½ pounds total)

   Additional basil, for garnish (optional)

1. In medium-size bowl, mix tomato, mozzarella, 2 tablespoons of the olive oil, the chopped basil, balsamic vinegar, ¼ teaspoon of the salt and ⅛ teaspoon of the pepper. Cover with plastic wrap and reserve until ready to serve.

2. Place flour on a large plate. Lightly beat eggs in a shallow bowl. Spread the bread crumbs on another plate.

3. Coat chicken with the flour, dip in the egg and then into the bread crumbs, pressing to adhere. Sprinkle all sides with the remaining salt and pepper. Place on a large plate.

4. In a large nonstick skillet, heat remaining 3 tablespoons oil over medium-high heat. Add chicken and cook about 10 minutes or until an instant-read meat thermometer inserted in the chicken registers 160°. Turn chicken as needed to avoid burning.

5. To serve, spoon tomato mixture over chicken. If desired, garnish with additional basil.

Top lightly breaded cutlets with a caprese salad of fresh mozzarella, tomatoes and basil.

PREP: 15 minutes
COOK: 10 minutes
MAKES: 4 servings

Per serving: 571 calories, 31 g total fat (9 g sat.), 238 mg cholesterol, 572 mg sodium, 16 g carbohydrate, 1 g fiber, 52 g protein.

How to
Dredge, dip
and coat

Place the chicken in flour and pull both sides through to coat. Shake or brush off excess flour.

Dip both sides of chicken in beaten egg and allow any excess to drip off.

Coat both sides of the egg-dipped chicken with bread crumbs, pressing gently to adhere coating.

Eggs Benedict

Hollandaise Sauce:
- 4 egg yolks
- ⅓ cup water
- 1 to 2 tablespoons lemon juice
- ½ cup (1 stick) cold butter, cut up
- ¼ teaspoon salt
- Pinch of white or black pepper

Egg Poaching and Assembly:
- 3 cups water
- 8 eggs
- 4 English muffins, split
- 8 slices Canadian bacon

1. **Hollandaise Sauce:** In small saucepan, whisk together egg yolks, water and lemon juice. Heat over medium-low heat, whisking constantly, until mixture registers 145° on an instant-read thermometer. The mixture will just begin to bubble around the edges (12 to 15 minutes).

2. Increase heat to medium and whisk in butter, one piece at a time, whisking for 3 to 5 minutes or until melted and thickened. Whisk in salt and pepper. Remove from heat; cover and keep warm.

3. **Egg Poaching:** Heat broiler. In a medium saucepan, bring water to a simmer. Break one of the eggs into a custard cup or small bowl. Slip into water; repeat with three more eggs. Cook for 3 to 5 minutes or until egg whites are firm. Remove with a slotted spoon to a paper towel-lined plate. Repeat with a second batch.

4. Meanwhile, arrange English muffins on baking sheet and toast under broiler for 3 minutes. Spread the bacon on a microwave-safe plate; microwave on HIGH for 30 seconds. **Assembly:** Place two muffin halves on each plate. Top each with Canadian bacon slice and an egg. Spoon 2 tablespoons Hollandaise Sauce over each egg.

Heavenly news! In about 30 minutes you can create this impressive dish of poached eggs and creamy hollandaise sauce for a weekend brunch.

PREP: 10 minutes
COOK: 21 to 30 minutes
MICROWAVE: 30 seconds
BROIL: 3 minutes
MAKES: 4 servings

Per serving: 485 calories, 29 g total fat (13 g sat.), 610 mg cholesterol, 863 mg sodium, 29 g carbohydrate, 2 g fiber, 27 g protein.

How to
Cook sauce and poach eggs

1

Whisk in butter pieces, one at a time, cooking for 3 to 5 minutes or until melted and thickened.

2

Place eggs, one at a time, in a small bowl and carefully slip into simmering water.

3

With a slotted spoon, remove egg from simmering water to a paper towel-lined plate.

Gnocchi

1½ pounds all-purpose potatoes, peeled and cut into 2-inch pieces
2¼ teaspoons salt
2 tablespoons butter, melted, plus 2 tablespoons unmelted
1 egg, lightly beaten
1 egg yolk, lightly beaten
⅛ teaspoon black pepper
⅛ teaspoon ground nutmeg
1 cup bread flour
2⅓ cups bottled pasta sauce (optional)
  Shredded Parmesan cheese, for garnish (optional)
  Fresh basil sprigs, for garnish (optional)

1. Place potatoes in large pot and cover with cold water. Add 1 teaspoon salt. Bring to a boil. Reduce heat; simmer about 25 minutes or until fork-tender. Drain. Return potatoes to pot; cook over medium heat about 1 minute or until dry.

2. Pass potatoes through food mill over large bowl or use a spatula to push through medium sieve. Add melted butter, egg, egg yolk, ¼ teaspoon salt, the pepper and nutmeg. Mix in enough of the bread flour to make stiff dough. Knead a few times in bowl to blend.

3. Heat oven to 200°. Line baking sheet with waxed paper. Lightly dust with flour.

4. Divide dough into six equal pieces. With well-floured hands, roll each piece into rope 1 inch in diameter. Cut each rope into ½-inch pieces. Place on prepared baking sheet. You should have about 90 gnocchi.

5. Place 2 tablespoons butter in heatproof dish; place in oven. Bring large skillet or pot of water to a boil. Add remaining 1 teaspoon salt. Drop in about one-quarter of the gnocchi. When they float (about 2 minutes), remove with skimmer. Transfer to warm dish in oven; stir to coat with butter. Cook remaining gnocchi in batches. Reserve 1 cup of the gnocchi cooking water.

6. If using pasta sauce, heat it in medium-size saucepan. Stir in as much of the reserved cooking water as needed to thin the sauce. Serve over cooked gnocchi; if desired, sprinkle with Parmesan cheese and garnish with basil.

Make Ahead: Uncooked gnocchi can be prepared 1 day ahead through step 4. Cover baking sheet with plastic wrap; refrigerate.

Tender homemade gnocchi are hard to come by even in restaurants—all the more reason to make them one of your house specialties.

PREP: 30 minutes
COOK: 34 minutes
MAKES: 6 servings (about 15 gnocchi per serving)

Per serving: 246 calories, 10 g total fat (5 g sat.), 92 mg cholesterol, 307 mg sodium, 31 g carbohydrate, 3 g fiber, 7 g protein.

How to
Roll and cut

Divide the dough into six equal pieces. With floured hands, roll each piece into a rope 1 inch in diameter. Cut each rope into ½-inch pieces.

Asparagus Risotto

1 quart (4 cups) chicken broth
1 bunch fresh asparagus (1 pound)
3 tablespoons unsalted butter
1 medium-size onion, chopped
1½ cups Arborio rice
½ cup dry white wine
Zest of 1 lemon
¼ cup grated Parmesan cheese

1. In medium-size saucepan, bring broth to a simmer. Snap off and discard tough ends of asparagus, letting each stalk break where it is tender. Cut into 1½-inch-long pieces. Add to simmering broth; cook for 3 minutes. Transfer asparagus to bowl; reduce heat under broth to medium-low.

2. In a second medium-size saucepan, melt 2 tablespoons butter over medium heat. Add onion; cook about 5 minutes or until softened. Stir in rice and coat with butter; cook about 2 minutes or until fragrant and slightly translucent.

3. Add wine and cook about 3 minutes or until almost all of the liquid has evaporated. Add one small ladleful of warm broth (about ½ cup); cook, stirring until broth is absorbed. Continue adding broth, one ladleful at a time, until rice begins to swell and a creamy sauce starts to appear (you should have about 1 cup of the broth remaining). Add remaining broth, ⅓ cup at a time, until very creamy.

4. Taste rice. If it is almost tender, stir in remaining 1 tablespoon butter and the lemon zest. If not yet tender, add ⅓ to ½ cup water and continue to cook for 3 minutes longer; add the remaining 1 tablespoon butter and the lemon zest. Then stir in grated Parmesan cheese and asparagus. Heat for 2 minutes. Stir in a few tablespoons of water if risotto is too thick. Serve warm.

Yes—you can master a spring-fresh version of Italy's classic rice dish. We'll show you the secrets!

PREP: 10 minutes
COOK: about 40 minutes
MAKES: 4 servings

Per serving: 500 calories, 15 g total fat (8 g sat.), 36 mg cholesterol, 1,131 mg sodium, 74 g carbohydrate, 3 g fiber, 14 g protein.

How to
Prep, scoop and stir

Snap off and discard tough ends of asparagus.

Scoop asparagus out of cooking water into a bowl.

Stir rice into melted butter, stirring to coat.

Caesar Salad

Dressing:
- 3 tablespoons water
- 2 tablespoons shredded Parmesan cheese
- 2 tablespoons lemon juice
- 2 teaspoons anchovy paste or 4 flat anchovy fillets smashed to equal 2 teaspoons
- 1 teaspoon Dijon mustard
- 2 cloves garlic, mashed
- ½ teaspoon sugar
- ⅛ teaspoon black pepper
- ⅓ cup extra-virgin olive oil
- 3 hard-cooked egg yolks

Salad and Croutons:
- 1 package (18 ounces) romaine hearts, rinsed, patted dry and torn into bite-size pieces
- 1 small loaf French bread (about 8 inches long) or ½ of a full-size loaf
- ¼ teaspoon garlic salt
- ½ cup shredded Parmesan cheese

1. Dressing: In a blender, combine water, Parmesan cheese, lemon juice, anchovy paste, mustard, garlic, sugar and pepper. Cover and blend until mixture is smooth. Slowly add oil and yolks. Cover and blend until smooth. Refrigerate.

2. Salad and Croutons: Place romaine in bowl. Cover with damp paper towel; refrigerate.

3. Heat broiler. Spread bread slices out on baking sheet. Coat with nonstick cooking spray. Sprinkle with ⅛ teaspoon garlic salt. Flip slices over. Repeat with nonstick cooking spray and garlic salt. Broil bread slices about 2 minutes or until toasted and crispy, turning once.

4. Sprinkle each toast with 2 teaspoons Parmesan cheese. Broil for 1 to 2 minutes or until cheese is melted and browned. Add dressing to romaine; toss. Serve with toasted bread slices.

If you've never tasted a from-scratch Caesar salad—sparked with a lemon, anchovy and garlic zip—you're in for a treat!

PREP: 30 minutes
BROIL: 3 to 4 minutes
MAKES: 6 servings

Per serving: 308 calories, 19 g total fat (5 g sat.), 116 mg cholesterol, 826 mg sodium, 24 g carbohydrate, 3 g fiber, 11 g protein.

How to
Pour, broil and toss

1. Carefully and slowly pour the oil into the dressing mixture in the blender.

2. Place bread slices on baking sheet and broil. Sprinkle with Parmesan and broil again.

3. Add dressing to romaine and toss to evenly coat the romaine.

Cinnamon-Sugar Doughnuts

When everyone gets bored on a rainy weekend afternoon, make doughnuts!

PREP: 15 minutes
REST: 15 minutes
FRY: in 365° oil for 2 to 3 minutes per batch
MAKES: 18 doughnuts plus "holes"

Per 1 doughnut plus "hole": 248 calories, 12 g total fat (2 g sat.), 39 mg cholesterol, 214 mg sodium, 31 g carbohydrate, 1 g fiber, 3 g protein.

Doughnuts:
- 3½ cups sifted all-purpose flour, plus more for rolling
- 3½ teaspoons baking powder
- 1 teaspoon salt
- ¼ teaspoon ground cinnamon
- ¼ teaspoon ground nutmeg
- 3 egg yolks
- ⅔ cup granulated sugar
- 3 tablespoons unsalted butter, melted
- ¾ cup milk
- 6 cups vegetable oil, for frying

Coating:
- ½ cup superfine sugar mixed with 1 teaspoon ground cinnamon

1. **Doughnuts:** In medium-size bowl, whisk together 3½ cups flour, the baking powder, salt, cinnamon and nutmeg. Set aside.

2. In large bowl, with electric mixer on medium speed, lightly beat egg yolks. Gradually add granulated sugar, beating about 3 minutes or until pale and slightly thickened. Stir in melted butter. Add flour mixture alternately with milk, stirring with wooden spoon until combined.

3. On well-floured surface, with floured rolling pin, roll dough to ½-inch thickness. Let rest for 15 minutes.

4. Meanwhile, in heavy-duty saucepan, heat oil over medium-high heat until it registers 365° on deep-fry thermometer (a cube of bread will be browned and crisp in 1 minute).

5. Cut doughnuts with 2¾-inch round cutter along with ¾-inch round cutter for the centers. Gather scraps and reroll if needed.

6. **Coating:** Place cinnamon-sugar in small bowl.

7. Carefully slip doughnuts and doughnut holes, 3 or 4 at a time, into the hot oil. Fry, turning once, for 2 to 3 minutes total or until golden brown. Drain doughnuts on paper towels, then transfer still-warm doughnuts to coating and roll to cover completely. Serve warm.

How to
Remove doughnuts

Using a slotted spoon, transfer doughnuts to paper towels to drain.

Florentine Focaccia

3 cups all-purpose flour
1 envelope quick-rise yeast
¾ teaspoon salt
1 cup water
3 tablespoons extra-virgin olive oil
1 tablespoon chopped fresh rosemary
4 ounces diced bacon (about 5 strips)
1 package (10 ounces) frozen chopped
   spinach, thawed and squeezed dry
½ teaspoon sea salt or coarse salt
1½ cups shredded fontina cheese (6 ounces)

1. In bowl, combine 1 cup flour, yeast and salt. In small saucepan, heat water, 2 tablespoons oil and the rosemary until very warm (125° to 130°). With wooden spoon, gradually beat water mixture into flour mixture. Beat in another 1½ cups flour, ½ cup at a time, to make soft dough.

2. Knead dough on floured surface until smooth and elastic (about 10 minutes), working in remaining ½ cup flour as needed to prevent sticking. Shape into ball. Cover; let rest for 10 minutes.

3. In large nonstick skillet, sauté bacon over medium-high heat for 4 to 5 minutes or until crisp. Add spinach; cook for 1 to 2 minutes longer. Remove from heat and set aside.

4. On a floured surface, roll out the dough into a 15×11-inch rectangle. Fit in greased 15×11×1-inch jelly-roll pan, gently pushing dough up into corners. With fingertips, make indentations over surface, pressing almost to bottom of pan. Scatter spinach mixture and sea salt over top. Drizzle with remaining 1 tablespoon oil. Cover with plastic wrap. Let rise in warm place until almost doubled (30 minutes).

5. Heat oven to 400°. Sprinkle cheese over focaccia. Bake for 20 to 25 minutes or until browned. Cut into 12 pieces. Serve warm.

Surprise! This classic Italian bread couldn't be simpler. You'll love serving it as a party appetizer all year.

PREP: 10 minutes
KNEAD: 10 minutes
REST: 10 minutes
RISE: 30 minutes
BAKE: at 400° for 20 to 25 minutes
MAKES: 12 servings

Per serving: 251 calories, 12 g total fat (5 g sat.), 21 mg cholesterol, 433 mg sodium, 26 g carbohydrate, 2 g fiber, 8 g protein.

How to
Combine, knead and form

Before adding the warm liquid, be sure the yeast and salt are distributed throughout the flour.

To knead, push the dough away from you with the heel of one hand. Fold the dough back onto itself and repeat.

With fingers, make indentations all over surface of dough, pressing almost to bottom of pan.

Coconut Shrimp

If you've fallen in love with this sweet and crunchy restaurant favorite, you'll also love how easy it is to make at home.

PREP: 20 minutes
FRY: in 375° oil for 1 to 2 minutes
MAKES: 24 shrimp

Per shrimp with ½ tablespoon sauce:
123 calories, 8 g total fat (2 g sat.), 42 mg cholesterol, 132 mg sodium, 9 g carbohydrate, 1 g fiber, 5 g protein.

How to
Coat shrimp

Coat each egg-dipped shrimp with coconut mixture, gently pressing with your fingers to help the coconut mixture adhere.

Dipping Sauce:
- 1 bottle (7.25 ounces) duck sauce
- ¼ cup ketchup
- 1 tablespoon reduced-sodium soy sauce

Coconut Shrimp:
- 24 jumbo shrimp (1½ pounds total), shelled and deveined (leave tails on)
- 1 bag (7 ounces) sweetened flake coconut (2⅔ cups)
- ¾ cup blanched whole almonds
- ½ cup all-purpose flour
- 2 eggs, lightly beaten
- ¼ teaspoon salt
  Vegetable oil, for frying

1. **Dipping Sauce:** In small bowl, stir together duck sauce, ketchup and soy sauce until smooth. Set aside until ready to serve; if refrigerating, return to room temperature before serving.

2. **Coconut Shrimp:** Rinse shrimp in cool water and pat dry with paper towels.

3. In food processor, combine ⅔ cup coconut and the almonds. Pulse until finely ground. In medium-size shallow dish, stir together ground coconut-almond mixture, the remaining coconut and the flour. In small bowl, whisk together eggs and salt. Set up an assembly line for coating shrimp.

4. Dip a few shrimp in egg mixture, allowing excess to drip back into bowl. Transfer egg-dipped shrimp to coconut mixture, gently pressing with fingertips to help mixture adhere. Place on waxed paper-lined plate. Repeat with all of the shrimp.

5. Meanwhile, in heavy-duty saucepan, heat oil over medium-high heat until it registers 375° on deep-fry thermometer (a cube of bread will be browned and crisp in 30 to 40 seconds). Carefully add shrimp, a few at a time, to hot oil; fry for 1 to 2 minutes or until golden brown. Remove with a slotted spoon, allowing excess oil to drip back into pan. Transfer to a paper towel-lined platter. Serve warm shrimp with dipping sauce.

Dill Pickles

- 4 quart-size wide-mouth jars
- 1 large pot with tight-fitting lid and rack
- 1 set tongs to remove jars from pot
- 4 pounds kirby cucumbers, each about 4½ inches long
- 5 cups white vinegar
- 3½ cups water
- 8 teaspoons sea salt
- 1 small bunch fresh dill
- 4 bay leaves
- 4 cloves garlic, peeled and smashed
- 24 whole black peppercorns
- ½ teaspoon dried red pepper flakes

1. Place clean jars on rack in pot. Fill pot with water and cover. Bring to a boil; boil for 10 minutes. Remove jars. Keep water boiling.

2. Rinse the cucumbers and scrub well. Trim cucumber ends and cut in half lengthwise. In large measuring cup, stir together half of the vinegar, water and sea salt until salt is dissolved. Pack two jars: Add 2 tablespoons dill sprigs, 1 bay leaf, 1 clove garlic, 6 peppercorns and ⅛ teaspoon red pepper flakes to each jar. Add one-quarter of the cucumber halves. Top each with 2 more tablespoons dill. Divide vinegar mixture evenly between packed jars, leaving ½ inch of space below rim.

3. Blend remaining vinegar, water and salt until salt is dissolved. Pack remaining two jars with dill, bay leaves, garlic, peppercorns and red pepper flakes, topped with remaining cucumber halves and more dill. Cover with vinegar mixture.

4. Warm lids in hot water; dry and put on jars, then screw on caps. Place jars on rack and process 15 minutes. Remove and cool overnight. Lids will be flat and have no give when pressed.

With a minimum of prep, you can turn petite kirby cucumbers into crisp, garlicky pickles. They'll come in handy when gift-giving season rolls around! Store pickles in a cool place for up to 1 year.

PREP: 30 minutes
PROCESS: 15 minutes
COOL: overnight
MAKES: 4 quarts

Per pickle spear: 8 calories, 0 g total fat (0 g sat.), 0 mg cholesterol, 140 mg sodium, 2 g carbohydrate, 0 g fiber, 0 g protein.

How to
Sterilize, brine and process

Sterilize jars for 10 minutes in boiling water. The pot should have enough space for the water to rise over the tops of the jars.

When salt dissolves in the vinegar-water mixture, pour mixture over the cucumbers and seasonings in jars.

Place lids and caps on filled jars and process in at least 200° water for 15 minutes. Remove with tongs.

Angel Food Cake

12 large eggs
1½ teaspoons cream of tartar
¼ teaspoon salt
1⅓ cups superfine sugar
1 teaspoon vanilla extract
1 cup sifted cake flour (not self-rising)

1. Heat oven to 350°.

2. Using an egg separator, separate one of the eggs into small bowl or measuring cup. Then transfer egg white to large bowl. Repeat with remaining eggs (this keeps any yolk from accidentally getting into all your whites). Discard yolks. Let egg whites warm to room temperature. Add cream of tartar and salt to egg whites.

3. With an electric mixer on medium to high speed, beat egg whites until frothy. Gradually beat in superfine sugar, 2 tablespoons at a time, beating for 5 to 7 minutes or until stiff and glossy peaks form. Beat in vanilla.

4. Fold flour into egg whites, in two additions, until incorporated. Spoon batter into an ungreased 10-inch tube pan.

5. Bake at 350° for 35 to 40 minutes or until top has risen very high and is lightly browned and cracked. Remove from oven and immediately invert onto a countertop. Cool completely.

Marbled Angel Food Cake: Prepare as directed through step 3. Transfer half of the batter to a medium-size bowl. Reduce cake flour to ¾ cup. Fold ½ cup of the flour into the batter in one of the bowls. Sift ⅓ cup unsweetened cocoa powder and the remaining ¼ cup flour over the second half of the batter in the other bowl and fold in until incorporated. Spoon batters alternately into an ungreased 10-inch tube pan. Swirl together with a knife to marble. Bake and cool as directed in step 5.

Whip egg whites to airy perfection, fold in flour and bake into a delicate, fat-free cake.

PREP: 20 minutes
BAKE: at 350° for 35 to 40 minutes
MAKES: 10 servings

Per serving: 168 calories, 0 g total fat (0 g sat.), 0 mg cholesterol, 124 mg sodium, 37 g carbohydrate, 0 g fiber, 5 g protein.

How to
Separate, fold and cool

Place egg separator over a small bowl. Break egg into separator and let yolk separate from egg white. Pour egg white into a large bowl.

Gently fold flour into whipped egg white mixture just until incorporated. Try not to deflate batter.

Once cake is finished baking, remove from oven and immediately invert to cool and keep from collapsing.

Lemon Curd-Coconut Cake

2½ cups unsifted cake flour (not self-rising)
2½ teaspoons baking powder
 ½ teaspoon salt
 1 cup milk
 ¼ cup cold water
1½ teaspoons vanilla extract
 4 egg whites
1½ cups sugar
 ½ cup (1 stick) butter, at room temperature
 ¼ cup bottled lemon curd
   Fluffy White Frosting (recipe follows)
 2 cups shaved fresh coconut, shredded
   unsweetened coconut or canned coconut
   Bottled lemon curd, for garnish (optional)

1. Heat oven to 350°. Grease two 9-inch round cake pans; dust with flour and tap out excess.

2. Sift together cake flour, baking powder and salt onto sheet of waxed paper. In small bowl, combine milk, water and vanilla.

3. In clean bowl, beat egg whites until frothy. Gradually beat in ½ cup sugar until soft peaks form.

4. In large bowl, with electric mixer on medium-high speed, beat butter and remaining 1 cup sugar about 2 minutes or until fluffy and light colored. On low speed, beat in flour mixture alternately with milk mixture. Fold in beaten whites, half at a time. Divide between prepared pans.

5. Bake at 350° for 20 to 25 minutes or until edges start to pull away from sides of pans. Cool cakes in pans on wire racks for 10 minutes. Turn out onto wire racks and cool completely.

6. With a serrated knife, carefully trim the rounded top of one cake layer to create a flat surface. Place cake layer, cut side down, on serving plate. Spread with the ¼ cup lemon curd. Top with second cake layer, rounded side up. Spread top and sides with Fluffy White Frosting. Press coconut onto top and sides. If desired, garnish with additional lemon curd.

Fluffy White Frosting: In the top of a double boiler, combine 1 cup sugar, 4 teaspoons pasteurized dried egg whites, ⅛ teaspoon cream of tartar and ⅛ teaspoon salt. Stir in ½ cup cold water. With clean beaters of electric mixer on medium to high speed, beat for 1 minute; beat over simmering water 6 minutes or until thick, shiny and firm peaks form. Remove from simmering water. Beat until cool. Beat in 1½ teaspoons vanilla extract.

What's a birthday without a cake? This one is sure to delight.

PREP: 45 minutes
BAKE: at 350° for 20 to 25 minutes
COOL: 10 minutes
COOK: 6 minutes
MAKES: 14 servings

Per serving: 393 calories, 15 g total fat (11 g sat.), 20 mg cholesterol, 215 mg sodium, 62 g carbohydrate, 2 g fiber, 5 g protein.

How to
Prep cake plate

Arrange waxed paper strips to cover edge of plate. Place cake layer, cut side down, on plate. After frosting and adding coconut, remove paper strips.

Lattice-Topped Nectarine-Plum Pie

- 4 small nectarines (about 1¼ pounds total), pitted and sliced
- 4 red plums (about 1¼ pounds total), pitted and sliced
- ½ cup granulated sugar
- ½ cup chopped walnuts
- ⅓ cup packed light-brown sugar
- 3 tablespoons cornstarch
- 1 tablespoon lemon juice
- ½ teaspoon ground cinnamon
- ¼ teaspoon ground nutmeg
- ⅛ teaspoon white pepper
- 1 package (15 ounces) refrigerated ready-to-use rolled 9-inch piecrust
- 2 tablespoons milk
- 1 teaspoon granulated sugar

Learn to weave a lattice and you can beautifully top just about any of your family's favorite double-crust pies.

PREP: 30 minutes
BAKE: at 400° for 15 minutes; at 375° for 50 to 55 minutes
COOL: 45 minutes
MAKES: 12 servings

1. Heat oven to 400°. In large bowl, mix nectarines, plums, ½ cup granulated sugar, nuts, brown sugar, cornstarch, lemon juice, cinnamon, nutmeg and white pepper.

2. Roll out one of the piecrust rounds to 12-inch circle. Transfer to deep-dish pie plate. Roll out the second piecrust round to 12-inch circle. With sharp knife or pastry cutter, cut circle into ¾-inch-wide strips.

3. Spoon nectarine mixture into pie plate. On top of pie, weave piecrust strips in lattice pattern. Crimp edge of crust together with ends of strips. Brush crust with milk; sprinkle with the 1 teaspoon granulated sugar.

4. Bake at 400° for 15 minutes. Reduce oven temperature to 375°. Cover edge with aluminum foil. Bake for 50 to 55 minutes longer or until filling is bubbly and thickened. Let cool on wire rack for at least 45 minutes. Serve slightly warm or let cool completely.

Per serving: 303 calories, 13 g total fat (4 g sat.), 7 mg cholesterol, 137 mg sodium, 45 g carbohydrate, 2 g fiber, 3 g protein.

How to
Weave lattice

1

To create a lattice top, lay half of the pastry strips over the filling at 1-inch intervals, with a slight overhang on both ends of each strip.

2

Fold every other pastry strip back halfway. Place a pastry strip across the middle, perpendicular to the first strips. Unfold the folded strips.

3

Repeat with additional pastry strips to cover top, rotating pie as needed. There will be extra pastry strips. Crimp ends of strips to crust.

Chocolate Soufflé

- 5 tablespoons superfine sugar
- ¼ cup unsweetened Dutch-process cocoa powder
- 1 tablespoon all-purpose flour
- ⅛ teaspoon ground cinnamon
- ¼ cup milk
- 2 tablespoons unsalted butter, cut up
- 2 egg yolks
- ½ teaspoon vanilla extract
- 3 egg whites
- ⅛ teaspoon cream of tartar
- ⅛ teaspoon salt
  Confectioners' sugar

1. Coat a 1- to 1½-quart soufflé dish with nonstick cooking spray. Using 1 tablespoon superfine sugar, coat all areas of dish. Set aside. In a small saucepan, whisk together cocoa powder, flour and cinnamon; whisk in milk. Over low heat, whisk in butter. Continue to cook, whisking constantly, for 2 to 3 minutes or until consistency of sour cream. Remove from heat. Place yolks in small bowl. Whisk in vanilla. Whisk in a heaping spoonful of the cocoa mixture. Whisk yolk mixture back into saucepan until smooth. Transfer to a large bowl.

2. In a second clean large bowl, with an electric mixer on medium to high speed, beat egg whites, cream of tartar and salt until frothy. Add remaining 4 tablespoons superfine sugar, 1 tablespoon at a time, beating until firm, glossy peaks form. Gently whisk about one-third of the egg whites into cocoa-yolk mixture. Gently fold in remaining egg whites.

3. Transfer batter to prepared dish. Bake at 350° for 22 to 25 minutes or until top is dry but cracks look moist. Dust with confectioners' sugar.

Once you master the technique, you'll want to make this extraordinary low-cal dessert all the time.

PREP: 20 minutes
BAKE: at 350° for 22 to 25 minutes
MAKES: 4 servings

Per serving: 167 calories, 10 g total fat (5 g sat.), 124 mg cholesterol, 86 mg sodium, 20 g carbohydrate, 0 g fiber, 3 g protein.

How to
Temper, beat and fold

1

After stirring a spoonful of the cocoa mixture into egg yolks, whisk the yolk mixture back into pan.

2

Beat egg whites until frothy. Then slowly add sugar, beating until firm, glossy peaks form.

3

Gently whisk one-third of the whites into cocoa mixture. Fold in remaining egg whites until evenly blended.

Fruit-Filled Jelly Roll

Roll a tender, chiffon-like cake around a luscious fruit filling for a decadent dessert.

PREP: 20 minutes
BAKE: at 375° for 15 minutes
COOL: 10 minutes
CHILL: 2 hours
MAKES: 8 servings

Per serving: 207 calories, 7 g total fat (3 g sat.), 117 mg cholesterol, 143 mg sodium, 24 g carbohydrate, 2 g fiber, 6 g protein.

How to
Roll up cake

Spread cooled cake with filling. Arrange berries on filling, alternating rows of blackberries and raspberries. Carefully roll up cake.

Cake:
   4 egg yolks
   ⅓ cup granulated sugar
   ½ teaspoon vanilla extract
   ¼ teaspoon lemon extract
   ½ cup lemon yogurt
   6 egg whites
   ¼ teaspoon cream of tartar
   ¼ teaspoon salt
   ¾ cup cake flour (not self-rising)
       Confectioners' sugar, for dusting
Filling:
   ¼ cup heavy cream
   ⅓ cup bottled lemon curd
   28 small blackberries or 14 large
       blackberries, each halved
   28 small raspberries

1. **Cake:** Heat oven to 375°. Line bottom of 15×10×1-inch jelly-roll pan with waxed paper. Lightly coat paper with nonstick cooking spray.

2. In large bowl, beat egg yolks, granulated sugar, vanilla and lemon extract 2 minutes or until lemon color. Add yogurt; beat until smooth.

3. In large bowl with clean beaters, beat egg whites on medium-high speed until foamy. Beat in cream of tartar and salt; beat about 3 minutes or until firm and glossy peaks form. Stir one-third of the beaten egg whites into egg yolk mixture to lighten. Fold in remaining beaten egg whites. Sift cake flour over batter; fold in. Scrape into prepared pan; smooth top.

4. Bake at 375° for 15 minutes or until light golden and center springs back when touched. Cool in pan on wire rack 10 minutes. Dust clean kitchen towel with 2 tablespoons confectioners' sugar. Turn cake out onto towel; dust with additional confectioners' sugar. Roll up cake with towel. Place, seam side down, on wire rack; cool.

5. **Filling:** In a small bowl, beat cream until stiff peaks form. Fold in lemon curd. Refrigerate until ready to assemble (up to 1 hour).

6. **Assembly:** Unroll cake. Spread with filling; leave ¼-inch border at one short end. Beginning at short end of cake without border, arrange alternate rows of blackberries and raspberries (7 berries per row), spacing rows ½ inch apart (8 rows total, 4 of each berry). Carefully roll up cake without towel. Wrap cake roll in plastic wrap; refrigerate at least 2 hours. Unwrap cake; dust with confectioners' sugar before serving.

Chocolate Ganache Cake

Cake:
- ½ cup (1 stick) butter, at room temperature
- ⅔ cup granulated sugar
- ⅓ cup packed light-brown sugar
- 5 eggs
- 1 can (16 ounces) chocolate syrup
- 2 teaspoons vanilla extract
- 1 teaspoon almond extract
- 1¼ cups all-purpose flour
- ⅛ teaspoon salt

Ganache:
- 1 cup heavy cream
- 1 teaspoon instant espresso coffee powder
- 1 tablespoon almond-flavored liqueur (optional)
- ½ pound semisweet chocolate, chopped
- ¾ cup sliced almonds, toasted, for garnish

1. **Cake:** Heat oven to 325°. Coat 9×2-inch round cake pan (straight sided) with nonstick cooking spray. Line bottom with waxed paper; coat waxed paper with nonstick cooking spray.

2. In large bowl, with electric mixer on medium-high speed, beat butter about 1 minute or until fluffy. Add both sugars; beat about 3 minutes or until smooth. Add eggs, one at a time, beating well after each addition. Add chocolate syrup, vanilla and almond extract; beat for 1 minute. On low speed, beat in flour and salt; beat on medium speed for 1 minute. Pour batter into prepared pan.

3. Bake at 325° for 55 to 60 minutes or until wooden toothpick inserted in center comes out clean. Let cake cool in pan on wire rack for 15 minutes. Turn cake out onto rack; remove paper (keep bottom side up). Cool completely.

4. **Ganache:** In small saucepan, bring cream to a boil. Stir in espresso powder to dissolve. Stir in almond liqueur, if using. Place chocolate in medium-size bowl. Pour hot cream mixture over top; let stand for 1 minute. Stir until very smooth. Cover; refrigerate about 45 minutes or until good spreading consistency.

5. Place cooled cake on wire rack over baking pan. (The smooth bottom becomes the top. Do not turn it right side up.) Spread ganache over side, then pour ganache over the top of the cake. Spread the ganache evenly over the top.

6. Before ganache sets, press almonds onto the side of the cake, using enough to cover. Refrigerate for at least 1 hour or overnight.

Make this restaurant-quality chocolate cake the star of your dessert tray.

PREP: 35 minutes
BAKE: at 325° for 55 to 60 minutes
COOL: 15 minutes
CHILL: ganache for 45 minutes; frosted cake for 1 hour or overnight
MAKES: 16 servings

Per serving: 383 calories, 21 g total fat (11 g sat.), 102 mg cholesterol, 62 mg sodium, 46 g carbohydrate, 2 g fiber, 6 g protein.

How to
Spread ganache

With an offset metal spatula, spread ganache evenly over the side of the cake.

Crème Brûlée

½ vanilla bean
2 cups half-and-half
2 eggs
2 egg yolks
⅓ cup granulated sugar
¼ cup turbinado sugar (such as Sugar in the Raw)

1. Heat oven to 325°. Place six 4- to 6-ounce ramekins in a large baking pan.

2. With tip of sharp paring knife, slit open vanilla bean and scrape out seeds. Place seeds in small, heavy-bottomed saucepan with half-and-half (save bean for another use). Heat just until small bubbles appear at the edge of the pan. Remove from heat.

3. In medium-size bowl, whisk together eggs, egg yolks and granulated sugar. Whisk a small amount of the warm half-and-half into egg mixture. Whisk egg mixture back into half-and-half in saucepan. Return to medium-low heat and cook for 7 to 8 minutes, stirring, until mixture coats the back of a spoon.

4. Divide mixture evenly among ramekins. Pour hot water halfway up sides of ramekins. Bake at 325° for 18 to 22 minutes or until custards are set but still jiggly in centers. Remove ramekins from baking pan; cool completely. Refrigerate until just before serving.

5. To serve: Remove ramekins from refrigerator. Heat broiler. Sprinkle each ramekin with 2 teaspoons turbinado sugar. Place under broiler for 2 to 3 minutes (depending on your oven) or just until sugar melts; watch carefully so sugar doesn't burn. Cool slightly and serve.

With just a handful of ingredients yet over-the-moon results, Crème Brûlée is one of the most magical desserts in the world.

PREP: 10 minutes
COOK: 7 to 8 minutes
BAKE: at 325° for 18 to 22 minutes
BROIL: 2 to 3 minutes
MAKES: 6 servings

Per serving: 224 calories, 11 g total fat (6 g sat.), 182 mg cholesterol, 67 mg sodium, 22 g carbohydrate, 0 g fiber, 6 g protein.

How to
Whisk, bake and top

Whisk some of the warm half-and-half into the egg mixture.

Make a water bath by pouring hot water halfway up the sides of the ramekins in the baking pan.

Sprinkle turbinado sugar on baked custards. Broil just until sugar melts.

Chocolate-Cherry Truffles

48 glacé red cherries (about 8 ounces, 1⅓ cups)
2 teaspoons plus 2 tablespoons brandy, bourbon, cognac or rum
4 teaspoons vanilla extract
12 ounces bittersweet or semisweet chocolate, coarsely chopped
1 cup heavy cream
2 tablespoons butter, at room temperature
Coatings (as desired) (see Note)
½ cup unsweetened cocoa powder
½ cup confectioners' sugar
2 cups finely chopped nuts (pecans, walnuts, hazelnuts or macadamia nuts)
2 cups sweetened flake coconut

1. Line 8-inch square pan with aluminum foil. In plastic food-storage bag, mix cherries, 2 teaspoons brandy and 2 teaspoons vanilla. Let stand at room temperature for at least 12 hours or up to 2 days.

2. Food Processor Method: Place chocolate in food processor fitted with metal blade. In small saucepan, heat cream until tiny bubbles form around edge. Pour over chocolate; let stand for 10 seconds. Cover and whirl until mixture is smooth. Add butter, the 2 tablespoons brandy and the remaining 2 teaspoons vanilla. Process until smooth. (Non-Processor Method: In large bowl, pour heated cream over chocolate; let stand for 1 minute. Add butter, the 2 tablespoons brandy and the remaining 2 teaspoons vanilla; whisk.)

3. Pour chocolate mixture into prepared pan; smooth top. Refrigerate 1 hour or until firm.

4. Lift foil and chocolate from pan. Cut into 48 equal pieces. Working with one piece of chocolate and one cherry at a time (keep remaining chocolate refrigerated until needed), press each piece of chocolate around one cherry. Roll quickly between hands into a ball (mixture will be very soft). Roll truffle in one of the coatings; place on waxed paper-lined baking sheet and refrigerate. Store in airtight container in refrigerator for up to 2 weeks. To give or serve: If necessary, reroll in desired coating; place in paper cups.

Note: Quantity for each coating is enough for the 4 dozen truffles.

Whirling the mixture in a food processor makes these brandy-infused, cherry-centered truffles a snap to prepare.

PREP: 1 hour
STAND: 12 hours to 2 days
CHILL: 1 hour
MAKES: 48 truffles

Per truffle: 80 calories, 5 g total fat (3 g sat.), 8 mg cholesterol, 6 mg sodium, 8 g carbohydrate, 1 g fiber, 1 g protein.

How to
Fill truffles

Use fingers to neatly wrap a piece of chocolate around each cherry.

Offer family and friends these fancy pastries filled with a decadent mocha cream. No one will ever guess what a cinch they are to make.

PREP: 15 minutes
COOL: 5 minutes
BAKE: at 400° for 15 minutes; at 350° for 15 minutes
STAND: 15 minutes
MAKES: 12 cream puffs

Per cream puff: 231 calories, 17 g total fat (10 g sat.), 119 mg cholesterol, 93 mg sodium, 15 g carbohydrate, 0 g fiber, 5 g protein.

How to
Form dough

Add flour all at once to the butter mixture, stirring briskly until a ball of dough forms and pulls away from the side of the pan.

Cream Puffs

1 cup fat-free milk
½ cup (1 stick) unsalted butter
½ teaspoon sugar
¼ teaspoon salt
1 cup all-purpose flour
4 eggs
1 cup heavy cream
2 teaspoons freeze-dried coffee granules
6 tablespoons purchased chocolate sauce
1 tablespoon confectioners' sugar,
for dusting

1. Heat oven to 400°. In medium-size saucepan, bring milk, butter, sugar and salt to a boil over medium-high to high heat. Add flour all at once; stir until ball forms and pulls away from side of pan. Cook, stirring constantly, for 1 minute. Remove from heat; transfer to large bowl. Let cool for 5 minutes, stirring occasionally.

2. Add eggs, one at a time, beating well after each addition with wooden spoon or electric mixer set on low speed. When all eggs are added, beat well about 1 minute or until mixture is shiny and smooth. Spoon into large pastry bag without a tip. Pipe 12 puffs, each about 3 inches in diameter, onto ungreased baking sheet.

3. Bake at 400° for 15 minutes, then reduce oven temperature to 350° and bake for 15 minutes longer or until puffed and golden brown. Turn oven off; place baking sheet on wire rack. Remove puffs from sheet; poke a small hole in the bottom of each puff. Place upside down on baking sheet; return to oven and let stand for 10 minutes with door slightly ajar (this will help dry out moist inner dough). Remove to a wire rack; cool completely.

4. In large bowl, combine cream and coffee granules. Let stand for 5 minutes. Add 2 tablespoons chocolate sauce. Beat with an electric mixer or by hand until medium-stiff peaks form.

5. Cut puffs in half horizontally. Remove any moist dough from the centers. Spoon whipped cream mixture into puffs (about 2 heaping tablespoons each). Replace tops of cream puffs. Drizzle plates with remaining chocolate sauce; place puffs on top. Dust with confectioners' sugar. Serve immediately.

Outdoor Grilling

Beef Fajitas p. 193

You'll find terrific new takes on burgers,
ribs, seafood, chicken and steaks, of course,
but this chapter also taps into an innovative side
of grilling, with wings, quesadillas, polenta
and veggie melts too.

Beef Roulades with Fresh Tomato Sauce

6 thin-cut beef round steaks
  (about 1½ pounds total)
½ cup plus 2 tablespoons extra-virgin olive oil
6 tablespoons balsamic vinegar
3 tablespoons Worcestershire sauce
4 cloves garlic, chopped
½ teaspoon salt
¼ teaspoon black pepper
1½ pounds zucchini, ends trimmed
6 plum tomatoes, cored, seeded and chopped
1 tablespoon chopped fresh basil leaves

Roulade Filling:
2 tablespoons extra-virgin olive oil
6 scallions, trimmed and chopped
½ cup packaged plain dry bread crumbs
2 tablespoons grated Parmesan cheese
1 tablespoon chopped fresh basil leaves
6 slices Virginia ham (3 ounces)
6 slices fontina cheese (3 ounces)

1. Place each piece of meat between two sheets of plastic wrap and pound to ⅛ inch thick; place in plastic food-storage bag. In bowl, whisk together the ½ cup oil, the vinegar, Worcestershire sauce, garlic, salt and pepper. Add the 2 tablespoons oil to ½ cup of the vinegar mixture. Add to meat in plastic bag; seal.

2. Cut each zucchini lengthwise into quarters, then cut crosswise in half. Place in clean plastic food-storage bag with ¼ cup of the remaining vinegar mixture; seal. In large bowl, toss together tomato, basil and remaining vinegar mixture; cover. Marinate meat, zucchini and tomato in refrigerator for 3 hours to overnight.

3. **Roulade Filling:** In medium-size skillet, heat oil over medium-high heat. Add scallion; sauté for 3 minutes. Remove from heat; add bread crumbs, Parmesan cheese and basil.

4. Heat gas grill to high or prepare charcoal grill with hot coals. Remove meat from marinade; discard marinade. On one piece of meat, place one slice ham and one slice cheese; spread 2 rounded tablespoons of bread crumb mixture over top. From short end, roll up meat, jelly-roll style. Secure with wooden picks. Repeat with remaining meat, ham, cheese and bread crumb mixture. Drain zucchini.

5. Cover and grill roulades 10 minutes or until cooked through, turning every 3 to 4 minutes. Grill zucchini about 6 minutes or until tender; turn once. Serve with the tomato mixture.

Tap into an elegant and unexpected side of grilling with steak rolled around ham and cheese and an irresistible filling of basil, scallions and Parmesan cheese.

PREP: 30 minutes
MARINATE: 3 hours to overnight
GRILL: roulades for 10 minutes; zucchini for 6 minutes
MAKES: 6 servings

QUICK TIP

THE HERB EXCHANGE

When substituting dried herbs for fresh, use one-third the amount called for in the recipe. Crush the dried herbs to release their flavors. To substitute ground herbs for dried leaf herbs, use about half of the amount called for in the recipe. If possible, add dried herbs at the beginning of cooking time to allow their flavors to develop.

Per serving: 515 calories, 33 g total fat (7 g sat.), 91 mg cholesterol, 463 mg sodium, 19 g carbohydrate, 3 g fiber, 37 g protein.

Beef Fajitas

Marinade and Steak:
- ⅓ cup lime juice
- ¼ cup vegetable oil
- 1 teaspoon hot-pepper sauce
- 4 cloves garlic, minced
- 1 teaspoon dried oregano
- ½ teaspoon sugar
- ¼ teaspoon black pepper
- 1 beef flank steak (about 1½ pounds)
- 1 large sweet onion (¾ pound), cut into wedges
- 1 large sweet red pepper, seeded and cut into bite-size strips
- 1 large green pepper, seeded and cut into bite-size strips
- 12 fajita-size flour tortillas, warmed according to package directions

Garnishes (optional):
- ½ cup guacamole
- 2 tomatoes (1 pound), cored, seeded and chopped
- 1 cup shredded Mexican-flavored cheese (4 ounces)
- ½ cup sour cream
- Lime wedges

1. **Marinade and Steak:** In small bowl, stir together lime juice, oil, hot-pepper sauce, garlic, oregano, sugar and black pepper. Place steak in large plastic food-storage bag. Place onion and peppers in second bag. Divide marinade between the two bags (about ⅓ cup in each); seal bags and turn to coat steak and vegetables. Marinate in refrigerator several hours to overnight, turning bags occasionally.

2. Heat gas grill to high or prepare charcoal grill with hot coals. Remove meat and vegetables from plastic bags; discard marinade.

3. Grill onions and peppers about 10 minutes or until tender, turning over about halfway through cooking time. Grill meat for 17 to 21 minutes or until internal temperature registers 145° on instant-read meat thermometer inserted in center of meat, turning over halfway through cooking time.

4. Place meat on cutting board. When cool enough to handle, cut into thin strips. Arrange meat and vegetables on platter; serve with tortillas.

5. **Garnishes:** If desired, serve meat and vegetables with guacamole, tomato, cheese, sour cream and lime wedges.

Who doesn't love fajitas? You get to choose what goes inside as well as what goes on top.

PREP: 10 minutes
MARINATE: several hours to overnight
GRILL: vegetables for 10 minutes; meat for 17 to 21 minutes
MAKES: 6 servings (2 fajitas each)

QUICK TIP

KIDS AND MANNERS

There's no better way to teach table manners to children than to eat meals with them every day. When you practice good table manners yourself, your kids will learn by example. Such skills will benefit them greatly as they mature.

Per serving: 583 calories, 29 g total fat (8 g sat.), 77 mg cholesterol, 680 mg sodium, 43 g carbohydrate, 4 g fiber, 37 g protein.

Blue Cheese Steaks with Grilled Zucchini Salad

- ⅓ cup balsamic vinegar
- 1 tablespoon coarse-grain mustard
- 1 teaspoon honey
- 1 clove garlic, finely chopped
- ½ teaspoon salt
- ¼ teaspoon black pepper
- ¼ teaspoon dried thyme
- ⅓ cup extra-virgin olive oil
- 6 ounces blue cheese, crumbled (about 1½ cups)
- 4 bone-in beef shell steaks (about 1¾ pounds total, ½ inch thick) (see Note)
- 2 zucchini, halved crosswise, then cut lengthwise into slices
- 6 ounces assorted baby leafy greens or packaged salad blend
- ½ red onion, halved and thinly sliced

1. In small bowl, whisk balsamic vinegar, mustard, honey, garlic, salt, pepper and thyme. Gradually whisk in oil until well blended. Stir in ½ cup of the crumbled cheese, mashing slightly. Remove ⅔ cup of the vinegar mixture to plastic food-storage bag. Add the steaks; seal. Turn to coat; marinate for 10 minutes.

2. Heat gas grill to high or prepare charcoal grill with hot coals.

3. In medium-size bowl, gently toss zucchini and 2 tablespoons of the remaining vinegar mixture.

4. Remove the steaks from marinade; discard marinade. Grill steaks for 5 minutes. Flip over. Top each with 1½ tablespoons of the remaining crumbled cheese. Grill about 5 minutes longer or until internal temperature registers 145° (medium rare) on instant-read meat thermometer inserted in centers of steaks. Remove to platter.

5. Grill zucchini slices about 2 minutes per side or until tender.

6. In large bowl, toss together greens, red onion, zucchini, remaining vinegar mixture and remaining crumbled cheese. Serve salad alongside grilled steaks.

Note: Shell steaks are called by a variety of names including skirt steak, Kansas City strip and the New York strip. This cut is what is left when the tenderloin strip is cut from the short loin.

The deep, rich combo of balsamic vinegar and blue cheese takes grilled steak to another level.

PREP: 15 minutes
MARINATE: 10 minutes
GRILL: steaks for 10 minutes; zucchini for 4 minutes
MAKES: 4 servings

QUICK TIP

TOSSING SALAD GREENS

Ever toss a salad and have many of the greens end up on the counter? That likely has nothing to do with clumsiness and everything to do with the bowl. When tossing greens, use a larger bowl than you think you need—that way the leaves stay in the bowl.

Per serving: 596 calories, 41 g total fat (14 g sat.), 117 mg cholesterol, 1,064 mg sodium, 13 g carbohydrate, 2 g fiber, 43 g protein.

Mesquite Steak with Grilled Sweet Onions

6 beef T-bone steaks (14 to 16 ounces each)
1 can (8 ounces) tomato sauce
½ cup mesquite-flavor steak sauce
   or mesquite grilling sauce
2 cloves garlic, chopped
2 tablespoons red-wine vinegar
2 teaspoons liquid smoke
¼ teaspoon plus ⅛ teaspoon salt
⅛ teaspoon plus pinch of black pepper
2 large Vidalia or other sweet onions
   (about 1 pound total)
1 tablespoon vegetable oil

1. Place steaks in large plastic food-storage bag or glass dish. In small bowl, whisk together tomato sauce, steak sauce, garlic, vinegar, liquid smoke, ¼ teaspoon salt and ⅛ teaspoon pepper. Add to steaks in bag or dish; seal bag or cover dish. Marinate in refrigerator for at least 30 minutes.

2. Heat gas grill to medium-high or prepare charcoal grill with medium-hot coals. Cut onions into ⅓-inch-thick slices. Secure onion slices with metal skewers to keep rings from separating. Brush with oil and season with the remaining ⅛ teaspoon salt and the pinch of pepper.

3. Drain steaks, reserving marinade. Grill steaks, covered, for 5 minutes. Transfer marinade to small saucepan; bring to a boil. Boil for 3 minutes; set aside.

4. Flip over steaks; add onions to grill. Grill steaks for 5 to 6 minutes longer or until internal temperature registers 145° (medium rare) on instant-read meat thermometer inserted in centers of steaks. Grill onions about 8 minutes or until done, turning once.

5. Remove steaks from grill; let stand for 10 minutes. Meanwhile, remove skewers from onion slices and separate into rings. Serve steaks with onions and boiled marinade.

No need to fuss with wood chips—the mesquite flavoring here comes from a convenient bottle of steak sauce.

PREP: 10 minutes
MARINATE: 30 minutes
GRILL: steak for 10 to 11 minutes; onions for 8 minutes
STAND: 10 minutes
MAKES: 6 servings

QUICK TIP

WINE WITH BARBECUE

Syrah (also called Shiraz) and Zinfandel both have a good mix of fruit and spice that meshes well with steaks coming off the grill. However, when the heat rises, leave the higher-alcohol Zins on the shelf—they may be too heavy for the hottest summer nights.

Per serving: 777 calories, 54 g total fat (20 g sat.), 147 mg cholesterol, 782 mg sodium, 19 g carbohydrate, 1 g fiber, 52 g protein.

Maple-Glazed Beef with Spiced Couscous

Maple-Glazed Beef:
- 1 cup maple syrup
- ½ cup cider vinegar
- 2 tablespoons soy sauce
- 1 teaspoon Chinese five-spice powder
- ¾ teaspoon red pepper flakes
- 1 beef flank steak (1½ pounds)
- 2 teaspoons cornstarch

Spiced Couscous:
- 1 can (14 ounces) chicken broth
- ¼ cup water
- 1 medium-size carrot, peeled and finely chopped
- ⅓ cup seedless golden raisins
- 1 tablespoon vegetable oil
- ½ teaspoon Chinese five-spice powder
- 1 box (10 ounces) plain couscous
- 2 scallions, trimmed and finely chopped
  Scallions, trimmed (optional)

You'll be amazed at how well an American favorite—maple syrup—complements classic Asian ingredients.

PREP: 20 minutes
SOAK: 30 minutes
MARINATE: 30 minutes to 1 hour
GRILL: 2 to 3 minutes
COOK: about 5 minutes
STAND: 5 minutes
MAKES: 6 servings

1. **Maple-Glazed Beef:** Soak twenty-four 10-inch bamboo skewers in enough hot water to cover for 30 minutes. In large plastic food-storage bag or large glass dish, combine maple syrup, vinegar, soy sauce, five-spice powder and red pepper flakes. Add steak; seal bag or cover bowl. Marinate in refrigerator for 30 minutes to 1 hour, turning occasionally.

2. Remove steak from marinade, letting excess drip back into container. Place steak on cutting board. Transfer marinade to saucepan. Slice steak diagonally across grain into ¼-inch-thick slices. Thread onto skewers.

3. Stir cornstarch into marinade in saucepan. Bring to boil; boil 3 minutes. Reserve half of the marinade for serving and half for basting.

4. Heat gas grill to high or prepare charcoal grill with hot coals. Brush skewers lightly with heated marinade. Grill skewers for 2 to 3 minutes or until beef is no longer pink, turning once and brushing with marinade halfway through grilling. Discard remainder of marinade used for basting.

5. **Spiced Couscous:** Meanwhile, in medium-size saucepan, bring chicken broth, water, carrot, raisins, oil and five-spice powder to a boil. Stir in couscous; remove from heat and cover saucepan. Let stand for 5 minutes. Fluff with fork. Stir in chopped scallion. Serve couscous with meat skewers and the reserved marinade. If desired, serve with additional scallions.

Per serving: 516 calories, 10 g total fat (3 g sat.), 41 mg cholesterol, 700 mg sodium, 84 g carbohydrate, 3 g fiber, 23 g protein.

BBQ Bacon Cheeseburger

BBQ Sauce:
- ¾ cup tomato sauce
- ⅓ cup cider vinegar
- ⅓ cup packed dark-brown sugar
- 3 tablespoons Worcestershire sauce
- 3 tablespoons sweet pickle relish
- ½ teaspoon garlic powder
- ¼ teaspoon black pepper

Burgers:
- 8 strips bacon (about 8 ounces)
- 1¾ pounds ground beef (91% lean)
- ½ teaspoon garlic powder
- ¼ teaspoon black pepper
- 6 slices reduced-fat American cheese
- 6 hamburger buns, sliced
- 1 head Boston or green leaf lettuce
- 1 large tomato, sliced
- 1 red onion, thinly sliced

1. **BBQ Sauce:** In medium-size saucepan, combine tomato sauce, vinegar, brown sugar, Worcestershire sauce, pickle relish, garlic powder and pepper. Heat over medium-high heat until bubbly. Cook for 5 minutes. Set sauce aside.

2. Heat gas grill to medium-high heat or prepare charcoal grill with medium-hot coals.

3. **Burgers:** In large skillet, cook bacon over medium-high heat about 5 minutes or just until crisp. Cool on paper towel-lined plate, then crumble. In large bowl, combine ½ cup of the BBQ Sauce, the bacon, ground beef, garlic powder and pepper. Mix until well mixed; shape into six patties, each ¾ inch thick.

4. Grill burgers for 10 minutes, turning once. Top with cheese and continue to grill for 1 minute longer or until internal temperature registers 160° on instant-read meat thermometer inserted in centers of burgers. Meanwhile, prepare buns: Spread some of the BBQ Sauce onto buns followed by a lettuce leaf, tomato and onion. Top each with cooked burger, then spread with a little more of the BBQ Sauce. Serve with remaining BBQ Sauce.

A juicy burger is even better with a special brown sugar-and-cider vinegar sauce.

PREP: 20 minutes
GRILL: 11 minutes
MAKES: 6 burgers

QUICK TIP

BURGERS ARE #1!

If you went straight to the burger recipe in this grilling chapter, you're not alone! According to a recent survey, America's number-one favorite food to grill is burgers, followed by steak, chicken, hot dogs and ribs. Remember that fun fact when coming up with a crowd-pleasing menu for your next get-together.

Per burger: 572 calories, 21 g total fat (9 g sat.), 56 mg cholesterol, 1,118 mg sodium, 54 g carbohydrate, 3 g fiber, 41 g protein.

Honey-Mustard Ribs

A mustardy rub does double duty as a base for a rich honey sauce.

PREP: 15 minutes
BAKE: at 425° for 1¼ hours
GRILL: 9 to 10 minutes
MAKES: about 28 ribs (2 full racks)

Per rib: 193 calories, 13 g total fat (4 g sat.), 48 mg cholesterol, 241 mg sodium, 9 g carbohydrate, 1 g fiber, 10 g protein.

Rub:
- ¼ cup dry mustard
- ¼ cup paprika
- 1 tablespoon dried oregano
- 1 tablespoon plus 1 teaspoon seasoned salt
- 1 tablespoon sugar
- 2 teaspoons black pepper

Ribs:
- 2 full racks baby back pork ribs (5 to 6 pounds total)
- 2 tablespoons all-purpose flour

Honeyed Sauce:
- ¾ cup honey
- ¾ cup cider vinegar
- 1 tablespoon cold water
- 1 teaspoon cornstarch

1. **Heat oven to 425°. Rub:** In small bowl, stir together dry mustard, paprika, oregano, seasoned salt, sugar and pepper.

2. **Ribs:** Remove rib racks from packaging and rinse in cool water. Pat dry with paper towels. Turn over ribs so they curve upward (meaty sides down). Insert a small knife under the edge of the thin white membrane, then grip membrane with a paper towel and remove from ribs. Discard and repeat with second rack.

3. Season ribs with ⅓ cup of the dry rub, pressing into ribs with your hands. Sprinkle flour into a heavy-duty foil oven bag set in a jelly-roll pan. Add ribs to bag; fold up edge to seal tightly.

4. Bake at 425° for 1¼ hours.

5. **Honeyed Sauce:** In small saucepan, combine the remaining dry rub, the honey and vinegar. Bring to a boil over high heat. Reduce heat to medium; simmer for 6 minutes, stirring frequently. In small bowl, stir together water and cornstarch. Add to saucepan, stirring constantly. Cook for 4 minutes longer.

6. Heat gas grill to medium-high or prepare charcoal grill with medium-hot coals. Carefully remove ribs from foil bag because steam will be escaping. Grill ribs for 9 to 10 minutes, turning and basting with sauce every 3 to 4 minutes. Serve with the remaining sauce on the side.

Pork Medallions with Sweet Chili Sauce

½ cup bottled chili sauce (such as Heinz brand)
½ cup peach preserves
2 tablespoons peach-flavored brandy or orange juice
2 tablespoons Dijon mustard
½ teaspoon salt
¼ teaspoon black pepper
8 boneless pork loin chops (about 1¼ pounds total)

1. In medium-size bowl, stir together chili sauce, preserves, brandy, mustard, salt and pepper. Pour ½ cup of the chili sauce mixture into plastic food-storage bag; add pork chops. Seal; turn pork chops to coat. Marinate in refrigerator for 1 hour. Reserve remaining chili sauce mixture for serving.

2. Heat gas grill to high or prepare charcoal grill with hot coals. Remove pork chops from marinade; discard marinade.

3. Grill pork chops, covered, about 5 minutes or until internal temperature registers 160° on instant-read meat thermometer inserted in centers of chops. Turn chops once during grilling. Serve with the reserved chili sauce mixture.

Peach preserves bring an intriguing fruitiness to a zippy mixture that works both as a marinade and as a sauce to pass.

PREP: 10 minutes
MARINATE: 1 hour
GRILL: 5 minutes
MAKES: 4 servings

QUICK BITE

A MULTIPURPOSE MUSTARD

Originally from the Burgundy region of France, Dijon mustard possesses an elegant, velvety texture and a clean, sharp taste. This versatile mustard is ideal both as a condiment and in cooking. Unopened mustard should be stored in a cool place. Once open, it should be refrigerated. Mustard will lose flavor and may discolor over time, so for optimum freshness, use it promptly.

Per serving: 319 calories, 4 g total fat (1 g sat.), 78 mg cholesterol, 1,222 mg sodium, 40 g carbohydrate, 0 g fiber, 32 g protein.

Kabobs with Saté Sauce

    1 cup ketchup
    ½ cup reduced-sodium teriyaki sauce
    ¼ cup packed light-brown sugar
    ¼ cup lime juice
    2 tablespoons vegetable oil
    1 clove garlic, finely chopped
    1 tablespoon chopped fresh ginger
    1 teaspoon dark Asian sesame oil
    ¾ teaspoon red pepper flakes
    2½ pounds pork tenderloin, 2½ pounds
       boneless, skinless chicken breasts
       or 2 pounds beef sirloin
    ¾ cup creamy peanut butter
       Chopped peanuts, for garnish (optional)

Sparked with fresh lime juice, this nutty hot sauce makes your favorite kabob even better.

PREP: 15 minutes
MARINATE: 4 hours
SOAK: 30 minutes
GRILL: 6 minutes for pork, 4 minutes for chicken, or 3 to 4 minutes for beef
MAKES: 6 servings

1. In large plastic food-storage bag, combine ketchup, teriyaki sauce, brown sugar, lime juice, vegetable oil, garlic, ginger, sesame oil and red pepper flakes. Cut pork, chicken or beef into ¼-inch-thick strips; place in bag and seal. Marinate in refrigerator for at least 4 hours.

2. Soak bamboo skewers in enough hot water to cover for 30 minutes. Heat gas grill to medium-high or prepare charcoal grill with medium-hot coals. Drain meat, reserving marinade. Thread meat on skewers. Grill until done, turning once. Allow 6 minutes for pork, 4 minutes for chicken or 3 to 4 minutes for beef.

3. Meanwhile, pour reserved marinade into medium-size saucepan and bring to a boil; reduce heat to medium and cook for 3 minutes. Stir in peanut butter. Transfer to a serving bowl. If desired, sprinkle with chopped peanuts. Serve alongside skewers.

Per serving: 344 calories, 14 g total fat (4 g sat.), 123 mg cholesterol, 464 mg sodium, 11 g carbohydrate, 1 g fiber, 43 g protein.

Polenta with Sausage and Fennel

Polenta:
- 3 cups milk
- ¾ teaspoon salt
- ¼ teaspoon fennel seeds, chopped
- ⅛ teaspoon black pepper
- 1 cup yellow cornmeal
- ⅓ cup grated Parmesan cheese

Sausages and Vegetables:
- 2 tablespoons lemon juice
- 2 tablespoons extra-virgin olive oil
- ¼ teaspoon salt
- ⅛ teaspoon black pepper
- 2 small bulbs fennel
- 2 medium-size red onions
- 6 links Italian sausage (1½ pounds total)

1. **Polenta:** Line 11×7×2-inch baking pan with aluminum foil; coat foil with nonstick cooking spray. In large saucepan, bring milk, salt, fennel seeds and pepper to a simmer. Whisk in cornmeal; cook, whisking, about 3 minutes or until polenta is thick and smooth. Stir in Parmesan cheese. Spread in foil-lined pan; cover. Refrigerate about 1 hour or until firm.

2. **Sausages and Vegetables:** In large bowl, whisk lemon juice, oil, salt and pepper. Remove stalks and fronds from fennel. Leaving cores intact, cut fennel and onions into 1-inch wedges; add to the lemon juice mixture.

3. In saucepan of boiling water, cook sausages for 5 minutes. Drain; cut the sausages in half lengthwise.

4. Heat gas grill to medium or prepare charcoal grill with medium coals. Cut firm polenta into six equal pieces.

5. Grill sausages, fennel and onion for 10 minutes; grill polenta for 4 minutes, turning each item halfway through grilling. Drizzle with any remaining lemon juice mixture.

Choose sweet or hot Italian sausage links to suit your taste—or use some of each.

PREP: 20 minutes
COOK: 8 minutes
CHILL: 1 hour
GRILL: sausages and vegetables for 10 minutes; polenta for 4 minutes
MAKES: 6 servings

QUICK BITE
PRODUCE POINTERS

It looks like pale, potbellied celery, but the flavors of fennel are much more refined and fragrant. Look for crisp, clean, blemish-free bulbs with bright green, fresh-looking fronds. Store tightly wrapped, in the refrigerator, for up to 5 days.

Per serving: 473 calories, 26 g total fat (10 g sat.), 66 mg cholesterol, 1,164 mg sodium, 39 g carbohydrate, 7 g fiber, 22 g protein.

Sweet and Hot Skewered Chicken Thighs

Sauce:
- 3 tablespoons vegetable oil
- 1 medium onion, chopped
- 4 cloves garlic, chopped
- 1⅓ cups honey
- ¾ cup ketchup
- ⅓ cup lemon juice
- ¼ cup light soy sauce
- 2 tablespoons oyster sauce
- 2 teaspoons hot Asian chili paste

Skewers:
- 6 large boneless, skinless chicken thighs (about 2¼ pounds total)
- 2 sweet red peppers, cut into 1-inch pieces
- 2 green peppers, seeded and cut into 1-inch pieces
- 1 large red onion, cut into ½-inch wedges
- 1 box (8 ounces) rice noodles

1. **Sauce:** In medium-size saucepan, heat oil over medium heat. Add onion; cook for 5 minutes. Add garlic; cook for 2 minutes longer, stirring so that garlic does not burn.

2. In medium-size bowl, whisk together honey, ketchup, lemon juice, soy sauce, oyster sauce and chili paste. Add to onion mixture; bring to a simmer. Simmer, uncovered, for 15 minutes (you should have about 3¼ cups). Cover; refrigerate until ready to use.

3. **Skewers:** Place chicken in a microwave-safe glass baking dish. Cover with plastic wrap, venting in one corner. Microwave on HIGH for 5 minutes. Turn chicken over and rotate dish. Microwave for 5 minutes longer. Let chicken cool slightly, then cut into 1-inch pieces.

4. Wipe out baking dish. Place peppers and onion wedges in dish. Cover with plastic wrap and vent. Microwave on HIGH for 3 minutes.

5. On six metal skewers, evenly divide chicken pieces, peppers and onion wedges.

6. Prepare rice noodles following package directions. Drain; toss with ¾ cup of the sauce.

7. Meanwhile, heat gas grill to medium-high or prepare charcoal grill with medium-hot coals. Liberally brush skewers with some of the remaining sauce. Grill for 8 minutes, turning once and brushing with additional sauce.

8. Divide noodles among six plates. Arrange skewers over noodles. Boil any remaining sauce for 3 minutes and serve on the side.

If your family loves barbecue sauce, try this dish—it combines honey and a few Asian ingredients for a sassy kick.

PREP: 30 minutes
COOK: about 25 minutes
MICROWAVE: 13 minutes
GRILL: 8 minutes
MAKES: 6 servings

QUICK BITE

WHY NOT TRY ...

Popular in Asian cooking, rice noodles are thin noodles made from finely ground rice and water; they're usually soaked before using (unless they're going to be fried). If you can't find rice noodles, substitute capellini or vermicelli.

Per serving: 679 calories, 14 g total fat (3 g sat.), 79 mg cholesterol, 988 mg sodium, 117 g carbohydrate, 4 g fiber, 26 g protein.

Spicy Asian Wings

½ cup soy sauce
¼ cup red-wine vinegar
2 tablespoons honey
2 tablespoons extra-virgin olive oil
4 cloves garlic, minced
2 tablespoons peeled, minced fresh ginger
1½ teaspoons red pepper flakes
¼ teaspoon black pepper
4 pounds chicken wings, wing tips removed

1. In medium-size bowl, whisk together soy sauce, vinegar, honey, oil, garlic, ginger, red pepper flakes and black pepper. Add chicken wings; turn to coat. Marinate, covered, in refrigerator for at least 2 hours to overnight.

2. Heat gas grill to high or prepare charcoal grill with hot coals. Remove wings from marinade; discard marinade.

3. Grill wings, covered, for 12 to 16 minutes or until internal temperature registers 180° on instant-read meat thermometer inserted in thickest parts of wings (not touching bone). Turn wings once during grilling.

Spicy wings, a favorite appetizer, are elevated to main-dish status—perfect for a casual get-together.

PREP: 15 minutes
MARINATE: 2 hours to overnight
GRILL: 12 to 16 minutes
MAKES: 8 servings

QUICK TIP

BEST BBQ TOOLS

Reliable tools are a must for safe grilling. You will never regret investing in sturdy, long-handled tongs and brushes; look for rugged wide spatulas for handy turning of delicate foods. Pick up a long instant-read thermometer to gauge doneness. And purchase a grill pan and/or wok to put on top of the grates so small items don't fall through.

Per serving: 303 calories, 21 g total fat (6 g sat.), 94 mg cholesterol, 550 mg sodium, 3 g carbohydrate, 0 g fiber, 24 g protein.

Summertime Chicken

Chicken:
- 1 container (8 ounces) low-fat plain yogurt
- 3 tablespoons balsamic vinegar
- 8 thin-cut boneless, skinless chicken breast halves (about 1½ pounds total)

Tomato-Mozzarella Topping:
- 1 tablespoon extra-virgin olive oil
- 1 medium-size onion, cut into 16 wedges
- ¼ cup balsamic vinegar
- 2 tablespoons water
- 1 pound plum tomatoes, cored, seeded and chopped (about 4 cups)
- 1 teaspoon salt
- ½ teaspoon black pepper
- 8 ounces fresh mozzarella cheese, cut into ½-inch dice
- 1 cup loosely packed fresh basil leaves, chopped

The classic trio of fresh mozzarella, basil and tomatoes makes a summer-fresh topping for grilled marinated chicken.

PREP: 15 minutes
MARINATE: 20 minutes
COOK: about 15 minutes
GRILL: 12 to 16 minutes
MAKES: 8 servings

1. **Chicken:** In small bowl, whisk together yogurt and balsamic vinegar until well blended. In a plastic food-storage bag, combine chicken and yogurt mixture; seal and turn to coat. Marinate in refrigerator for 20 minutes.

2. Meanwhile, heat gas grill to medium-high or prepare charcoal grill with medium-hot coals.

3. **Tomato-Mozzarella Topping:** In large skillet, heat oil over medium heat. Add onion; sauté about 5 minutes or until slightly softened (the wedges will fall apart into pieces). Add balsamic vinegar and water. Bring to a simmer. Reduce heat to medium-low; cook about 7 minutes or until liquid is reduced and onion is tender.

4. Increase heat to medium-high. Add tomato, salt and pepper; cook for 2 minutes. Remove skillet from heat; let cool for 2 to 3 minutes. Stir in mozzarella cheese and basil.

5. Remove chicken from bag; discard marinade. Gently rinse chicken; pat dry with paper towels.

6. Grill for 6 to 8 minutes per side or until internal temperature registers 170° on instant-read meat thermometer inserted in centers, turning once. Serve immediately or let cool to room temperature. Serve chicken with topping.

QUICK TIP

STORE IT RIGHT

Unlike most other herbs, basil will blacken in the refrigerator. To store, cut ½ inch from the stems; store with the stems submerged in a jar of fresh water on your counter.

Per serving: 224 calories, 11 g total fat (6 g sat.), 68 mg cholesterol, 527 mg sodium, 6 g carbohydrate, 1 g fiber, 24 g protein.

Chipotle Chicken Quesadillas

1½ pounds boneless, skinless chicken thighs, rinsed and patted dry

Chipotle Marinade:
- 1 bottle (12 ounces) chili sauce
- 4 chipotle chile peppers in adobo sauce (from 7-ounce can) plus 1 tablespoon sauce
- ¼ cup lime juice
- ½ cup vinegar
- ⅓ cup packed dark-brown sugar
- ⅓ cup molasses

Quesadillas:
- 1 large sweet onion
- 2 tablespoons vegetable oil
- 16 fajita-size flour tortillas
- 8 ounces pepper-Jack cheese, shredded (about 2 cups)
- Sour cream (optional)

1. Place chicken in a large plastic food-storage bag or glass dish.

2. **Chipotle Marinade:** In food processor, blend chili sauce, chipotle chiles plus adobo sauce and lime juice. Add to chicken; turn to coat. Seal bag or cover dish. Marinate in refrigerator for 30 minutes to several hours.

3. Remove chicken to a plate; scrape off and reserve marinade. For sauce, transfer reserved marinade to saucepan. Add vinegar, brown sugar and molasses. Bring to a boil; boil for 4 minutes. Set aside until ready to use.

4. **Quesadillas:** Heat gas grill to medium-high heat or prepare charcoal grill with medium-hot coals. Cut onion into ½-inch-thick slices. Slide a skewer through each onion slice sideways to keep rings together. Using 1 tablespoon oil, brush both sides of each onion slice. Grill about 16 minutes or until lightly charred and tender, turning once. Transfer to a bowl; remove skewers. Separate into rings; cover. Set aside.

5. Grill chicken for 10 to 16 minutes or until internal temperature registers 180° on instant-read meat thermometer inserted in the thickest part. Turn chicken once during grilling. Remove to cutting board; slice thinly and place in a bowl. Stir in ½ cup of the sauce.

6. Top one tortilla with 2 tablespoons cheese, ¼ cup chicken, some onion, 2 tablespoons more cheese and a second tortilla. Brush both sides lightly with remaining 1 tablespoon oil. Grill 1 minute per side. Repeat with remaining ingredients. If desired, serve with sour cream.

Canned chipotle chiles are an instant way to lend slow-smoked intensity to cheesy quesadillas.

PREP: 30 minutes
MARINATE: 30 minutes to several hours
GRILL: onions for 16 minutes; chicken for 10 to 16 minutes; quesadillas for 2 minutes
MAKES: 8 quesadillas

QUICK TIP

EXTRA CHIPOTLES?

Few recipes call for an entire can of chipotle peppers; fortunately, you can freeze leftovers for future use. Just pack in a freezer container with a little sauce from the can. Cover, seal, label and freeze for up to 2 months, then thaw in the refrigerator when needed.

Per quesadilla: 516 calories, 22 g total fat (9 g sat.), 113 mg cholesterol, 1,093 mg sodium, 49 g carbohydrate, 3 g fiber, 30 g protein.

BBQ Chicken Quarters

If you've never made a homemade barbecue sauce, now's your chance. It's simple—and it makes all the difference.

PREP: 25 minutes
COOK: 1 hour
GRILL: 1 hour
MAKES: 8 servings

Per serving: 597 calories, 31 g total fat (10 g sat.), 220 mg cholesterol, 979 mg sodium, 26 g carbohydrate, 2 g fiber, 54 g protein.

BBQ Sauce:
- 3 tablespoons butter
- 1 large onion, finely chopped
- 1 small green pepper, seeded and finely chopped
- 4 cloves garlic, finely chopped
- 1 can (14½ ounces) diced tomatoes
- 1½ cups ketchup
- 1 cup water
- ¼ cup red-wine vinegar
- ¼ cup packed dark-brown sugar
- 2 tablespoons spicy brown mustard
- 1 tablespoon paprika
- 1 teaspoon ground cumin
- 1 teaspoon hot-pepper sauce
- ½ teaspoon salt
- ¼ teaspoon black pepper

Chicken:
- 2 whole chickens (3½ to 4 pounds each), quartered

1. **BBQ Sauce:** In large saucepan, melt butter over medium-high heat. Add onion, green pepper and garlic; sauté for 5 minutes.

2. Stir undrained tomatoes, ketchup, water, vinegar, brown sugar, mustard, paprika, cumin, hot-pepper sauce, salt and black pepper into onion mixture. Bring to a simmer over medium-high heat. Cover; lower heat to medium-low. Simmer for 30 minutes, stirring occasionally. Uncover saucepan; cook, stirring occasionally, over medium-low heat for 30 minutes longer. Remove from heat until ready to use.

3. Heat gas grill to medium-high or prepare charcoal grill with medium-hot coals. Grease grill rack. Set aside half of the BBQ sauce (2¼ cups) for serving on the side and use remaining for brushing on chicken.

4. **Chicken:** Grill the chicken, uncovered, for 10 minutes, turning once. Spoon the BBQ Sauce generously over the chicken. Cover the grill; grill the chicken for 10 minutes. Spoon on more sauce; turn the chicken over. Continue to grill, covered, spooning on more sauce and turning every 5 to 10 minutes, for 40 minutes longer or until internal temperature registers 165° on instant-read meat thermometer inserted in the thickest parts (not touching bone). (The total cooking time will be 1 hour; do not spoon any sauce over the chicken during last 10 minutes of grilling.) Serve chicken with reserved BBQ Sauce.

Chili-Rubbed Chicken Thighs

Spice Rub:
- ¼ cup paprika
- 1 tablespoon dark-brown sugar
- 2 teaspoons hot chili powder
- 1 teaspoon ground cumin
- 1 teaspoon garlic salt
- ½ teaspoon salt

Potatoes and Chicken:
- 4 baking potatoes (about 6 ounces each), scrubbed and blotted dry
- 1 medium-size onion, thinly sliced
- 4 tablespoons (½ stick) butter
- 8 bone-in chicken thighs (about 2½ pounds total)

1. **Spice Rub:** In small bowl, stir together paprika, brown sugar, chili powder, cumin, garlic salt and salt. Set aside.

2. **Potatoes:** Heat gas grill to medium high or prepare charcoal grill with medium-hot coals. Cut each potato in half lengthwise. With a paring knife, score the flesh of each potato piece in a crisscross pattern. Place one-quarter of the onion, 1 tablespoon butter and ½ teaspoon of the spice rub on one exposed surface of each potato. Re-form each potato, pressing two pieces together. Seal each potato tightly in a double layer of aluminum foil. Place foil packets on grill over indirect heat; close lid. Grill for 45 to 60 minutes or until tender.

3. **Chicken:** Remove skin from thighs. Coat both sides of chicken with remaining spice rub. Place chicken in a 13×9×2-inch microwave-safe baking dish. Cover with plastic wrap and vent in one corner. Microwave on HIGH for 10 minutes.

4. Grill thighs about 6 minutes or until internal temperature registers 170° on instant-read meat thermometer inserted in thigh (not touching bone). Turn thighs once during grilling. Serve chicken thighs with grilled potatoes.

Chicken thighs take well to an assertive rub of hot chili powder and other seasonings. Serve them with potatoes cooked in foil packets right on the grill.

PREP: 15 minutes
GRILL: potatoes for 45 to 60 minutes; chicken thighs for 6 minutes
MICROWAVE: 10 minutes
MAKES: 4 servings

QUICK TIP

GIVE IT A REST

When you're finished grilling, allow the coals to completely burn down and let the ashes cool for 24 hours before disposing of them. Also be sure to let your grill cool completely before covering or storing it—never try to move it while it's still hot.

Per serving: 624 calories, 28 g total fat (12 g sat.), 162 mg cholesterol, 886 mg sodium, 53 g carbohydrate, 6 g fiber, 41 g protein.

Honey-Mustard Chicken

For family-pleasing appeal, you can't go wrong with chicken breasts brushed with a creamy honey-mustard sauce.

PREP: 15 minutes
MARINATE: 2 hours to overnight
GRILL: 10 to 12 minutes
MAKES: 6 servings

QUICK TIP

THE BEAUTY OF BUTTERMILK

A great marinade from the dairy case? Yes! Marinating chicken in buttermilk, which has a mild tang, helps keep the bird moist while adding flavor.

Marinade:
- 2 cups buttermilk
- ¼ teaspoon salt
- ¼ teaspoon black pepper
- Pinch of cayenne pepper
- 6 boneless, skinless chicken breast halves (about 2¼ pounds total)

Sauce:
- ¼ cup light mayonnaise
- ¼ cup honey
- ¼ cup Dijon mustard
- ¼ teaspoon dried thyme
- Fresh parsley leaves, chopped, for garnish (optional)

1. **Marinade:** In large plastic food-storage bag or glass dish, combine buttermilk, salt, black pepper and cayenne pepper. Add chicken; turn to coat. Seal bag or cover dish. Marinate in the refrigerator for 2 hours to overnight.

2. Heat gas grill to medium or prepare charcoal grill with medium-hot coals. Remove chicken from marinade and pat dry with paper towels; discard marinade. Grill for 8 minutes, turning chicken once during grilling.

3. **Sauce:** In small bowl, mix mayonnaise, honey, mustard and thyme until smooth.

4. Place chicken on a plate or shallow dish; brush with some of the honey-mustard sauce. Return to grill for 2 to 4 minutes or until internal temperature registers 160° on instant-read meat thermometer inserted in thickest part of breasts. Turn chicken once during grilling. Serve warm with remaining sauce on the side. If desired, garnish sauce with chopped parsley.

Per serving: 309 calories, 7 g total fat (2 g sat.), 105 mg cholesterol, 626 mg sodium, 17 g carbohydrate, 0 g fiber, 43 g protein.

Chicken Caesar Burgers

1 egg
1 pound ground chicken
1 cup fresh bread crumbs (2 slices)
¼ cup grated Parmesan cheese
2 teaspoons anchovy paste
1 teaspoon lemon juice
1 teaspoon Worcestershire sauce
1 clove garlic, finely chopped
¼ teaspoon black pepper
½ cup sour cream
½ cup bottled Caesar salad dressing
4 pitas (6-inch), split open a third of the way around
  Tomato slices (optional)
  Shredded romaine lettuce

1. Heat gas grill to medium-high or prepare charcoal grill with medium-hot coals.

2. Beat egg in large bowl. Mix in chicken, bread crumbs, Parmesan cheese, anchovy paste, lemon juice, Worcestershire sauce, garlic and pepper.

3. Between sheets of waxed paper coated with nonstick cooking spray, flatten rounded ½ cup mixture to 5-inch patty, making four burgers.

4. Grill burgers about 6 minutes or until internal temperature registers 165° on instant-read meat thermometer inserted in centers of burgers. Turn burgers once during grilling.

5. In small bowl, combine sour cream and dressing. In each pita, place a burger and, if desired, a tomato slice. Add some of the sour cream mixture and lettuce.

Chicken Caesar salad has become a restaurant favorite over the years, so it figures that Caesar salad dressing would taste great with grilled chicken patties.

PREP: 15 minutes
GRILL: 6 minutes
MAKES: 4 burgers

QUICK TIP

PREPPING ROMAINE

To prepare romaine lettuce, cut off the bottom core. Rinse the leaves in cold water and pat dry. The leaves can be stored in a plastic bag in the refrigerator for up to 5 days. Before using, remove the fibrous rib from each leaf. A one-pound head of romaine yields about 10 cups torn lettuce.

Per burger: 538 calories, 28 g total fat (7 g sat.), 167 mg cholesterol, 1,328 mg sodium, 36 g carbohydrate, 2 g fiber, 34 g protein.

Grilled Mango Chicken

Chicken:
- ½ cup mango nectar
- 6 tablespoons extra-virgin olive oil
- ¼ cup lime juice
- 2 cloves garlic, minced
- 1 tablespoon sugar
- ½ teaspoon salt
- 6 boneless, skinless chicken breast halves (about 2½ pounds total)

Mango Salsa:
- 1 mango
- 1 medium-size cucumber
- 1 firm, ripe avocado
- 1 jalapeño chile, seeded
- 2 tablespoons extra-virgin olive oil
- 2 tablespoons lime juice
- 1 tablespoon chopped fresh cilantro leaves
- ½ teaspoon salt

1. **Chicken:** In medium-size bowl, combine mango nectar, oil, lime juice, garlic, sugar and salt. Place chicken breast halves and mango mixture in large plastic food-storage bag; seal. Marinate in refrigerator for 2 hours.

2. **Mango Salsa:** Meanwhile, peel and dice mango, cucumber and avocado. Finely chop jalapeño. In large bowl, combine mango, cucumber, avocado, jalapeño, oil, lime juice, cilantro and salt. Refrigerate until serving.

3. Heat gas grill to high or prepare charcoal grill with hot coals. Remove chicken from marinade; discard marinade. Grill about 12 minutes or until internal temperature registers 160° on instant-read meat thermometer inserted in thickest part of breasts. Turn chicken once during grilling. Serve with Mango Salsa.

Mango nectar and fruit add a refreshing, exotic accent to a dish that will taste great on a hot summer night.

PREP: 20 minutes
MARINATE: 2 hours
GRILL: 12 minutes
MAKES: 6 servings

QUICK TIP

PRODUCE POINTERS

- Gently press against a mango with your thumb; it should give slightly. The stem end should smell fresh and sweet.
- If firm and green, leave the mango out on the counter to ripen. Do not refrigerate.

Per serving: 493 calories, 28 g total fat (5 g sat.), 104 mg cholesterol, 487 mg sodium, 16 g carbohydrate, 1 g fiber, 41 g protein.

Smoked Turkey Breast

Brine:
- ½ cup kosher or coarse salt
- ½ cup packed dark-brown sugar
- 1 cup hot water
- 3 cups cold water
- 1 medium-size onion, halved and thinly sliced
- 2 cloves garlic, slightly crushed
- 1 jalapeño chile, seeded and sliced
- 1 tablespoon chili powder
- 1 teaspoon ground cumin
- 12 whole black peppercorns

Turkey:
- 1 whole turkey breast, with bones and skin (about 5 pounds)
- 1½ cups mesquite wood chips
- Grilled Corn Salsa (recipe follows) (optional)

1. **Brine:** In large bowl, combine salt and brown sugar. Add hot water; stir to dissolve salt and sugar. Stir in cold water, onion, garlic, jalapeño, chili powder, cumin and peppercorns.

2. **Turkey:** Place turkey and brine in 2-gallon plastic food-storage bag; seal bag. Marinate in refrigerator overnight, turning occasionally.

3. Soak wood chips following package directions.

4. Remove turkey breast from brine; pat dry. Discard brine. Drain wood chips; place in small aluminum foil pan. Heat gas grill for indirect grilling with foil pan or prepare charcoal grill with hot coals arranged for indirect grilling, placing foil pan with chips in corner of grill and over direct heat. Grill is ready when chips begin to smoke (about 5 minutes). Grill turkey, breast side up, over indirect heat, covered, about 1½ hours or until internal temperature registers 160° on instant-read meat thermometer inserted in thickest part (not touching bone). Let turkey stand for 10 minutes before carving. If desired, serve with Grilled Corn Salsa.

Grilled Corn Salsa: Heat gas grill to high or prepare charcoal grill with hot coals. Husk and remove silk from 4 ears corn; coat with nonstick cooking spray. Grill corn over direct heat, covered, for 3 to 4 minutes on each side. Remove from heat; when cool enough to handle, cut kernels from cobs. (You should have about 2 cups.) In bowl, combine corn; ½ medium-size sweet red pepper, seeded and chopped; 1 small red onion, chopped; 1 jalapeño chile, seeded and chopped; ¼ cup chopped fresh cilantro; 2 tablespoons lime juice; 2 tablespoons extra-virgin olive oil; ½ teaspoon salt; and ¼ teaspoon pepper.

Don't think of turkey as only a Thanksgiving staple. It can also take center stage at a summer barbecue with fresh corn salsa.

PREP: 15 minutes
MARINATE: overnight
SOAK: wood chips following package directions
GRILL: 1½ hours
STAND: 10 minutes
MAKES: 10 servings

Per serving: 292 calories, 11 g total fat (3 g sat.), 111 mg cholesterol, 774 mg sodium, 2 g carbohydrate, 0 g fiber, 43 g protein.

Grilled Turkey-Tortellini Salad

½ cup vegetable oil
¼ cup lemon juice
1 large shallot, finely chopped
2 teaspoons sugar
1 teaspoon Dijon mustard
½ teaspoon salt
¼ teaspoon black pepper
1½ pounds turkey cutlets
2 packages (9 ounces each) refrigerated cheese tortellini
2 cups packed fresh spinach leaves, torn
1 cup cherry tomatoes, halved
½ cup toasted walnuts, chopped

1. Bring a pot of salted water to a boil (to cook the tortellini).

2. Meanwhile, for dressing, in small bowl, whisk oil, lemon juice, shallot, sugar, mustard, salt and pepper.

3. Transfer ¼ cup of the dressing to plastic food-storage bag or glass dish; add turkey and turn to coat. Marinate for 15 minutes at room temperature. Reserve remaining dressing.

4. Add tortellini to boiling water; cook following package directions. Drain; rinse and drain again.

5. Prepare charcoal grill with medium-hot coals or heat gas grill to medium-high.

6. In large serving bowl, combine spinach and cherry tomato.

7. Remove turkey from marinade; discard marinade. Grill about 10 minutes or until turkey is no longer pink and juices run clear, turning once. Cut the turkey into bite-size pieces.

8. Add drained pasta to spinach mixture in bowl. Add turkey, reserved dressing and walnuts; toss to mix. Serve slightly warm or chilled.

Tortellini make this salad extra hearty and satisfying.

PREP: 20 minutes
MARINATE: 15 minutes
GRILL: about 10 minutes
MAKES: 6 servings

QUICK BITE
WHY NOT TRY ...

When you want a mellow, onionlike tinge, reach for shallots. Sometimes you have to buy them in small bags. If you have any left over, keep them in a cool, dry place as you would onions. Use finely minced shallot as a replacement for garlic in your favorite vinaigrette recipe for a softer, but very flavorful, version.

Per serving: 614 calories, 30 g total fat (2 g sat.), 99 mg cholesterol, 662 mg sodium, 46 g carbohydrate, 1 g fiber, 39 g protein.

Tuna Steaks with Tomato Sauce

- 4 tuna steaks (about 5 ounces each)
- 5 tablespoons sweet-style teriyaki sauce (such as Maui Mountain)
- 3 medium-size tomatoes (about 1½ pounds total)
- ¼ teaspoon salt
- 1 small red onion, finely chopped
- 2 tablespoons chopped fresh cilantro leaves
- 2 tablespoons lime juice
- 1 tablespoon tequila (optional)

1. Place tuna steaks in large plastic food-storage bag. Add 3 tablespoons teriyaki sauce; seal. Marinate at room temperature for 30 minutes.

2. Cut tomatoes in half; squeeze out seeds. Chop tomatoes into ½-inch pieces. Spread out on paper towels; sprinkle with salt. Cover with a layer of paper towels; let stand for 15 minutes.

3. Pat chopped tomato dry; place in medium-size bowl. Stir in the remaining 2 tablespoons teriyaki sauce, the onion, cilantro, lime juice and tequila (if using). Let stand at room temperature until ready to serve.

4. Meanwhile, heat gas grill to medium-high or prepare charcoal grill with medium-hot coals. Remove tuna from bag; discard marinade. Grill about 6 minutes or until tuna flakes easily when tested with fork, turning once. Serve tuna with tomato mixture.

Fresh tuna right off the grill is a wonderful way to end a day, even more so when it has a sprightly teriyaki-tweaked topping.

PREP: 10 minutes
MARINATE: 30 minutes
STAND: 15 minutes
GRILL: 6 minutes
MAKES: 4 servings

QUICK BITE

TUNA TERRIFIC

Firm, mild to moderately flavored tuna is a particularly good choice for cookouts because it holds its shape well when grilled. If you can't find tuna steaks, substitute swordfish or shark steaks.

Per serving: 323 calories, 9 g total fat (2 g sat.), 69 mg cholesterol, 993 mg sodium, 12 g carbohydrate, 1 g fiber, 45 g protein.

Grilled Tuna Salad Niçoise

½ pound fresh green beans, trimmed

Dressing:
  3 tablespoons balsamic vinegar
  1 teaspoon Dijon mustard
  ⅛ teaspoon garlic salt
  ⅛ teaspoon black pepper
  ¼ cup extra-virgin olive oil

Tuna Salad:
  6 tuna steaks (4 ounces each, about
    ½ inch thick)
  ¼ teaspoon salt
  ⅛ teaspoon black pepper
  1 bag (10 ounces) European salad blend
  1 can (14½ ounces) fully cooked potatoes,
    drained and sliced
  1 large green pepper, seeded and cut into
    thin strips
  ⅓ cup Niçoise olives, pitted
  4 hard-cooked eggs, peeled and cut into
    quarters
  4 plum tomatoes (about 1 pound), sliced

Can you improve on a classic? Yes—when you use fresh grilled tuna instead of the canned version in this popular salad.

PREP: 20 minutes
COOK: 6 to 7 minutes
GRILL: 5 minutes
MAKES: 6 servings

1. Heat gas grill to high or prepare charcoal grill with hot coals.

2. In medium-size saucepan of salted boiling water, cook green beans for 6 to 7 minutes or until crisp-tender. Drain beans; let cool.

3. **Dressing:** In small bowl, whisk together balsamic vinegar, mustard, garlic salt and pepper. Gradually whisk in oil until dressing is thick, smooth and well blended.

4. **Tuna Salad:** Season tuna with salt and pepper. Grill for 3 minutes. Turn tuna over; grill about 2 minutes longer or until fish flakes easily when tested with a fork. Brush with 2 tablespoons dressing. Set aside.

5. In large bowl, combine green beans, salad blend, potato slices, green pepper and olives. Drizzle remaining dressing over top; toss to coat all ingredients.

6. Equally divide the salad among six plates. Add one tuna steak to each plate. Divide hard-cooked egg quarters and tomato slices among the plates.

QUICK TIP

THE FRESHNESS TEST

Did you know that a fresh egg will sink in a glass of water? If it stands upright, use it soon. If it floats in water, toss it!

Per serving: 342 calories, 17 g total fat (3 g sat.), 193 mg cholesterol, 542 mg sodium, 16 g carbohydrate, 4 g fiber, 31 g protein.

Halibut Chimichurri

Chimichurri Sauce:
- ½ cup extra-virgin olive oil
- ⅓ cup lime juice
- ½ small onion, chopped
- ¼ cup chopped fresh cilantro leaves
- 4 cloves garlic, minced
- ½ teaspoon dried oregano
- ½ teaspoon salt
- ¼ teaspoon cayenne pepper
- ¼ teaspoon black pepper

Halibut:
- 1 pound halibut fillet (with skin)

1. **Chimichurri Sauce:** In small bowl, mix oil, lime juice, onion, cilantro, garlic, oregano, salt, cayenne pepper and black pepper (can be made up to 3 days ahead and refrigerated, covered).

2. **Halibut:** Cut halibut fillet into four serving-size pieces. In a plastic food-storage bag, combine ⅓ cup of the Chimichurri Sauce and the halibut; seal. Reserve remaining Chimichurri Sauce. Marinate halibut in refrigerator for 30 minutes.

3. Heat gas grill to high or prepare charcoal grill with hot coals. Remove halibut from marinade; discard marinade.

4. Grill halibut, covered, about 10 minutes or until halibut flakes when tested with a fork, turning once. Serve with reserved Chimichurri Sauce.

Chimichurri is a boldly garlicky herb sauce from Argentina.

PREP: 15 minutes
MARINATE: 30 minutes
GRILL: 10 minutes
MAKES: 4 servings

QUICK BITE

HERB KNOW-HOW

Once a hard-to-find ingredient, cilantro has definitely gone mainstream! The leafy herb adds an intriguing flavor to foods that's at once lively and pungent but with a cooling finish.

Per serving: 396 calories, 31 g total fat (4 g sat.), 36 mg cholesterol., 355 mg sodium, 5 g carbohydrate, 1 g fiber, 24 g protein.

Grilled Shrimp on Brown Rice

2 cups instant brown rice
1 pound large shrimp, shelled and deveined
1 tablespoon apricot preserves
1 can (15¼ ounces) tropical fruit medley, drained with ¾ cup juice reserved
1 tablespoon rice vinegar
1 teaspoon dark Asian sesame oil
1 tablespoon vegetable oil
1 teaspoon grated fresh ginger
¼ teaspoon salt
⅛ teaspoon black pepper
1 cup grape tomatoes or cherry tomatoes, halved
1 can (8 ounces) whole water chestnuts, drained and sliced

1. Heat gas grill to high or prepare charcoal grill with hot coals.

2. Prepare rice following package directions, omitting butter and salt. Let cool.

3. Thread shrimp on six metal skewers. Brush with preserves.

4. Grill shrimp for 3 to 4 minutes or until they turn pink.

5. For dressing, in small bowl, whisk together reserved fruit juice, the vinegar, sesame oil, vegetable oil, ginger, salt and pepper.

6. In large bowl, combine cooled rice, drained fruit, tomato, water chestnuts and half of the dressing; toss to combine. To serve, place 1 cup of the rice mixture in each bowl or on each plate. Top with shrimp; drizzle with remaining dressing.

With fruity, nutty, tangy and spicy ingredients, this recipe hits all the right buttons.

PREP: 20 minutes
GRILL: 3 to 4 minutes
MAKES: 6 servings

QUICK TIP

STORE IT RIGHT

Unpeeled fresh ginger stays fresh
2 to 3 weeks in the refrigerator when wrapped loosely in a paper towel. For longer storage, place unpeeled ginger in a freezer bag and store it in the freezer. Ginger will keep indefinitely when frozen, and you can grate or slice the ginger while it's still frozen.

Per serving: 233 calories, 5 g total fat (0 g sat.), 90 mg cholesterol, 215 mg sodium, 35 g carbohydrate, 4 g fiber, 13 g protein.

Parmesan Shrimp Skewers

Seasoning:
- 2 anchovy fillets (optional)
- ¼ cup grated Parmesan cheese
- 2 tablespoons lemon juice
- 2 tablespoons white-wine vinegar
- 2 tablespoons water
- 4 teaspoons Dijon mustard
- 1 teaspoon Worcestershire sauce
- ¼ cup extra-virgin olive oil

Skewers:
- 1 pound large shrimp (about 20), shelled and deveined
- 2 each sweet red and yellow peppers, seeded and cut into 1-inch-square pieces
- Pinch of salt
- Pinch of black pepper
- 2 tablespoons grated Parmesan cheese
- 3 cups cooked white rice
- Lemon wedges (optional)

1. Heat gas grill to medium or prepare charcoal grill with medium coals.

2. **Seasoning:** In food processor or blender, combine anchovies (if using), Parmesan cheese, lemon juice, vinegar, water, mustard and Worcestershire sauce. Puree until smooth. With machine running, slowly add oil. Transfer to small measuring cup.

3. **Skewers:** In large bowl, combine shrimp, sweet pepper, half of the seasoning mixture, the salt and black pepper.

4. Skewer shrimp on four metal skewers, alternating with pieces of sweet pepper. Place any remaining sweet pepper on separate skewer. Sprinkle the skewers with 1 tablespoon Parmesan cheese.

5. Grill for 4 minutes. Flip skewers; sprinkle with remaining 1 tablespoon Parmesan cheese. Grill for 3 to 4 minutes longer or until shrimp turn pink.

6. Serve shrimp and sweet peppers over rice. Drizzle with remaining seasoning mixture. If desired, serve with lemon wedges.

If you love Caesar salad, chances are you'll appreciate the brisk mix of lemon, anchovy and Parmesan cheese in these skewers.

PREP: 15 minutes
GRILL: 7 to 8 minutes
MAKES: 4 servings

QUICK TIP

EXTRA ANCHOVIES?

When you have anchovies left over from a recipe and you won't be able to use them within 1 or 2 days, store them in moisture- and vaporproof wrap in the freezer for up to 3 months.

Per serving: 455 calories, 19 g total fat (4 g sat.), 169 mg cholesterol, 578 mg sodium, 45 g carbohydrate, 3 g fiber, 26 g protein.

Jalapeños add zip to pineapple juice for a glaze that's perfect on these kabobs.

PREP: 30 minutes
MARINATE: 1 hour
GRILL: 6 to 8 minutes
MAKES: 6 servings

Per serving: 273 calories, 3 g total fat (1 g sat.), 187 mg cholesterol, 405 mg sodium, 24 g carbohydrate, 1 g fiber, 34 g protein.

Hawaiian Kabobs

24 large shrimp (about 1½ pounds total), shelled and deveined
1¼ pounds boneless, skinless chicken breasts, cut into 1-inch pieces
Spicy Pineapple Marinade:
1 cup pineapple juice
2 tablespoons lime juice
2 medium-size jalapeño chiles, seeded and diced
Sauce:
¼ cup packed light-brown sugar
¼ cup white vinegar
4 teaspoons cornstarch
½ teaspoon salt
½ teaspoon black pepper
Kabobs:
2 cups fresh pineapple pieces (1-inch cubes)
1 large green pepper, seeded and cut into 1-inch pieces

1. In large plastic food-storage bag, combine shrimp and chicken.

2. **Spicy Pineapple Marinade:** In small bowl, combine pineapple juice, lime juice and jalapeño; add to bag. Seal; marinate in refrigerator for 1 hour.

3. Heat gas grill to medium-high or prepare charcoal grill with medium-hot coals. Soak 12 bamboo skewers for 30 minutes (if using). Remove chicken and shrimp from marinade to a large bowl.

4. **Sauce:** Pour marinade from bag into small saucepan. Whisk in brown sugar, vinegar, cornstarch, ¼ teaspoon salt and ¼ teaspoon pepper. Bring to a boil over medium-high heat. Boil for 3 minutes. Remove from heat and divide in half. Set aside half to serve with kabobs; use remaining half for basting.

5. **Kabobs:** Alternately thread the chicken, shrimp, pineapple and green pepper onto 12 metal or presoaked bamboo skewers. Season with the remaining ¼ teaspoon salt and ¼ teaspoon pepper.

6. Grill kabobs for 3 to 4 minutes. Turn over; brush with half of the basting sauce. Grill for 3 to 4 minutes longer or until the chicken and shrimp are cooked through. Serve kabobs with reserved sauce.

Quick-Fix Veggie Melts

1 medium-size eggplant (1½ pounds), cut lengthwise into 6 slices (½ inch thick)

3 yellow summer squash (¾ pound total), cut lengthwise into 6 slices (½ inch thick)

2 medium-size red onions, cut into 6 slices (½ inch thick)

1 package (10 ounces) large white mushrooms, stems removed

1 large sweet red pepper, seeded and cut into ½-inch slices

¼ cup vegetable oil

½ teaspoon salt

¼ teaspoon black pepper

Dressing:

1 tablespoon balsamic vinegar

1 clove garlic, finely chopped

1½ teaspoons light-brown sugar

½ teaspoon yellow mustard

⅛ teaspoon salt

⅛ teaspoon black pepper

3 tablespoons extra-virgin olive oil

1 large round loaf crusty bread (about 1 pound), cut into 6 slices (1 inch thick)

1 large clove garlic, peeled

½ pound fontina cheese, shredded

1. Heat gas grill to medium-high or prepare charcoal grill with medium-hot coals. Grease grill rack.

2. In large bowl, gently toss together eggplant, squash, onion, mushrooms, sweet pepper, vegetable oil, salt and pepper.

3. Grill eggplant, squash and onion for 6 to 8 minutes or until fork-tender, turning a few times. Transfer to large, clean bowl; cut up large pieces. Cover to keep warm.

4. Place mushrooms and sweet pepper in grilling basket. Grill for 6 to 8 minutes or until tender, turning a few times. Transfer to bowl with other vegetables, cutting up any large pieces.

5. Dressing: In small bowl, whisk together balsamic vinegar, garlic, brown sugar, mustard, salt and black pepper. Gradually drizzle in olive oil, whisking until thick and well blended. Add to vegetables; toss. Keep warm.

6. Grill bread slices for 4 to 6 minutes or until toasted. Rub with peeled garlic. Divide vegetables among bread slices. Top with cheese. Place sandwiches on grill over indirect heat. Grill about 5 minutes or until heated through.

Colorful grilled vegetables are tossed with a balsamic dressing, then served over toasted bread and topped with fontina cheese.

PREP: 25 minutes
GRILL: 21 to 27 minutes
MAKES: 6 servings

QUICK BITE

CHEESE, PLEASE: FONTINA

Originally from Italy, fontina has a subtle, nutty flavor that pairs well with many foods. It's a great melting cheese too. If you have any extra, tuck it between slices of bread with a thin piece of prosciutto for an Italian-inspired grilled cheese sandwich.

Per serving: 520 calories, 30 g total fat (9 g sat.), 44 mg cholesterol, 890 mg sodium, 47 g carbohydrate, 7 g fiber, 18 g protein.

Portabella Burgers with Basil

¾ cup light mayonnaise
¼ cup fresh basil leaves
4 tablespoons balsamic vinegar
½ teaspoon garlic powder
3 tablespoons extra-virgin olive oil
½ teaspoon salt
⅛ teaspoon black pepper
6 onion rolls, split
6 large portabella mushrooms (1½ pounds total), stems removed
6 slices (½ inch thick) tomatoes (from 2 large tomatoes)
1 bunch arugula, cleaned

1. In food processor, blend mayonnaise, basil, 1 tablespoon balsamic vinegar and the garlic powder. In small bowl, whisk together the remaining 3 tablespoons balsamic vinegar, the oil, salt and pepper.

2. Heat gas grill to medium or prepare charcoal grill with medium coals. Grill onion rolls, cut sides down, about 1½ minutes or until toasted. Brush mushrooms and tomato slices with some of the vinegar-oil mixture. Grill mushrooms for 16 to 20 minutes and tomatoes for 4 minutes or until tender, turning once and brushing with remaining vinegar-oil mixture.

3. Spread generous 1 tablespoon of the basil-mayonnaise mixture on each cut side of each onion roll. Evenly divide arugula among the onion roll bottoms. Top each with a portabella mushroom, a tomato slice and onion roll top. Serve immediately.

This hearty sandwich proves that meat isn't the only food that tastes great grilled and served in a bun!

PREP: 10 minutes
GRILL: about 20 minutes
MAKES: 6 servings

QUICK TIP

EXTRA ARUGULA?

Another night add any leftover arugula to other lettuces to bring a peppery accent to tossed salads. Or let the smaller, bright green leaves serve as a bed for grilled meats.

Per serving: 367 calories, 21 g total fat (5 g sat.), 10 mg cholesterol, 727 mg sodium, 39 g carbohydrate, 4 g fiber, 10 g protein.

So-Easy Baking

Apple-Raisin Sticky Buns p. 226

Think you don't have time to bake? You'll change your mind when you take a look at these tempting recipes for cakes, pies, quick breads, bars and other goodies. Many call on clever shortcuts; all are super-simple.

Tomato-Cheddar Bread

> 3 cups all-purpose baking mix (such as Bisquick)
> 1 cup shredded Cheddar cheese (4 ounces)
>   Salt
> 2 eggs, lightly beaten
> 1 can (14½ ounces) diced tomatoes, with juice
> ⅓ cup milk

1. Heat oven to 350°. Coat two 8½×4½×2½-inch loaf pans with nonstick cooking spray.

2. In large bowl, stir together baking mix, cheese and salt to taste; make a well in center of mixture. Add eggs, tomatoes and milk to well. Stir just until the dry ingredients are moistened. Divide batter evenly between the prepared loaf pans.

3. Bake at 350° about 45 minutes or until wooden toothpick inserted in centers comes out clean. Cool in pans on wire rack for 5 minutes. Remove pans. Serve warm.

This tomato-studded bread helps you turn a soup-and-salad supper into a hearty meal.

PREP: 5 minutes
BAKE: at 350° for 45 minutes
MAKES: 2 loaves (6 servings each)

QUICK TIP

CHEDDAR CHOICES

Whether to choose an aged Cheddar is a matter of personal taste. As cheese ages, it loses moisture, concentrating and sharpening its flavor. For those who love a Cheddar with deep character, a 2-year-aged variety is a good bet. However, many people prefer the cool, moist, almost buttery taste of new cheese. And, if you want neat slices for sandwiches, younger Cheddars are the way to go.

Per serving: 184 calories, 9 g total fat (4 g sat.), 46 mg cholesterol, 533 mg sodium, 20 g carbohydrate, 1 g fiber, 6 g protein.

Cumin-Cheesy Focaccia

1 sheet frozen puff pastry (from a 17.3-ounce package), thawed
2 tablespoons unsalted butter
2 medium-size onions, thinly sliced
1 teaspoon ground cumin
½ teaspoon sugar
¼ teaspoon salt
⅔ cup shredded Monterey Jack cheese

1. Heat oven to 425°. Unfold puff pastry onto baking sheet. Fold all edges over ½ inch to form border. Prick center of dough with fork. Bake at 425° for 15 minutes.

2. Meanwhile, in large skillet, melt butter over medium heat. Add onion; cook for 5 minutes. Sprinkle with cumin, sugar and salt. Cook about 6 minutes more or until onion is golden and fragrant.

3. Once crust is baked, sprinkle with cheese. Top with onion mixture; return to oven. Bake at 425° for 5 minutes. Cut into squares.

Caramelized onions and Monterey Jack cheese top a puff-pastry crust—serve it as a snack or appetizer.

PREP: 15 minutes
BAKE: at 425° for 20 minutes
MAKES: 6 servings

QUICK TIP

HANDLING FLAKY PASTRY

Because recipes made with puff pastry look so spectacular, many cooks think the pastry must be tricky to work with. It's not! The only trick is to keep it cool—if the dough becomes too warm, it will soften, making it sticky and unmanageable. Keep it frozen until you're ready to use it and thaw it no longer than the package directs before using it.

Per serving: 130 calories, 10 g total fat (5 g sat.), 21 mg cholesterol, 188 mg sodium, 8 g carbohydrate, 1 g fiber, 4 g protein.

Apple-Corn Muffins

- 2 boxes (8½ ounces each) corn muffin mix
- 2 small sweet apples (such as McIntosh, Empire or Jonagold), peeled, cored and grated
- 2 eggs
- ½ cup milk
- 3 tablespoons sugar
- 1 teaspoon pumpkin pie spice
- ½ cup chopped pecans

1. Heat oven to 400°. Coat the cups of a jumbo muffin pan with nonstick cooking spray.

2. In large bowl, combine muffin mix, grated apple, eggs, milk, 2 tablespoons sugar and the pumpkin pie spice. Stir until moistened, then divide evenly among prepared muffin cups, using a heaping ½ cup batter in each muffin cup. Sprinkle tops of muffins with remaining 1 tablespoon sugar and the chopped nuts.

3. Bake at 400° for 18 to 20 minutes or until lightly browned around edges. Slide a thin knife between muffin and pan; gently lift muffins from pan. Cool and serve.

Note: To make standard-size muffins, coat 12 cups of a standard-size muffin pan with nonstick cooking spray. Divide batter among prepared cups, using about ⅓ cup batter in each muffin cup. Sprinkle with sugar and nuts; bake at 400° for 18 minutes.

Jazz up corn muffins with a little fruit, nuts and spice—perfect with a steaming bowl of chili!

PREP: 10 minutes
BAKE: at 400° for 18 to 20 minutes
MAKES: 6 jumbo muffins

QUICK TIP

STIRRING ADVICE

After adding the liquid mixture to the flour mixture when making muffins, stir just until moistened. If you try to stir out all the lumps, your muffins will have peaks, tunnels and a tough texture.

Per jumbo muffin: 491 calories, 19 g total fat (4 g sat.), 75 mg cholesterol, 924 mg sodium, 71 g carbohydrate, 7 g fiber, 9 g protein.

Garlic-Herb Biscuits

1 head garlic
½ teaspoon extra-virgin olive oil
2¼ cups all-purpose or low-fat baking mix
   (such as Bisquick)
½ teaspoon dried minced onion
⅛ teaspoon black pepper
1 teaspoon fresh thyme leaves
⅔ cup milk

1. Drizzle whole head of garlic with oil and rub some into papery skin. Place in a microwave-safe dish and cover with plastic wrap. Microwave on HIGH for 3 minutes. Let stand, covered, for 5 minutes to soften.

2. Meanwhile, heat oven to 425°. In large bowl, combine baking mix, onion and pepper.

3. Uncover garlic and slice off top. Squeeze pulp from skin. Chop with thyme leaves, then whisk into dry ingredients in bowl. Stir in milk. Drop batter in ½-cupfuls onto an ungreased baking sheet for a total of 9 biscuits.

4. Bake biscuits at 425° for 10 to 12 minutes or until puffed and lightly browned. Remove to wire rack and cool slightly before serving.

Soften and mellow a head of garlic in your microwave, then stir the tasty pulp into the biscuit dough.

PREP: 10 minutes
MICROWAVE: 3 minutes
BAKE: at 425° for 10 to 12 minutes
MAKES: 9 biscuits

QUICK TIP

FREEZER FACTS

To freeze biscuits, scones or muffins, leave unfrosted and let them cool completely. Wrap tightly in heavy foil or place in a freezer container. Freeze for up to 3 months. Reheat, wrapped in foil, in a 300° oven. Reheat biscuits and scones for 20 to 25 minutes, muffins for 15 to 18 minutes.

Per biscuit: 139 calories, 2 g total fat (0 g sat.), 2 mg cholesterol, 209 mg sodium, 25 g carbohydrate, 3 g fiber, 6 g protein.

Apple-Raisin Sticky Buns

Topping:
- ¾ cup packed brown sugar
- 2 tablespoons unsalted butter, at room temperature
- ½ cup chopped pecans

Buns:
- ¼ cup packed brown sugar
- 1 teaspoon ground cinnamon
- 1 pound frozen bread dough, thawed
- 1 tablespoon butter, melted
- ½ cup chopped pecans
- ⅓ cup dark seedless raisins
- ⅓ cup chopped peeled apple

1. **Topping:** Lightly coat a 9-inch round cake pan with nonstick cooking spray.

2. In small bowl, stir together brown sugar and butter to make a paste. Spread over bottom of prepared pan; mixture may not cover bottom completely. Top with pecans.

3. **Buns:** In small bowl, mix brown sugar and cinnamon. On lightly floured surface, roll thawed bread dough out into 12×10-inch rectangle. Brush with melted butter. Sprinkle cinnamon mixture evenly on top, leaving ½-inch border around edge. Sprinkle pecans, raisins and apple on top.

4. Starting from a long side, roll dough up, jelly-roll style. With serrated knife, trim ends, then cut crosswise into 9 equal pieces. Place pieces, cut sides down, in prepared pan. With nonstick cooking spray, coat a piece of plastic wrap large enough to cover pan; place plastic wrap, coated side down, over buns. Refrigerate overnight.

5. Remove pan with buns from the refrigerator; let stand for 30 minutes. Heat oven to 350°. Remove plastic wrap.

6. Bake at 350° about 20 minutes or until golden. Cool buns in pan on wire rack for 5 minutes. Invert large serving platter over pan; carefully invert. Remove pan; let mixture in pan drip over buns. Serve buns warm or at room temperature.

Note: To prepare in one day: In step 4, cover buns with clean towel and let stand at room temperature for 1½ to 2 hours or until doubled in bulk. Proceed as directed.

Most of the work can be done in the evening. That way, in the morning it's easy to treat your family to warm sticky buns fresh from the oven.

PREP: 30 minutes
CHILL: overnight
STAND: 30 minutes
BAKE: at 350° for 20 minutes
MAKES: 9 buns

DRIED FRUIT DECISION

Almost any variety of dried fruit can be used in these gooey breakfast or brunch buns. Substitute golden raisins, dried cherries, dried cranberries, dried blueberries or even a mixture of dried fruit bits for the dark raisins. If you have big pieces of the dried fruit, you might want to snip them into smaller pieces.

Per bun: 382 calories, 16 g total fat (3 g sat.), 10 mg cholesterol, 292 mg sodium, 59 g carbohydrate, 4 g fiber, 7 g protein.

Cheese-and-Cherry Danishes

1 package (8 ounces) pot cheese or cream
    cheese, at room temperature (see Note)
¼ cup sugar
2 tablespoons all-purpose flour
2 teaspoons grated lemon zest
1 tablespoon lemon juice
1 teaspoon vanilla extract
2 packages (8 ounces each) refrigerated
    crescent-roll dough
¾ of 21-ounce can cherry pie filling
1 egg, lightly beaten with 1 tablespoon water
¼ cup sliced almonds

1. In medium-size bowl, stir together pot cheese, sugar, flour, lemon zest, lemon juice and vanilla with a wooden spoon until well blended and smooth.

2. Heat oven to 375°. Unroll one package of the crescent-roll dough and separate dough into four rectangles. On a lightly floured work surface, cut each rectangle in half crosswise, making two squares from each rectangle. Pinch together any perforations or holes in dough, then stretch two opposite corners of each square slightly to lengthen the dough and form the flaps that will enclose the filling. Transfer to ungreased baking sheet.

3. Spoon 1 tablespoon of the cheese mixture diagonally onto center of each square, at a right angle to stretched corners. Top with about 1 tablespoon pie filling. Fold one of the flaps across mixture. Fold other flap across, overlapping first flap. Brush each Danish with egg and water mixture. Sprinkle with some of the almonds. Continue making more Danishes with remaining dough, cheese mixture and pie filling, including the second package of dough. Brush with egg and water mixture; sprinkle with almonds.

4. Bake at 375° for 15 to 18 minutes or until golden brown. Remove to wire rack to cool.

Note: You can find pot cheese in the dairy section of some supermarkets and in specialty food shops.

Homemade Danishes that take just 15 minutes to assemble? Refrigerated crescent-roll dough makes it happen!

PREP: 15 minutes
BAKE: at 375° for 15 to 18 minutes
MAKES: 16 Danishes

QUICK TIP

COFFEE THOUGHTS

Few beverages go better with a flaky Danish than a robust cup of coffee. When making coffee, use the freshest beans possible, and grind the beans just before brewing. Buy beans in small amounts—just what you will use in a week. Store beans in an airtight container in a cool, dry place. Do not refrigerate them; moisture can damage their flavor.

Per Danish: 200 calories, 9 g total fat (3 g sat.), 17 mg cholesterol, 267 mg sodium, 24 g carbohydrate, 0 g fiber, 5 g protein.

Black-Bottom Raspberry Cheesecake

1 box (22½ ounces) brownie mix
⅓ cup water
3 tablespoons vegetable oil
6 eggs
1 cup chopped walnuts
1 package (10 ounces) frozen raspberries, thawed and drained
¾ cup seedless raspberry jam
3 packages (8 ounces each) cream cheese, at room temperature
1 cup granulated sugar
1 teaspoon vanilla extract
2 tablespoons confectioners' sugar
Fresh raspberries, for garnish (optional)

1. Heat oven to 350°. Grease bottom of 10-inch springform pan with removable bottom.

2. In large bowl, combine brownie mix, water, oil and 3 eggs. Stir in nuts. Pour into prepared pan.

3. Bake at 350° for 25 minutes. Cool on rack for 15 minutes.

4. In small bowl, combine thawed raspberries and ½ cup raspberry jam.

5. In large bowl, with electric mixer on medium speed, beat cream cheese until smooth. Add granulated sugar, vanilla and the remaining 3 eggs; beat until well blended.

6. Spoon raspberry mixture evenly over top of brownie in pan. Slowly pour cream cheese mixture on top.

7. Bake at 350° about 55 minutes or until cheesecake is slightly set in center. Remove to wire rack to cool. Refrigerate the cooled cheesecake overnight.

8. To serve, prepare raspberry drizzle. In small saucepan, heat remaining ¼ cup raspberry jam over low heat just until melted. Let cool for 10 minutes. Spoon confectioners' sugar into small sieve; sprinkle over each serving of cheesecake. Drizzle top of each serving with melted raspberry jam.

Welcome to dessert heaven! Here two favorites—brownies and cheesecake—are baked into one spectacular treat.

PREP: 20 minutes
BAKE: at 350° for 1 hour 20 minutes
COOL: 25 minutes
CHILL: overnight
MAKES: 16 servings

QUICK TIP

SWEET STIRRINGS

To further indulge guests at dessert time, offer chocolate-coated spoons when serving coffee. Dip the tips of 8 metal or plastic teaspoons into 2 ounces melted semisweet chocolate squares; refrigerate about 5 minutes or just until set.

Per serving: 490 calories, 24 g total fat (10 g sat.), 126 mg cholesterol, 286 mg sodium, 63 g carbohydrate, 4 g fiber, 10 g protein.

German Chocolate Bars

Bars:
- 1 box (17.6 ounces) brownie mix with milk-chocolate chunks
- 1 egg
- ⅓ cup vegetable oil
- ¼ cup water
- 1 teaspoon coconut extract
- ½ cup chopped sweetened flake coconut
- ½ cup chopped pecans

Frosting:
- ¾ cup sugar
- 1 can (5 ounces) evaporated milk
- 5 tablespoons unsalted butter, cut up
- 2 egg yolks
- 1 cup sweetened flake coconut
- ¾ cup chopped pecans
- ½ teaspoon vanilla extract

1. **Bars:** Heat oven to 350°. Line bottom and sides of a 13×9×2-inch baking pan with nonstick aluminum foil, leaving 2-inch overhang on the short sides.

2. In large bowl, stir together brownie mix, egg, oil, water and coconut extract just until smooth. Stir in coconut and nuts. Spoon into prepared pan, spreading to edges.

3. Bake at 350° for 20 to 25 minutes or until center is set.

4. **Frosting:** In small saucepan, combine sugar, evaporated milk, butter and egg yolks. Cook over medium-high heat, whisking, for 13 to 15 minutes or until very bubbly and thickened. Stir in coconut, nuts and vanilla; cook for 2 minutes longer.

5. After removing bar from oven, pour warm frosting over top, spreading to edges. Cool for 20 minutes on wire rack at room temperature. Chill slightly, or until ready to serve. Using foil overhang, lift bar from pan for easier slicing.

Tuck pecans into a brownie mix that bakes up into these moist bars; stud the coconut frosting with some nuts too.

PREP: 10 minutes
BAKE: at 350° for 20 to 25 minutes
COOK: 15 minutes
COOL: 20 minutes
MAKES: 24 bars

QUICK TIP

FOIL LINING TRICK

Ever have trouble getting aluminum foil to line a pan smoothly? Here's the secret: First flip the pan over and shape the foil around the outside of the pan, extending it about 1 inch past the edges, then place the foil lining in the pan.

Per bar: 244 calories, 15 g total fat (4 g sat.), 37 mg cholesterol, 168 mg sodium, 27 g carbohydrate, 1 g fiber, 2 g protein.

Apricot-Spice Upside-Down Cakes

1 tablespoon butter, for pan

Topping:
- ½ cup (1 stick) butter, melted
- ½ cup packed light-brown sugar
- 1 teaspoon ground cinnamon
- ½ teaspoon ground nutmeg
- 2 cans (15¼ ounces each) unpeeled apricots in syrup, drained, reserving ¼ cup syrup for cake

Cake:
- 1 box (18¼ ounces) spice cake mix
- 1 cup sour cream
- ½ cup (1 stick) butter, melted
- 2 eggs
- ¼ cup packed light-brown sugar
- ¼ cup reserved apricot syrup, from topping

1. Heat oven to 350°. Line two 8×2-inch round cake pans with aluminum foil; butter foil.

2. Topping: In small bowl, stir butter, brown sugar, cinnamon and nutmeg until sugar is dissolved. Spread over bottoms of pans, dividing equally.

3. Arrange a can of the apricots, cut sides down, in each pan.

4. Cake: In large bowl, combine cake mix, sour cream, butter, eggs, brown sugar and the ¼ cup reserved apricot syrup. Beat with electric mixer on low speed for 1 minute. Increase speed to medium; beat for 2 minutes. Spoon into pans, being careful not to move apricots.

5. Bake at 350° for 45 to 50 minutes or until wooden toothpick inserted in centers of cakes comes out clean. Let cakes cool in pans on wire racks for 3 minutes. Run knife around edge of cakes; carefully invert onto serving plates. Remove foil and pans. Serve cakes warm or at room temperature.

Move over, pineapple! Apricots are great in an upside-down cake too. A mix makes it easy, while sour cream makes it rich!

PREP: 15 minutes
BAKE: at 350° for 45 to 50 minutes
COOL: 3 minutes
MAKES: 18 servings
(two cakes, 9 servings each)

QUICK TIP

SPICE SAVVY

If you want the most distinctive flavor from your nutmeg, grate it yourself. First select whole, warm-brown nutmegs in a supermarket or specialty store. Rub them on the finest side of a grater. You can use a standard box grater or one designed for this purpose.

Per serving: 318 calories, 18 g total fat (10 g sat.), 66 mg cholesterol, 242 mg sodium, 39 g carbohydrate, 1 g fiber, 3 g protein.

Honey-Nut Mini Bundts

Bundt Cakes:
- 1 package (18¼ ounces) yellow cake mix
- 3 eggs
- ½ cup brewed coffee, cooled
- ¼ cup honey
- ¼ cup (½ stick) unsalted butter, at room temperature
- 1½ teaspoons pumpkin pie spice
- 1 Bartlett pear, peeled, cored and shredded (about 1 cup)
- ½ cup walnuts, chopped

Lemon Glaze:
- 1 cup canned vanilla frosting
- 1 teaspoon grated lemon zest
- 1 tablespoon lemon juice
- Chopped walnuts (optional)

1. Bundt Cakes: Heat oven to 350°. Generously coat two mini Bundt pans, each with six 1-cup indentations (preferably light pans, not dark), with nonstick cooking spray, making sure rim is well coated.

2. In large bowl, with electric mixer on low speed, beat cake mix, eggs, coffee, honey, butter and pie spice about 30 seconds or until moistened. Increase speed to medium; beat for 2 minutes. Stir in shredded pear and walnuts.

3. Spoon slightly rounded ½ cup batter into each prepared mini Bundt.

4. Bake at 350° about 20 minutes or until wooden toothpick inserted in centers comes out clean (cakes may rise over center indents).

5. Let cakes cool in pans on wire rack for 10 minutes. Turn cakes out onto wire rack; let cool completely.

6. Lemon Glaze: In small microwave-safe bowl, combine frosting, lemon zest and juice. Microwave on HIGH about 15 seconds or just until pourable. Drizzle 1 tablespoon of the glaze over each Bundt. If desired, sprinkle tops with chopped nuts. Let stand about 30 minutes or until frosting sets. Store in airtight container at room temperature for up to 3 days.

Cake mix and prepared vanilla frosting cut the prep time for these darling little baby cakes.

PREP: 15 minutes
BAKE: at 350° for 20 minutes
COOL: 10 minutes
MICROWAVE: 15 seconds
STAND: 30 minutes
MAKES: 12 mini Bundts

QUICK TIP

SPICE SAVVY

If you don't have pumpkin pie spice, substitute the following combination of spices: For each teaspoon called for in a recipe, use ½ teaspoon ground cinnamon, ¼ teaspoon ground ginger, ¼ teaspoon ground allspice and ⅛ teaspoon ground nutmeg. (For this recipe, stir together a double batch and then use 1½ teaspoons of the spice mixture.)

Per mini Bundt: 392 calories, 17 g total fat (5 g sat.), 64 mg cholesterol., 323 mg sodium, 58 g carbohydrate, 1 g fiber, 4 g protein.

Cinnamon Bread Pudding

3 Rome Beauty apples, peeled, cored and thinly sliced
1 tablespoon all-purpose flour
1 loaf (16 ounces) cinnamon-swirl bread
6 eggs
1¾ cups milk
½ cup bottled caramel sauce, plus more to drizzle
⅓ cup plus 2 tablespoons sugar
¼ teaspoon salt
   Ice cream (optional)

1. Coat a 2½-quart shallow baking dish with nonstick cooking spray. In small bowl, toss apples with flour.

2. Cut loaf of bread in half diagonally (to form triangle-shape slices). Layer half of the bread and half of the apple, overlapping, in bottom of prepared dish.

3. In medium-size bowl, whisk together eggs, milk, ½ cup caramel sauce, ⅓ cup sugar and salt. Pour half of the egg mixture over bread and apple in dish. Repeat layering, using all remaining bread and apple. Pour second half of the egg mixture over layers. Cover dish with plastic wrap; press lightly. Refrigerate to soak for 30 minutes to 1 hour.

4. Heat oven to 375°. Unwrap dish; sprinkle with remaining 2 tablespoons sugar. Bake at 375° for 30 minutes; cover with aluminum foil and bake about 15 minutes longer or until center registers 160° on an instant-read thermometer. Drizzle top with additional caramel sauce; let cool on wire rack for 15 minutes. Serve warm. If desired, serve with ice cream.

Cinnamon-swirl bread and bottled caramel sauce give you a jump-start on this old-fashioned favorite.

PREP: 20 minutes
CHILL: 30 minutes to 1 hour
BAKE: at 375° for 45 minutes
COOL: 15 minutes
MAKES: 8 servings

QUICK TIP

COFFEE WITH DESSERT

This dessert begs for a good cup of coffee to wash it down. Make Irish Coffee by adding a tablespoon or two of Irish whiskey to a cup of joe. Stir in sugar to taste and top with sweetened whipped cream. Other coffee stir-ins? Amaretto, Irish cream, coffee-flavor liqueur or good ol' half-and-half and sugar—even if you generally don't sweeten or whiten your coffee, sometimes doing so makes for a better partner with dessert.

Per serving: 378 calories, 11 g total fat (3 g sat.), 167 mg cholesterol, 451 mg sodium, 64 g carbohydrate, 5 g fiber, 13 g protein.

Golden Baked Alaska

1 **pint each strawberry and chocolate ice cream or frozen yogurt, softened**
½ **of 18-ounce tube refrigerated chocolate-chip cookie dough**
¼ **cup finely chopped toasted walnuts**
⅓ **cup pasteurized dried egg whites**
⅔ **cup warm water**
½ **cup sugar**

1. Line 1-quart round bowl with plastic wrap so there is enough overhang to cover top. Scoop one flavor of ice cream into bowl and pack, smoothing top evenly. Top with second flavor of ice cream, smoothing top. Bring sides of plastic wrap up and cover top of ice cream. Freeze several hours or overnight or until very firm.

2. Heat oven to 350°. Tear off 10-inch-wide sheet of aluminum foil. Place on large baking sheet; grease 8-inch circle in center.

3. In large bowl, combine cookie dough and walnuts with wooden spoon until well blended. (If dough becomes too soft, refrigerate about 10 minutes or until firm.) Shape dough into ball; place in center of greased foil. Pat or roll with floured rolling pin into 8-inch circle.

4. Bake at 350° for 12 to 15 minutes or until lightly browned at edges. Remove cookie, still on foil, to wire rack to cool completely. Increase oven temperature to 475°.

5. Remove bowl with ice cream from freezer; let stand until ice cream is softened enough to lift with plastic wrap from bowl—it may be necessary to loosen sides by gently running long, thin metal spatula between bowl and plastic wrap. (Also to speed loosening, you may dip bottom half of bowl into large bowl of warm water for a few seconds.)

6. In small bowl, stir dried egg whites into warm water to dissolve completely. Beat with electric mixer on high speed until fluffy. Gradually add sugar, beating until meringue forms stiff peaks.

7. Loosen cookie from foil, then return to same piece of foil. Place on cool insulated baking sheet. Lift ice cream from bowl. Fold sides of plastic wrap back from top of ice cream; invert ice cream onto center of cookie. Peel off plastic wrap. Cover ice cream with meringue.

8. Bake at 475° for 2 to 4 minutes or until meringue is lightly browned. Using wide spatula, gently slide Alaska from foil onto serving platter. Serve immediately.

Refrigerated cookie dough and pasteurized egg whites help make this always-impressive classic trick-free!

PREP: 20 minutes
FREEZE: several hours or overnight
BAKE: crust at 350° for 12 to 15 minutes; meringue at 475° for 2 to 4 minutes
MAKES: 8 servings

QUICK TIP

SAFETY & EASE

Pasteurized dried egg whites have two distinct advantages for cooks. First, because they're pasteurized, they alleviate the health concerns that come with undercooked eggs. Second, they save you from having to think of what to do with the egg yolks when your recipe calls for only the whites.

Per serving: 356 calories, 15 g total fat (7 g sat.), 27 mg cholesterol, 116 mg sodium, 51 g carbohydrate, 1 g fiber, 5 g protein.

Pear-Grape Jalousie

¼ cup plus 1 tablespoon sugar
1 tablespoon cornstarch
1½ cups red seedless grapes, halved
1 Bartlett pear, peeled, cored and cut into ½-inch pieces
1 teaspoon grated fresh ginger
⅛ teaspoon ground nutmeg
1 sheet frozen puff pastry (from a 17.3-ounce package), thawed
1 egg, lightly beaten

1. In small saucepan, stir together ¼ cup sugar and the cornstarch. Stir in grapes, pear, ginger and nutmeg. Bring to simmering over medium-high heat, stirring. Simmer about 8 minutes or until mixture has thickened. Let cool.

2. Heat oven to 400°. Cut pastry in half parallel to the fold lines. Roll out each half with a floured rolling pin on a floured surface, one into a 15×7-inch rectangle, the other into a 14×6-inch rectangle.

3. Place smaller rectangle on greased baking sheet. Spread fruit mixture lengthwise down center in a 3-inch-wide strip, leaving a 1½-inch border. Fold larger pastry rectangle lengthwise in half. Along folded edge, cut slits, about ¾ inch apart and 2½ inches long.

4. Brush edges of bottom pastry around filling with some of the egg. Top with unfolded larger pastry, pressing edges. Use tines of fork to seal. Brush top with egg. Sprinkle with the remaining 1 tablespoon sugar. Trim pastry edges with a sharp knife.

5. Bake at 400° for 20 to 25 minutes or until golden brown. Cool to room temperature.

Starting with prepared puff pastry saves time and effort; adding grated fresh ginger to the filling throws a party for your taste buds.

PREP: 20 minutes
COOK: 8 minutes
BAKE: at 400° for 20 to 25 minutes
MAKES: 8 servings

QUICK TIP

STORE IT RIGHT

To maintain the full flavors of the spices you purchase, store them in a dry place away from heat and light. Tightly close the containers after each use. To check freshness, look for a bright, appropriate color and strong aroma. Ground spices usually stay fresh for about 1 year.

Per serving: 103 calories, 2 g total fat (1 g sat.), 27 mg cholesterol, 26 mg sodium, 21 g carbohydrate, 1 g fiber, 1 g protein.

Apple Betty

1 packaged (12 ounces) all-butter loaf or pound cake

6 tablespoons (¾ stick) unsalted butter, melted

½ cup sliced almonds

1½ teaspoons pumpkin pie spice

2 pounds Rome apples, peeled, cored and thinly sliced (about 5 apples)

2 packages (4.4 ounces each) fresh blueberries, rinsed

½ cup packed light-brown sugar

2 tablespoons cold unsalted butter, cut up

1. Heat oven to 350°. Coat 11×7×1½-inch baking pan with nonstick cooking spray. Set aside.

2. Place cake in a food processor. Pulse until crumbs are formed (you may need to start with half of the cake and then add remaining half). Transfer to a large bowl. Stir in melted butter, almonds and 1 teaspoon pumpkin pie spice.

3. In second large bowl, combine apples, blueberries, brown sugar and remaining ½ teaspoon pumpkin pie spice. Toss to combine ingredients.

4. Spoon ½ cup of the crumb mixture into bottom of prepared baking dish. Top with half of the apple mixture and half of the remaining crumb mixture. Repeat, ending with crumb mixture. Dot top of crumbs with butter pieces and cover dish with aluminum foil.

5. Bake at 350° for 30 minutes; uncover and bake 30 minutes longer. Remove from oven; cool for at least 15 minutes before serving.

A betty is typically made with bread crumbs, but this one is made extra rich and buttery with cake crumbs.

PREP: 15 minutes
BAKE: at 350° for 1 hour
COOL: 15 minutes
MAKES: 12 servings

QUICK TIP

STORE IT RIGHT

Store unopened packages of nuts in a cool, dark place. Keep opened packages in an airtight container in the refrigerator for up to 6 months or in the freezer for up to 1 year.

Per serving: 284 calories, 15 g total fat (8 g sat.), 60 mg cholesterol, 150 mg sodium, 38 g carbohydrate, 2 g fiber, 3 g protein.

Caramel-Nut Brownie Delight

2 packages (21 to 22½ ounces each) brownie mix
⅔ cup chopped pecans
½ cup instant coffee crystals
1 tablespoon ground cinnamon

Caramel:
⅓ cup heavy cream
½ cup packed light-brown sugar
6 tablespoons (¾ stick) unsalted butter
2 tablespoons light corn syrup
½ teaspoon vanilla extract

Filling and Topping:
1 jar (13 ounces) chocolate-nut spread (such as Nutella brand)
⅓ cup chopped pecans
3 cups pecan halves

1. Heat oven to 350°. Lightly grease two 9-inch round cake pans. Line bottoms of pans with waxed paper. Lightly grease waxed paper. Set aside.

2. Prepare each brownie mix according to package directions for fudgy brownies, stirring ⅓ cup of the chopped pecans, ¼ cup of the instant coffee crystals and 1½ teaspoons of the cinnamon into each brownie batter. Spoon batter into the prepared pans, spreading evenly. Bake at 350° for 45 minutes. Cool completely in pans on wire racks. Loosen edges and carefully remove from pans.

3. **Caramel:** Meanwhile, for caramel, in heavy medium-size saucepan, combine cream, brown sugar, butter and corn syrup. Bring to boiling over medium-high heat, whisking occasionally. Reduce heat to medium. Boil gently for 3 minutes longer. Stir in vanilla. Transfer to a bowl. Cool completely (at least 2 hours).

4. **Filling and Topping:** Place one brownie layer, top side up, on a cake plate. Top with chocolate-nut spread, spreading evenly. Spoon ⅓ cup of the caramel over chocolate, spreading evenly. Sprinkle with ⅓ cup chopped pecans. Add the second brownie layer, top side up. Spoon remaining caramel over top of cake. Top with pecan halves. Let stand for 30 minutes before serving.

5. To serve, use a long serrated knife to cut torte into wedges.

This luscious deep chocolate showstopper is elegant enough for even the fanciest gathering.

PREP: 10 minutes
BAKE: at 350° for 45 minutes
COOL: 2 hours
STAND: 30 minutes
MAKES: 16 servings

QUICK TIP

SWEET SUCCESS

When making treats from cake or brownie mixes, for best results use salted butter, not unsalted. If whole milk is called for, don't substitute, but if the recipe just says "milk," any kind is fine. Use large eggs. Finally, if a recipe requires vegetable oil, use a light flavorless one like soybean or canola.

Per serving: 680 calories, 35 g total fat (7 g sat.), 72 mg cholesterol, 305 mg sodium, 92 g carbohydrate, 2 g fiber, 7 g protein.

Cappuccino Pecan Pie

- 1 refrigerated ready-to-use rolled 9-inch piecrust (half of 15-ounce package)
- ⅓ cup packed dark-brown sugar
- 4 eggs
- 1 jar (about 18 ounces) butterscotch or caramel dessert sauce
- 6 tablespoons instant cappuccino coffee mix
- ½ teaspoon ground cinnamon
- 2 cups pecan halves (about 7 ounces)

1. Heat oven to 350°. Unroll the piecrust into 9-inch pie plate. Turn edge under to form standup edge; if desired, decoratively crimp the edge. Crumble brown sugar in even layer over crust.

2. In large bowl, slightly whisk eggs to break up. Stir in butterscotch sauce, cappuccino coffee mix and cinnamon until well blended. Stir in pecan halves. Pour pecan mixture into crust.

3. Bake at 350° for 45 to 50 minutes or just until center of filling is set.

4. Transfer pie to wire rack; let pie cool completely. Refrigerate about 3 hours or until pie is firm. To serve, allow pie to come to room temperature.

If you're into the flavor of caramel and coffee (as in caramel lattes), you'll love this coffee-and-caramel dessert!

PREP: 10 minutes
BAKE: at 350° for 45 to 50 minutes
CHILL: 3 hours
MAKES: 12 servings

QUICK TIP

SWEETENED WHIPPED CREAM

It's hard to resist any dessert that comes topped with a dollop of whipped cream! Here's how to make some fresh: First chill the beaters and the mixing bowl you'll be using. Then, in the chilled bowl, stir together 1 cup heavy cream, 2 tablespoons sugar and ½ teaspoon vanilla extract. Beat with an electric mixer on medium speed until soft peaks form.

Per serving: 405 calories, 21 g total fat (5 g sat.), 75 mg cholesterol, 311 mg sodium, 53 g carbohydrate, 2 g fiber, 5 g protein.

Boston Cream Pie

- 1 box (18¼ ounces) yellow cake mix
- 1 box (3 ounces) cook-and-serve vanilla pudding mix
- 1⅓ cups water
- ⅓ cup vegetable oil
- 3 eggs
- ¾ cup plus 2 tablespoons milk

Topping:
- 6 tablespoons heavy cream
- 6 squares (1 ounce each) semisweet baking chocolate, finely chopped

1. Heat oven to 350°. Coat two 9-inch round cake pans with nonstick cooking spray.

2. Place the cake mix in large bowl. Add 4½ tablespoons of the pudding mix. Add water, oil and eggs; beat with electric mixer on low speed for 30 seconds. Increase speed to medium-high; beat for 2 minutes. Transfer batter to the prepared pans. Bake at 350° for 28 to 31 minutes or until toothpick inserted in centers comes out clean.

3. Meanwhile, in small saucepan, combine remaining pudding mix and all of the milk. Cook over medium heat, stirring constantly, about 8 minutes or until mixture comes to a full boil. Transfer to small bowl; cover and chill.

4. Remove cakes from oven. Cool in pans on wire racks for 15 minutes. Remove from pans; cool completely. Place one layer on serving platter; spread with pudding. Top with second layer.

5. **Topping:** In small microwave-safe bowl, microwave cream on HIGH about 45 seconds or until steaming and slightly bubbly. Place chopped chocolate in a small bowl; pour in steaming cream. Let stand for 1 minute, then whisk to blend until smooth. Cool to 90° on an instant-read thermometer. Pour on top of filled cake, spreading with a spatula until topping dribbles slightly over sides. Store in refrigerator until serving time.

Cake and pudding mixes make one of America's all-time favorite desserts a breeze to prepare. Kids love this sweet treat!

PREP: 10 minutes
BAKE: at 350° for 28 to 31 minutes
COOK: 8 minutes
COOL: 15 minutes
MICROWAVE: 45 seconds
MAKES: 16 servings

QUICK TIP

BLOOMING CHOCOLATE

If stored at higher-than-ideal temperatures, chocolate can develop a grayish film known as "bloom." While this may look unappetizing, it is harmless and will not affect the flavor of the chocolate. To help prevent chocolate from blooming, store in a tightly covered container or sealed plastic bag in a cool, dry place (under 78°).

Per serving: 303 calories, 16 g total fat (5 g sat.), 53 mg cholesterol, 270 mg sodium, 38 g carbohydrate, 2 g fiber, 4 g protein.

Lemon Curd Tart

- ½ of 18-ounce tube refrigerated sugar cookie dough
- 2 teaspoons grated lemon zest
- ½ cup bottled lemon curd
- 3 cups fresh raspberries (about 1 pint)
  Fresh mint leaves, for garnish (optional)

1. Heat oven to 350°. Lightly grease 9-inch springform pan with removable bottom.

2. In large bowl, work together dough and lemon zest with wooden spoon until well blended. (If dough becomes too soft to work with, refrigerate to firm for 10 minutes.) Press dough evenly over bottom and ½ inch up sides of prepared pan.

3. Bake at 350° about 20 minutes or until golden brown and center springs back when lightly touched. Remove springform pan to wire rack. Using thin metal spatula, carefully loosen crust from side of pan. Remove side of pan; cool crust completely on wire rack.

4. Place crust on serving platter. Spread lemon curd over crust. Top with raspberries. If desired, garnish with mint.

Four wisely chosen ingredients add up to a luscious lemon tart that you can make in about half an hour.

PREP: 10 minutes
BAKE: at 350° for 20 minutes
MAKES: 8 servings

QUICK TIP

WHEN LIFE GIVES YOU LEMON CURD

With a jar of lemon curd on hand, you are halfway to dessert. Use it as a dipping sauce for purchased shortbread or sugar cookies. You can also make quick lemon tartlets by filling purchased baked miniature phyllo dough shells with 2 teaspoons of lemon curd each. Top with raspberries and dust with confectioners' sugar just before serving.

Per serving: 229 calories, 9 g total fat (2 g sat.), 10 mg cholesterol, 167 mg sodium, 40 g carbohydrate, 3 g fiber, 2 g protein.

Plum Galette

1 box (11 ounces) piecrust mix
⅔ cup chopped pecans
3 tablespoons plus ⅓ cup packed brown
   sugar
1¼ pounds fresh plums
1 tablespoon all-purpose flour

1. Heat oven to 375°.

2. In medium-size bowl, combine piecrust mix, ⅓ cup pecans and 3 tablespoons brown sugar. Stir in amount of water recommended on the crust box for making a double-crust pie; continue stirring until dough forms.

3. On lightly floured surface, roll dough out to 13-inch circle. Transfer to large ungreased baking sheet.

4. Halve and pit plums; cut each half into four slices. Toss slices in bowl with the remaining ⅓ cup pecans, the remaining ⅓ cup brown sugar and the flour. Mound plum mixture in center of pastry circle, topping with any sugar mixture left in bowl. Fold border up over filling, working around circle.

5. Bake at 375° for 35 to 40 minutes or until filling is hot and crust is golden brown. Cool on baking sheet on wire rack. Serve slightly warm.

Although they're less common in baking than other fruits, plums turn out beautifully! Taste for yourself with this free-form pie.

PREP: 20 minutes
BAKE: at 375° for 35 to 40 minutes
MAKES: 12 servings

QUICK TIP

PRODUCE POINTERS

Find plums that are firm, plump and well shaped. Note that bloom (a light gray cast) on the skin is natural and doesn't affect quality. Plums should give slightly when gently pressed. If they don't, place them in a small, clean, loosely closed paper bag and store at room temperature until ripe. Once ripened, store in the refrigerator for up to 3 days.

Per serving: 243 calories, 13 g total fat (3 g sat.), 0 mg cholesterol, 200 mg sodium, 31 g carbohydrate, 2 g fiber, 3 g protein.

Pear Tart Tatin

¼ cup plus 2 tablespoons packed dark-brown
    sugar
2 cans (15¼ ounces each) pear halves, in
    syrup
1 prepared single-crust pie pastry
¼ cup pecans, finely chopped

1. Heat oven to 425°. Sprinkle ¼ cup brown sugar
over bottom of an ovenproof 10-inch nonstick
skillet. Drain pears; blot dry with paper towels.

2. Place 9 pear halves, cut sides up, in circle
in skillet. Fill center with remaining pears.
Sprinkle the remaining 2 tablespoons brown
sugar over pears.

3. Roll out crust to 11-inch circle. Spread nuts
over crust. Using rolling pin, press nuts into
crust; be careful not to tear crust.

4. Invert crust, nut side down, onto pears in skillet.
Tuck crust overlap between pears and edge of
pan, forming lip.

5. Bake at 425° about 25 minutes or until crust is
golden brown. Transfer skillet to wire rack; let
stand about 15 minutes or until skillet is cool
enough to handle. Invert serving platter on top
of skillet and flip tart onto platter. Let stand,
loosely covered, at room temperature until
serving time.

Pears work just as nicely as
apples in this simplified version
of a French classic.

PREP: 10 minutes
BAKE: at 425° for 25 minutes
STAND: 15 minutes
MAKES: 8 servings

QUICK TIP

PASTRY ON CALL

To get a quick start on your next pie
project, prepare pastry ahead and freeze
it. Simply prepare as directed in your
recipe but do not roll out. Flatten the ball
into a disk. Freeze in a freezer bag for up
to 2 months. Thaw overnight in the
refrigerator, then continue as directed
in the recipe.

Per serving: 267 calories, 9 g total fat (3 g sat.),
5 mg cholesterol, 113 mg sodium, 44 g carbohydrate,
1 g fiber, 1 g protein.

Crumb Cake

Cake:
- 1 box (18¼ ounces) yellow cake mix
- 1¼ cups sour cream
- ⅓ cup vegetable oil
- 3 eggs
- 1 teaspoon ground cinnamon
- ½ teaspoon ground nutmeg

Crumb Topping:
- 3¾ cups all-purpose flour
- ¾ cup packed light-brown sugar
- 2 teaspoons ground cinnamon
- ½ teaspoon ground nutmeg
- 1½ cups (3 sticks) butter or margarine, melted

Sour Cream Glaze:
- ½ cup plus 2 tablespoons confectioners' sugar
- 2 tablespoons sour cream

1. Heat oven to 350°. Grease 15×10×1-inch baking pan. Lightly dust pan with all-purpose flour; gently shake out any excess flour.

2. **Cake:** In large bowl, combine cake mix, sour cream, oil, eggs, cinnamon and nutmeg. Beat according to package directions. Pour batter into prepared pan. Bake at 350° about 20 minutes or until wooden toothpick inserted in center of cake comes out clean.

3. **Crumb Topping:** In medium-size bowl, stir together flour, brown sugar, cinnamon and nutmeg; stir in melted butter until mixture is evenly moistened and comes together in clumps.

4. Remove cake from oven. Sprinkle crumbs over top (this will be a thick covering). Return to oven; bake about 15 minutes longer or until crumbs are slightly set. Remove pan to wire rack and let cool completely.

5. **Sour Cream Glaze:** In small bowl, whisk together ½ cup confectioners' sugar and sour cream until well blended. Dust top of cake evenly with remaining 2 tablespoons confectioners' sugar. Drizzle evenly with glaze.

A buttery, spicy crumb topping is a much-loved feature of many coffee cakes—here it's the star!

PREP: 25 minutes
BAKE: at 350° for 35 minutes
MAKES: 25 servings

QUICK TIP

MEASURING FLOUR

It's important to measure flour correctly in baking because too much flour can cause the results to be dry. To measure, first stir the flour in the bag or canister to lighten its volume. Gently spoon the flour into a dry measuring cup or measuring spoon. Level off the top with the straight side of a knife. Note that sifting flour is not necessary, except when specified in a recipe or when you're using cake flour.

Per serving: 354 calories, 20 g total fat (9 g sat.), 61 mg cholesterol, 157 mg sodium, 40 g carbohydrate, 4 g fiber, 4 g protein.

Chocolate "Soufflé" Cake

1 box (19 ounces) dark-chocolate cake mix
3½ cups strong brewed coffee
3 eggs
¼ cup freeze-dried coffee crystals
3 tablespoons vegetable oil
½ cup mini semisweet chocolate chips
¾ cup packed dark-brown sugar
¼ cup unsweetened cocoa powder
   Confectioners' sugar, for dusting
Coffee Cream:
¾ cup heavy cream
2 tablespoons coffee liqueur

1. Heat oven to 350°. Coat 3-quart baking dish with nonstick cooking spray.

2. In large bowl, combine cake mix, 1 cup brewed coffee, eggs, coffee crystals and oil. Beat with electric mixer on low speed about 30 seconds or until moistened. Increase speed to medium-high; beat for 2 minutes. Stir in chocolate chips. Spread in prepared baking dish.

3. In small saucepan, bring remaining 2½ cups brewed coffee to simmering. Sprinkle brown sugar and cocoa powder over batter. Pour hot coffee over top. Transfer dish to oven.

4. Bake at 350° about 40 minutes or until top is puffed (center still jiggly). Transfer to wire rack; dust with confectioners' sugar.

5. **Coffee Cream:** In small bowl, with electric mixer on low speed, beat cream and liqueur until soft peaks form. Serve warm cake in bowls with cream mixture.

This dessert is puffy and moist in the middle—just like a soufflé. But unlike most soufflés, it's a cinch to make.

PREP: 10 minutes
BAKE: at 350° for 40 minutes
MAKES: 12 servings

QUICK TIP

OIL IN BAKING

Unless a recipe calls for another type of oil, vegetable oils are better for baking because they are light in color and have a neutral flavor that won't clash with other flavors in the recipe. Store vegetable oils at room temperature and use within 6 months.

Per serving: 390 calories, 17 g total fat (6 g sat.), 74 mg cholesterol, 441 mg sodium, 58 g carbohydrate, 3 g fiber, 5 g protein.

Banana Cream Cake

- 4 medium-size bananas
- 1 box (18¼ ounces) yellow cake mix
- 4 eggs
- 1⅓ cups water
- 1 tablespoon vegetable oil
- ⅓ cup finely chopped walnuts
- ⅓ cup mini semisweet chocolate chips
- 2 boxes (about 3 ounces each) instant banana cream pudding mix
- 3¾ cups cold milk
- 1 cup heavy cream
- 2 tablespoons confectioners' sugar
- 2 tablespoons unsweetened cocoa powder
  Mini semisweet chocolate chips, for garnish (optional)

1. Heat oven to 350°. Coat two 9-inch round cake pans with nonstick cooking spray.

2. In large bowl, mash 1 banana. Add cake mix, eggs, water and oil. Beat with electric mixer on low speed until blended, then beat on medium-high speed for 2 to 3 minutes, scraping down sides of bowl, if necessary. Fold in nuts. Scrape batter into prepared pans. Sprinkle ⅓ cup mini chocolate chips evenly over top of each cake.

3. Bake at 350° for 32 to 35 minutes or until a wooden toothpick inserted in the centers of the cakes comes out clean. Cool cakes in pans on wire racks about 10 minutes. Carefully invert the cakes onto wire racks to cool completely. Remove pans.

4. In medium-size bowl, prepare pudding mix with the milk, following the package directions. Trim top of each cake layer evenly; slice each layer in half horizontally for a total of four layers. Thinly slice remaining 3 bananas. Place one cake layer on cake stand. Spread top of the layer evenly with one-third of the pudding mixture. Arrange 1 sliced banana over the pudding. Top with the second cake layer. Continue layering with pudding, banana slices and cake. Top with final cake layer.

5. In medium-size bowl, with electric mixer on medium speed, beat together cream, confectioners' sugar and cocoa powder until well blended and peaks form. Spread the whipped cream mixture evenly over top of the cake. If desired, garnish with additional mini chocolate chips.

Creamy banana pudding separates tender layers, and a chocolate-kissed whipped cream frosting is the crowning touch.

PREP: 15 minutes
BAKE: at 350° for 32 to 35 minutes
COOL: 10 minutes
MAKES: 12 servings

QUICK TIP

TROPICAL BARGAINS

Did you know that tropical fruits, such as bananas, papayas and mangoes, don't fluctuate much in price? That's because growers close to the equator enjoy a year-round growing season. Remember this when you're trying to pack your diet with healthful fruits while on a budget.

Per serving: 473 calories, 22 g total fat (9 g sat.), 109 mg cholesterol, 563 mg sodium, 65 g carbohydrate, 3 g fiber, 8 g protein.

Cream Cheese-Streusel Pound Cake

Streusel:
- 1 cup packed light-brown sugar
- ¼ cup all-purpose baking mix (such as Bisquick)
- ½ teaspoon ground cinnamon
- ¼ cup (½ stick) unsalted butter, at room temperature, cut into pieces

Cake:
- 3½ cups all-purpose baking mix (such as Bisquick)
- 1½ cups granulated sugar
- ¾ cup (1½ sticks) unsalted butter, at room temperature
- 1 package (8 ounces) cream cheese, at room temperature
- 6 eggs
- 1 teaspoon vanilla extract
- Confectioners' sugar (optional)

1. Heat oven to 350°. Grease and flour 10-inch tube pan with removable bottom.

2. **Streusel:** In small bowl, stir together brown sugar, baking mix and cinnamon; cut in butter with a fork until mixture is crumbly. Set aside.

3. **Cake:** In large bowl, combine baking mix, granulated sugar, butter, cream cheese, eggs and vanilla. With electric mixer on low speed, beat about 1 minute or until blended, scraping down sides of bowl. On high speed, beat for 3 minutes.

4. Spread one-third (2 cups) of the batter into prepared pan. Sprinkle with one-third (⅓ cup) of the streusel. Repeat twice with remaining batter and streusel.

5. Bake at 350° for 70 to 80 minutes or until wooden skewer inserted in center of cake comes out clean. Remove pan to wire rack; let cake cool in pan for 15 minutes. Remove side of pan. Let cake cool completely. Remove cake from bottom of pan and tube. If desired, dust with confectioners' sugar.

Whether you're looking for a treat to bring to the office or a dessert for a potluck, this cake will serve a crowd.

PREP: 10 minutes
BAKE: at 350° for 70 to 80 minutes
COOL: 15 minutes
MAKES: 16 servings

QUICK TIP

EGG SUBSTITUTES

Use large eggs for the recipes in this book. If you open your fridge only to find small, medium or extra-large eggs, here are the equivalents:

2 large eggs = 2 extra-large, 2 medium or 3 small eggs

3 large eggs = 3 extra-large, 3 medium or 4 small eggs

4 large eggs = 4 extra-large, 5 medium or 5 small eggs

5 large eggs = 4 extra-large, 6 medium or 7 small eggs

6 large eggs = 5 extra-large, 7 medium or 8 small eggs

Per serving: 435 calories, 19 g total fat (11 g sat.), 126 mg cholesterol, 373 mg sodium, 61 g carbohydrate, 2 g fiber, 8 g protein.

Orange-Brownie Torte

Layers:
- 1 large orange
- 1 box (21 ounces) family-style brownie mix
- 3 eggs
- ½ cup vegetable oil

Frosting:
- 1½ cups milk
- 1 envelope whipped topping mix (1.3 ounces; from a 2.6-ounce package)
- 1 box (3.4 ounces) instant vanilla pudding mix
  Orange food coloring
- 1 can (15 ounces) mandarin oranges in light syrup

1. **Layers:** Heat oven to 350°. Coat two 9-inch round cake pans with nonstick cooking spray. Remove peel from orange with a zester, avoiding pith (about 2½ teaspoons zest). Juice the orange (about ⅓ cup juice).

2. In large bowl, stir together brownie mix, eggs, 2 teaspoons orange zest, the ⅓ cup orange juice and oil about 1 minute or until well mixed. Divide between prepared pans.

3. Bake at 350° about 25 minutes or until wooden toothpick inserted at edge of pans comes out clean. Cool in pans on wire racks for 5 minutes. Invert layers on wire racks; cool completely.

4. **Frosting:** In medium-size bowl, with electric mixer on low speed, beat milk, whipped topping mix and pudding mix until blended. Increase speed to high; beat about 4 minutes or until soft peaks form. Stir in a drop of food coloring and the remaining ½ teaspoon orange zest.

5. Place one cake layer on serving platter. Spread with ¾ cup of the frosting. Drain mandarin oranges; pat dry with paper towels. Arrange ¾ cup orange segments over frosting. Top with second brownie layer. Spread remaining frosting on top and sides of torte. Decoratively place remaining orange segments on top and around sides of torte. Refrigerate for 1 hour before serving.

Packaged brownie mix goes upscale, thanks to simple add-ins of orange juice and zest and mandarin oranges.

PREP: 10 minutes
BAKE: at 350° for 25 minutes
COOL: 5 minutes
CHILL: 1 hour
MAKES: 16 servings

QUICK TIP

PRODUCE POINTERS

Look for oranges that are firm and heavy for their size. Don't worry about brown specks or a slight greenish tinge on the surface—these will not affect the quality of the flesh inside. Refrigerate oranges for up to 2 weeks.

Per serving: 301 calories, 13 g total fat (3 g sat.), 47 mg cholesterol, 371 mg sodium, 42 g carbohydrate, 1 g fiber, 3 g protein.

Spectacular Desserts

Tiramisù p.254

Rich pies, creamy cheesecakes, fruit-filled tarts, impressive tiramisù—here are more than 25 desserts you'd expect to pay top dollar for at fancy restaurants. You can make them easily and inexpensively at home.

Irish Pots de Crème

6 egg yolks
¼ cup sugar
1¾ cups whole milk
¼ cup Irish cream liqueur
½ teaspoon vanilla extract
⅛ teaspoon ground nutmeg
4 cups hot water

1. Heat oven to 325°. In medium-size bowl, whisk together egg yolks and sugar until the mixture is well blended. In small saucepan, heat the milk gently just until it reaches simmering. Remove the saucepan from the heat.

2. Whisk a small amount of the hot milk into the egg yolk mixture; whisk the egg yolk mixture into the hot milk in the saucepan. Stir in liqueur and vanilla. Pour milk mixture through a fine-mesh sieve into a 4-cup glass measure to remove any cooked pieces of egg.

3. Pour milk mixture into six 4-ounce cups, ramekins or custard cups, dividing the milk mixture equally among the cups. Sprinkle tops of the custards evenly with nutmeg.

4. Place the cups in a 9×9×2-inch baking dish. Place baking dish with cups on middle rack in oven. Carefully pour enough hot water (about 4 cups) into baking dish to come halfway up the sides of the cups.

5. Bake pots de crème in water bath at 325° about 35 minutes or just until centers are set. Remove baking dish from oven; remove ramekins from water bath to wire racks. Refrigerate for 3 hours or overnight or until well chilled.

The French dessert gets a touch of Irish charm, thanks to a little Irish cream liqueur.

PREP: 15 minutes
BAKE: at 325° for 35 minutes
CHILL: 3 hours or overnight
MAKES: 6 servings

QUICK TIP

EGGCELLENT ADVICE

Any dish that contains eggs should be cooked until it registers 160° on an instant-read thermometer. If a recipe calls for raw or undercooked eggs (such as homemade ice cream), use shell eggs that are clearly labeled as having been pasteurized to destroy salmonella. If you have a recipe that calls for raw or undercooked egg whites, use pasteurized dried egg whites or pasteurized refrigerated liquid egg whites.

Per serving: 138 calories, 8 g total fat (3 g sat.), 222 mg cholesterol, 43 mg sodium, 12 g carbohydrate, 0 g fiber, 5 g protein.

Butterscotch Poached Pears

Poached Pears:
- 1 bottle (750 ml) white wine
- 1½ cups granulated sugar
- 1 (2-inch) strip lemon peel
- 2 tablespoons lemon juice
- 1 whole cinnamon stick
- 6 whole cloves
- 6 firm ripe Bosc pears

Butterscotch Sauce:
- 1 cup packed light-brown sugar
- ¼ cup (½ stick) unsalted butter
- ¼ cup light corn syrup
- ¼ teaspoon salt
- ½ cup heavy cream
- 2 teaspoons vanilla extract

1. **Poached Pears:** In large saucepan, bring wine, granulated sugar, lemon peel, lemon juice, cinnamon and cloves to a boil; boil about 5 minutes or until sugar is dissolved. Peel pears, leaving stems on. Core from bottom. Add pears to pan; cover and simmer for 10 to 15 minutes or until tender. Cool to room temperature. Refrigerate pears in liquid about 4 hours or until cold. (Can be prepared up to a day ahead.)

2. **Butterscotch Sauce:** In small saucepan, combine brown sugar, butter, corn syrup and salt. Over medium-low heat, stir about 3 minutes or until blended. Over medium-high heat, bring to a gentle boil; boil for 2 minutes without stirring. Remove from heat; stir in cream and vanilla. Let cool. Cover; refrigerate about 1 hour or until thickened.

3. Spoon sauce over drained pears.

A luscious sauce transforms pears into a grand finale for a glamorous dinner party.

PREP: 10 minutes
COOK: pears for 10 to 15 minutes; sauce for 5 minutes
CHILL: pears for 4 hours; sauce for 1 hour
MAKES: 6 servings (1½ cups sauce)

QUICK TIP

STORE IT RIGHT

Store cinnamon sticks and whole cloves in airtight containers in a dry place away from sunlight and heat. Replace them when their aroma fades. Whole stick cinnamon and whole cloves will keep for up to 2 years when stored at 70°.

Per serving: 425 calories, 16 g total fat (9 g sat.), 48 mg cholesterol, 133 mg sodium, 72 g carbohydrate, 3 g fiber, 1 g protein.

Black-and-White Cookies

Cookies:
- 1⅓ cups all-purpose flour
- ½ teaspoon baking soda
- ½ teaspoon salt
- ½ cup granulated sugar
- ⅓ cup unsalted butter, at room temperature
- 1 egg
- ⅓ cup buttermilk

Black and White Icing:
- 2 cups confectioners' sugar
- 2 tablespoons light corn syrup
- ½ teaspoon vanilla extract
- 2 tablespoons plus 4 teaspoons milk
- 2 tablespoons unsweetened cocoa powder

1. **Cookies:** Heat oven to 350°. Coat two cookie sheets with nonstick cooking spray. In medium-size bowl, combine flour, baking soda and salt. In large bowl, with electric mixer on medium speed, beat together sugar and butter about 1 minute or until smooth and creamy. Beat in egg until well mixed. On low speed, alternately beat in flour mixture and the buttermilk, ending with flour mixture; beat until smooth.

2. Onto prepared sheets, drop ¼ cup dough for each cookie, spacing about 3 inches apart. Refrigerate one of the sheets of cookies.

3. Bake the remaining sheet of cookies at 350° about 13 minutes or until wooden pick inserted in centers comes out clean. Transfer cookies to wire rack, placing rounded sides down; let cool. Repeat with remaining sheet of cookies.

4. **Black and White Icing:** In medium-size bowl, stir together confectioners' sugar, corn syrup and vanilla; stir in 2 tablespoons plus 1 to 2 teaspoons milk until smooth but thick enough to coat cookie. Remove ¼ cup icing to small bowl; stir in cocoa powder and remaining 2 teaspoons milk until smooth.

5. Using a metal spatula, spread white icing over one half of the flat side of each cookie. Clean spatula and spread chocolate icing over the other halves of cookies. Let stand at room temperature until set. Store in airtight container at room temperature for up to 3 days.

The two-tone icing complements these tender drop cookies that are a New York bakery tradition.

PREP: 20 minutes
BAKE: at 350° for 13 minutes per batch
MAKES: 8 large cookies

QUICK TIP

MIX NOW, BAKE LATER

If you can't get all your baking done in one step, divide and conquer the task by mixing one day, then baking another. Most cookie doughs (except bar batters and meringue mixtures) can be mixed, then refrigerated or frozen. Pack your favorite dough into freezer containers or shape slice-and-bake doughs into rolls and wrap. Store in tightly covered containers in the refrigerator for up to 1 week or freeze up to 6 months. Before baking, thaw frozen dough in the refrigerator. If dough is too stiff, let stand at room temperature to soften.

Per cookie: 325 calories, 9 g total fat (5 g sat.), 49 mg cholesterol, 254 mg sodium, 59 g carbohydrate, 1 g fiber, 4 g protein.

Cookies 'n' Cream Delights

1½ cups all-purpose flour
¾ cup confectioners' sugar
⅓ cup unsweetened cocoa powder
½ teaspoon salt
10 tablespoons butter, cut into small pieces and chilled
1 tablespoon instant espresso coffee powder
2 tablespoons cold water
2 egg yolks
1½ teaspoons vanilla extract
Cream Filling (recipe, page 276)
84 fresh raspberries (about ½ pint)

1. Sift together flour, confectioners' sugar, cocoa powder and salt into large bowl. Using pastry blender, cut in butter until mixture looks like coarse cornmeal.

2. In small bowl, sprinkle espresso powder over the cold water. Lightly beat in egg yolks and vanilla. Using a fork, stir egg yolk mixture into flour mixture until dough comes together. Shape into disk; wrap in plastic wrap. Refrigerate overnight or up to 2 days.

3. Heat oven to 400°. Working with half of the dough at a time, roll out between two sheets of waxed paper to ³⁄₁₆-inch thickness. Remove top sheet of paper. Using 3-inch-round biscuit cutter with fluted or scalloped edge, dip edge in flour and cut out as many cookies as possible, leaving cookies on paper. Slide cookies on waxed paper onto cookie sheet. Freeze for 10 minutes.

4. Use a small metal spatula dipped in flour to move the cookies from the waxed paper to clean cookie sheets. Gather the scraps together; re-roll and cut out additional cookies as above and place on cookie sheets. You will need a total of 21 cookies.

5. Bake at 400° for 8 to 10 minutes. Let cool on cookie sheets on wire racks for 2 minutes. Remove from sheets to wire rack to cool.

6. Prepare Cream Filling. Place a cookie on a serving plate. Spoon about 3 tablespoons of the filling onto cookie. Top with about 6 raspberries. Place a second cookie on top; spoon on another layer of filling; top with 6 more raspberries. Place another cookie on top. Add a third layer of filling. Repeat with remaining cookies, filling and raspberries (total of 7 stacks).

Delight is right! Who isn't going to love a mini tower of mocha cookies and a raspberry-vanilla cream filling?

PREP: 45 minutes
CHILL: overnight or up to 2 days
FREEZE: 10 minutes
BAKE: at 400° for 8 to 10 minutes per batch
COOL: 2 minutes
MAKES: 7 servings

QUICK TIP

ESPRESSO EXTRA

Coffee enhances the flavor of both chocolate and vanilla, and the espresso coffee powder—brewed espresso that has been dehydrated to make a fine powder—in these treats highlights that flavor combo. Espresso coffee powder is especially suited for baking because it dissolves easily. Look for it in the coffee aisle of most supermarkets.

Per serving: 602 calories, 37 g total fat (21 g sat.), 283 mg cholesterol, 225 mg sodium, 59 g carbohydrate, 3 g fiber, 10 g protein.

Hazelnut Macaroons

4 ounces whole skinless hazelnuts (about ¾ cup)
¾ cup sugar
1 package (7 ounces) almond paste
2 egg whites
24 whole skinless hazelnuts
6 squares (1 ounce each) semisweet chocolate, melted

1. Heat oven to 325°. Coat cookie sheets with nonstick cooking spray or line sheets with nonstick aluminum foil. Fit large pastry bag with large ¾-inch star tip.

2. In food processor, process the 4 ounces hazelnuts and ¼ cup of the sugar until finely ground. Add remaining ½ cup sugar, the almond paste and egg whites. Process until thoroughly blended.

3. Spoon hazelnut mixture into pastry bag. Pipe rosettes (about 1¼ inches round) 1 inch apart onto prepared sheets. Top each rosette with a whole hazelnut.

4. Bake at 325° about 14 minutes or until light golden brown. Transfer cookie sheets to wire racks; let stand for 1 minute. With metal spatula, remove macaroons to wire racks and let cool. (If macaroons stand too long on cookie sheet, they may stick. If so, place in oven for 1 minute before removing.)

5. Dip bottoms of macaroons in melted chocolate; place on waxed-paper-lined baking sheets. Let stand until set.

Coconut isn't the only ingredient that makes a great macaroon—as the use of hazelnuts and chocolate proves!

PREP: 10 minutes
BAKE: at 325° for 14 minutes per batch
STAND: 1 minute
MAKES: 24 macaroons

QUICK TIP

SKINNING HAZELNUTS

In most cases, hazelnuts taste better in recipes when their bitter brown skins have been removed. Here's how to do it: Spread shelled hazelnuts on an ungreased baking sheet and toast in a 350° oven for 10 to 15 minutes, stirring occasionally until the skins begin to flake. Remove from the oven and place nuts (a handful at a time) in a clean, dry cotton kitchen towel. Rub the nuts vigorously until the skins come off.

Per macaroon: 146 calories, 9 g total fat (2 g sat.), 0 mg cholesterol, 5 mg sodium, 16 g carbohydrate, 2 g fiber, 3 g protein.

Butterscotch Parfaits

Butterscotch Pudding:
- ½ cup packed dark-brown sugar
- 3 tablespoons cornstarch
- ¼ teaspoon salt
  - Pinch of ground cinnamon
- ½ cup heavy cream
- 1½ cups milk
- 3 tablespoons butter
- 1 teaspoon vanilla extract

Vanilla Pudding:
- ½ cup granulated sugar
- 2 tablespoons cornstarch
- ¼ teaspoon salt
- 2 cups milk
- 1 teaspoon vanilla extract

1. **Butterscotch Pudding:** In heavy-bottomed medium saucepan (not nonstick), stir together with wooden spoon the brown sugar, cornstarch, salt and cinnamon. Stir in cream until smooth. Stir in milk. Cook over medium heat, stirring constantly, about 5 minutes or just until mixture begins to bubble and thicken. Reduce heat; simmer 3 minutes longer. Remove from heat. Stir in butter and vanilla. Cover and set aside.

2. **Vanilla Pudding:** In second saucepan, stir together granulated sugar, cornstarch and salt. Stir in ½ cup milk until smooth. Stir in the remaining 1½ cups milk. Cook over medium heat, stirring constantly, about 5 minutes or just until mixture begins to bubble and thicken. Reduce heat; simmer 3 minutes longer. Remove from heat. Stir in vanilla.

3. In dessert glasses, alternate layers of both puddings. Cover with plastic wrap; chill until ready to serve.

Introduce the kids to an old-timey pudding parfait just like Grandma used to make!

PREP: 20 minutes
COOK: 20 minutes
MAKES: 6 servings

QUICK BITE
VANILLA POWER

Vanilla extract is made from a liquid extracted from the seed of a particular species of orchid. Real vanilla extract can be pricey; imitation vanilla extract, an artificial flavoring, makes an inexpensive substitute.

Per serving: 369 calories, 18 g total fat (11 g sat.), 62 mg cholesterol, 280 mg sodium, 48 g carbohydrate, 0 g fiber, 5 g protein.

Tiramisù

8 ounces mascarpone cheese, softened
⅓ cup sugar
⅓ cup coffee liqueur
1 cup heavy cream
2 packages (3 ounces each) ladyfingers (24 total)
⅔ cup strong coffee
¼ cup unsweetened cocoa powder
4 ounces bittersweet chocolate, shaved
¼ cup sliced almonds, toasted

1. In large bowl, with electric mixer on low speed, beat together mascarpone and sugar about 3 minutes or until smooth. Beat in liqueur.

2. In small bowl, beat cream until stiff peaks form. Fold into mascarpone mixture.

3. Line an 8×8×2-inch square baking dish with aluminum foil, leaving extra foil above the edge of the dish. Arrange 12 ladyfingers in bottom of pan, opening up some of the ladyfingers to cover bottom. Brush with half of the coffee. Spread half of the mascarpone mixture over top. Sift half of the cocoa powder over top; sprinkle with half of the shaved chocolate. Repeat layering. Cover and refrigerate for 4 hours or overnight.

4. To serve, using foil lift the tiramisù from the baking dish; garnish with toasted almonds. Cut into squares.

We fell in love with this Italian creation—literally "carry me up"—in Italian restaurants. Who knew it was this easy to make at home?

PREP: 25 minutes
CHILL: 4 hours to overnight
MAKES: 9 servings

Per serving: 441 calories, 28 g total fat (16 g sat.), 83 mg cholesterol, 40 mg sodium, 38 g carbohydrate, 3 g fiber, 6 g protein.

Coconut Flan

⅓ cup sugar
¼ cup water
   Butter
2 cups half-and-half
1 cup canned cream of coconut, well stirred
4 eggs
2 egg yolks
¼ cup dark rum
1 teaspoon vanilla extract
¼ teaspoon ground allspice
½ cup sweetened flake coconut, toasted

1. Place 8-inch round cake pan in oven. Heat oven to 200°.

2. In small, heavy-bottomed saucepan, boil sugar and water over medium heat without stirring, about 13 minutes or until amber color.

3. With oven mitts, remove cake pan from oven. Carefully pour sugar mixture into pan, turning pan until bottom and sides of pan are coated. Set aside on wire rack to cool. Lightly butter any uncoated spots on pan.

4. Increase oven temperature to 350°. In small saucepan, bring half-and-half and cream of coconut to a boil, stirring occasionally.

5. In medium-size bowl, whisk eggs and egg yolks. Slowly whisk coconut cream mixture into eggs; add rum, vanilla and allspice.

6. Place coated cake pan in small roasting pan. Pour egg mixture into coated pan. Place on middle rack in oven. Pour enough boiling water into roasting pan to come halfway up sides of custard-filled pan.

7. Bake at 350° for 35 to 45 minutes or just until custard is set and knife inserted near center comes out clean. Transfer cake pan to wire rack to cool. Refrigerate for at least 2 hours.

8. To serve, run knife around edge of cake pan. Invert serving platter on top of cake pan; invert flan onto platter, letting caramel run over top and sides. Sprinkle toasted coconut on top.

Coconut inside and out—along with a bit of rum—elevates the always-popular flan to top-flight status.

PREP: 20 minutes
COOK: 13 minutes
BAKE: at 350° for 35 to 45 minutes
CHILL: 2 hours
MAKES: 10 servings

QUICK TIP

WHY A WATER BATH?

A water bath is a method of cooking a flan, custard or other recipes in a baking dish that's placed in a larger pan of hot water. When such a method is specified in a recipe, don't be tempted to skip this step—it helps delicate dishes cook without curdling.

Per serving: 206 calories, 15 g total fat (10 g sat.), 146 mg cholesterol, 71 mg sodium, 13 g carbohydrate, 1 g fiber, 5 g protein.

Petite Choco-Raspberry Mousse Cups

Mousse:
- 2 tablespoons brewed coffee
- 1½ cups heavy cream
- 10 ounces bittersweet chocolate, chopped
- 2 tablespoons coffee liqueur
- 1 teaspoon vanilla extract
- ¼ cup confectioners' sugar
- 36 fresh raspberries
- 12 round chocolate wafer cookies

Ganache:
- 8 ounces bittersweet chocolate, chopped
- 1 cup heavy cream
- 3 tablespoons unsalted butter

Glossy chocolate enrobes individual mousse cups filled with fresh raspberries. They look and taste as though they were made by a master pastry chef!

PREP: 10 minutes
COOK: 13 minutes
COOL: about 2 hours
CHILL: 2 hours 20 minutes
MAKES: 6 mousse cups

1. **Mousse:** Coat cups of a 12-cup muffin pan with nonstick cooking spray. Line cups with plastic wrap, letting wrap overhang cups; press wrap into cups by stacking second cup inside each. Remove second cup; coat plastic wrap with nonstick cooking spray.

2. In saucepan, stir together coffee, ¼ cup of the heavy cream and the chocolate. Cook over medium-low heat 8 minutes, stirring frequently until smooth. Stir in coffee liqueur and vanilla; cook 1 minute longer. Remove from heat; cool on wire rack 1½ hours, stirring occasionally.

3. When chocolate is cool, beat the remaining 1 cup heavy cream with an electric mixer on medium speed until soft peaks form; add confectioners' sugar and continue beating until stiff peaks form. Gently fold whipped cream into chocolate until no streaks remain.

4. Place chocolate mixture in large resealable plastic bag. Snip corner off one edge. Pipe chocolate into each cup, filling about half full. Top chocolate with 3 raspberries per cup. Pipe remaining chocolate into cups until full. Place a cookie on top of each cup. Cover entire muffin pan with plastic wrap. Chill for 2 hours.

5. **Ganache:** Place chocolate in a small bowl. In a small saucepan, heat cream over medium-high heat about 4 minutes or until steaming. Pour over chocolate and stir until smooth. Stir in butter. Let cool at room temperature about 20 minutes, stirring occasionally.

6. Remove muffin pan from refrigerator. Remove top piece of plastic wrap. Place wire rack on top and invert. Place rack over large baking sheet. Gently remove plastic wrap. Spoon ganache over mousse, covering mousse completely. Chill for 20 minutes or up to several hours.

QUICK TIP

SEMISWEET VERSUS BITTERSWEET

Semisweet chocolate blends chocolate liquor, cocoa butter and enough sugar to soften the bitterness. Bittersweet chocolate uses the same ingredients but has less sugar for a more intense flavor. Generally, bittersweet and semisweet chocolate can be used interchangeably in recipes.

Per mousse cup: 418 calories, 32 g total fat (19 g sat.), 68 mg cholesterol, 66 mg sodium, 32 g carbohydrate, 3 g fiber, 4 g protein.

New York-Style Cheesecake

Crust:
- 1⅔ cups graham cracker crumbs (about 12 boards)
- 2 tablespoons granulated sugar
- 2 tablespoons light-brown sugar
- ¼ teaspoon ground cinnamon
- 3 tablespoons butter, melted

Filling:
- 4 packages (8 ounces each) cream cheese (2 pounds total), at room temperature
- 1 cup granulated sugar
- ¼ cup all-purpose flour
- ¼ cup heavy cream
- 4 eggs, at room temperature
- 1 teaspoon vanilla extract
- ½ teaspoon grated orange zest
- ½ teaspoon grated lemon zest
- ¼ teaspoon salt
- Topping (recipe, right)
- Orange zest strips, for garnish (optional)

1. Heat oven to 325°. Wrap outside of 9-inch springform pan with aluminum foil.

2. **Crust:** In small bowl, combine graham cracker crumbs, granulated sugar, brown sugar and cinnamon; stir in butter until well blended. Press the crumb mixture over bottom and halfway up the sides of the springform pan.

3. **Filling:** In large bowl, with electric mixer on medium speed, beat together cream cheese, granulated sugar and flour about 2 minutes or until smooth and creamy. Add cream; beat for 30 seconds. Add the eggs, one at a time, beating well after each addition. Beat in vanilla, orange zest, lemon zest and salt until well combined. Scrape filling into the prepared pan, smoothing top. Place pan in large baking pan on oven shelf. Pour enough hot water into larger pan to come halfway up sides of springform pan.

4. Bake at 325° about 1½ hours or until center is set. Remove springform pan from water bath. Pour topping over top of cake and spread evenly with spatula. Return springform pan to water bath. Bake at 325° about 15 minutes longer or until the topping is set. Remove the springform pan from the water bath; carefully remove aluminum foil. Run knife around edge of cake. Cool pan on wire rack. Cover pan and refrigerate for 6 hours or overnight.

5. To serve, remove side of springform pan. If desired, garnish with orange zest strips.

This is it! The perfect choice for those who like the traditional style of cheesecake.

PREP: 20 minutes
BAKE: at 325° for 1¾ hours
CHILL: 6 hours or overnight
MAKES: 16 servings

CHEESECAKE TOPPING

In small bowl, stir together 1 cup sour cream, 2 tablespoons granulated sugar and ½ teaspoon vanilla extract.

Per serving: 392 calories, 28 g total fat (17 g sat.), 133 mg cholesterol, 284 mg sodium, 28 g carbohydrate, 0 g fiber, 7 g protein.

Black and White Flips

Cupcakes:
- 1½ cups all-purpose flour
- 1¾ teaspoons baking powder
- ¼ teaspoon salt
- ½ cup (1 stick) unsalted butter, softened
- ¾ cup granulated sugar
- 3 egg whites
- ½ cup milk
- 1 teaspoon vanilla extract
- 1 square (1 ounce) semisweet chocolate, melted

Frosting:
- 3 cups confectioners' sugar
- ¼ cup (½ stick) unsalted butter, softened
- ¼ cup solid vegetable shortening
- 3 tablespoons milk (plus more if needed)
- ½ teaspoon vanilla extract
- 2 squares (1 ounce each) milk chocolate, melted

1. Heat oven to 350°. Line cups of a standard-size cupcake pan with 12 paper or foil liners.

2. **Cupcakes:** In small bowl, whisk together flour, baking powder and salt.

3. In large bowl, beat butter with an electric mixer on medium speed. Gradually add granulated sugar; beat until lightened. Slowly beat in egg whites. Add flour mixture, alternating with milk, beginning and ending with flour. Beat in vanilla.

4. Place half of the batter in small bowl. Stir in melted chocolate. Fill six prepared liners with white batter and six with chocolate. Bake at 350° for 20 to 25 minutes or until crowned and lightly colored. Remove cupcakes from pan; cool on wire rack.

5. Remove cupcake liners and slice cupcakes in half horizontally (separate tops from bottoms).

6. **Frosting:** In medium-size bowl, with an electric mixer on low speed, beat together confectioners' sugar, butter, shortening, milk and vanilla. Remove ¾ cup frosting to a small bowl; stir in melted chocolate. Add additional milk, if necessary.

7. Spread white frosting on white cupcake bottoms and chocolate frosting on chocolate bottoms. Top white bottoms with chocolate tops. Frost with additional white frosting. Repeat with white cupcake tops and chocolate frosting.

Can't decide whether to take the vanilla or chocolate route? These cuties offer the best of both worlds.

PREP: 15 minutes
BAKE: at 350° for 20 to 25 minutes
MAKES: 12 cupcakes

QUICK TIP

SMOOTH GOING

To melt chocolate on the range top, place it in a heavy saucepan or double boiler. Place the saucepan over low heat or place the double boiler over hot, but not boiling, water. Stir the chocolate often to keep it from burning. Make sure your utensils are dry and avoid splashing any water into the pan because even a little water can cause the chocolate to seize up and become grainy.

Per cupcake: 393 calories, 19 g total fat (10 g sat.), 34 mg cholesterol, 131 mg sodium, 54 g carbohydrate, 2 g fiber, 4 g protein.

Brown Sugar Cake Roll

1¼ cups all-purpose flour
1 teaspoon baking powder
¼ teaspoon baking soda
¾ teaspoon ground ginger
½ teaspoon grated orange zest
½ teaspoon salt
4 eggs
¾ cup packed dark-brown sugar
⅓ cup vegetable oil
½ cup low-fat buttermilk
1 teaspoon vanilla extract
2 tablespoons confectioners' sugar
   Filling and Frosting (recipe, right)
½ cup orange marmalade

1. Heat oven to 350°. Coat 15×10×1-inch jelly-roll pan with nonstick cooking spray. Line bottom of pan with waxed paper; coat waxed paper with nonstick spray.

2. In medium-size bowl, whisk together flour, baking powder, baking soda, ginger, orange zest and salt.

3. In large bowl, with electric mixer on medium speed, beat eggs about 3 minutes or until foamy and slightly thickened. Add brown sugar gradually, breaking apart with hands. Beat in oil, followed by buttermilk and vanilla. Stir in the flour mixture. Pour batter into prepared pan, spreading to edges.

4. Bake at 350° for 20 minutes. Remove cake from oven. Dust top with confectioners' sugar. Immediately invert cake onto clean kitchen towel and remove waxed paper. Roll up cake with towel, beginning with short end. Let cool to room temperature (about 1 hour).

5. Meanwhile, prepare Filling and Frosting. Once cake has cooled, carefully unroll. Gently spread marmalade over the unrolled cake. Top marmalade with 1 cup of the whipped cream mixture, leaving a ½-inch border on short ends. Roll up cake without towel, enclosing filling. Transfer to serving tray. Frost cake with remaining whipped cream mixture. Refrigerate for up to 24 hours.

Brown sugar adds a rich, butterscotchlike flavor that goes beautifully with the orange flavors in the filling and frosting.

PREP: 15 minutes
BAKE: at 350° for 20 minutes
COOL: 1 hour
CHILL: up to 24 hours
MAKES: 12 servings

FILLING AND FROSTING

In large bowl, combine 1¼ cups heavy cream, 2 tablespoons plus 1 teaspoon confectioners' sugar and ¼ teaspoon grated orange zest. With electric mixer on low to medium speed, beat until stiff peaks form but texture is still smooth.

Per serving: 312 calories, 17 g total fat (7 g sat.), 105 mg cholesterol, 211 mg sodium, 36 g carbohydrate, 0 g fiber, 4 g protein.

Glazed Plum Cake

½ cup milk
1 teaspoon sugar
1 envelope active dry yeast
2⅓ cups all-purpose flour, plus ¼ cup for dusting
¼ teaspoon salt
1 egg, lightly beaten
¼ cup vegetable oil
3 tablespoons honey
2 plums
1 teaspoon sugar
Lemon Glaze (recipe, left)

Peak season for plums is June and July—take advantage by baking the sweet summer fruit into a lovely cake.

PREP: 35 minutes
RISE: 1½ to 2 hours
CHILL: overnight
BAKE: at 375° for 40 to 45 minutes
COOL: 10 minutes
COOK: 5 minutes
MAKES: 8 servings

1. In small saucepan, heat together milk and 1 teaspoon sugar until the temperature registers 105° to 115° on an instant-read thermometer. Remove from heat. Sprinkle yeast over top milk. Let stand 5 minutes. Stir to dissolve yeast.

2. Meanwhile, in medium-size bowl, mix 2 cups flour and the salt. In small bowl, whisk egg, oil and honey. Whisk ⅓ cup flour into egg mixture; stir in yeast mixture.

3. Add egg mixture to flour mixture; stir until dough comes together. Transfer dough to floured surface. Knead for 5 minutes, using as much of remaining ¼ cup flour as needed to prevent sticking.

4. Transfer dough to greased bowl, turning dough to coat. Cover bowl loosely with waxed paper and clean kitchen towel. Let rise in warm place, away from drafts, for 1½ to 2 hours or until doubled in bulk.

5. Punch down dough; let rest for 3 minutes. Coat 8½-inch round springform pan with nonstick cooking spray. Pat out dough on lightly floured surface. Fit into bottom of prepared pan. Cover pan with plastic wrap; refrigerate overnight.

6. Remove springform pan from refrigerator; remove the plastic wrap. Heat oven to 375°.

7. Slice plums in half. Remove the pits and discard. Slice each plum into 12 equal slices. Fan plum slices in concentric circles over the top of the dough; sprinkle with 1 teaspoon sugar.

8. Bake at 375° for 40 to 45 minutes or until the edge of the cake is browned and the plums are soft. Let the cake cool in the pan on a wire rack for 10 minutes.

9. Prepare Lemon Glaze. Run a thin knife around the side of the springform pan. Release side of the pan and remove. Brush top of cake with Lemon Glaze. Serve slightly warm.

LEMON GLAZE

In small saucepan, bring ⅓ cup sugar and ⅓ cup water to a boil over medium-high heat. Reduce heat to medium; simmer for 5 minutes. Remove saucepan from heat; let cool. Stir in 1 teaspoon grated lemon zest.

Per serving: 286 calories, 9 g total fat (1 g sat.), 29 mg cholesterol, 90 mg sodium, 48 g carbohydrate, 2 g fiber, 6 g protein.

Chocolate Fudge Cake

- ½ cup (1 stick) unsalted butter
- 4 squares (1 ounce each) unsweetened chocolate, broken up
- 2½ cups all-purpose flour
- 2¼ cups sugar
- 1 cup unsweetened cocoa powder
- 2 teaspoons baking soda
- ½ teaspoon baking powder
- 1½ teaspoons salt
- 1½ cups sour cream
- 3 eggs
- 1 cup water
- 2 teaspoons vanilla extract
- Chocolate Frosting (recipe, right)

Garnish (optional):
- Chocolate curls
- Fresh raspberries

1. Heat oven to 350°. Grease and flour three 9-inch round cake pans.

2. In microwave-safe bowl, combine butter and chocolate; microwave on HIGH for 1 to 1½ minutes or until melted and smooth, stirring halfway through microwaving. Set aside. In large bowl, combine flour, sugar, cocoa powder, baking soda, baking powder and salt until blended.

3. Add sour cream, eggs, water, chocolate mixture and vanilla; beat with electric mixer on low speed about 30 seconds or until dry ingredients are moistened. Increase speed to medium; beat for 2 minutes. Pour into prepared pans.

4. Bake at 350° about 40 minutes or until cake layers spring back when pressed.

5. Cool layers in pans on wire rack for 10 minutes. Remove cakes to wire rack to cool.

6. Prepare Chocolate Frosting. Place a cake layer on pedestal. Spread with about ⅔ cup of the frosting. Top with second cake layer; spread with about ⅔ cup more frosting. Top with remaining cake layer. Frost top and sides, swirling decoratively. If desired, garnish with chocolate curls and raspberries.

Sour cream in the cake and the frosting—there's nothing better.

PREP: 20 minutes
BAKE: at 350° for 40 minutes
COOL: 10 minutes
MAKES: 12 servings

CHOCOLATE FROSTING

Place 4 squares (1 ounce each) unsweetened chocolate, broken up, in small microwave-safe bowl. Microwave on HIGH about 1 minute or until melted. Stir until smooth. In bowl, with electric mixer on medium speed, beat ½ cup solid vegetable shortening; ½ cup (1 stick) unsalted butter, softened; ⅓ cup milk; ¼ cup sour cream; 2 teaspoons vanilla extract; and ¼ teaspoon salt. Using 1 box (1 pound) confectioners' sugar, measure 1 cup sugar. Beat the 1 cup confectioners' sugar and ½ cup unsweetened cocoa powder into butter mixture. Gradually beat in the remainder of the box of confectioners' sugar and the chocolate.

Per serving: 889 calories, 46 g total fat (24 g sat.), 111 mg cholesterol, 612 mg sodium, 115 g carbohydrate, 11 g fiber, 14 g protein.

Pecan Pound Cake

Cake:
- 2½ cups all-purpose flour
- ½ cup finely ground pecans
- 1 tablespoon baking powder
- ½ teaspoon salt
- ¾ cup buttermilk
- ¼ cup hazelnut liqueur
- 1 teaspoon vanilla extract
- ¾ cup (1½ sticks) unsalted butter or regular margarine, at room temperature
- 2 cups sugar
- 4 eggs

Dark Chocolate Glaze:
- ⅓ cup evaporated milk
- ⅛ teaspoon salt
- 5 squares (1 ounce each) bittersweet chocolate, chopped

White Chocolate Glaze:
- 5 squares (1 ounce each) white baking chocolate, chopped
- 3 tablespoons solid vegetable shortening
- ⅛ teaspoon salt

A handful of pecans teamed with white and dark chocolate glazes adds a festive final flourish.

PREP: 30 minutes
BAKE: at 350° for 50 minutes
COOL: 23 minutes
MAKES: 16 servings

1. Heat oven to 350°. Coat 12-cup Bundt pan with nonstick cooking spray. Dust with flour.

2. **Cake:** In medium-size bowl, combine flour, pecans, baking powder and salt. In a small bowl, combine buttermilk, liqueur and vanilla. In large bowl, with electric mixer on medium speed, beat butter and sugar about 4 minutes or until creamy. Beat in eggs, one at a time, beating well after each addition. Beat in flour mixture in three additions, alternating with buttermilk mixture (beginning and ending with flour), beating until smooth. Pour into prepared pan. Bake at 350° about 50 minutes or until wooden pick inserted in center comes out clean. Let cake cool in pan 15 minutes. Remove cake from pan to wire rack; cool completely.

3. **Dark Chocolate Glaze:** In small saucepan, combine evaporated milk and salt. Bring just to a boil over medium heat. Add bittersweet chocolate; stir until melted and smooth. Spoon over cake; let stand until set.

4. **White Chocolate Glaze:** In small, heavy saucepan, combine white chocolate, vegetable shortening and salt. Heat over very low heat, stirring occasionally, until melted and smooth. Let cool slightly (about 8 minutes). Spoon over top of Dark Chocolate Glaze; let set.

QUICK TIP

BUTTERMILK SUBSTITUTE

Here's how to make a homemade sour milk mixture to substitute for buttermilk in baking: For each cup of sour milk needed, place 1 tablespoon lemon juice or vinegar in a glass measuring cup. Add enough milk to make 1 cup total liquid (increase or decrease measures proportionately to get the amount called for in the recipe). Let mixture stand for 5 minutes before using it.

Per serving: 369 calories, 18 g total fat (9 g sat.), 79 mg cholesterol, 216 mg sodium, 47 g carbohydrate, 2 g fiber, 5 g protein.

Flourless Almond-Chocolate Cake

8 ounces semisweet chocolate, coarsely chopped

10 tablespoons (1¼ sticks) butter, cut into small pieces

1 can (8 ounces) almond paste

3 tablespoons confectioners' sugar

¾ cup granulated sugar

4 eggs

1 teaspoon vanilla extract

½ teaspoon salt

⅓ cup Dutch-process cocoa powder or regular unsweetened cocoa powder

16 blanched whole almonds, for top

1 tablespoon confectioners' sugar, for garnish

1. Coat 9-inch springform pan with nonstick cooking spray.

2. In large microwave-safe bowl, combine chocolate and butter. Microwave on HIGH about 1 minute or until melted; stir until smooth. If needed, microwave 30 seconds to 1 minute longer, then stir. Let cool slightly.

3. Meanwhile, heat oven to 375°. On flat work surface, knead together almond paste and the 3 tablespoons confectioners' sugar. Roll out into 8-inch circle.

4. Beat granulated sugar into chocolate mixture about 1 minute or until smooth. Add eggs, one at a time, beating after each addition until blended; beat on high speed about 2 minutes or until slightly airy. Beat in vanilla and salt until blended. Sift the cocoa powder over the top of chocolate mixture; beat on low speed about 1 minute or until blended. Pour half of the batter into prepared pan. Carefully fit the almond paste circle on top of the batter in the pan. Scrape remaining chocolate batter into pan; spread to cover the circle and smooth the top. Carefully arrange whole almonds on top.

5. Bake at 375° for 30 minutes. Remove the pan to wire rack and let cool to room temperature. Refrigerate for 2 hours. Remove side of pan. Sprinkle the top with the 1 tablespoon confectioners' sugar. Slice and serve.

This flourless chocolate cake has a surprise contrasting layer of almond paste.

PREP: 20 minutes
BAKE: at 375° for 30 minutes
CHILL: 2 hours
MAKES: 16 servings

QUICK BITE
GO DUTCH

Dutch-process cocoa powder, also called European-style cocoa powder, is unsweetened cocoa powder that has been treated to neutralize its naturally occurring acids. Its flavor is more mellow and the color more red than unsweetened cocoa powder. Dutch-process and unsweetened cocoa powder can be used interchangeably in recipes.

Per serving: 268 calories, 19 g total fat (9 g sat.), 73 mg cholesterol, 92 mg sodium, 24 g carbohydrate, 2 g fiber, 5 g protein.

Strawberry Layer Cake

When strawberry season rolls around, show off the fruit between tender layers and fluffy whipped cream.

PREP: 25 minutes
BAKE: at 350° for 35 minutes
COOL: 15 minutes
MAKES: 12 servings

CHOOSING AND STORING STRAWBERRIES

Strawberries do not ripen after they're picked. Therefore, choose with care. Look for well-shaped, plump, bright red berries with fresh, green caps. Avoid any with green or white around the cap. To store, remove berries from their container and place in a bowl. Store in the coldest part of the refrigerator, loosely covered with plastic wrap, for up to 3 days. Do not wash until ready to use.

Per serving: 364 calories, 13 g total fat (7 g sat.), 112 mg cholesterol, 184 mg sodium, 57 g carbohydrate, 1 g fiber, 5 g protein.

3 cups cake flour (not self-rising), sifted
2½ teaspoons baking powder
¼ teaspoon salt
1 cup (2 sticks) butter, at room temperature
1½ cups granulated sugar
4 eggs
1 teaspoon vanilla extract
¾ cup cranberry-strawberry juice
 Strawberry Syrup (recipe, below)
1½ cups heavy cream plus 1½ tablespoons sugar, whipped
1 quart fresh strawberries, hulled and sliced (3 cups)
 Confectioners' sugar, for garnish (optional)
 Whole strawberries, for garnish (optional)

1. Heat oven to 350°. Coat two 8×2-inch round cake pans with nonstick cooking spray. Line bottoms with waxed paper. Coat waxed paper with nonstick cooking spray.

2. In medium bowl, mix cake flour, baking powder and salt. In large bowl, with electric mixer on medium speed, beat butter and granulated sugar for 2 minutes. Beat in eggs, one at a time. Beat in vanilla, then flour mixture in three additions, alternating with juice and beginning and ending with flour; beat for 1 minute. Divide between prepared pans.

3. Bake at 350° about 35 minutes or until wooden toothpick inserted in center comes out clean. Cool in pans on wire racks for 15 minutes. Invert onto wire racks; remove waxed paper. Cool. Slice each cake in half horizontally into two layers.

4. Brush cut sides of cake layers with Strawberry Syrup. Top the cut side of one cake layer with one third of the whipped cream, one-third of the sliced berries and another cake layer. Repeat layering once more, ending with cake, cut side down. If desired, sift with confectioners' sugar. If desired, garnish with whole strawberries.

Strawberry Syrup: In small saucepan, heat ¼ cup water, 3 tablespoons sugar and 2 tablespoons strawberry liqueur until sugar dissolves.

Piña Colada Party Cakes

Cakes:
- 1⅔ cups all-purpose flour
- ⅓ cup sugar
- 2¼ teaspoons baking powder
- ¼ teaspoon salt
- ¾ cup canned cream of coconut, well stirred
- 1 egg
- ¼ cup vegetable oil
- 1 can (8 ounces) crushed pineapple, drained, reserving ¼ cup juice for frosting

Frosting:
- ⅔ cup sugar
- ¼ cup reserved pineapple juice (from cakes)
- 1 egg white
- 1 tablespoon light corn syrup
- Pinch of cream of tartar
- Pinch of salt
- ½ teaspoon coconut extract
- Toasted shaved coconut, for garnish

1. **Cakes:** Heat oven to 400°. Coat a popover pan with nonstick cooking spray and line each of 6 indentations with two paper cupcake liners.

2. In large bowl, whisk together flour, sugar, baking powder and salt.

3. In small bowl, whisk together cream of coconut, egg and oil. Make a well in the flour mixture; add coconut mixture. Stir until flour mixture is moistened. Fold in drained crushed pineapple.

4. Transfer batter to popover cups, a heaping ⅓ cup per indentation.

5. Bake cakes at 400° for 15 minutes. Reduce oven temperature to 350°; bake for 8 minutes longer. Remove cakes immediately from pan; cool completely on a wire rack.

6. Once cakes are cool, prepare **Frosting:** In small saucepan (not nonstick), mix sugar, reserved pineapple juice, egg white, corn syrup, cream of tartar and salt. Heat over medium-low to medium heat, beating continuously with an electric mixer about 7 minutes or until medium-stiff white peaks are formed and an instant-read thermometer registers 150°. Remove from heat. Beat in coconut extract for 1 minute.

7. Spread cakes generously with frosting (about 3 tablespoons per cake; there will be frosting left over). If desired, run flat edge of knife around tops of cakes to create smooth edges. Top with toasted coconut.

A popover pan is the secret to making these sweet and petite beauties rise to the occasion!

PREP: 15 minutes
BAKE: at 400° for 15 minutes; at 350° for 8 minutes
COOK: 7 minutes
MAKES: 6 cakes

QUICK TIP

COCONUT CONFUSION

Don't confuse cream of coconut with coconut milk. Cream of coconut is a sweetened coconut concoction often used to make mixed drinks such as piña coladas; it's usually found alongside other drink mixes near the wine and spirits aisle of the supermarket.

Per cake: 447 calories, 17 g total fat (7 g sat.), 35 mg cholesterol, 315 mg sodium, 69 g carbohydrate, 2 g fiber, 6 g protein.

Lemon Poppy Seed Cake

Lemon and poppy seeds are natural partners in a buttery layer cake. The buttercream frosting is a best-loved favorite.

PREP: 30 minutes
STAND: 1 hour
BAKE: at 350° for 30 to 35 minutes
MAKES: 16 servings

LEMON BUTTERCREAM FROSTING

In clean large bowl, with electric mixer on high speed, beat 1¼ cups (2½ sticks) unsalted butter or regular margarine, at room temperature, until fluffy. On low speed, beat in 2½ boxes (1 pound each) confectioners' sugar alternately with ½ cup lemon juice until smooth and creamy. Stir in 2 tablespoons grated lemon zest and ⅛ teaspoon salt.

Per serving: 827 calories, 33 g total fat (19 g sat.), 82 mg cholesterol, 368 mg sodium, 130 g carbohydrate, 2 g fiber, 7 g protein.

3 jars (1¼ ounces each) poppy seeds (¾ cup)
2¼ cups milk
4½ cups cake flour (not self-rising)
1½ tablespoons baking powder
1½ teaspoons salt
6 egg whites
2½ cups granulated sugar
1¼ cups (2½ sticks) unsalted butter or regular margarine, at room temperature
2 tablespoons grated lemon zest
Lemon Buttercream Frosting (recipe, left)
Lemon zest strips, for garnish (optional)

1. In a small saucepan, combine poppy seeds and 1 cup milk. Heat to a boil. Remove from heat; cover and let stand 1 hour.

2. Heat oven to 350°. Grease and flour three 9×2-inch round cake pans. Sift together cake flour, baking powder and salt.

3. In large bowl, with electric mixer on high speed, beat egg whites until foamy. Beat in 1 cup sugar, 1 tablespoon at a time, until soft peaks form.

4. In another large bowl, on medium speed, beat together butter and the remaining 1½ cups sugar about 3 minutes or until smooth and creamy. Blend in poppy seed mixture and lemon zest. On low speed, beat in flour mixture in three additions, alternating with remaining 1¼ cups milk and beginning and ending with flour. Fold in egg whites until no white streaks remain. Divide batter among prepared pans.

5. Bake at 350° for 30 to 35 minutes or until centers spring back and wooden pick inserted in centers comes out clean. Using thin metal spatula, gently loosen sides of cakes. Cool layers in pans on wire racks for 10 minutes. Invert layers onto wire racks to cool completely.

6. Prepare Lemon Buttercream Frosting. Rub your hand around the edges of the cake layers to loosen and rub off any crumbs. Trim the rounded tops of the layers with serrated knife.

7. Place one cake layer, top side down, on serving platter. Spread top evenly with about ¾ cup of the frosting. Place second layer, bottom side down, on top. Spread top of the second layer with about ¾ cup of the frosting. Place third layer, bottom side down, on top. Frost top and sides of whole cake with the remaining frosting. If desired, garnish with lemon zest strips.

Buttermilk-Chocolate Chunk Cake

Cake:
- 3½ cups cake flour (not self-rising), sifted
- 2¼ teaspoons baking powder
- 1 teaspoon baking soda
- ½ teaspoon salt
- 1 cup (2 sticks) butter, at room temperature
- 2 cups granulated sugar
- 4 eggs
- 2 teaspoons vanilla extract
- 1½ cups buttermilk
- 8 ounces good-quality bittersweet chocolate, chopped

Assembly:
- Bittersweet Frosting (recipe, right)

1. **Cake:** Heat oven to 350°. Coat three 8-inch round cake pans with nonstick cooking spray. Line bottoms with waxed paper rounds. Coat waxed paper with nonstick cooking spray.

2. In large bowl, whisk together flour, baking powder, baking soda and salt.

3. In second large bowl, with electric mixer on medium-high speed, beat butter and sugar for 3 to 4 minutes or until smooth and light; scrape down sides halfway through. Add eggs, one at a time, beating well after each addition. Add vanilla; beat to mix.

4. On low speed, beat in flour mixture in three additions, alternating with buttermilk and beginning and ending with flour. Scrape down sides of bowl; beat on medium speed for 3 minutes. Fold in chocolate. Divide batter among pans, using scant 3 cups batter per pan; spread evenly in pans.

5. Bake on two racks at 350° for 30 to 35 minutes or until cakes spring back when lightly touched and a toothpick inserted in the centers comes out clean. (The layer on the bottom rack may take up to 5 minutes longer.) Let cakes cool in pans on wire racks for 20 minutes. Run sharp knife around edge of pans; turn out cake. Let cool completely. Remove waxed paper.

6. **Assembly:** Place one cake layer on cake stand or platter. Frost top with 1 cup Bittersweet Frosting. Place another cake layer on top; frost top with 1 cup of the frosting. Top with third cake layer. Reserve 1 cup of the frosting for top. Frost side of cake with remaining frosting, then frost top with reserved 1 cup. Refrigerate for at least 1 hour before serving.

Is there a birthday coming up? This beauty will make the person being honored feel extra special.

PREP: 20 minutes
BAKE: at 350° for 30 to 35 minutes
CHILL: 1 hour
MAKES: 16 servings

BITTERSWEET FROSTING

In large bowl, with electric mixer on medium-high speed, beat 1 cup (2 sticks) butter, softened, about 2 minutes or until smooth. On low speed, beat in 1 box (1 pound) confectioners' sugar and ¼ cup buttermilk for 1 to 2 minutes or until blended; scrape down sides of bowl. Beat in another box (1 pound) confectioners' sugar, another ¼ cup buttermilk and 2 teaspoons vanilla extract; beat for 1 to 2 minutes. Beat in 4 ounces bittersweet chocolate, melted and cooled. Cover bowl with plastic wrap and let stand at room temperature until needed (up to 1 hour).

Per serving: 759 calories, 33 g total fat (20 g sat.), 117 mg cholesterol, 258 mg sodium, 113 g carbohydrate, 2 g fiber, 6 g protein.

Apple Meringue Tart

1 package (11 ounces) piecrust mix
¼ teaspoon ground cinnamon
2 tablespoons ice water
1 egg white
  Pinch of salt
⅓ cup plus 2 tablespoons sugar
½ cup sliced almonds, chopped
1 tablespoon plus 2 teaspoons all-purpose flour
3 Golden Delicious apples (about 1¼ pounds total)
2 tablespoons apple jelly (optional)

1. Heat oven to 425°. Place 1¼ cups (about half) of the piecrust mix (reserve remainder for another recipe) in medium-size bowl. Add cinnamon; stir with a fork to combine. Add ice water and stir until dough comes together in a ball.

2. Transfer dough to a floured surface; roll out to a 10-inch circle. Drape into a 9-inch fluted tart pan with removable bottom. Fit into bottom, then fold over edge to come halfway up side of pan. Pierce with a fork; line with nonstick aluminum foil. Fill foil with dried beans, rice or pie weights; bake crust at 425° for 8 minutes.

3. While crust bakes, place egg white and salt in medium-size bowl. Add ⅓ cup sugar (1 tablespoon at a time), beating constantly with an electric mixer on medium to high speed. Once sugar is added, beat for 1 minute. Stir in almonds and 1 tablespoon flour.

4. Remove crust from oven and remove foil and beans. Spread almond mixture over bottom of crust. Set aside.

5. Peel and core apples. Cut into ¼-inch-thick slices. In large bowl, toss apple slices with the remaining 2 tablespoons sugar and the remaining 2 teaspoons flour. Arrange apple slices in concentric circles in crust, packing as closely together as possible.

6. Bake tart at 425° for 30 to 35 minutes or until apples are knife-tender. Meanwhile, if desired, melt jelly in microwave on HIGH about 20 seconds; stir until smooth and brush jelly onto warm tart. Slice and serve.

Sliced apples are baked atop a layer of tempting almond-infused meringue.

PREP: 15 minutes
BAKE: at 425° for 38 to 43 minutes
MAKES: 12 servings

QUICK TIP

PICKING THE BEST APPLES

When baking with apples, use the variety specified in the recipe. If no variety is specified, use a combination of these sweet and tart varieties:
Sweet: Braeburn, Golden Delicious, Jonagold
Tart: Cortland, Granny Smith, Jonathan (Jonathan apples do not perform well when baked whole.)

Per serving: 229 calories, 12 g total fat (3 g sat.), 0 mg cholesterol, 210 mg sodium, 28 g carbohydrate, 1 g fiber, 3 g protein.

Pineapple Tart

Crust:
- 1½ cups all-purpose flour
- ½ cup macadamia nuts, finely ground
- ⅓ cup sugar
- 1 teaspoon grated orange zest (optional)
- ¼ teaspoon salt
- ½ cup (1 stick) unsalted butter, cut into small pieces and chilled
- 1 egg yolk

Pastry Cream:
- 1 cup milk
- 5 tablespoons sugar
- 2 egg yolks
- 2½ tablespoons all-purpose flour
- 1 tablespoon unsalted butter
- 1½ teaspoons vanilla extract

Topping:
- ½ of 3-pound pineapple, peeled and cored
- ½ pint fresh raspberries

1. **Crust:** In medium-size bowl, mix flour, nuts, sugar, zest (if using) and salt. Using pastry blender, cut in butter until mixture is consistency of peas. Stir in egg yolk until dough begins to come together. Shape into ball; wrap in plastic wrap. Refrigerate for 20 minutes.

2. Heat oven to 400°. Select a 14×4×¼-inch tart pan with removable bottom or a 9-inch round tart pan with removable bottom. Roll out dough to 15×5-inch rectangle for rectangular pan or 10-inch circle for round pan. Fit dough into pan. Prick bottom and sides of dough with a fork. Bake at 400° about 20 minutes or until golden brown. Cool on wire rack.

3. **Pastry Cream:** In small saucepan, bring milk and 3 tablespoons sugar to boiling, stirring to dissolve sugar. Remove from heat. In bowl, whisk egg yolks and the remaining 2 tablespoons sugar until lemon color and smooth. Whisk in flour until smooth. Whisk in a little of the hot milk mixture. Whisk egg yolk mixture into milk mixture in saucepan. Bring to a boil, whisking; simmer about 2 minutes or until thickened, whisking. Remove from heat. Stir in butter and vanilla. Strain through sieve over bowl. Cover pastry cream surface directly with plastic wrap; refrigerate about 2 hours or until chilled.

4. **Topping:** Cut pineapple into thin slices. Spoon pastry cream into tart shell, spreading to edges. Top with pineapple and berries.

A buttery crust combines with vanilla-scented pastry cream and fresh fruit for a refreshing treat.

PREP: 15 minutes
BAKE: at 400° for 20 minutes
COOK: 10 to 15 minutes
CHILL: 2 hours
MAKES: 12 servings

QUICK TIP

PRODUCE POINTERS

A symbol of hospitality, pineapple is in peak season from December through February (from the Caribbean) and then again in April and May (from Hawaii). Look for firm fruit with green leaves. It should be heavy for its size, with flat "eyes" and no bruises. It will not ripen once picked; however, keeping it at room temperature will reduce its acidity. To store, wrap it in plastic and keep in the warmest part of the refrigerator for several days. Enjoy pineapple as soon as possible.

Per serving: 269 calories, 15 g total fat (7 g sat.), 79 mg cholesterol, 62 mg sodium, 31 g carbohydrate, 2 g fiber, 4 g protein.

Hazelnut Fruit Tart

Use your imagination to arrange four different types of fruit in a creative way on top of this nutty tart.

PREP: 40 minutes
CHILL: crust for 1 hour to 2 days; tart for 1 hour
BAKE: at 350° for 25 minutes
MAKES: 8 servings

QUICK TIP

PRODUCE POINTERS

When choosing fruit, look for those that are heavy for their size, an indication of juiciness. Avoid fruits with bruises, mold, mildew or other blemishes. When making this tart, suit your taste when it comes to fruit choices. For example, try topping it with pitted sweet cherries and sliced nectarines—a surefire fruit combo.

Crust:
- 1 cup all-purpose flour
- ¼ cup sugar
- 2 tablespoons ground hazelnuts
- ¼ teaspoon salt
- ¼ cup (½ stick) butter, cut into small pieces and chilled
- 1 egg, lightly beaten
- Pastry Cream (recipe, page 276)

Topping:
- 1 pint strawberries, hulled and sliced (1½ cups)
- 2 kiwifruits, peeled and sliced
- 2 bananas, sliced
- 1 container (½ pint) raspberries
- 2 tablespoons currant jelly
- 2 tablespoons ground hazelnuts, for garnish

1. **Crust:** In large bowl, mix flour, sugar, hazelnuts and salt. Using pastry blender, cut in butter until mixture resembles cornmeal.

2. Make a well in center of flour mixture; add egg to well. Mix egg into flour with fork just until dough comes together. Pat into bottom and up sides of ungreased 9-inch tart pan with removable bottom. Cover; refrigerate at least 1 hour or up to 2 days.

3. Heat oven to 350°. Line dough with foil. Fill with dried beans, rice or pie weights. Bake at 350° for 15 minutes. Remove foil and beans. Bake about 10 minutes longer or just until crust starts to brown. Let cool in pan on wire rack for 5 minutes. Remove crust from pan to wire rack and let cool completely.

4. **Topping:** Prepare Pastry Cream. Spread cooled Pastry Cream over bottom of cooled tart shell. Arrange fruit over top.

5. In small saucepan, melt jelly. Cool slightly; brush over fruit. Garnish with nuts. Refrigerate for at least 1 hour.

Per serving: 357 calories, 13 g total fat (6 g sat.), 157 mg cholesterol, 118 mg sodium, 53 g carbohydrate, 4 g fiber, 8 g protein.

Pecan Pie Tartlets

Crust:
- ¾ cup pecan pieces
- 2 cups all-purpose flour
- 2 teaspoons granulated sugar
- 1 teaspoon salt
- ½ cup (1 stick) butter, cut into pieces
- ⅓ cup water
- 2 egg yolks

Filling:
- ½ cup mini semisweet chocolate chips
- 5 eggs
- 1½ cups light corn syrup
- ¾ cup granulated sugar
- ¾ cup packed dark-brown sugar
- 1½ teaspoons vanilla extract
- 1 cup chopped pecans
- ½ cup pecan halves

1. **Crust:** Heat oven to 350°. Toast pecans on baking sheet at 350° about 8 minutes or until slightly darkened. Cool. (Turn oven off.) Pulse nuts in food processor until ground. Add flour, granulated sugar and salt; pulse to combine. Add butter; pulse to form fine crumbs.

2. In small bowl, whisk water and egg yolks. Add to flour mixture; process until dough is moistened. Remove from processor; shape into 8×6-inch rectangle. Wrap; refrigerate for 1 hour.

3. Heat oven to 350°. Divide dough into eight equal pieces. On floured surface with floured rolling pin, roll out one piece of dough to 6-inch circle. Drape into 5×1-inch-deep pie plate or pan. Tuck rim under; flute edge. Repeat with remaining dough for eight tartlets.

4. **Filling:** Sprinkle 1 tablespoon chocolate chips over bottom of each crust. In large bowl, whisk eggs, corn syrup, granulated sugar, brown sugar and vanilla; stir in chopped pecans. Divide mixture among pie pans, about ½ cup per pie. Sprinkle tops with pecan halves. Place tartlets on baking sheets.

5. Bake at 350° about 45 minutes or until crusts are golden brown and centers are puffed and browned; switch positions and rotate sheets halfway through baking time. Transfer tartlets to wire racks; let cool. Cut tartlets in half for two servings each.

All the yummy goodness of pecan pie served in oh-so-cute mini versions—each studded with just a sprinkling of chocolate.

PREP: 30 minutes
CHILL: 1 hour
BAKE: nuts at 350° for 8 minutes; tartlets at 350° for 45 minutes
MAKES: 16 servings (8 tartlets)

QUICK TIP

MEASURING SUGAR

To measure granulated or confectioners' sugar, spoon it into a dry measuring cup and level it off with the straight side of a knife. To measure brown sugar, press it firmly into a dry measure so it holds the shape of the cup when it is turned out.

Per serving: 460 calories, 24 g total fat (6 g sat.), 109 mg cholesterol, 199 mg sodium, 60 g carbohydrate, 2 g fiber, 6 g protein.

Chocolate Cream Pie

This pie is so deliciously decadent you'll need only a small slice.

PREP: 30 minutes
CHILL: crust for 30 minutes; pie for 3 hours
BAKE: at 425° for 23 to 25 minutes
COOK: about 25 minutes
MAKES: 10 servings

CHOCOLATE FILLING

In small, heavy saucepan, combine 2½ squares (1 ounce each) unsweetened chocolate and ½ cup milk; heat over low heat, stirring constantly, until chocolate melts. In large saucepan, combine 1½ cups granulated sugar, ⅔ cup cornstarch and ¾ teaspoon salt. Gradually stir in 3½ cups milk until smooth. Stir in chocolate mixture. Cook over medium heat, stirring constantly, for 15 to 20 minutes or until mixture is thickened and begins to bubble; cook 2 to 3 minutes longer, stirring constantly.

Pie Pastry:
- 1⅓ cups all-purpose flour
- 2 tablespoons granulated sugar
- ½ teaspoon salt
- ½ cup solid vegetable shortening, chilled
- 3 tablespoons cold water
- Chocolate Filling (recipe, left)

Cream Topping:
- 2 cups heavy cream
- ¼ cup confectioners' sugar
- 1½ teaspoons vanilla extract

1. **Pie Pastry:** In medium-size bowl, mix together flour, sugar and salt until well blended. Using pastry blender or two knives, cut shortening into flour mixture until coarse crumbs form. Gradually add water, tossing with a fork until the mixture begins to come together. With your hands, shape pastry into a ball.

2. Roll pastry out on lightly floured surface into 13-inch circle. Roll pastry up on rolling pin; unroll into 9-inch pie plate. Gently fit pastry into pie plate, being careful not to stretch pastry. Roll edge of the pastry under to form a stand-up edge; with your fingers, flute edge. Place crust in refrigerator for 30 minutes to chill.

3. To bake crust, heat oven to 425°. Remove pie plate from refrigerator. Prick pastry all over with a fork. Line pastry shell with aluminum foil; fill with dried beans, rice or pie weights.

4. Bake pastry at 425° for 15 minutes. Carefully remove the aluminum foil with the beans. Bake crust for 8 to 10 minutes longer or until edge of the crust is golden brown. Let cool while preparing filling.

5. Prepare Chocolate Filling. Pour filling into cooled pastry shell. Place a sheet of plastic wrap directly on the surface of the filling. Refrigerate about 3 hours or until well chilled.

6. **Cream Topping:** Just before serving, in small bowl, with electric mixer on low to medium speed, beat together cream, confectioners' sugar and vanilla until stiff peaks form. Spread topping evenly over surface of the pie. Refrigerate until ready to serve.

Per serving: 611 calories, 38 g total fat (19 g sat.), 185 mg cholesterol, 362 mg sodium, 64 g carbohydrate, 2 g fiber, 8 g protein.

Lemon Meringue Pie

Pastry:
- 1⅓ cups all-purpose flour
- 2 tablespoons sugar
- ½ teaspoon salt
- ½ cup (1 stick) butter or margarine
- 3 tablespoons cold water

Lemon Filling:
- 3 to 4 large lemons
- 1¾ cups sugar
- ¾ cup cornstarch
- ¼ teaspoon salt
- 2¼ cups water
- 6 eggs, separated
- 2 tablespoons butter or margarine
- Meringue (recipe, right)

1. **Pastry:** In medium-size bowl, mix flour, sugar and salt. Using pastry blender, cut in butter until coarse crumbs form. Gradually add water, tossing with fork, until pastry comes together. Roll pastry out on floured surface to 13-inch circle. Roll pastry up on rolling pin; unroll into 9-inch pie plate. Fit into pie plate. Roll edge under; flute. Chill 30 minutes. Heat oven to 425°. Prick crust all over with fork. Line with aluminum foil; fill with dried beans or pie weights. Bake at 425° for 15 minutes. Remove foil and beans. Bake for 8 to 10 minutes or until edge is golden. Cool.

2. **Lemon Filling:** Grate 2 tablespoons lemon zest and squeeze ¾ cup juice from lemons. In large saucepan, mix sugar, cornstarch and salt. Stir in water and lemon juice. Cook over medium heat, stirring, for 15 to 20 minutes or until thickened and bubbly. Cook for 2 to 3 minutes longer, stirring. Remove from heat.

3. In small bowl, use fork to beat egg yolks (reserve egg whites for Meringue); stir in ½ cup of the hot lemon mixture. Stir egg yolk mixture into lemon mixture in saucepan. Cook over low, stirring, for 1 minute (don't overcook). Turn off heat; stir in butter and lemon zest. Pour into crust. Place oven rack in lower third of oven. Heat oven to 325°. Spoon Meringue over filling, spreading to edge of crust to seal to prevent shrinkage. Swirl in peaks.

4. Bake pie in lower third of oven at 325° about 30 minutes or until instant-read thermometer inserted in meringue registers 140°. Bake for 3 minutes longer. Cool on wire rack at room temperature for up to 2 hours. Refrigerate for at least 1 hour. (Pie may be refrigerated longer, but you will need a wet knife to cut it.)

Offer a piece of cool and tangy lemon meringue after a big, hearty meal.

PREP: 35 minutes
CHILL: crust for 30 minutes; pie for 1 hour
BAKE: crust at 425° for 23 to 25 minutes; pie at 325° for 33 minutes
COOK: 20 minutes
COOL: 2 hours
MAKES: 8 servings

MERINGUE

In a large bowl, using electric mixer on medium-high speed, beat 6 egg whites from Lemon Filling plus 2 additional egg whites and ½ teaspoon cream of tartar until foamy. On high speed, slowly beat in ¾ cup sugar, a tablespoon at a time, until stiff peaks form.

Per serving: 568 calories, 18 g total fat (9 g sat.), 190 mg cholesterol, 397 mg sodium, 95 g carbohydrate, 1 g fiber, 8 g protein.

Mocha Bars

Crust:
- 14 cream-filled chocolate sandwich cookies, finely crushed in food processor
- ¼ cup chocolate-covered espresso beans, finely crushed in plastic bag with rolling pin
- 1 teaspoon instant espresso coffee powder
- ¼ cup (½ stick) butter, melted

Filling:
- 1 tablespoon instant espresso coffee powder
- 1 tablespoon milk
- 2 cups sifted confectioners' sugar
- ¼ cup (½ stick) butter, at room temperature
- 1 teaspoon vanilla extract
- ¼ cup chocolate-covered espresso beans, chopped

Topping:
- 4 ounces semisweet chocolate, chopped
- ⅓ cup heavy cream
- 2 ounces white baking chocolate, chopped

Mixing in crushed chocolate-covered espresso beans makes for an out-of-this-world crust.

PREP: 35 minutes
CHILL: 1 hour
MAKES: 30 bars

1. **Crust:** In a medium-size bowl, stir together crushed cookies, espresso beans and espresso powder. Stir in melted butter until mixture is evenly moistened. Press mixture over the bottom of an 8×8×2-inch baking pan.

2. **Filling:** In a bowl, stir together espresso powder and milk. Add 1 cup of the confectioners' sugar and the butter; beat, with an electric mixer on medium-high speed, until smooth. On low speed, gradually add the remaining 1 cup confectioners' sugar, beating until incorporated. Beat in vanilla. Stir in espresso beans. Spread over top of crust in pan. Chill about 30 minutes or until slightly firm.

3. **Topping:** Place semisweet chocolate in a small bowl. In a small saucepan, heat cream just until simmering. Pour cream over chocolate, stirring until smooth. Let cool to 80°. Pour over filling in pan; spread out smoothly.

4. Place white chocolate in a small microwave-safe bowl. Microwave on HIGH for 45 seconds. Stir; microwave on HIGH for 30 seconds longer. Stir until smooth. Transfer melted white chocolate to a small pastry bag fitted with a medium writing tip. (Or place melted white chocolate in a small heavy-duty plastic bag; snip off one corner.) Pipe white chocolate in parallel lines, ½ inch apart, across chocolate topping. Run the tip of a knife across the white stripes, alternating directions with each pass to form a feathered pattern. Chill about 30 minutes or until firm. Cut into bars.

Per bar: 130 calories, 8 g total fat (4 g sat.), 12 mg cholesterol, 38 mg sodium, 15 g carbohydrate, 0 g fiber, 1 g protein.

Cappuccino Chiffon Pie

- 1 **cup all-purpose flour**
- ½ **cup unsweetened cocoa powder**
- 3 **tablespoons sugar**
- ¼ **teaspoon salt**
- ½ **cup (1 stick) butter, cut into small pieces and chilled**
- 1 **egg yolk**
- 3 **tablespoons cold water**
  Espresso Filling (recipe, page 276)
  Chocolate curls, for garnish (optional)

1. In food processor, pulse together flour, cocoa powder, sugar and salt to blend. Add cold butter; pulse until coarse crumbs form and no large pieces of butter remain. Add egg yolk and the cold water; pulse until dough begins to come together. Transfer dough to sheet of plastic wrap. Shape into disk; wrap disk with plastic wrap. Refrigerate about 30 minutes or until firm.

2. Once dough has chilled, heat oven to 425°. Using a paper towel moistened with vegetable oil, lightly grease edge of 10-inch pie plate.

3. Roll out dough between two sheets of waxed paper into 14-inch circle. Remove top sheet of waxed paper; invert crust into pie plate and remove paper. Gently press crust over bottom and up sides of pie plate. Crimp edge of crust as desired. Prick crust all over with fork. Place in freezer for 10 minutes to firm.

4. Line crust with aluminum foil; fill with dried beans, rice or pie weights.

5. Bake at 425° for 10 minutes. Carefully remove from oven. Remove foil and beans. Return piecrust to oven; bake for 8 to 10 minutes longer or until set and dry to the touch. Let crust cool in pie plate on wire rack.

6. Prepare Espresso Filling. Dollop 1 cup of the coffee-flavored chiffon into cooled piecrust. Top with the vanilla chiffon. Place small dollops of the remaining coffee chiffon on top. Swirl with thin knife or spatula to marbleize chiffon. Refrigerate, covered, about 2 hours or until filling is set (cover by inverting large bowl over top of pie).

7. Before serving, if desired, garnish with chocolate curls. Store pie, refrigerated and covered, for up to 1 week.

If you need an all-out dazzler for your next get-together with friends, this is it. Make it up to one week ahead of time.

PREP: 30 minutes
CHILL: crust for 30 minutes; pie for 2 hours
FREEZE: 10 minutes
BAKE: at 425° for 18 to 20 minutes
MAKES: 12 servings

QUICK TIP

THE FINISHING TOUCH

Chocolate curls are simple to make and add that "this is really special" element to desserts. To create curls, grab your trusty vegetable peeler and run it down the long side of a chocolate bar. Presto— an instant, deliciously edible garnish!

Per serving: 283 calories, 19 g total fat (11 g sat.), 126 mg cholesterol, 102 mg sodium, 25 g carbohydrate, 2 g fiber, 5 g protein.

Cream Filling

For Cookies 'n' Cream Delights (recipe, page 251)

- 2 **cups milk**
- 7 **tablespoons sugar**
- ½ **of a vanilla bean**
- 4 **egg yolks**
- 2 **tablespoons all-purpose flour**
- 2 **tablespoons cornstarch**
- 1½ **teaspoons unflavored gelatin**
- 3 **tablespoons raspberry-flavored liqueur**
- 1 **cup heavy cream**

1. In medium-size saucepan combine milk and 2 tablespoons sugar. Scrape seeds from vanilla bean into milk mixture; add bean. Bring to a boil over medium heat. Remove from heat. Let steep for 15 minutes. Discard vanilla bean.

2. In medium-size bowl, whisk together egg yolks and 2 tablespoons sugar until lemon colored and smooth. Sift in flour and cornstarch; whisk until blended and smooth.

3. Whisk ½ cup of the hot milk mixture into egg yolk mixture. Pour egg yolk mixture into milk in saucepan. Bring to a boil, stirring constantly. Boil for 2 minutes, stirring. Remove from heat.

4. In small glass measuring cup, sprinkle gelatin over raspberry liqueur. Let stand for 5 minutes to soften gelatin. Bring small saucepan of water to boiling. Place measuring cup in water; stir gelatin mixture to dissolve gelatin. Stir gelatin mixture into egg yolk mixture. Pour into bowl, straining if necessary to remove any lumps. Place bowl in ice-water bath about 5 minutes or until cooled and slightly thickened, stirring occasionally. Remove from heat.

5. In medium-size bowl, beat together heavy cream and remaining 3 tablespoons sugar until stiff peaks form. Stir one-quarter of the whipped cream into egg yolk mixture. Gently fold in remaining whipped cream. Place plastic wrap directly on surface. Refrigerate about 1 hour or until completely cooled. Makes about 4 cups.

Pastry Cream

For Hazelnut Fruit Tart (recipe, page 270)

- 2 **cups milk**
- ⅓ **cup sugar**
- ½ **of a vanilla bean**
- 4 **egg yolks**
- 2 **tablespoons all-purpose flour**
- 2 **tablespoons cornstarch**
- 1 **teaspoon unflavored gelatin**
- 2 **tablespoons hazelnut liqueur**

1. In small saucepan, mix milk and half of the ⅓ cup sugar. Scrape seeds and pulp from the vanilla bean into saucepan; add vanilla bean. Bring to a boil. Remove from heat; steep for 15 minutes. Discard vanilla bean.

2. In bowl, whisk egg yolks and remaining sugar until lemon colored and smooth. Sift in flour and cornstarch; whisk until blended and smooth.

3. Whisk ½ cup of hot milk mixture into the egg yolk mixture. Pour egg yolk mixture into milk mixture in saucepan. Bring to boil, whisking constantly. Boil 2 minutes; whisk occasionally. Remove from heat.

4. In a medium-size bowl, sprinkle gelatin over hazelnut liqueur. Stir to dissolve gelatin, gently heating if necessary. Stir in egg yolk mixture; strain if lumpy. Place bowl in ice bath; cool, gently stirring occasionally, for 15 minutes. Place plastic wrap directly on surface of pastry cream. Refrigerate to chill thoroughly (up to 1 day).

Espresso Filling

For Cappuccino Chiffon Pie (recipe, page 275)

- 1 **envelope (0.25 ounce) unflavored gelatin**
- ⅓ **cup sugar**
- ⅛ **teaspoon salt**
- ⅓ **cup water**
- 3 **egg yolks**
- 1 **teaspoon vanilla extract**
- 1¼ **cups heavy cream**
- 2 **tablespoons pasteurized dried egg whites**
- 6 **tablespoons warm water**
- ⅓ **cup sugar**
- 1 **tablespoon instant espresso coffee powder**
- 1 **tablespoon hot water**

1. In saucepan, stir together gelatin, ⅓ cup sugar and salt; add ⅓ cup water and yolks. Let stand 3 minutes or until gelatin is softened. Heat over medium-low heat, whisking gently, until mixture thickens and registers 160° on an instant-read thermometer. Strain through fine-mesh sieve into large bowl. Stir in vanilla. Chill 5 minutes.

2. In large bowl, beat cream until soft peaks form. Chill. Whisk gelatin mixture; let stand at room temperature. Using clean bowl and beaters, beat whites and warm water until foamy. Gradually add ⅓ cup sugar; beat until stiff peaks form. Fold beaten whites into gelatin mixture. Fold in whipped cream. Reserve 1½ cups whipped cream mixture. Dissolve espresso in hot water; fold into reserved whipped cream mixture.

Great Gatherings

Tex-Mex Spicy Meatballs p. 279

From Valentine's Day, Easter Sunday
and summer picnics to tailgates, Thanksgiving and
Christmas, whatever you're celebrating, you'll find
all the menus, recipes and tips you need
to make the occasion easy and unforgettable.

Crispy Fried Chicken

Chicken:
- 2 cups buttermilk
- 2 tablespoons hot-pepper sauce
- 2 tablespoons Dijon mustard
- 1 egg
- 1½ teaspoons dried oregano
- 8 thin-sliced chicken breast cutlets (about 1½ pounds total)
- 2 cups panko (Japanese) bread crumbs
- ½ teaspoon salt
- ½ teaspoon black pepper

Honey-Mustard Sauce:
- 3 tablespoons honey
- 2 tablespoons Dijon mustard
- 1 tablespoon white-wine vinegar
- 1½ quarts (6 cups) vegetable oil, for frying

1. **Chicken:** For marinade, in large glass bowl, whisk together buttermilk, hot-pepper sauce, Dijon mustard, egg and 1 teaspoon oregano. Add chicken cutlets and submerge in marinade. Cover with plastic wrap; refrigerate for 1 to 2 hours.

2. In shallow dish, toss together bread crumbs, the remaining ½ teaspoon oregano, the salt and pepper. Set the mixture aside.

3. **Honey-Mustard Sauce:** In small bowl, whisk together honey, Dijon mustard and vinegar until smooth. Set aside until serving.

4. In deep pot, heat oil over medium heat until it registers 350° on deep-fat frying thermometer. Remove chicken from refrigerator. One at a time, remove cutlets from marinade, letting excess marinade drip back into bowl. Discard marinade. Coat cutlets with bread crumb mixture.

5. Add three chicken cutlets at a time to hot oil. Fry about 3 minutes or until lightly browned. Transfer cutlets to a paper towel-lined platter; tent with aluminum foil to keep warm.

6. Let oil return to 350° before continuing with the frying. Repeat as above with remaining chicken and bread crumbs. Serve cutlets warm with the Honey-Mustard Sauce.

This headliner has everything going for it—buttermilk to add moisture, panko crumbs for a gorgeous crust and a memorable honey-mustard dipping sauce.

PREP: 10 minutes
CHILL: 1 to 2 hours
COOK: 3 minutes per batch
MAKES: 8 servings

QUICK TIP

CHICKEN KNOW-HOW

Keep a stash of chicken cutlets on hand for last-minute get-togethers. At the store avoid packages with a lot of juice in them. Refrigerate chicken as soon as you get it home. If you plan to use the cutlets within 2 days, keep them in the original wrapping and set them on a plate in the refrigerator. Otherwise wrap individual pieces in plastic and place them in a resealable freezer bag. Store them in the freezer for up to 1 year.

Per serving: 267 calories, 9 g fat (1 g sat.), 57 mg cholesterol, 355 mg sodium, 22 g carbohydrate, 1 g fiber, 22 g protein.

Tex-Mex Spicy Meatballs

½ cup packaged plain dry bread crumbs
½ cup milk
1½ pounds lean ground beef
2 eggs
2 tablespoons dried minced onion
1 teaspoon ground cumin
1 teaspoon dried oregano
½ teaspoon garlic salt
¼ teaspoon cayenne pepper
1 cup beef broth
¾ cup chili sauce (such as Heinz brand)

1. Heat oven to 350°. Line a baking sheet with nonstick aluminum foil.

2. In small bowl, combine bread crumbs and milk. Let stand until bread crumbs absorb the milk.

3. In large bowl, combine ground beef, bread crumb mixture, eggs, dried minced onion, cumin, oregano, garlic salt and cayenne pepper. Mix with clean hands until combined. Form into 30 meatballs, each about 1 inch in diameter; place on prepared baking sheet.

4. Bake meatballs at 350° for 20 minutes.

5. In large skillet, mix together broth and chili sauce. Add meatballs and simmer, covered, over medium heat for 10 minutes. Stir occasionally. Remove cover; cook for 5 minutes longer.

Make Ahead: Can be made ahead, cooked, covered and refrigerated for 1 to 2 days; reheat before serving. To transport, place in an insulated container. Serve within 2 hours (within 1 hour if the outside temperature is above 90°).

Every bowl-game party needs a great batch of meatballs. This is yours!

PREP: 20 minutes
BAKE: at 350° for 20 minutes
COOK: 15 minutes
MAKES: 30 meatballs

QUICK TIP

PARTY PLANNING

Before the crowd arrives,
be sure to:
- Empty the dishwasher.
- Set out serving plates and utensils.
- Line up music so it's ready to play.
- Arrange plates of food that can be served cold.
- Clear out the fridge to make room for any dishes that guests may bring.

Per meatball: 63 calories, 3 g fat (1 g sat.), 23 mg cholesterol, 192 mg sodium, 4 g carbohydrate, 0 g fiber, 6 g protein.

Chocolate Cheesecake

Crust:
- 1 **box (11 ounces) sweet tea biscuits (such as Social Tea biscuits) (about 66 cookies, 2 sleeves), finely crushed (about 3 cups)**
- 6 **tablespoons (¾ stick) butter, melted**
- ½ **teaspoon ground cinnamon**

Filling:
- 3 **packages (8 ounces each) cream cheese, at room temperature**
- 1 **cup sugar**
- 1 **tablespoon cornstarch**
- 4 **eggs**
- 12 **squares (1 ounce each) semisweet chocolate, melted**
- 1 **cup sour cream**
- 1 **teaspoon vanilla extract**
- ¾ **cup sour cream, for garnish (optional)**

1. **Crust:** Heat oven to 325°. In medium-size bowl, stir together crumbs, butter and cinnamon until crumbs are evenly moistened. Press mixture over bottom and halfway up sides of 9-inch springform pan.

2. Bake at 325° about 7 minutes or until lightly browned. Let cool slightly in pan on wire rack.

3. **Filling:** In large bowl, with electric mixer on medium-high speed, beat together cream cheese, sugar and cornstarch about 2 minutes or until smooth. Add eggs, one at a time, beating well after each addition. Beat in melted chocolate, the 1 cup sour cream and vanilla.

4. Wrap aluminum foil around bottom and up sides of springform pan to prevent any leakage. Pour filling into the pan; smooth with rubber spatula. Place springform pan into large baking pan; place on oven rack. Pour hot water into baking pan to come halfway up sides of springform pan.

5. Bake at 325° for 60 to 70 minutes or until center of cheesecake is set. Remove springform pan from water bath. Run knife around edge of cheesecake. Remove aluminum foil from pan. Place pan on wire rack; let cool. Cover and refrigerate for 6 hours or overnight.

6. To serve, release side of springform pan and remove. Cut cheesecake into wedges. If desired, garnish wedges with spoonfuls of the ¾ cup sour cream.

It's hard to beat a smooth chocolate cheesecake when you want to indulge friends and family at a special party.

PREP: 25 minutes
BAKE: crust at 325° for 7 minutes; cheesecake at 325° for 60 to 70 minutes
CHILL: 6 hours or overnight
MAKES: 20 servings

QUICK TIP

CHOCOLATE-DIPPED STRAWBERRIES

To make the strawberries shown in the photo above, cut up 3 squares (1-ounce each) semisweet chocolate. In small microwave-safe bowl, microwave chocolate on MEDIUM power 1 to 1½ minutes or until melted, stirring occasionally. Tilt bowl to pool chocolate; dip desired number of small whole strawberries in chocolate to coat half of each berry. Place on waxed paper; let harden at room temperature.

Per serving: 392 calories, 26 g fat (15 g sat.), 94 mg cholesterol, 180 mg sodium, 35 g carbohydrate, 2 g fiber, 6 g protein.

Salsa Verde Dip

1 jar (15 ounces) green salsa (about 1½ cups)
1 pound Monterey Jack cheese, cut into
   ½-inch cubes
1 avocado, halved, pitted, peeled and diced
½ cup pickled sliced jalapeño chiles
2 tablespoons chopped fresh cilantro leaves
1 large bag (about 20 ounces) tortilla chips

1. Heat oven to 350°. Coat a 1-quart shallow dish, an 8×8×2-inch glass baking dish or a 9-inch pie plate with nonstick cooking spray.

2. Spoon salsa over bottom of prepared dish. Top with cheese.

3. Bake at 350° about 30 minutes or until bubbly. Remove from oven. Sprinkle with avocado, jalapeños and cilantro. Serve with chips.

Don't be surprised if sports fans actually pay more attention to this dip than to the game—it's that good!

PREP: 10 minutes
BAKE: at 350° for 30 minutes
MAKES: 12 servings

QUICK TIP

BEYOND BEER

Yes—beer is often the beverage of choice for game-day get-togethers, but if you're not a fan, consider a sparkling wine that will be just as refreshing with the savory nibbles. Two inexpensive choices include Prosecco from Italy, a light and fruity sparkling wine, or cava, the Spanish version of Champagne that's much less expensive than its French cousins.

Per serving: 420 calories, 27 g fat (10 g sat.), 33 mg cholesterol, 638 mg sodium, 34 g carbohydrate, 5 g fiber, 13 g protein.

Red Velvet Cupcakes

¾ cup sour cream
⅔ cup vegetable oil
2½ cups self-rising flour (such as Presto)
¼ cup unsweetened cocoa powder
1½ cups sugar
2 eggs
1 bottle (1 ounce) red food coloring
1 teaspoon vanilla extract
1 can (1 pound) prepared vanilla icing
Additional red food coloring
¼ cup unsweetened cocoa powder
2 teaspoons water

1. Line 18 standard-size muffin cups with cupcake liners. Heat oven to 350°.

2. In large bowl, whisk sour cream and oil (it will look curdled). Sift flour and ¼ cup cocoa powder into the bowl. Add sugar. Beat, with electric mixer on low speed, just until moistened. Add eggs; beat on medium-high speed about 2 minutes or until smooth and fluid. Stir in the bottle of food coloring and the vanilla. Fill cupcake liners two-thirds full.

3. Bake cupcakes at 350° for 22 to 25 minutes or until wooden toothpick inserted in centers comes out clean. Cool in pans on wire rack for 10 minutes; remove cupcakes and let cool completely on rack.

4. Divide frosting in half. Tint half light pink with additional red food coloring. Stir ¼ cup cocoa powder and the water into the remaining half. Frost half of the cupcakes with chocolate icing and remaining half with pink icing. Chill slightly before serving.

Food coloring gives the rich chocolate batter a lovely red hue—how perfect for Valentine's Day.

PREP: 10 minutes
BAKE: at 350° for 22 to 25 minutes
COOL: 10 minutes
MAKES: 18 cupcakes

QUICK TIP

LET THEM EAT CUPCAKES

To convert a two-layer cake recipe into cupcakes, follow these guidelines:
• Grease and flour muffin cups (or line the cups with cupcake liners).
• Fill cups half full with batter.
• Bake at the same temperature called for in the cake recipe but reduce baking time by about one-half. Almost any cake that starts with beating sugar and butter or shortening until fluffy can be made into cupcakes. A two-layer cake recipe yields about 24 to 30 cupcakes.

Per cupcake: 344 calories, 16 g fat (3 g sat.), 28 mg cholesterol, 297 mg sodium, 49 g carbohydrate, 1 g fiber, 3 g protein.

Heart-Shape Sandwich Cookies

Cookies:
- 3 cups all-purpose flour
- 2 teaspoons baking powder
- ¼ teaspoon salt
- 1 cup (2 sticks) unsalted butter
- 1 cup granulated sugar
- 3 egg yolks
- 1 teaspoon vanilla extract

Decorating:
- 1¾ cups confectioners' sugar, sifted
- 1 tablespoon pasteurized dried egg whites
- 2 tablespoons plus 1 teaspoon water
- Red food coloring
- Mini heart-shape candies
- ½ cup raspberry jam

1. **Cookies:** In medium-size bowl, mix flour, baking powder and salt. In large bowl, with electric mixer on medium speed, beat butter and sugar about 3 minutes or until creamy. Beat in yolks and vanilla. On low speed, beat in flour mixture in three batches, beating until dough forms. Divide dough in half; cover. Refrigerate 1 hour.

2. Heat oven to 350°. Coat two large cookie sheets with nonstick cooking spray.

3. On floured surface, roll half of the dough to ⅛-inch thickness. With a 2-inch heart-shape cutter, cut out cookies. Place on prepared sheets. Gather scraps and re-roll; cut out for a total of 40 cookies. Refrigerate for 20 minutes.

4. Bake at 350° for 8 minutes; don't let brown. Let stand for 1 minute. Remove to racks to cool.

5. Roll out remaining dough. With the 2-inch heart-shape cutter, cut out 40 cookies, re-rolling scraps. Using 1-inch heart-shape cutter, cut out centers. Place cookies with cutout centers and small cookies on separate cookie sheets. Refrigerate for 20 minutes.

6. Bake at 350° for 5 to 6 minutes for small cookies and 8 minutes for large cookies. Cool as above.

7. **Decorating:** In small bowl, with electric mixer on low speed, beat confectioners' sugar, dried egg whites and water for 2 minutes to combine; increase to high speed and beat about 4 minutes or until thickened and creamy. Tint half pink. Frost small hearts with pink or white icing. Use icing to attach candies to cutout heart cookies as desired. Spread 1 teaspoon jam on each of the large solid heart cookies; top each with a cutout heart cookie.

Your favorite jam works as the glue to attach the cutout heart-shape layer to the base of each appealing sandwich.

PREP: 30 minutes
CHILL: 1 hour 40 minutes
BAKE: at 350° for 8 minutes per batch (large cookies), 5 to 6 minutes per batch (small cookies)
MAKES: 40 filled heart-shape cookies and 40 small heart cookies

QUICK TIP

TOUGH COOKIES?

If your cutout cookies are less than tender, perhaps you've used too much flour or handled the dough too much. Try rolling the dough on a pastry cloth with a stockinette-covered rolling pin; use only enough flour to keep the dough from sticking. Make cutouts as close together as possible so less rerolls are needed.

Per filled cookie plus 1 small cookie:
137 calories, 5 g fat (3 g sat.), 28 mg cholesterol, 40 mg sodium, 22 g carbohydrate, 0 g fiber, 1 g protein.

Tropical Bonbon Bites

1 can (8 ounces) marzipan (such as Solo)
¼ cup sweetened condensed milk
1 package (3 ounces) pineapple-flavored gelatin dessert mix (see Note)
4 drops yellow food coloring (see Note)
1½ cups sweetened flake coconut
½ cup confectioners' sugar
½ cup clear sugar decorating crystals

1. Line a 13×9×2-inch baking pan with waxed paper. In large bowl, knead marzipan with fingers to soften. Stir in sweetened condensed milk until well combined.

2. Add dry gelatin mix and food coloring, stirring until blended. Add coconut, breaking up large clumps with fingers. Stir in confectioners' sugar a little at a time, using fingers if necessary when the mixture becomes stiff.

3. Place sugar crystals in small shallow bowl. Pinch off heaping teaspoons of the dough and roll into ¾-inch balls. Roll in sugar crystals and place on prepared pan. Refrigerate, lightly covered, for 8 hours or overnight. Store in airtight container, with waxed paper between layers, at cool room temperature for up to 2 weeks.

Note: You can substitute lime- or orange-flavored gelatin mix and green or orange food coloring.

Reminiscent of gumdrops—but even prettier—these sugar-coated candies take no time to make.

PREP: 15 minutes
CHILL: 8 hours or overnight
MAKES: 60 bites

QUICK BITE

A NUTTY CONFECTION

Marzipan is a creamy almond confection that is easy to color and shape into a variety of fanciful, eye-catching treats. Look for it in your grocery store or a gourmet or specialty shop.

Per bite: 40 calories, 1 g fat (1 g sat.), 0 mg cholesterol, 10 mg sodium, 7 g carbohydrate, 0 g fiber, 1 g protein.

Do-Ahead French Toast

1 loaf egg bread (challah)
6 eggs
1 cup half-and-half
½ cup milk
1 teaspoon vanilla extract
½ teaspoon freshly grated nutmeg
¼ teaspoon salt
6 tablespoons (¾ stick) unsalted butter
¾ cup packed dark-brown sugar
¾ cup chopped pecans
1 tablespoon confectioners' sugar

1. Coat two 13×9×2-inch baking dishes with nonstick cooking spray.

2. Slice bread into 12 equal slices, each about 1 inch thick. Arrange slices in prepared dishes.

3. In large bowl, beat together eggs, half-and-half, milk, vanilla, nutmeg and salt. Pour mixture over the bread in the two baking dishes, dividing equally. Cover and refrigerate for at least 4 hours or overnight.

4. Heat oven to 350°. In small saucepan, melt butter over low heat. Stir in brown sugar and pecans until combined. Spoon evenly over all bread slices.

5. Bake at 350° for 30 to 40 minutes or until lightly browned and cooked through.

6. Dust with confectioners' sugar; serve warm.

Oven-baking French toast is a no-hassle way to serve a delicious breakfast.

PREP: 10 minutes
CHILL: 4 hours or overnight
BAKE: at 350° for 30 to 40 minutes
MAKES: 12 servings

QUICK TIP

IN A PINCH

When you run out of a key ingredient, here are a few handy substitutions:
• For 1 cup half-and-half, use 1 tablespoon melted butter or margarine plus enough whole milk to make 1 cup.
• For 1 ounce of unsweetened chocolate, use 3 tablespoons unsweetened cocoa powder plus 1 tablespoon butter.
• For 1 cup corn syrup, use 1 cup granulated sugar plus an additional ¼ cup of the liquid used in the recipe.

Per serving: 336 calories, 18 g fat (7 g sat.), 152 mg cholesterol, 287 mg sodium, 35 g carbohydrate, 2 g fiber, 8 g protein.

Chocolate Silver-Dollar Pancakes

1 cup 2% milk
2 eggs
⅓ cup packed light-brown sugar
2 cups reduced-fat baking mix (such as Bisquick)
⅓ cup unsweetened cocoa powder
Sliced bananas and maple syrup (optional)

1. In blender, combine milk, eggs and brown sugar; whirl until smooth. Sift together baking mix and cocoa powder. Add to blender and whirl to blend.

2. Coat silver-dollar pancake skillet or large nonstick skillet with nonstick cooking spray. Heat over medium heat.

3. For each pancake, drop one generous tablespoon of the batter onto skillet. Cook for 1 to 2 minutes or until small bubbles form on top. Flip pancakes over and cook for 1 to 2 minutes longer or until browned. Remove from skillet and keep warm until all pancakes are cooked.

4. If desired, serve with bananas and maple syrup.

Make Ahead: Cook the pancakes as directed. Let cool and refrigerate, covered with plastic wrap, for up to 2 days. To serve, microwave on HIGH for 30 seconds.

These chocolaty pancakes taste great topped with syrup and sliced bananas. Kids will love them!

PREP: 10 minutes
COOK: 2 to 4 minutes per batch
MAKES: 6 servings (4 pancakes each)

Per serving: 255 calories, 6 g fat (2 g sat.), 74 mg cholesterol, 513 mg sodium, 45 g carbohydrate, 2 g fiber, 7 g protein.

Denver Frittata

1 tablespoon butter
1 small onion, chopped
1 small green pepper, seeded and chopped
1 small sweet red pepper, seeded and chopped
8 eggs
¼ cup milk
¾ cup shredded Cheddar cheese (3 ounces)
2 slices ham (2 ounces), cut into thin strips (about ½ cup)
¼ teaspoon salt
¼ teaspoon black pepper

1. Heat oven to 350°. Coat a 10-inch nonstick skillet (with ovenproof handle) with nonstick cooking spray.

2. In the skillet, heat butter over medium heat. Add onion and green and red peppers; cook for 5 minutes, stirring occasionally.

3. In large bowl, whisk together eggs and milk; whisk in ½ cup cheese, ham, salt and black pepper. Pour into skillet and stir to combine. Cook over medium-low heat for 5 minutes, stirring gently halfway through cooking.

4. Sprinkle the remaining ¼ cup cheese on top. Place skillet in oven; bake at 350° for 15 minutes.

5. Remove from oven. To serve, gently slide frittata onto serving plate and cut into 8 wedges.

Wake up to the best of both worlds. Here you can have a Denver omelet in an easier-to-make Italian frittata.

PREP: 15 minutes
COOK: 10 minutes
BAKE: at 350° for 15 minutes
MAKES: 8 servings

QUICK TIP

WHAT'S IN A NAME?

A frittata is an Italian omelet. Both frittatas and omelets are prepared in skillets. However, omelets are cooked on the stovetop and folded over assorted fillings, while frittatas have the fillings stirred into the egg mixture. Frittatas are started on top of the stove but often finished in the oven, so use a skillet with an ovenproof handle.

Per serving: 156 calories, 11 g fat (5 g sat.), 232 mg cholesterol, 309 mg sodium, 4 g carbohydrate, 1 g fiber, 11 g protein.

Sweet-Tart Fruit Salad

½ cup lime juice
½ cup sugar
4 whole Jamaican allspice berries
4 whole cloves
1 cinnamon stick (3 inches long)
½ vanilla bean
1 fresh pineapple, peeled, cored and cut into 1-inch pieces
2 ruby red grapefruit
2 navel oranges
1 cup seedless green grapes (about 26), halved
1 cup seedless red grapes (about 26), halved
Fresh mint leaves, for garnish (optional)

1. In small saucepan, combine lime juice, sugar, allspice, cloves and cinnamon stick. Split vanilla bean in half lengthwise; add to saucepan. Bring to a boil over medium-high heat to dissolve the sugar. Reduce heat to medium; simmer, stirring occasionally, for 5 minutes. Remove from heat; let syrup cool slightly.

2. Place the pineapple in a large glass serving bowl. With sharp knife, cut off rind and white pith from one grapefruit. Cut into separate sections, discarding membranes and seeds. Place in serving bowl. Repeat with other grapefruit and navel oranges. Add grapes.

3. Pour the lime syrup through a strainer over the fruit in the bowl. Discard solids in strainer. Gently stir the fruit to evenly coat with the syrup. Cover the bowl tightly with plastic wrap; refrigerate overnight. Gently stir fruit before serving. If desired, garnish with mint.

Made sweet with sugar, oranges and grapes, and tart with lime juice and grapefruit, this colorful salad will be a real eye-opener at brunch.

PREP: 20 minutes
COOK: 5 minutes
CHILL: overnight
MAKES: 8 servings

QUICK BITE

RED GRAPEFRUIT

Grapefruit flourish in a few Southern states, but Texas is noted for the ruby red variety. In fact, the red grapefruit is the official state fruit of Texas. Look for red grapefruit starting in November; its peak season is between Christmas and April.

Per serving: 154 calories, 1 g fat (0 g sat.), 0 mg cholesterol, 2 mg sodium, 40 g carbohydrate, 3 g fiber, 2 g protein.

Asparagus Soup

1 bunch fresh asparagus, ends trimmed
2 tablespoons unsalted butter
1 medium-size onion, diced
3 cups chicken broth
1 medium-size potato, peeled and diced
¼ teaspoon salt
¼ teaspoon dried dill
⅛ teaspoon white or black pepper
1 tablespoon water
½ cup heavy cream

1. Cut tips from asparagus. Set aside. Chop remaining stalks into ½-inch pieces. In 4-quart saucepan, melt butter over medium heat. Add onion; cook for 3 minutes. Add asparagus stalk pieces; cook for 2 minutes longer. Add chicken broth, potato, salt, dill and pepper. Bring to a boil.

2. Reduce heat to medium-high; cook, uncovered, for 10 to 12 minutes or until potato is very tender. Meanwhile, in small glass bowl, combine asparagus tips and water. Cover with plastic wrap; microwave on HIGH for 1 minute.

3. Remove soup from heat and puree until smooth. Stir in cream. Serve warm or chilled; garnish with asparagus tips.

Kick off your Easter celebration with one of spring's most beloved tastes, asparagus. The soup will look lovely on your table too.

PREP: 10 minutes
COOK: about 20 minutes
MICROWAVE: 1 minute
MAKES: 8 appetizer servings

QUICK TIP

SOME LIKE IT HOT

When serving hot soup, make sure it arrives at the table still pleasantly warm by serving it in a warm bowl. To warm bowls, run them under warm running water from the tap and wipe them dry.

Per serving: 130 calories, 10 g fat (6 g sat.), 30 mg cholesterol, 456 mg sodium, 8 g carbohydrate, 1 g fiber, 3 g protein.

Honey-Herbed Cornish Hens

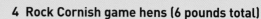

4 Rock Cornish game hens (6 pounds total)
2 tablespoons extra-virgin olive oil
2 tablespoons lemon juice
2 tablespoons honey
2 teaspoons chopped fresh thyme leaves
2 teaspoons chopped fresh oregano leaves
½ teaspoon salt
⅛ teaspoon black pepper
  Fresh fruit, for garnish (optional)
  Fresh herb sprigs, for garnish (optional)

1. Using kitchen shears or a sharp chef's knife, cut out backbone of each hen and split through each breastbone. Trim off excess fat and skin.

2. Brush the olive oil onto a large shallow pan (15×10×1-inch) and place in the oven. Heat oven to 400°.

3. In small bowl, whisk together lemon juice, honey, thyme and oregano. Season game hen halves with salt and pepper. Once pan has heated, carefully remove from oven. Place hens, skin sides down, into pan. Brush with half of the honey mixture.

4. Bake at 400° for 30 minutes. Remove pan from oven and turn over hens. Brush with remaining honey mixture. Return to oven and bake for 20 to 30 minutes longer or until instant-read meat thermometer inserted in thighs (not touching bone) registers 180°. Transfer to serving platter.

5. Drain pan drippings into a fat separator (or skim off as much fat as possible). Pour into a gravy boat; serve alongside hens. If desired, garnish with fresh fruit and fresh herb sprigs.

Easy-to-prepare Cornish hens offer an ideal balance of white and dark meat.

PREP: 15 minutes
BAKE: at 400° for 50 to 60 minutes
MAKES: 8 servings

QUICK TIP

BE READY FOR HELPERS

When guests offer to help in the kitchen, never say no—let's face it, we all can use a little help! Ask them to:
• Finish setting the table.
• Fill glasses with ice and water.
• Reheat vegetable dishes in the microwave oven.
• Carry food to the table or sideboard.
• Gather diners for the meal.
• Lead a prayer.
• Offer a toast at the meal.

Per serving (with skin): 895 calories, 63 g fat (17 g sat.), 427 mg cholesterol, 354 mg sodium, 5 g carbohydrate, 0 g fiber, 73 g protein.

Per serving (skin removed): 485 calories, 16 g fat (3 g sat.), 346 mg cholesterol, 351 mg sodium, 5 g carbohydrate, 0 g fiber, 76 g protein.

New-Potato Bake

- 3 small red-skin new potatoes, quartered
- 2 teaspoons salt
- 1 bag (9 ounces) baby spinach leaves
- 3 tablespoons unsalted butter
- 1 bunch scallions or spring onions, trimmed and chopped
- 3 tablespoons all-purpose flour
- 2 cups milk, warmed
- ¾ teaspoon salt
- ⅛ teaspoon white or black pepper
- ⅛ teaspoon cayenne pepper
- Pinch of ground nutmeg
- ½ pound Swiss cheese, shredded (about 2 cups)
- 1 tablespoon packaged plain dry bread crumbs

1. Heat oven to 375°. In large saucepan, combine potatoes and salt. Add enough cold water to cover. Bring to a boil; simmer for 8 minutes. Just before draining, add spinach. Drain.

2. In a small saucepan, melt butter over medium heat. Add scallion; cook about 5 minutes or until softened. Sprinkle flour over scallion and whisk to blend. In two additions, whisk in warm milk until smooth. Add salt, white or black pepper, cayenne pepper and nutmeg. Bring to a boil over medium heat, whisking occasionally. Remove from heat. Whisk in 1 cup Swiss cheese.

3. Coat 13×9×2-inch baking dish with nonstick cooking spray. Layer half of the potatoes and spinach in dish; spoon half of the sauce over. Sprinkle with half of the remaining cheese. Top with remaining potatoes, spinach and sauce. Sprinkle with remaining cheese.

4. Bake at 375° for 20 minutes. Top with bread crumbs. Bake about 10 minutes longer or until browned. Let stand for 10 to 15 minutes.

Spinach and scallions dot the tasty casserole for a spring-fresh style of au gratin potatoes.

PREP: 15 minutes
COOK: about 15 minutes
BAKE: at 375° for 30 minutes
STAND: 10 to 15 minutes
MAKES: 8 servings

QUICK TIP

HAM HOW-TOS

Ham is another Easter favorite. Here are some hints you need to know:

- Plan on about ⅓ pound boneless ham or ⅔ pound bone-in ham per person.
- Remove the ham from the fridge about 30 minutes before heating. Once it's done, let it stand 10 minutes before slicing.
- A "ready to eat" ham will taste best if warmed to 140°.
- Bake a "cook before eating" ham to an internal temperature of 155° to 160°.

Per serving: 253 calories, 12 g fat (7 g sat.), 37 mg cholesterol, 521 mg sodium, 24 g carbohydrate, 3 g fiber, 13 g protein.

Strawberry-Rhubarb Cheesecake

A popular duo in springtime pies, strawberries and rhubarb also make a just-right topping for a lemon-scented cheesecake.

PREP: 15 minutes
BAKE: crust at 325° for 10 minutes; cheesecake at 325° for 40 to 45 minutes
CHILL: at least 2 hours
MAKES: 12 servings

QUICK TIP

1–2–3 GLAZES

When you can't find rhubarb for the topping, these other fruity fix-ups will work quite nicely:

- Spread purchased lemon curd on top. Chill for 30 minutes before cutting.
- Melt 2 tablespoons orange marmalade or grape jelly with 1 teaspoon water. Let cool and spread on cheesecake. Chill until set. Garnish with orange peel or fresh grape halves.

Per serving: 309 calories, 17 g fat (10 g sat.), 83 mg cholesterol, 234 mg sodium, 33 g carbohydrate, 0 g fiber, 6 g protein.

Crust:
- 32 vanilla wafer cookies, crushed
- ¼ cup (½ stick) unsalted butter

Filling:
- 2½ packages (8 ounces each) reduced-fat cream cheese (⅓ less fat), softened
- ⅔ cup sugar
- 2 eggs
- 2 tablespoons all-purpose flour
  Zest of 1 lemon
- 2 teaspoons lemon juice

Topping:
- ¼ pound fresh rhubarb, trimmed and cut into ¼-inch-thick slices (¾ cup)
- ⅔ cup sugar
- ¾ cup fresh strawberries, hulled and chopped
  Fresh whole strawberries, for garnish (optional)

1. Heat oven to 325°. **Crust:** Place cookie crumbs in a bowl. Melt butter and stir into crumbs. Press mixture into bottom of an 8-inch springform pan. Bake at 325° for 10 minutes. Remove to a wire rack to cool.

2. **Filling:** In large bowl, with electric mixer on low to medium speed, beat together cream cheese and sugar until smooth. Beat in eggs, one at a time, until blended; beat in flour. Stir in lemon zest and juice. Pour into pan; smooth top with rubber spatula.

3. Bake at 325° for 40 to 45 minutes or until lightly golden around edges. Remove to rack to cool.

4. **Topping:** In small saucepan, combine rhubarb, sugar and ¼ cup chopped strawberries. Bring to a low boil over medium-high heat. Continue to cook, stirring, for 6 to 7 minutes longer. One minute before topping is finished, stir in the remaining ½ cup chopped strawberries. Remove from heat.

5. As soon as cheesecake is baked, spread with warm topping, leaving a border around edge. Run a thin knife between pan and cake; cool to room temperature. Chill for at least 2 hours or until serving time. If desired, garnish with whole strawberries.

Pomegranate Cosmos

Ice
¾ cup vodka
⅓ cup triple sec
⅓ cup Rose's sweetened lime juice
⅓ cup pomegranate juice
Coarse sugar, for garnish (optional)
Lime slices, for garnish (optional)

1. Fill a pitcher with ice. Add vodka, triple sec, sweetened lime juice and pomegranate juice. Stir until well combined and mixture is chilled. If desired, dip rims of four glasses in water; dip in coarse sugar to coat. Strain vodka mixture into glasses. If desired, garnish with lime slices.

To get the conversation going, have everyone guess this drink's "secret ingredient"—pomegranate juice.

PREP: 5 minutes
MAKES: 4 servings

QUICK TIP

STOCKING A BAR

The standard rundown for a bar includes vodka, tequila, scotch, bourbon and gin. Other options include white rum, vermouth and triple sec. For mixers, set out regular and diet cola, club soda and tonic water. It's also nice to have ginger ale, lemon-lime soda, fruit juices (orange, grapefruit, pineapple and cranberry) and tomato juice. Look for individual sizes of mixers and juice. They may cost more per ounce, but you'll have much less waste from leftover half-empty bottles.

Per serving: 151 calories, 0 g fat (0 g sat.), 0 mg cholesterol, 7 mg sodium, 11 g carbohydrate, 0 g fiber, 0 g protein.

Sunset Sippers

3 cups orange juice
1½ cups rum or white cranberry juice
¾ cup prepared lemonade or triple sec
12 ounces ginger ale
   Juice of 1 lime
6 to 12 teaspoons grenadine

1. In large pitcher, combine orange juice, rum or white cranberry juice, prepared lemonade or triple sec, ginger ale and lime juice. Using six champagne flutes or tall glasses, carefully pour 1 to 2 teaspoons grenadine syrup into each glass. Divide juice mixture among glasses.

A thrilling cocktail is a great way to kick off a party with aplomb. This one has a dashing swirl of grenadine for extra loveliness.

PREP: 5 minutes
MAKES: 6 servings

QUICK TIP

PARTIES 101

When you want to be sure you'll have enough of everything for all your guests:
• Figure most drinks will be served in ½-cup portions. Plan on two drink servings per guest in the first hour and one serving for each additional hour.
• Plan on four to six appetizers per person. When serving dips with fresh fruits and veggies, count on ½ cup produce and ¼ cup dip per guest.

Per serving: 264 calories, 0 g fat (0 g sat.), 0 mg cholesterol, 31 mg sodium, 32 g carbohydrate, 0 g fiber, 0 g protein.

Swiss Cheese Fondue

1½ cups dry white wine
¾ pound Swiss cheese, grated (about 3 cups)
¼ pound mild cheese (such as Monterey Jack), grated (about 1 cup)
¼ teaspoon salt
¼ teaspoon white or black pepper
⅛ teaspoon cayenne pepper
Pinch of ground nutmeg
2 tablespoons cornstarch blended with 2 tablespoons cold water
Italian bread, cut in cubes
Granny Smith and Gala apples, cut in chunks or sliced
1 bag (7½ ounces) mixed root-vegetable chips (such as Terra Chips)

1. In flameproof fondue pot or nonaluminum saucepan, bring wine to a simmer. Add cheeses, stirring until melted; mixture will not be smooth.

2. Stir in salt, white or black pepper, cayenne pepper and nutmeg. Stir cornstarch-water mixture and stir into pot. Simmer over medium-low heat about 2 minutes or until thickened and smooth. Serve immediately with bread cubes, apple pieces and chips; keep fondue warm over a low flame.

The best appetizers usually have a little cheese in the mix. Fondue gets right to the point and stars the ever-popular ingredient front and center.

PREP: 10 minutes
COOK: about 10 minutes
MAKES: 8 servings

QUICK TIP

BEYOND BREAD

Fun dippers for fondue and other hot dips include toasted pita or flour tortilla wedges, cut or broken flatbread, pretzels and breadsticks. Apples and pears work with dips; to keep them looking fresh, brush the cut sides with lemon juice.

Per serving: 450 calories, 21 g fat (13 g sat.), 53 mg cholesterol, 538 mg sodium, 45 g carbohydrate, 5 g fiber, 19 g protein.

Spinach Pinwheels

2 tablespoons unsalted butter
1 medium-size onion, finely chopped
1 large clove garlic, finely chopped
1 box (10 ounces) frozen chopped spinach, thawed and squeezed dry
¼ teaspoon salt
¼ teaspoon black pepper
1 package (4 ounces) crumbled goat cheese
1 box (17.3 ounces) frozen puff pastry, thawed

1. In large nonstick skillet, melt butter over medium heat. Add onion and garlic; sauté for 5 minutes, stirring. Add spinach, salt and pepper. Cook for 2 minutes. Remove from heat; stir in goat cheese. Let cool.

2. Unroll one sheet puff pastry. Spread with half of the spinach mixture, leaving a ½-inch border on edges. Roll up from a long side. Repeat with second sheet and remaining spinach mixture. Wrap both logs in plastic wrap. Freeze for 30 minutes. (Can be frozen for up to a month; slice while frozen and bake without thawing.)

3. Heat oven to 400°. Line two large baking sheets with aluminum foil. Unwrap logs. Cut into ½-inch-thick slices; place slices, cut sides down, on prepared baking sheets. (Roll log after 4 or 5 slices to keep pinwheels as round as possible.)

4. Bake at 400° for 20 minutes, rotating pans halfway through (if frozen, bake a little longer). Cool on wire rack. Serve pinwheels warm or at room temperature.

You can't go wrong with these delectable spirals combining goat cheese and greens wrapped in puff pastry.

PREP: 15 minutes
COOK: 7 minutes
FREEZE: 30 minutes
BAKE: at 400° for 20 minutes
MAKES: about 48 pinwheels

QUICK TIP

APPETIZERS ON CALL

Be prepared to entertain anytime by keeping various party snacks on hand. These include ready-made dips and spreadables, such as jars of tapenade, salsa or tins of pâté; jars of olives; and firm and hard cheeses—properly wrapped and stored in the refrigerator, they generally keep longer than softer cheeses. Remember, too, to have a supply of crackers to go with your offerings.

Per pinwheel: 70 calories, 5 g fat (2 g sat.), 2 mg cholesterol, 51 mg sodium, 5 g carbohydrate, 0 g fiber, 1 g protein.

Pork and Pear Toasts

Pear Compote:
- 2 pounds Bartlett pears (about 4), peeled, cored and diced
- ⅔ cup packed light-brown sugar
- ½ cup dried cherries
- 2 tablespoons water
- ⅛ teaspoon ground cinnamon
- 3 tablespoons cider vinegar
- 2 teaspoons cornstarch
  Pinch of salt
  Pinch of black pepper

Pork Tenderloin and Toasts:
- 2 boneless pork tenderloins (2 to 2½ pounds total)
- ½ teaspoon salt
- ¼ teaspoon black pepper
- 2 tablespoons plus ½ cup honey mustard
- 2 tablespoons extra-virgin olive oil
- ½ cup water
- 1 large baguette (about 12 ounces)
  Fresh herb sprigs, for garnish (optional)

1. **Pear Compote:** In small saucepan, bring pears, brown sugar, cherries, water and cinnamon to a simmer. Cook over medium heat for 25 minutes.

2. In small bowl, combine vinegar and cornstarch. Add to saucepan with salt and pepper; cook about 2 minutes or until thickened. Remove from heat; cool.

3. **Pork Tenderloin and Toasts:** Heat oven to 400°. Rinse tenderloins and pat dry with paper towels. Season with salt and pepper; spread each tenderloin with 1 tablespoon mustard. In large ovenproof skillet, heat oil over high heat. Add pork; cook about 4 minutes or until browned on all sides, turning to brown evenly. Add water to skillet; transfer to oven. Bake at 400° for 12 to 15 minutes or until instant-read meat thermometer inserted in centers of tenderloins registers 160°. Remove from oven; let stand for 20 minutes.

4. Heat broiler. Slice baguette into 48 slices. Toast under broiler for 2 minutes, turning once. Store in a plastic food-storage bag for up to a day.

5. Spread each toast with ½ teaspoon mustard. Thinly slice pork on a slight diagonal. Place one or two pork slices on each toast. Spoon a little pear compote on top of each and serve. If desired, garnish with fresh herb sprigs.

When you want to provide a hearty appetizer along with other nibbles, treat guests to succulent pork tenderloin topped with a sweet-tart compote.

PREP: 20 minutes
COOK: about 30 minutes
BAKE: at 400° for 12 to 15 minutes
STAND: 20 minutes
BROIL: 2 minutes
MAKES: 48 toasts

QUICK TIP

THE BEST BITES

Since most people will be holding a drink, whatever you serve must be easy to eat with the remaining hand. Don't make it bigger than one or two bites. Salty and spicy foods tend to complement drinks best, which is why chips and dip are naturals. Skip juicy nibbles that will wind up dripping down a sleeve.

Per toast: 99 calories, 3 g fat (1 g sat.), 13 mg cholesterol, 85 mg sodium, 14 g carbohydrate, 1 g fiber, 5 g protein.

Creamy Ranch Dip

⅓ cup light mayonnaise
⅓ cup reduced-fat sour cream
1 tablespoon lemon juice
½ teaspoon garlic salt
½ teaspoon lemon pepper
⅔ cup buttermilk
1 tablespoon chopped fresh parsley
1 tablespoon chopped fresh chives
Crudités, for serving

1. In medium-size bowl, whisk together mayonnaise, sour cream, lemon juice, garlic salt and lemon pepper. Gradually whisk in buttermilk. Stir in parsley. Cover and refrigerate for at least 1 hour or up to several days.

2. Sprinkle with chopped chives. Serve with assorted crudités.

Green beans, celery sticks, sweet pepper wedges, cucumber slices and carrot sticks are all terrific dippers.

PREP: 10 minutes
CHILL: 1 hour to several days
MAKES: 1½ cups

QUICK TIP

A DUET OF DIPS

You can never have too many dip recipes. Here are two extra-easy options:
• In a food processor, combine 1 cup prepared hummus; 1 bottled roasted red sweet pepper, ¼ teaspoon ground cumin and a pinch cayenne pepper. Cover and whirl until smooth.
• In a small bowl, stir together ½ cup ricotta and ½ cup crumbled goat cheese. Stir in 5 tablespoons prepared pesto and 1 tablespoon milk.

Per 1 tablespoon dip: 19 calories, 1 g fat (0 g sat.), 3 mg cholesterol, 83 mg sodium, 1 g carbohydrate, 0 g fiber, 1 g protein.

Cheese-Stuffed Cherry Tomatoes

36 cherry tomatoes
 1 package (4 ounces) garlic-and-herb
    spreadable cheese (such as Alouette)
 2 tablespoons buttermilk
 ½ cup grated sharp Cheddar cheese
    (2 ounces)

1. Cut tops off tomatoes. Gently remove seeds and pulp with a small melon baller or measuring spoon. Invert onto a paper towel-lined baking sheet and let drain.

2. In food processor, combine spreadable cheese and buttermilk. Whirl until smooth. Add cheddar cheese; pulse two or three times.

3. Place cheese mixture into a pastry bag fitted with a medium-size star tip. Pipe cheese mixture into tomatoes.

4. Refrigerate for at least 1 hour.

Sweet cherry tomatoes balance an herbed-cheese filling, and with just four ingredients, they're ready in no time!

PREP: 20 minutes
CHILL: 1 hour
MAKES: 36 stuffed tomatoes

QUICK TIP

SAFE PICNIC POINTERS

- Chill cold foods before placing them in a cooler. Pack a second cooler with beverages and snacks.
- If possible, place coolers with the iced-down food in the backseat instead of the much-hotter trunk.
- When the outside temperature climbs above 90°, throw out uneaten food within 1 hour; otherwise, you can leave it out for up to 2 hours.

Per tomato: 17 calories, 1 g fat (0 g sat.), 3 mg cholesterol, 27 mg sodium, 1 g carbohydrate, 0 g fiber, 1 g protein.

Muffaletta Wedges

1 large tomato, seeded and chopped
¾ cup pimiento-stuffed green olives, drained and chopped (4½ ounces)
2 ribs celery, diced
¼ cup extra-virgin olive oil
2 cloves garlic, chopped
1 tablespoon red-wine vinegar
1 tablespoon chopped fresh oregano leaves
1 tablespoon chopped fresh parsley leaves
⅛ teaspoon black pepper
1 medium-size round Italian or sourdough bread (about 9-inch diameter, 1¼ pounds and no more than 3 inches in height), cut horizontally in half
¼ pound sliced salami
¼ pound sliced provolone cheese
¼ pound sliced honey-roasted turkey
¼ pound sliced American cheese

1. In medium-size bowl, mix together tomato, olives, celery, oil, garlic, vinegar, oregano, parsley and pepper. Cover and refrigerate for 1 hour.

2. Spoon 1 cup of the olive mixture over the bottom half of the bread. Layer on salami, provolone cheese, turkey and American cheese. Top with remaining olive mixture. Cover with top of bread. Wrap in plastic wrap and place on baking sheet. Weigh down with heavy pot. Let stand for 1 hour at room temperature. If desired, remove plastic wrap and cut into 8 wedges. Place wedges back together to form round and rewrap in plastic wrap. Refrigerate until ready to serve.

Ever so moist and chock-full of popular meats and cheeses, this take on a classic New Orleans sandwich is sure to please.

PREP: 10 minutes
CHILL: 1 hour
STAND: 1 hour
MAKES: 8 servings

QUICK TIP

TERRIFIC PICNIC WINES

Here are two go-to choices for picnics:
Riesling: With a sensuous fruitiness—yet a racy streak of acidity—Riesling pairs beautifully with all kinds of picnic foods, including rich cured meats like salami, cheeses and potato salad.
Beaujolais: One of the few red wines that actually taste great chilled, Beaujolais is lighter than most reds and goes with so many foods. Beaujolais Nouveau, a wine released in November, is meant to be drunk when very young.

Per serving: 462 calories, 25 g fat (8 g sat.), 40 mg cholesterol, 1,524 mg sodium, 40 g carbohydrate, 3 g fiber, 19 g protein.

Zesty Potato Salad

2 **pounds mixed small red and
fingerling potatoes**
1 **small red onion, thinly sliced**
6 **tablespoons sherry-wine vinegar**
1 **tablespoon grainy mustard**
½ **teaspoon salt**
¼ **teaspoon black pepper**
6 **tablespoons extra-virgin olive oil**
2 **tablespoons chopped fresh parsley leaves**
1 **tablespoon chopped fresh oregano leaves**

1. Bring a large pot of lightly salted water to a boil. Add potatoes. Cover and return to a boil. Boil, uncovered, about 20 minutes or until fork tender. Drain.

2. Cut warm potatoes into bite-size pieces and place in bowl. Stir in onion.

3. In small bowl, stir together vinegar, mustard, salt and pepper. Drizzle in oil, whisking continuously. Stir in parsley and oregano. Pour vinegar mixture over warm potatoes and onion. Stir gently. Serve warm or at room temperature (or cover and refrigerate for up to a day).

This no-fuss salad is simply a variety of small potatoes and red onions tossed in a vinegar-and-mustard dressing.

PREP: 10 minutes
COOK: 20 minutes
MAKES: 8 servings

QUICK TIP

THE RIGHT BOWL

When making a salad containing acidic ingredients such as tomatoes, lemon or vinegar, choose a container that is not made from aluminum, copper or cast iron. Those metals react detrimentally with acidic ingredients, giving a metallic flavor to the food.

Per serving: 184 calories, 10 g fat (1 g sat.), 0 mg cholesterol, 184 mg sodium, 22 g carbohydrate, 2 g fiber, 3 g protein.

Old-Fashioned Lemonade

12 **large lemons**
8 **cups cold water**
1¼ **cups superfine sugar**
Fresh mint leaves, for garnish (optional)

1. Microwave the 12 lemons on HIGH for 10 seconds. Cut in half and juice; you should have about 3 cups juice.

2. In large pitcher or container, stir together lemon juice, cold water and superfine sugar until sugar is dissolved.

3. Refrigerate for at least 1 hour or up to a day. Stir before serving. If desired, garnish with mint leaves.

Treat everyone to the homemade, fresh-squeezed version of this all-time-best sipper soon.

PREP: 10 minutes
MICROWAVE: 10 seconds
CHILL: 1 hour to 1 day
MAKES: 12 cups

QUICK TIP

SETTING THE SCENE FOR YOUR PICNIC

- Put up an umbrella to keep food out of direct sunlight and to signal your location to friends.
- If picnic tables are unavailable, bring a breakfast-in-bed tray or lap table for your meal.
- Pick up stylish platters, plates and silverware in sturdy plastic—it's fun to mix and match colors.

Per cup: 90 calories, 0 g fat (0 g sat.), 0 mg cholesterol, 1 mg sodium, 25 g carbohydrate, 0 g fiber, 0 g protein.

Berry Daiquiris

1 container (6 ounces) fresh raspberries
1 container (6 ounces) fresh blackberries
   Fresh strawberries
½ cup rum (4 ounces)
3 tablespoons lime juice
3 to 4 tablespoons superfine sugar
   Crushed ice

1. Clean and chop raspberries and blackberries. Clean and chop strawberries; add enough strawberries to raspberries and blackberries to equal 3 cups. Puree in blender. Push through fine mesh strainer (you should have 2 cups). Return to blender; add rum, lime juice and superfine sugar. Blend until smooth. Add ¼ cup crushed ice (or to taste) and blend. If desired, garnish with strawberries.

Mango Daiquiris: Slice 1 large unpeeled mango from stem end to bottom, parallel to flat seed on both sides. Cut down to, but not through, skin of each slice in a cross-hatch pattern. Push skin side up and out; cut cubes off. In blender, combine cubed mango, 3 to 4 ounces rum, ¼ cup lime juice and 2 tablespoons superfine sugar. Blend until smooth. Add ¼ cup crushed ice (or to taste) and blend. If desired, garnish with lime wedges. Makes 4 servings.

Hosting a range of ages? Juicy mango or bright berry daiquiris are delicious with or without rum.

PREP: 15 minutes
MAKES: 4 servings

QUICK TIP

ICE IT UP

It's amazing how quickly you can go through ice at a party. For mixed drinks and sodas, expect to use about 4 ice cubes per drink. Either start filling up plastic bags from your home freezer a day or two before the party or pick up a 10-pound bag of ice. Better yet, if you have the freezer space, get two.

Per serving (berry): 158 calories, 1 g fat (0 g sat.), 0 mg cholesterol, 1 mg sodium, 24 g carbohydrate, 6 g fiber, 1 g protein.

Per serving (mango): 122 calories, 1 g fat (0 g sat.), 0 mg cholesterol, 1 mg sodium, 16 g carbohydrate, 1 g fiber, 0 g protein.

Wings, Two Ways

1 package (5 pounds) frozen chicken wingettes (such as Tyson brand) or 5 pounds chicken wings, each cut into 2 pieces (70 pieces total)

Buffalo Sauce:
- ¾ cup hot-pepper sauce (such as Frank's Red Hot)
- 4 tablespoons unsalted butter, melted

Maple BBQ Sauce:
- 1 cup ketchup
- ½ cup maple syrup
- 6 tablespoons cider vinegar

For serving (optional):
- 3 scallions
- 4 ribs celery, cut in 4-inch sticks
- Thick blue cheese dressing

1. Heat oven to 425°. Place wing pieces in large deep roasting pan—no need to thaw. Bake at 425° about 1 hour or until cooked through and meat begins to pull away from the ends, stirring frequently. Remove pan to a wire rack. Using tongs, divide wing pieces between two 15×10×1-inch jelly-roll pans, shaking excess fat back into roasting pan.

2. Heat oven to broil. Stir together ingredients for Buffalo Sauce; stir together ingredients for Maple BBQ Sauce. Brush enough Buffalo Sauce onto wing pieces in one pan to coat. Broil about 7 minutes or until crispy. Turn wing pieces over; brush with more sauce. Broil 7 minutes longer. Remove and let cool briefly on wire rack. Repeat with Maple BBQ Sauce on wings in second pan, broiling each side for 8 minutes. Remove and let cool briefly. Reserve any leftover Maple BBQ Sauce. Serve immediately or cover when completely cool and refrigerate for up to 1 day.

3. To serve, uncover and reheat if necessary at 350° about 20 minutes or until hot, turning occasionally. If desired, place on platter with scallions and celery. If desired, serve with blue cheese dressing and reserved Maple BBQ Sauce (boiled for 3 minutes).

Our options are hot and spicy or sweet and tangy—two kinds of wings for all kinds of people! Most will love both.

PREP: 10 minutes
BAKE: at 425° for 1 hour
BROIL: 14 to 16 minutes per batch
MAKES: 70 wings

QUICK BITE

HOORAY FOR BUFFALO

The wildly popular Buffalo chicken wings got their start at the Anchor Bar in Buffalo, New York, back in 1964. Owners Teressa and Frank Bellissimo fried up wings and served them drenched in hot sauce along with celery sticks and blue cheese dressing. Restaurants and bars across the country took to serving wings Buffalo-style, and the rest is history.

Per wing with Buffalo Sauce: 76 calories, 6 g fat (2 g sat.), 26 mg cholesterol, 122 mg sodium, 0 g carbohydrate, 0 g fiber, 5 g protein.

Per wing with Maple BBQ Sauce: 76 calories, 5 g fat (1 g sat.), 26 mg cholesterol, 144 mg sodium, 3 g carbohydrate, 0 g fiber, 5 g protein.

Do-Ahead Tortellini Salad

- 1 package (9 ounces) refrigerated cheese tortellini
- 1 package (9 ounces) refrigerated spinach tortellini
- 1 pound fresh green beans, trimmed and cut into 1½-inch pieces
- 1 small red onion, diced
- 1 cup quartered grape tomatoes
- ½ cup pitted kalamata olives, diced

Dressing:
- ½ cup extra-virgin olive oil
- 1 teaspoon minced garlic
- 2 tablespoons white-wine vinegar
- 1 tablespoon balsamic vinegar
- ½ teaspoon salt
- ½ teaspoon dried basil
- ¼ teaspoon dried oregano
- ¼ teaspoon black pepper

1. Bring a large pot of salted water to a boil. Add cheese tortellini and spinach tortellini and cook for 3 minutes; add beans and continue cooking about 5 minutes or until tortellini are tender. Drain; rinse under cool water. Drain well. Place mixture in serving bowl. Stir in onion, tomato and olives.

2. **Dressing:** In small jar or plastic container with tight-fitting lid, combine oil and garlic. Let stand for 10 minutes, then add white wine vinegar, balsamic vinegar, salt, basil, oregano and pepper. Shake well. Stir half into salad.

3. Cover salad with plastic wrap and refrigerate for up to 1 day. Remove from refrigerator 30 minutes before serving; stir in remaining dressing if needed.

Two kinds of tortellini make this a filling salad that will help add heartiness to the spread.

PREP: 15 minutes
COOK: about 8 minutes
STAND: 40 minutes
CHILL: up to 1 day
MAKES: 12 servings

QUICK TIP

ENTERTAINING DOS AND DON'TS

- Do ask guests ahead of time about dietary restrictions.
- Don't depend on people to bring wine; keep some on hand.
- Do expect the unexpected; have extra food just in case someone brings a surprise guest.
- Don't set up the bar and buffet next to each other.
- Do serve tried-and-true recipes; this isn't the time to experiment.

Per serving: 192 calories, 9 g fat (3 g sat.), 13 mg cholesterol, 281 mg sodium, 21 g carbohydrate, 1 g fiber, 6 g protein.

Fourth-of-July Cupcakes

Cake:
- **Zest and juice of 2 lemons**
- **2 boxes (18.25 ounces each) white cake mix**
- **6 egg whites**
- **1 teaspoon lemon extract**

Frosting:
- **½ cup (1 stick) unsalted butter, at room temperature**
- **½ cup solid vegetable shortening, at room temperature**
- **2 boxes (1 pound each) confectioners' sugar**
- **¼ cup milk**
- **2 tablespoons lemon juice**

Decoration:
- **¾ cup fresh blueberries, washed and dried**
- **3 cups large fresh raspberries, washed and dried**

1. **Cake:** Heat oven to 350°. Line 48 standard-size muffin cups with cupcake liners; set aside. Pour lemon juice into 4-cup measuring cup; add enough water to equal 2⅔ cups.

2. In large bowl, with electric mixer on medium speed, beat cake mixes, egg whites, lemon zest, juice-water mixture and lemon extract about 3 minutes or until combined. Fill each cupcake liner two-thirds full with batter.

3. Bake at 350° for 18 to 21 minutes or until a toothpick inserted in centers comes out clean. Remove cupcakes from muffin cups to wire racks; let cool to room temperature.

4. **Frosting:** In large bowl, with electric mixer on low to medium speed, beat butter and shortening for 1 to 2 minutes or until fluffy. Add confectioners' sugar, milk and lemon juice. Continue beating on low speed until well blended and good spreading consistency, adding more milk if needed.

5. Frost cupcakes. Top cupcakes with berries.

Show your patriotic colors in the sweetest of ways! Top these lemony, white-frosted cupcakes with red- and blue-hued fruit.

PREP: 10 minutes
BAKE: at 350° for 18 to 21 minutes
DECORATE: 15 minutes
MAKES: 48 cupcakes

QUICK TIP

A SWEET FINISH

If you don't feel like making dessert for your pool party, bring out a tray of the ripest fruit you can find—grapes, cherries, pears, oranges, kiwifruit and pineapple are reliable—to serve with assorted chocolates. It's a refreshing way to end the get-together.

Per cupcake: 210 calories, 7 g fat (3 g sat.), 5 mg cholesterol, 161 mg sodium, 36 g carbohydrate, 0 g fiber, 2 g protein.

Savory Deviled Eggs

12 hard-cooked eggs, peeled
½ cup light mayonnaise
1 tablespoon honey mustard
¼ teaspoon black pepper
½ cup large pimiento-stuffed olives (about 8), chopped

1. Cut eggs in half lengthwise and spoon yolks into a bowl. Reserve whites. Mash yolks with a fork. Stir mayonnaise, honey mustard and pepper into yolks.

2. Reserve 1 tablespoon olives. Fold remaining olives into yolk mixture.

3. Fill whites with the yolk mixture. Place reserved olives on top of eggs. Refrigerate for at least 1 hour.

Bacon-Cheese Deviled Eggs: Prepare filling, omitting olives. Instead stir in 4 strips cooked, crumbled bacon and 2 tablespoons shredded Cheddar cheese.

Curried Deviled Eggs: Prepare filling, omitting olives. Instead stir in 1 tablespoon curry powder, 1 teaspoon grated lemon zest and pinch of cayenne pepper.

Make Ahead: Can be made up to 1 day ahead; cover and refrigerate until ready to serve.

Who's the famous deviled egg maker in your extended family? With this recipe, it could be you!

PREP: 20 minutes
CHILL: 1 hour
MAKES: 24 pieces

QUICK TIP

PERFECT PEELING

To peel a hard-cooked egg, let cool, then gently tap it on the countertop. Roll it between the palms of your hands. Peel off the shell, starting at the large end.

Per piece: 59 calories, 5 g fat (1 g sat.), 108 mg cholesterol, 115 mg sodium, 1 g carbohydrate, 0 g fiber, 3 g protein.

Classic Pulled Pork

1 can (14½ ounces) diced tomatoes with jalapeños
1 can (16 ounces) tomato sauce
⅔ cup packed brown sugar
⅔ cup vinegar
⅔ cup ketchup
¼ teaspoon hot-pepper sauce
1 bone-in pork butt or shoulder roast (about 6 pounds)
12 hamburger buns

1. Heat oven to 375°. In medium-size saucepan, combine tomatoes (undrained), tomato sauce, brown sugar, vinegar, ketchup and hot-pepper sauce. Bring to a boil; reduce heat to medium and simmer 10 minutes. Remove from heat.

2. Trim pork of excess fat. Place pork in a large foil cooking bag. Remove ½ cup of the ketchup mixture; set aside remaining ketchup mixture. Brush the ½ cup ketchup mixture on the pork in cooking bag. Seal foil bag tightly.

3. Place pork in bag in large shallow baking pan. Bake at 375° for 3 hours. Remove from oven; carefully open foil. Let stand about 30 minutes or until cool enough to handle. Using forks or your hands, pull meat into shreds, discarding excess fat. (Use paper towels to help remove fat from meat.) Place in large oven-safe serving pan. Stir in remaining ketchup mixture. Serve on buns.

Make Ahead: Refrigerate shredded meat mixture for up to 1 day or freeze for up to 2 months. To serve, thaw if necessary; heat oven to 325°. Bake, covered, at 325° for 20 to 30 minutes or until heated through, stirring occasionally.

All the work can be done in advance! Just chill the filling, then reheat and savor irresistible pork sandwiches.

PREP: 25 minutes
BAKE: at 375° for 3 hours
STAND: 30 minutes
MAKES: 12 servings

QUICK TIP

COOL COLESLAW

Serve slaw alongside or even on top of the sandwich. In a large serving bowl, combine ½ cup light mayonnaise, ⅓ cup buttermilk, ⅓ cup sugar, 2 tablespoons white vinegar, ½ teaspoon salt and 1 teaspoon celery seeds. Stir in 1 package (16 ounces) shredded coleslaw mix, ½ package (10 ounces) shredded carrot mix and 1 chopped scallion. Cover and refrigerate for at least 4 hours or overnight, stirring occasionally. Before serving, pour off excess liquid.

Per serving: 397 calories, 12 g fat (4 g sat.), 98 mg cholesterol, 663 mg sodium, 39 g carbohydrate, 1 g fiber, 31 g protein.

Bagel Chip Salad

¼ cup red-wine vinegar
1 tablespoon Dijon mustard
½ teaspoon garlic salt
½ teaspoon dried oregano
¼ teaspoon black pepper
⅔ cup extra-virgin olive oil
2 large heads romaine lettuce, trimmed, washed, dried and cut into bite-size pieces (about 18 cups)
1 medium-size red onion, halved and thinly sliced
1½ cups garlic bagel chips, coarsely broken up
½ cup grated Parmesan cheese

1. For dressing, in small bowl, combine vinegar, mustard, garlic salt, oregano and pepper. Whisk to combine. Gradually drizzle in oil while whisking continuously. Whisk until mixture is emulsified. Set aside.

2. In large bowl, mix together lettuce and onion. Toss with dressing. Stir in broken bagel chips and cheese.

Make Ahead: Dressing can be made several days ahead. Salad ingredients can be prepped up to 1 day ahead. To transport, place dressing in a jar fitted with a tight lid. Pack remaining ingredients in separate plastic food-storage bags. Toss just before serving.

Crisp romaine is dressed with a tangy mustard vinaigrette, and bagel chips stand in for the usual salad croutons.

PREP: 15 minutes
MAKES: 12 servings

QUICK TIP

MORE WITH ROMAINE

Romaine lettuce is best known for its role in Caesar salad, but it goes well in other salads too. Here are two more ways to use this crisp, crunchy lettuce:
• Top with slices of mango and/or papaya (found in refrigerated jars in the produce section), plus slices of avocado. A vinaigrette made with lime juice will liven this one up.
• Greek Treat: Toss a romaine blend with tomatoes, feta cheese, red onions, pitted kalamata olives and a lemon-sparked olive-oil dressing.

Per serving: 150 calories, 12 g fat (2 g sat.), 2 mg cholesterol, 229 mg sodium, 11 g carbohydrate, 2 g fiber, 3 g protein.

Lemon-Blueberry Bundt

Lemon and blueberry make great partners, as this simply delicious cake demonstrates.

PREP: 20 minutes
BAKE: at 350° for 50 minutes
COOL: 20 minutes
MAKES: 16 servings

Cake:
- 2¾ cups all-purpose flour
- 1½ teaspoons baking powder
- ¼ teaspoon baking soda
- ¼ teaspoon salt
- 1 cup (2 sticks) unsalted butter, at room temperature
- 1¾ cups granulated sugar
- 4 eggs
- 1 tablespoon grated lemon zest
- 2 tablespoons lemon juice
- 1½ teaspoons vanilla extract
- 1 cup buttermilk
- 1¼ cups fresh blueberries tossed with 1¼ tablespoons all-purpose flour

Glaze:
- 1½ cups confectioners' sugar
- 2 tablespoons lemon juice
- 1 tablespoon corn syrup
- Shredded lemon zest, for garnish (optional)

1. **Cake:** Heat oven to 350°. Butter and flour a 12-cup Bundt pan.

2. In large bowl, whisk together flour, baking powder, baking soda and salt. Set aside.

3. In another large bowl, with electric mixer on medium speed, beat butter until smooth. Add granulated sugar and beat for 2 to 3 minutes or until fluffy. Beat in eggs, one at a time, beating well after each addition. Add lemon zest, lemon juice and vanilla; beat until combined. Beat in flour mixture in three additions, alternating with buttermilk and beginning and ending with flour. Beat for 2 minutes on medium-high speed. Fold in blueberry-flour mixture. Spoon into prepared pan.

4. Bake at 350° about 50 minutes or until wooden toothpick inserted in the center of the cake comes out clean. Cool on wire rack for 20 minutes. Run a sharp knife around edges of the pan. Turn out and cool completely.

5. **Glaze:** In small bowl, mix together confectioners' sugar, lemon juice and corn syrup until smooth. Drizzle over top of cake and let it roll down the sides. If desired, garnish with lemon zest.

QUICK TIP

EASY OUT

To butter and flour baking pans, use a paper towel or pastry brush to spread the butter evenly in the pan. Add a tablespoon or two of flour to the buttered pan, tilt the pan and tap it so the flour covers all the greased surfaces, then tap out the excess flour.

Per serving: 345 calories, 13 g fat (8 g sat.), 85 mg cholesterol, 128 mg sodium, 53 g carbohydrate, 1 g fiber, 5 g protein.

Burgers, Three Ways

¼ **pound fresh white button mushrooms,
    stemmed and finely chopped**
¼ **cup prepared balsamic vinaigrette dressing
    and marinade**
1 **teaspoon dried onion flakes**
½ **teaspoon adobo seasoning**
¼ **teaspoon black pepper**
½ **pound ground beef**
½ **pound ground turkey**
½ **pound ground pork**
    American cheese (optional)
6 **soft hamburger buns or 12 slices bread
    Green leaf lettuce, separated into leaves
    and rinsed**
1 **large red onion, sliced**
1 **large tomato, sliced**

1. In medium-size bowl, mix mushrooms, dressing, onion flakes, adobo seasoning and pepper. Divide into thirds. Place different ground meats in three separate bowls. Add one-third of the mushroom mixture to each bowl; mix gently with your hands. Shape into six patties (two for each meat, about ¾ inch thick) and refrigerate until time to grill.

2. Heat gas grill to medium-high or prepare charcoal grill with medium-hot coals. Add patties and grill for 5 minutes. Flip over; continue to grill about 5 minutes longer or until an instant-read meat thermometer inserted in centers of patties registers 160° for beef, 165° for turkey and 160° for pork. Top with cheese, if using, during last minute of cooking.

3. Place lettuce on bun bottoms or on half of the bread slices; top with burgers, onion and tomato slices. Add bun tops or remaining bread slices.

Some people like beef, others prefer pork and then there's the turkey crowd. Please them all with this three-in-one recipe.

PREP: 15 minutes
GRILL: 10 minutes
MAKES: 6 servings

QUICK TIP

TAKE IT WITH YOU

Advance planning is key to making it easy to leave the tailgating site the way you found it. Be sure to pack all the food in disposable containers or resealable bags and throw a roll of paper towels in for cleanup. Don't forget napkins, paper plates and utensils. Tuck a large garbage bag into the trunk so you can pack up all the trash at the end.

Per serving (beef): 481 calories, 30 g fat (11 g sat.), 85 mg cholesterol, 532 mg sodium, 27 g carbohydrate, 2 g fiber, 25 g protein.

Per serving (turkey): 351 calories, 16 g fat (4 g sat.), 90 mg cholesterol, 560 mg sodium, 27 g carbohydrate, 2 g fiber, 24 g protein.

Per serving (pork): 480 calories, 31 g fat (10 g sat.), 82 mg cholesterol, 517 mg sodium, 27 g carbohydrate, 2 g fiber, 24 g protein.

Macaroni Salad

1 pound shell macaroni, cooked, rinsed
   and chilled
12 ounces assorted sweet pepper strips,
   cut into bite-size pieces
1 package (8 ounces) Cheddar and
   Monterey Jack cheese cubes
1 jar (9½ ounces) light tartar sauce
½ cup light mayonnaise
⅓ cup cider vinegar
2½ teaspoons sugar
2 teaspoons Dijon mustard
¼ teaspoon salt
¼ teaspoon black pepper
3 scallions, trimmed and chopped

1. In large bowl, stir together macaroni, sweet pepper, cheese, tartar sauce, mayonnaise, vinegar, sugar, mustard, salt and black pepper. Stir in scallion. Store chilled.

Choice add-ins—including sweet pepper strips and tartar sauce—take this favorite to new heights.

PREP: 20 minutes
MAKES: 8 servings

QUICK TIP

VARIATIONS ON A THEME

Once you have a basic recipe for macaroni salad, you can adjust the ingredients to match your family's preferences. For example, any semisoft to semifirm cheese will do—try cubes of Gouda, Muenster, provolone or mozzarella if that's what you have in the fridge. Take out the pepper strips and add frozen peas, sliced radishes and/or celery. Or use a couple tablespoons of finely chopped red onion or sweet yellow onion instead of the scallion.

Per serving: 336 calories, 21 g fat (8 g sat.), 40 mg cholesterol, 588 mg sodium, 28 g carbohydrate, 1 g fiber, 11 g protein.

Quick Brownies

Graham cracker squares
1 family-size box (about 21 ounces) brownie mix
1 cup semisweet chocolate chips
1 cup chopped walnuts
1½ cups mini marshmallows

1. Heat oven to 350°. Line 13×9×2-inch baking pan with nonstick aluminum foil.

2. Line bottom of pan with graham crackers, breaking apart to fit.

3. Prepare brownie mix, following package directions for cakey brownies; stir in chocolate chips and walnuts. Spread over crackers.

4. Bake at 350° for 28 minutes. Top with marshmallows; return to oven. Bake for 2 minutes longer. Cool in pan on wire rack. Cut into bars with a lightly greased knife.

A graham cracker base and marshmallow topping set these treats apart from other brownies.

PREP: 10 minutes
BAKE: at 350° for 30 minutes
MAKES: 16 brownies

QUICK TIP

MOBILE MUNCHIES

Here's a foolproof way to transport brownies. Once they're completely cooled and cut, line a cardboard shirt box with waxed paper. Arrange the brownies in a single layer, crumpling extra waxed paper around the edges to keep the squares from sliding. If you need to stack the brownies, put a sheet of waxed paper between the layers.

Per brownie: 363 calories, 19 g fat (4 g sat.), 27 mg cholesterol, 161 mg sodium, 44 g carbohydrate, 2 g fiber, 6 g protein.

Sausage and Pepper Lasagna

- 1 tablespoon extra-virgin olive oil
- 1 medium-size green pepper, seeded and diced
- 1 small onion, diced
- 2 cloves garlic, sliced
- 5 links sweet Italian sausage (about 1⅓ pounds total), casings removed
- 1 can (28 ounces) fire-roasted crushed tomatoes in puree
- 1 tablespoon balsamic vinegar
- 2¼ teaspoons dried Italian seasoning
- 2 teaspoons sugar
- 1 container (15 ounces) ricotta cheese
- 1 egg
- 4 tablespoons grated Parmesan cheese
- ¼ teaspoon black pepper
- 12 no-boil lasagna noodles
- 2 cups shredded mozzarella cheese (8 ounces)

1. Heat oven to 350°. Coat a 13×9×2-inch baking dish with nonstick cooking spray.

2. Heat oil in 12-inch skillet over medium-high heat. Add green pepper, onion and garlic. Cook for 5 minutes, stirring constantly. Add sausage; cook about 5 minutes or until no longer pink, breaking apart with a spoon. Add tomatoes, vinegar, 2 teaspoons Italian seasoning and sugar. Reduce heat to medium; simmer for 10 minutes.

3. In medium-size bowl, stir together ricotta cheese and egg. Stir in 2 tablespoons grated Parmesan cheese, the black pepper and the remaining ¼ teaspoon Italian seasoning.

4. Begin layering: Place 1 cup of the sausage mixture on bottom of prepared baking dish. Top with three noodles (do not overlap). Top with ¾ cup of the ricotta cheese mixture and 1 cup of the mozzarella cheese. Ladle on 1 cup of the sausage mixture, then three noodles and another 1 cup sausage mixture. Top with three more noodles, then top with remaining ricotta cheese mixture. Spread with 1 cup sausage mixture; top with the final three noodles. Top noodles with the remaining sausage mixture, the remaining 1 cup mozzarella cheese and the remaining 2 tablespoons Parmesan cheese.

5. Cover dish with nonstick aluminum foil; bake at 350° for 30 minutes. Uncover dish; bake for 20 to 25 minutes longer or until top is browned. Cool for 10 to 15 minutes before serving.

A great lasagna is a dish that everyone appreciates. This one has it all—creamy cheeses, robust sausage and a tangy tomato sauce.

PREP: 15 minutes
COOK: 20 minutes
BAKE: at 350° for 50 to 55 minutes
COOL: 10 to 15 minutes
MAKES: 8 servings

QUICK TIP

FREEZER FACTS

To freeze leftover lasagna, divide it into smaller portions, if needed. Transfer to airtight containers designed for the freezer. Seal and freeze for up to 3 months.

Per serving: 478 calories, 23 g fat (10 g sat.), 94 mg cholesterol, 818 mg sodium, 36 g carbohydrate, 4 g fiber, 28 g protein.

Garlic Knots

2 tablespoons extra-virgin olive oil
2 tablespoons unsalted butter
4 cloves garlic, finely chopped
⅛ teaspoon salt
1 pound frozen bread dough, thawed
¼ teaspoon salt

1. In 10-inch skillet, heat oil and butter over medium-low heat about 4 minutes or until butter is melted. Add garlic and the ⅛ teaspoon salt. Cook for 3 to 4 minutes. Set aside.

2. Roll out thawed dough to a 12×10-inch rectangle. Cut lengthwise into 12 strips, then in half crosswise (for a total of twenty-four 5×1-inch strips).

3. Tie each strip into a knot, stretching dough slightly. Transfer dough knots to two large baking sheets (12 per sheet). Sprinkle with the ¼ teaspoon salt. Cover with a clean towel; let stand in warm place to rise for 30 minutes.

4. Heat oven to 375°. Uncover knots; brush each with a little of the garlic butter. Bake at 375° for 20 minutes, rotating pans halfway through baking. Once baked, immediately transfer to a large bowl and toss with remaining garlic butter.

Frozen bread dough is your ticket to a fresh-baked garlic bread that will go well with all kinds of meals.

PREP: 10 minutes
COOK: 7 to 8 minutes
RISE: 30 minutes
BAKE: at 375° for 20 minutes
MAKES: 24 knots

QUICK BITE

BIG YET MILD

Sometimes at farmer's markets or larger supermarkets, you might spot elephant garlic alongside regular garlic. As its name suggests, elephant garlic is larger. It's also milder in flavor and more closely related to the leek than regular garlic.

Per knot: 72 calories, 3 g fat (1 g sat.), 3 mg cholesterol, 142 mg sodium, 10 g carbohydrate, 1 g fiber, 2 g protein.

Spiced Apple Cider

1 quart (4 cups) apple cider
½ teaspoon ground ginger
   Pinch of ground allspice
6 ounces apple brandy (optional)
   Licorice twists, for garnish (optional)

1. In medium-size saucepan, combine cider, ginger and allspice. Heat over medium heat about 5 minutes or until warm.

2. Divide cider mixture among four mugs. If desired, add 1½ ounces apple brandy to each mug. If desired, garnish each serving with a licorice twist.

What lemonade is to summer, hot apple cider is to autumn— the quintessential drink of the season!

PREP: 5 minutes
COOK: 5 minutes
MAKES: 4 servings

QUICK BITE
APPLES WITH A KICK

Calvados is a world-famous apple brandy made in Normandy, France. It's more expensive than domestic apple brandy but is a good choice if, in addition to using it to spike cider, you wish to keep some on hand for after-dinner sipping during the year-end holidays.

Per serving: 247 calories, 0 g fat (0 g sat.), 0 mg cholesterol, 1 mg sodium, 35 g carbohydrate, 0 g fiber, 1 g protein.

Halloween Cookies

Vanilla Cookies:
- 2¼ cups all-purpose flour
- Pinch of salt
- ¾ cup (1½ sticks) unsalted butter, at room temperature
- ¾ cup sugar
- 1 egg
- 1 teaspoon vanilla extract

Decorations:
- Royal Icing (recipe, right)
- Assorted food coloring, pastry bags and writing tips

1. **Vanilla Cookies:** In small bowl, mix flour and salt. In medium-size bowl, with electric mixer on medium speed, beat together butter and sugar about 2 minutes or until fluffy. Beat in egg and vanilla. On low speed, beat in flour mixture in thirds. Shape into disk; divide in half. Wrap and refrigerate overnight.

2. Heat oven to 350°. Using half of the dough at a time, roll out between 2 sheets of waxed paper to ¼-inch thickness. (You can also roll out on well-floured surface.) Remove top waxed paper sheet; cut out shapes. Reserve scraps. Transfer cookies from paper to ungreased cookie sheets.

3. Bake at 350° for 11 to 13 minutes or until browned around edges. Transfer to wire rack and let cool. Repeat with scraps.

4. **Decorate:** Add food coloring to thin Royal Icing for base coat as desired. Use a thin spatula to spread icing to edges of cookies. Add food coloring to thick Royal Icing for piping as desired. Place in pastry bags with writing tips. Using the cookies pictured as a guide, pipe edging and designs on cookies. To make a spider web: Paint cookies with icing. Pipe contrasting spiral on top. Draw a knife through spiral, starting at center.

Chocolate Cookies: Make the dough as in step 1 above, except substitute ¼ cup unsweetened cocoa powder for ¼ cup of the all-purpose flour. Cut out cookies and bake following steps 2 and 3 above. Decorate following step 4 above.

Why save the prettiest cookies for Christmas? Roll out a batch for another favorite family holiday!

PREP: 15 minutes
CHILL: overnight
BAKE: at 350° for 11 to 13 minutes per batch
DECORATE: 25 minutes
MAKES: 48 cookies

ROYAL ICING

For thin icing for base coat, in small bowl, with electric mixer on low to medium speed, beat together 1 box (1 pound) confectioners' sugar, sifted; ½ cup warm water; and 3 tablespoons pasteurized dried egg whites about 6 minutes or until consistency of honey.

For thick icing for piping, make a second batch as above, but use only 6 tablespoons warm water; beat until consistency of sour cream.

Per cookie (vanilla without icing): 99 calories, 3 g fat (2 g sat.), 12 mg cholesterol, 8 mg sodium, 17 g carbohydrate, 0 g fiber, 1 g protein.

Per cookie (chocolate without icing): 59 calories, 3 g fat (2 g sat.), 12 mg cholesterol, 8 mg sodium, 7 g carbohydrate, 0 g fiber, 1 g protein.

Roast Turkey Breast and Gravy

Turkey:
- 1 **whole turkey breast on the bone (about 7 pounds)**
- 2 **tablespoons lemon juice**
- 2 **tablespoons extra-virgin olive oil**
- 2½ **tablespoons Holiday Spice Rub (recipe follows)**

Gravy:
- ¾ **cup dry white wine**
- 3 **tablespoons all-purpose flour**
- 3 **cups chicken broth**

1. Heat oven to 350°. Coat large roasting pan with nonstick cooking spray.

2. **Turkey:** Rinse turkey breast under cold water; pat dry with paper towels. Rub on all sides with lemon juice and oil. Rub Holiday Spice Rub on turkey, including under the skin.

3. Place the turkey in prepared pan. Roast at 350° about 2 hours or until instant-read meat thermometer inserted in center of breast (not touching bone) registers 170°. Transfer turkey to serving platter. Let stand for 10 to 15 minutes in a warm place.

4. **Gravy:** Pour off all but about 2 tablespoons of the drippings from pan. Add wine and cook over medium-high heat, scraping up any browned bits from bottom of the pan. Cook for 1 minute. Sprinkle flour into pan; cook for 1 minute. Gradually whisk in chicken broth; cook, stirring, about 2 minutes or until thickened. Strain gravy into a gravy boat.

5. To serve, slice turkey and accompany with the warm gravy.

Holiday Spice Rub: In small bowl, combine 4 teaspoons onion salt, 2 teaspoons garlic powder, 2 teaspoons dried oregano, 2 teaspoons dried sage, 2 teaspoons paprika, 2 teaspoons black pepper, 1 teaspoon dried thyme and ½ teaspoon ground allspice. Store in a tightly covered jar for up to 3 months. Makes about 5 tablespoons (enough to season 2 whole turkey breasts).

Note: For a whole turkey, follow directions as in step 2. Roast at 350° following timing suggestion on package. Prepare gravy as directed.

Looking to simplify the holiday? A turkey breast is much more manageable and cooks more quickly than a whole turkey.

PREP: 15 minutes
ROAST: at 350° for 2 hours
STAND: 10 to 15 minutes
COOK: 4 minutes
MAKES: 12 servings

QUICK TIP

GRAVY Rx

If your gravy is too thin, stir in a thickener such as a beurre manié (flour mixed into softened butter), cornstarch blended with a little water or quick-cooking tapioca. Add the thickener slowly, just 1 teaspoon at a time, then blend the mixture well. Add too much thickener and your gravy will become jellylike!

Per serving: 327 calories, 8 g fat (2 g sat.), 168 mg cholesterol, 514 mg sodium, 2 g carbohydrate, 0 g fiber, 55 g protein.

Cheesy Broccoli and Cauliflower

2 large heads fresh broccoli
   (3 to 3½ pounds total)
1 medium-size head cauliflower
   (about 2 pounds)
3 tablespoons unsalted butter
3 tablespoons all-purpose flour
1¾ cups milk
2 cups shredded sharp Cheddar cheese
   (8 ounces)
1 can (4¼ ounces) diced green chiles, drained
1 tablespoon Dijon mustard
¼ teaspoon hot-pepper sauce
⅛ teaspoon salt
   Additional milk, if needed, to thin sauce

1. Cut broccoli and cauliflower into flowerets, discarding outer leaves and stems. You should have about 8 cups broccoli flowerets and 4 cups cauliflower flowerets. (If desired, save stems for soup.)

2. In large pot, bring 8 cups lightly salted water to a boil. Add cauliflower; cook for 2 minutes. Add broccoli; cook about 6 minutes longer or until vegetables are crisp-tender. Drain.

3. While vegetables are cooking, in medium-size saucepan, melt butter over medium heat. Whisk in flour and cook for 1 minute. Gradually whisk in the 1¾ cups milk; continue to whisk until smooth. Bring to a boil. Remove from heat and stir in cheese, chiles, mustard, hot-pepper sauce and salt. Stir until smooth. If a thinner sauce is desired, stir in a few more tablespoons of milk.

4. To serve, place broccoli and cauliflower in large serving dish and pour cheese sauce over the top. Serve immediately.

Make Ahead: Cook vegetables; rinse under cold water to stop cooking. Drain and refrigerate. Prepare sauce; let cool, then cover and refrigerate for up to 1 day. To serve, uncover; remove from refrigerator and let stand for 30 minutes. Reheat vegetables and sauce separately in microwave oven (adding more milk to sauce as needed).

Thanks to a creamy cheese sauce studded with green chiles, don't be surprised if even the kids say, "These veggies rock!"

PREP: 15 minutes
COOK: about 8 minutes
MAKES: 12 servings

QUICK TIP

THE BIG DAY

When you're hosting a houseful of guests at Thanksgiving, it's a good idea to offer both red and white wines because many guests will prefer one over the other. A good choice for a red is a Pinot Noir from California or Oregon; the bright berry flavors and silky softness will please a lot of palates and go well with just about everything on the table. For a white, you can't go wrong with a dry Riesling; however, you might also consider a California style of Chenin Blanc for those who like a little more sweetness.

Per serving: 163 calories, 11 g fat (7 g sat.), 33 mg cholesterol, 340 mg sodium, 9 g carbohydrate, 1 g fiber, 9 g protein.

Whipped Potato Casserole

- 5 **pounds all-purpose potatoes, peeled and quartered**
- 1¼ **cups half-and-half**
- 1 **tub (8 ounces) whipped cream cheese with chives (or 1 tub plain cream cheese mixed with 2 tablespoons chopped fresh chives)**
- ½ **cup (1 stick) unsalted butter, at room temperature**
- 1 **teaspoon garlic salt**
- ¼ **teaspoon ground nutmeg**
- 1 **cup sliced almonds**

1. Heat oven to 350°. Coat 3-quart baking dish with nonstick cooking spray.

2. Place potatoes in large pot with enough water to cover. Lightly salt and bring to a boil. Lower heat to simmering; cook for 15 to 20 minutes or until fork-tender. Drain.

3. In large bowl, mash potatoes with hand mixer. Add half-and-half, cream cheese, butter, garlic salt and nutmeg. With mixer on medium-high speed, beat potatoes until very smooth. Spoon into prepared baking dish.

4. Bake, uncovered, at 350° for 30 minutes. Sprinkle almonds over casserole; bake, uncovered, for 15 minutes longer or until lightly browned.

5. Let stand for 15 minutes before serving.

Make Ahead: Prepare as above through step 3 and allow to cool. Cover with plastic wrap and refrigerate for up to 2 days. To serve, unwrap and allow to stand at room temperature for at least 30 minutes. Begin with step 4 and bake until instant-read thermometer inserted in center of baking dish registers 140°.

Call on the make-ahead directions and you can forget all that last-minute boiling and mashing.

PREP: 15 minutes
COOK: 15 to 20 minutes
BAKE: at 350° for 45 minutes
STAND: 15 minutes
MAKES: 12 servings

QUICK TIP

POTLUCK POINTERS

When someone asks if he or she can bring a dish to a holiday dinner, say, "Yes, please!" But instead of being vague by asking guests to bring some sort of side dish or dessert, request specific foods that will complement your menu, such as dressing or apple pie. This will prevent an all-green-bean-casserole buffet but still allow for some creative freedom.

Per serving: 364 calories, 21 g fat (11 g sat.), 54 mg cholesterol, 232 mg sodium, 37 g carbohydrate, 4 g fiber, 8 g protein.

Sausage and Corn Bread Stuffing

2 tablespoons extra-virgin olive oil
1 pound sweet Italian sausage links, casing removed, crumbled
1 large onion, finely chopped
4 ribs celery (including leaves), thinly sliced
1 cup shredded carrot
3 cups water
1 cup apple juice
1 Granny Smith apple, peeled, cored and diced
½ teaspoon poultry seasoning
2 boxes (6 ounces each) corn bread stuffing mix
Fresh sage, for garnish (optional)

1. In large skillet or large deep pot, heat oil over medium-high heat. Add sausage, onion, celery and carrot. Break up sausage with wooden spoon. Sauté for 12 minutes, stirring occasionally. Add water, juice, diced apple and poultry seasoning, stirring to combine. Bring to a simmer.

2. Turn off heat and stir in stuffing mix. Cover and allow to stand for 5 minutes. Fluff with a fork. If desired, garnish with sage.

Make Ahead: Prepare as above. Spoon into a casserole and let cool. Cover with plastic wrap and refrigerate for up to 2 days. To serve, unwrap and allow to stand at room temperature for 30 minutes. Heat oven to 325°. Bake at 325° about 40 minutes or until instant-read meat thermometer inserted in center of casserole registers 140°.

Jazz up packaged stuffing mix with homespun extras to make a side dish everyone will love.

PREP: 15 minutes
COOK: 12 minutes
STAND: 5 minutes
MAKES: 12 servings

QUICK BITE

GREAT GRANNIES

Ever wonder why so many recipes call for Granny Smith apples? The firm apple holds its shape well when cooked. And its puckery, sharp and zingy flavor—a little like sour-apple-flavor hard candies—adds a distinctive appeal in both sweet and savory recipes. If you can't find Granny Smith, substitute another tart cooking or baking apple, such as Cortland.

Per serving: 223 calories, 10 g fat (2 g sat.), 15 mg cholesterol, 698 mg sodium, 27 g carbohydrate, 2 g fiber, 7 g protein.

Spicy Sweet Potatoes

- 3 tablespoons vegetable oil
- 2 medium-size onions, halved and thinly sliced
- 3½ pounds large sweet potatoes (about 6 large), peeled and cut up
- 2 cups water
- 1 cup golden raisins
- 2 tablespoons light-brown sugar
- 1½ teaspoons salt
- 1 teaspoon ground ginger
- ½ teaspoon ground cinnamon
- ¼ teaspoon cayenne pepper

1. In large skillet, heat oil over medium-high heat. Add onion and cook, stirring occasionally, about 3 minutes or until golden brown. Add sweet potatoes and cook, stirring occasionally, for 10 minutes.

2. Add water, raisins, brown sugar, salt, ginger, cinnamon and cayenne pepper. Cook, covered, over medium heat about 12 minutes or until tender. Stir occasionally.

3. Serve warm or at room temperature.

Make Ahead: Spoon fully prepared potatoes into a casserole dish and let cool. Cover with plastic wrap and refrigerate for up to 2 days. To serve, unwrap and allow to stand at room temperature for at least 30 minutes. Heat oven to 325°. Bake at 325° about 30 minutes or until instant-read thermometer inserted in center of casserole registers 140°.

A yummy sweet potato recipe is a must at Thanksgiving. Try this adaptation, with plump golden raisins and warm baking spices.

PREP: 15 minutes
COOK: 25 minutes
MAKES: 12 servings

QUICK TIP

SETTING THE STAGE

For your holiday table:
- Be sure to keep flowers or other centerpieces low enough so that guests can see each other. Ditto for candles.
- Tuck dried leaves and pinecones into floral arrangements.
- Fill a large glass bowl with a combination of whole fruits, nuts in the shell and pinecones.
- Place a small potted herb at each place with a bold ribbon tied around the container.

Per serving: 235 calories, 4 g fat (0 g sat.), 0 mg cholesterol, 312 mg sodium, 49 g carbohydrate, 5 g fiber, 3 g protein.

Chocolate Pumpkin Chiffon Pie

Crust:
- 6 tablespoons (¾ stick) unsalted butter, melted
- 24 cream-filled chocolate sandwich cookies (such as Oreo), finely ground

Filling:
- 1 envelope (0.25 ounce) unflavored gelatin
- 2 tablespoons brandy or water
- 1¼ cups canned pumpkin puree
- 1 cup evaporated milk
- ¾ cup packed light-brown sugar
- 4 egg yolks
- 2 teaspoons pumpkin pie spice
- ¼ teaspoon salt
- ¾ cup heavy cream
- Chocolate curls, for garnish (optional)

1. **Crust:** In medium-size bowl, stir melted butter into ground cookies until moistened. Press into the bottom and up the sides of a 9-inch deep-dish pie plate. Refrigerate until ready to fill.

2. **Filling:** In small glass measuring cup, sprinkle gelatin over brandy. Let stand for 5 minutes.

3. In heavy-bottomed medium-size saucepan, whisk together pumpkin puree, milk, brown sugar, egg yolks, pumpkin pie spice and salt until smooth. Cook over medium heat, whisking, about 8 minutes or until temperature registers 140° on an instant-read thermometer. Continue stirring over low heat for 3 minutes, maintaining 140°.

4. Microwave gelatin mixture on HIGH about 10 seconds or until melted. Whisk into the pumpkin mixture and remove from heat.

5. Pour filling into large bowl. Set into larger bowl of ice water and cool, stirring occasionally, for 10 to 12 minutes or until consistency of honey.

6. In small bowl, with electric mixer on medium-high speed, whip cream until stiff peaks form. Gently fold cream into cooled pumpkin mixture. Pour into cooled crust. Refrigerate overnight.

7. If desired, garnish with chocolate curls. Allow to stand at room temperature for 15 minutes before serving. With a sharp knife, cut into slices.

No need to choose between a traditional pumpkin dessert and a chocolate treat! This recipe offers the best of both worlds.

PREP: 30 minutes
STAND: 20 minutes
COOK: 11 minutes
MICROWAVE: 10 seconds
COOL: 10 to 12 minutes
CHILL: overnight
MAKES: 8 servings

QUICK TIP

CRUSHING COOKIES

To crush sandwich cookies, place them in a large resealable food-storage bag; seal bag well. Lay the bag flat on your counter and, using a rolling pin, crush the cookies until crumbs are about the consistency of cornmeal.

Per serving: 486 calories, 29 g fat (14 g sat.), 170 mg cholesterol, 438 mg sodium, 50 g carbohydrate, 2 g fiber, 7 g protein.

Gingerbread Cookies

Cookies:
- 2½ cups all-purpose flour
- 2 teaspoons ground ginger
- 1 teaspoon ground cinnamon
- ½ teaspoon salt
- ¼ teaspoon ground cloves
- 14 tablespoons (1¾ sticks) unsalted butter, at room temperature
- 1 cup packed dark-brown sugar
- 2 egg yolks
- 1 teaspoon vanilla extract

Icing:
- 2½ cups confectioners' sugar
- ¼ cup orange juice
- ½ teaspoon orange extract
- Assorted soft gel paste food coloring
- Assorted colors gel decorator icing

1. **Cookies:** Sift together flour, ginger, cinnamon, salt and cloves into a medium-size bowl.

2. In large bowl, with electric mixer on medium speed, beat together butter and brown sugar until creamy. Beat in egg yolks and vanilla. Stir flour mixture into butter mixture. Divide dough in half. Shape each half into a disk; wrap each in plastic wrap. Chill about 1 hour or until firm enough to roll.

3. Heat oven to 350°. Line cookie sheet with parchment paper or aluminum foil.

4. On floured surface, using half the dough at a time, roll out dough to ⅜-inch thickness. Cut out cookies using gingerbread people cookie cutters. Using wide metal spatula, transfer cookies to the prepared cookie sheet, spacing 1 inch apart. Reroll the scraps; if too soft, chill about 10 minutes.

5. Bake at 350° about 15 minutes or until golden brown. Cool on cookie sheet on wire rack.

6. **Icing:** In medium-size bowl, whisk together confectioners' sugar, orange juice and orange extract. Divide into several batches; tint as desired with food coloring. If icing is too thick, whisk in a drop or two of water or milk to thin to icing consistency. If icing is too thin, whisk in ¼ to ½ cup additional confectioners' sugar. Transfer icings to pastry bags fitted with writing tips. Using colored icings and gel decorator icings, decorate cookies as desired. Let stand until icing is completely dry. Store cookies in an airtight container at room temperature for up to 3 days.

All hands on deck! Get everyone involved in decorating these charming little fellows.

PREP: 20 minutes
CHILL: 1 hour
BAKE: at 350° for 15 minutes per batch
MAKES: about 16 cookies

QUICK TIP

A COOKIE SWAP

Invite your baker friends over for a good old-fashioned cookie swap. Have everyone bring a dozen or two of a favorite holiday cookie. Provide plates and plastic wrap and let everyone select a variety of cookie shapes and flavors to take home. Also make a pot of coffee and have some hot tea and hot chocolate on hand so you can sip while you make up your plates (some cookie sneaking is to be expected, so you'll need beverages to wash them down).

Per cookie: 284 calories, 11 g fat (7 g sat.), 54 mg cholesterol, 81 mg sodium, 45 g carbohydrate, 1 g fiber, 3 g protein.

Santa's Sandwiches

Cookies:
- 1¼ cups all-purpose flour
- ½ cup unsweetened cocoa powder
- ¾ teaspoon baking soda
- ¼ teaspoon salt
- 1 cup granulated sugar
- ½ cup (1 stick) unsalted butter, at room temperature
- 1 egg
- ½ teaspoon vanilla extract
- ¼ teaspoon mint extract

Filling:
- 2½ cups sifted confectioners' sugar
- ½ cup (1 stick) unsalted butter, softened
- 2 tablespoons milk
- ½ teaspoon mint extract
- Red and green food coloring

1. **Cookies:** Sift together flour, cocoa powder, baking soda and salt into small bowl; set aside. In large bowl, with electric mixer on medium speed, beat granulated sugar and butter until smooth. Beat in egg, then vanilla and mint extract. On low speed, beat flour mixture into butter mixture. Divide in half; shape each half into a log about 1½ inches in diameter. Wrap each in plastic wrap; refrigerate for 4 hours.

2. Heat oven to 375°. Cut each log into 36 slices, each about ⅛ inch thick; place on ungreased cookie sheet. Bake at 375° for 6 to 8 minutes or until almost firm. Transfer cookies to wire rack and let cool.

3. **Filling:** In medium-size bowl, with electric mixer on low to medium speed, beat confectioners' sugar, butter, milk and mint extract until spreading consistency. Tint half with red food coloring and other half with green food coloring. Spread flat sides of one-quarter of the cookies with red filling and another quarter with green filling. Top each with a plain cookie. Chill until serving time.

Santa's not the only one who's going to adore these chocolaty, buttery delights.

PREP: 20 minutes
CHILL: 4 hours
BAKE: at 375° for 6 to 8 minutes per batch
MAKES: 36 sandwich cookies

QUICK TIP

BEST-EVER COOKIES

To turn out picture-perfect goodies every time, keep these pointers in mind:
- Make sure all ingredients are at room temperature before combining, unless the recipe says otherwise.
- Don't substitute reduced-fat margarine for full-fat because its increased water content will adversely affect the results.
- For even baking, form cookies on the same sheet to a uniform size.
- Let cookie sheet cool thoroughly before placing a second batch on it.

Per sandwich cookie: 115 calories, 6 g fat (3 g sat.), 20 mg cholesterol, 46 mg sodium, 16 g carbohydrate, 1 g fiber, 1 g protein.

Cranberry Crescents

1 cup (2 sticks) butter, at room temperature
½ cup granulated sugar
1 package (8 ounces) cream cheese
2 egg yolks
½ teaspoon vanilla extract
½ teaspoon orange extract
¼ teaspoon salt
2½ cups all-purpose flour
1 package (6 ounces) dried sweetened cranberries
⅔ cup golden raisins
3 tablespoons orange juice
1 egg, lightly beaten
Clear sugar decorating crystals, for garnish

1. In large bowl, with electric mixer on medium speed, beat butter and granulated sugar about 1 minute or until creamy. Beat in cream cheese, egg yolks, vanilla, orange extract and salt; beat for 1 minute. On low speed, beat in flour just until combined. Divide dough into quarters; shape into disks. Wrap in plastic wrap; refrigerate about 2 hours or until firm.

2. In food processor, chop cranberries and raisins. Add orange juice.

3. Heat oven to 350°. Grease large cookie sheet.

4. On floured surface, roll one disk of dough into 8-inch round. Spread with ¼ cup of the cranberry mixture. Cut into 12 wedges. Starting at outside edge, roll up each wedge to enclose filling. Transfer to prepared cookie sheet. Repeat with remaining dough (48 cookies total). Brush with egg; top with sugar crystals.

5. Bake at 350° about 20 minutes or until lightly browned. Transfer to wire racks and let cool.

Dried cranberries add a refreshing tartness and a colorful hue to these roll-ups.

PREP: 25 minutes
CHILL: 2 hours
BAKE: at 350° for 20 minutes per batch
MAKES: 48 crescents

QUICK TIP

THE PERFECT CUPPA

How about a spot of tea with your Christmas cookies? To make a perfect cup, start by putting fresh, cool water on to boil. Just before it boils, pour some of the water into the teapot, swirling it around to warm up the pot. Pour it out and add tea leaves (custom dictates a teaspoon of loose leaf tea for each person, plus a teaspoon "for the pot"). Pour the boiling water over the tea. Let steep about 3 minutes, then strain into teacups.

Per crescent: 105 calories, 6 g fat (4 g sat.), 29 mg cholesterol, 29 mg sodium, 12 g carbohydrate, 1 g fiber, 1 g protein.

Holiday Biscotti

2¼ cups all-purpose flour
1½ teaspoons baking powder
    Pinch of salt
½ cup (1 stick) unsalted butter
½ cup packed light-brown sugar
2 eggs
1 teaspoon vanilla extract
½ cup dried sweetened cranberries
2 tablespoons grated orange zest
2 ounces white chocolate melted with
    1 teaspoon vegetable oil

1. Heat oven to 375°. Grease large cookie sheet.

2. In small bowl, mix flour, baking powder and salt. In large bowl, with electric mixer on medium speed, beat butter and brown sugar about 2 minutes or until creamy. Beat in eggs, one at a time. Add vanilla. Stir in flour mixture. Stir in cranberries and orange zest. Gather mixture into a ball. Divide in half.

3. Using floured hands, roll each portion into a 14-inch-long log. Place on prepared cookie sheet. Press dough slightly to flatten so each log is 2 inches wide.

4. Bake at 375° about 25 minutes or until lightly browned. Transfer logs to wire rack; let cool.

5. Reduce oven temperature to 325°. Cut loaves into ¾-inch-thick slices. Place slices, cut sides down, on cookie sheet. Bake for 10 minutes. Turn over; bake for 10 minutes longer. Cool biscotti on wire rack. Drizzle with the white chocolate mixture.

Package these slices with a bag of premium coffee for a gift anyone will appreciate.

PREP: 15 minutes
BAKE: at 375° for 25 minutes; at 325° for 20 minutes per batch
MAKES: 36 biscotti

QUICK TIP

BETTER BEANS

One way to ensure you're getting a high-quality coffee to enjoy with your cookies is to choose arabica coffee over robusta coffee. Most of the coffee found in the huge cans in supermarket aisles is made from beans from the robusta coffee plant, a hardy plant that offers high yields and, hence, a less expensive product. On the other hand, the arabica plant, which grows at higher altitudes than robusta, produces coffee that connoisseurs often describe as rich and complex. Look for arabica coffee at specialty coffee shops.

Per biscotti: 82 calories, 4 g fat (2 g sat.), 19 mg cholesterol, 31 mg sodium, 11 g carbohydrate, 0 g fiber, 1 g protein.

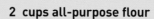

Candy Cane Puffs

2 cups all-purpose flour
¼ teaspoon salt
1 cup confectioners' sugar
½ cup (1 stick) unsalted butter, at room temperature
1 egg
½ teaspoon peppermint extract
½ teaspoon vanilla extract
8 ounces white chocolate baking pieces, melted
½ cup finely chopped candy canes

1. In medium-size bowl, combine flour and salt.

2. In large bowl, with electric mixer on medium speed, beat confectioners' sugar and butter until smooth and creamy. Beat in egg. Beat in peppermint extract and vanilla.

3. On low speed, beat in flour mixture. Wrap dough in plastic wrap; refrigerate for 1 hour.

4. Heat oven to 375°. Lightly grease cookie sheets. Shape dough into 1-inch balls; place on prepared cookie sheets.

5. Bake at 375° for 10 to 12 minutes or until bottoms are lightly browned. Transfer cookies to wire racks and let cool.

6. To top cookies, brush with melted white chocolate; dip lightly in chopped candy canes. Place on waxed paper to harden.

White chocolate and chopped candy canes make an extra-special topping for these buttery gems.

PREP: 10 minutes
CHILL: 1 hour
BAKE: at 375° for 10 to 12 minutes per batch
MAKES: about 48 puffs

QUICK TIP

HANDY CANDY

Make swift work of chopping candy canes by placing the candy canes in a heavy-duty resealable food-storage bag and crushing them with a rolling pin. This technique also works for making graham cracker or cookie crumbs for piecrusts.

Per puff: 84 calories, 4 g fat (2 g sat.), 11 mg cholesterol, 19 mg sodium, 12 g carbohydrate, 0 g fiber, 1 g protein.

Index

Index

Index

Index

Index

For a recipe to earn this "healthy" icon, it must meet certain nutritional requirements. Maximum levels per serving include: **One-dish meal:** 500 calories, 16 grams fat, 800 milligrams sodium and 150 milligrams cholesterol. **Side dish:** 200 calories, 9 grams fat and 300 milligrams sodium. **Dessert:** 250 calories, 9 grams fat and 350 milligrams sodium.

In-a-Pinch Substitutions

It can happen to the best of us: Halfway through a recipe, you find you're completely out of a key ingredient. Here's what to do:

Recipe Calls For:	You May Substitute:
1 square unsweetened chocolate	3 Tbs unsweetened cocoa powder + 1 Tbs butter/margarine
1 cup cake flour	1 cup less 2 Tbs all-purpose flour
2 Tbs flour (for thickening)	1 Tbs cornstarch
1 tsp baking powder	¼ tsp baking soda + ½ tsp cream of tartar + ¼ tsp cornstarch
1 cup corn syrup	1 cup sugar + ¼ cup additional liquid used in recipe
1 cup milk	½ cup evaporated milk + ½ cup water
1 cup buttermilk or sour milk	1 Tbs vinegar or lemon juice + enough milk to make 1 cup
1 cup sour cream (for baking)	1 cup plain yogurt
1 cup firmly packed brown sugar	1 cup sugar + 2 Tbs molasses
1 tsp lemon juice	¼ tsp vinegar (not balsamic)
¼ cup chopped onion	1 Tbs instant minced
1 clove garlic	¼ tsp garlic powder
2 cups tomato sauce	¾ cup tomato paste + 1 cup water
1 Tbs prepared mustard	1 tsp dry mustard + 1 Tbs water

How to Know What You Need

Making a shopping list based on a recipe can be tricky if you don't know how many tomatoes yields 3 cups chopped. Our handy translations:

When the Recipe Calls For:	You Need:
4 cups shredded cabbage	1 small cabbage
1 cup grated raw carrot	1 large carrot
2½ cups sliced carrots	1 pound raw carrots
4 cups cooked cut fresh green beans	1 pound beans
1 cup chopped onion	1 large onion
4 cups sliced raw potatoes	4 medium-size potatoes
1 cup chopped sweet pepper	1 large pepper
1 cup chopped tomato	1 large tomato
2 cups canned tomatoes	16 oz can
4 cups sliced apples	4 medium-size apples
1 cup mashed banana	3 medium-size bananas
1 tsp grated lemon rind	1 medium-size lemon
2 Tbs lemon juice	1 medium-size lemon
4 tsp grated orange rind	1 medium-size orange
1 cup orange juice	3 medium-size oranges
4 cups sliced peaches	8 medium-size peaches
2 cups sliced strawberries	1 pint
1 cup soft bread crumbs	2 slices fresh bread
1 cup bread cubes	2 slices fresh bread
2 cups shredded Swiss or Cheddar cheese	8 oz cheese
1 cup egg whites	6 or 7 large eggs
1 egg white	2 tsp egg white powder + 2 Tbs water
4 cups chopped walnuts or pecans	1 pound shelled